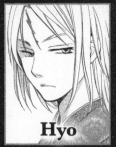

A merchant who sells black-market drugs across Shisen. He's cruel and has no qualms about treating addicts as his puppets.

Hyo

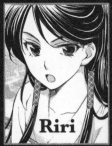

Daughter of Ahn Jung-gi, the Water Tribe Chief. When she learns that Water Tribe lands are under threat from the Kai Empire, she immediately tries to do what she can to protect her people, but she's been too sheltered to really grasp how the world works.

Riri

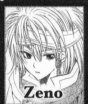

Zeno

The Yellow Dragon of the Four Dragon Warriors. He has the power of a dragon in his body...or at least he's supposed to! In practice, he's delicate and soft skinned. He left his village to go on a journey, and while traveling, he met and joined Yona's group.

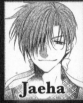

Jaeha

The Green Dragon of the Four Dragon Warriors. With the power of a dragon in his right leg, he can leap to tremendous heights. Due to his love of freedom and his hatred of his destined duty as one of the Four Legendary Dragons, he fled his village and joined a pirate crew.

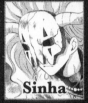

Sinha

The Blue Dragon of the Four Dragon Warriors. With the power of a dragon in his eyes, he can paralyze anyone he looks at. He grew up being hated and feared for his incredible power. He usually wears a mask.

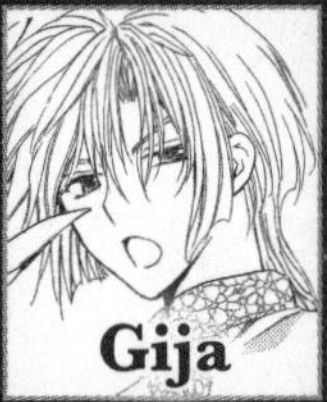

Gija

The White Dragon of the Four Dragon Warriors. His right hand contains a dragon's might and is more powerful than ten men. Though beloved by everyone in his village, he yearned for a master to serve. He adores Yona and finds fulfillment in his role as one of the Four Legendary Dragons.

The Four Dragon Warriors... In the Age of Myths, a dragon god took on human form and founded a nation. As the Crimson Dragon King, he was the first ruler of the Kingdom of Kohka. Four other dragons shared their blood with humans so that they could protect him. Those warriors became known as the Four Legendary Dragons, or the Four Dragon Warriors, and their power has been passed down for generations.

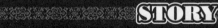

STORY

Yona, the princess of the Kingdom of Kohka, was raised by her kind, loving father, King Il. She has deep feelings for her cousin Su-won, a companion since childhood. On her 16th birthday, she sees her father being stabbed to death—by Su-won!

Driven from the palace, Yona and Hak meet a priest named Ik-su who tells Yona that her life will transform the nation and that she must locate the Four Dragon Warriors. And now, after overcoming many obstacles, she and the Four Dragon Warriors are together!

Yona decides to take up arms and defend her nation with the Four Dragon Warriors at her side. The group reaches the Water Tribe lands, said to be the most beautiful place in Kohka. However, its towns and people have been ravaged by the spread of a horrific drug called "nadai."

Yona soon meets Riri, the Water Tribe chief's daughter, who is traveling in secret. While Hak and the others are off on an information-gathering mission, Yona stays at an expensive inn with Riri. There, she encounters Hyo, the man responsible for nadai permeating the port towns. When things turn violent, Yona gets injured protecting Riri!

*The Kingdom of Kohka is a coalition of five tribes: Fire, Water, Wind, Earth and Sky. The throne is held by the tribe with the greatest influence, so the current royal family are of the Sky Tribe. The royal capital is Kuuto. Each tribe's chief also holds the rank of general, and the Meeting of the Five Tribes is the nation's most powerful decision-making body.

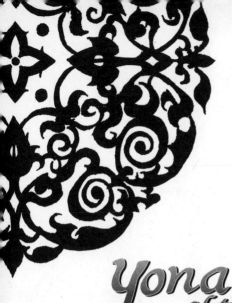

Yona of the Dawn
Volume 15

CONTENTS

Chapter 83 The Sound of
            Unseen Tears·····················5

Chapter 84 Parting Ways ···················· 35

Chapter 85 To Sensui ····························· 65

Chapter 86 Shaped by Those We Meet ··· 95

Chapter 87 Pursuit ·····························126

Chapter 88 Eyes the Color
            of the Same Sea ················159

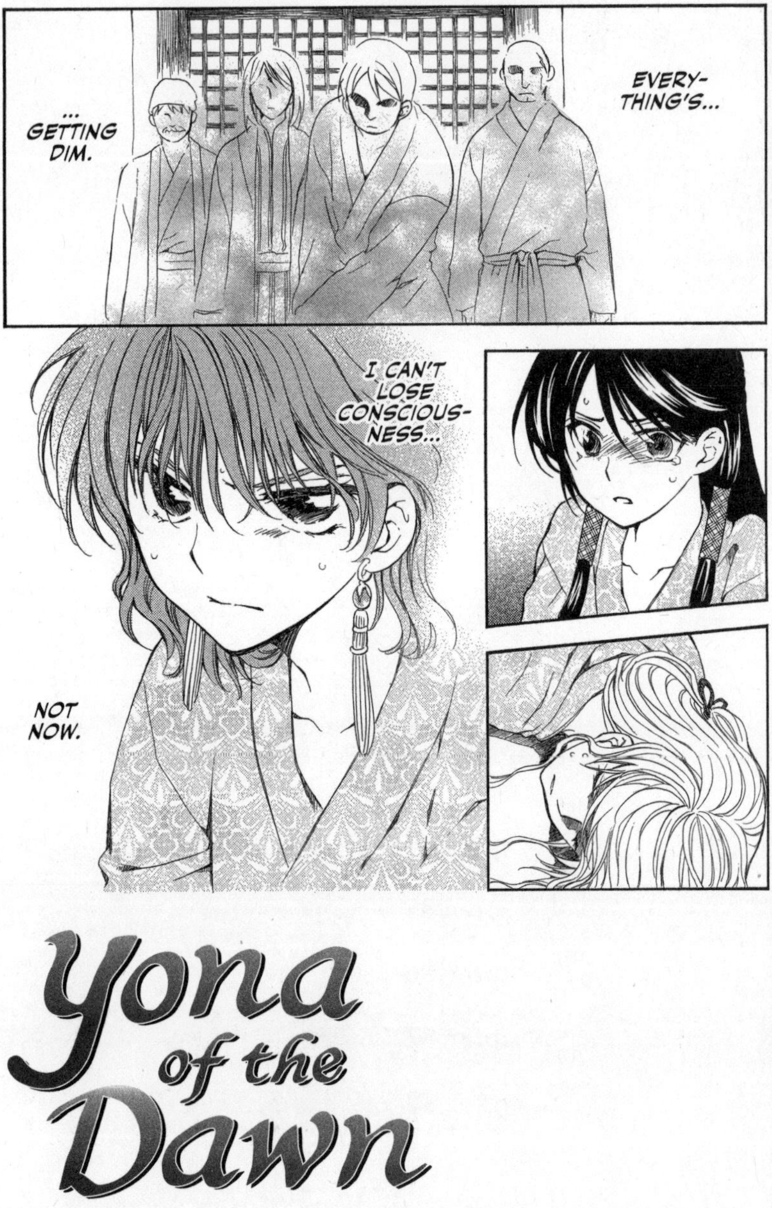
EVERY-THING'S...
...GETTING DIM.
I CAN'T LOSE CONSCIOUS-NESS...
NOT NOW.

Yona of the Dawn

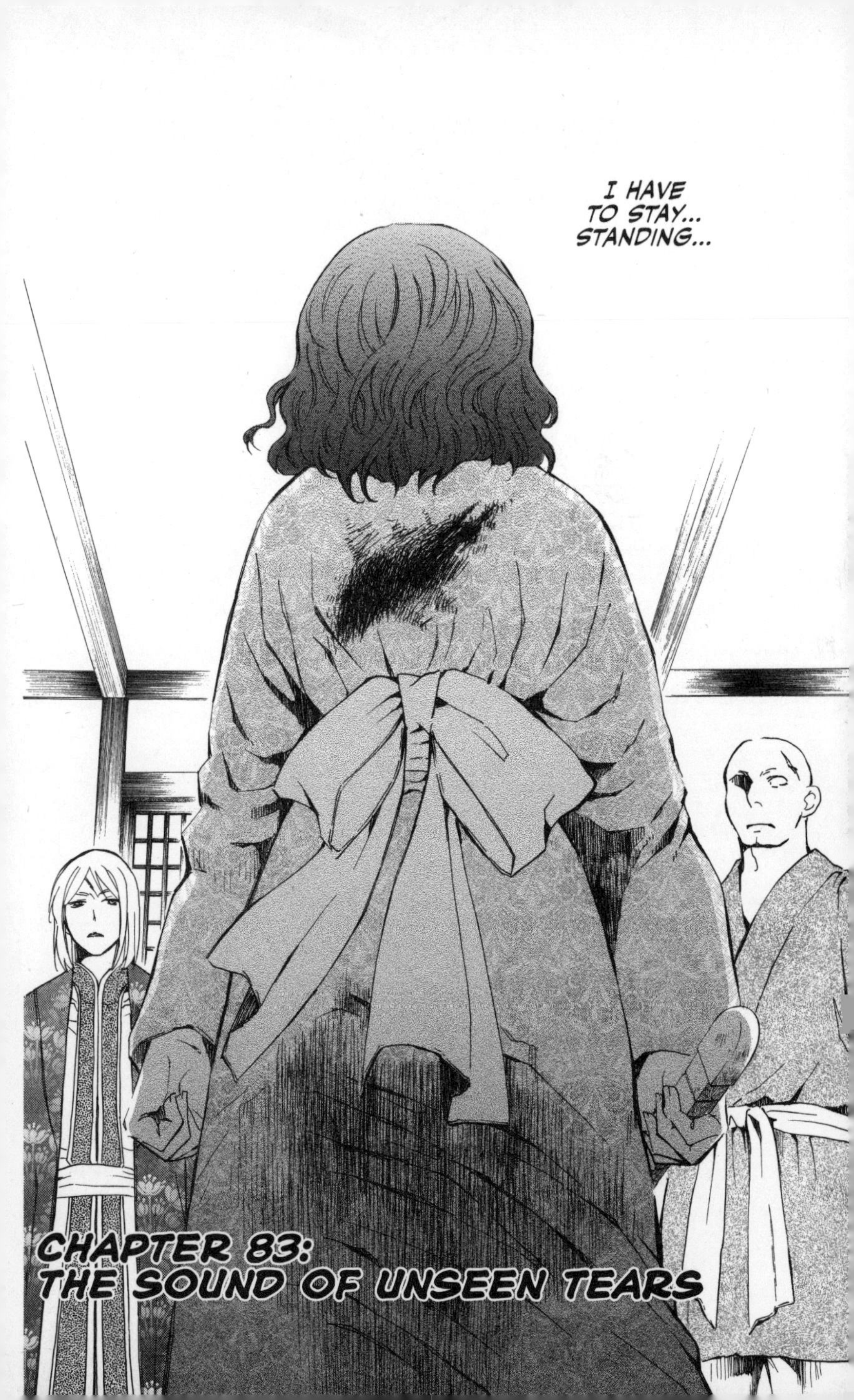
I HAVE TO STAY... STANDING...
CHAPTER 83: THE SOUND OF UNSEEN TEARS

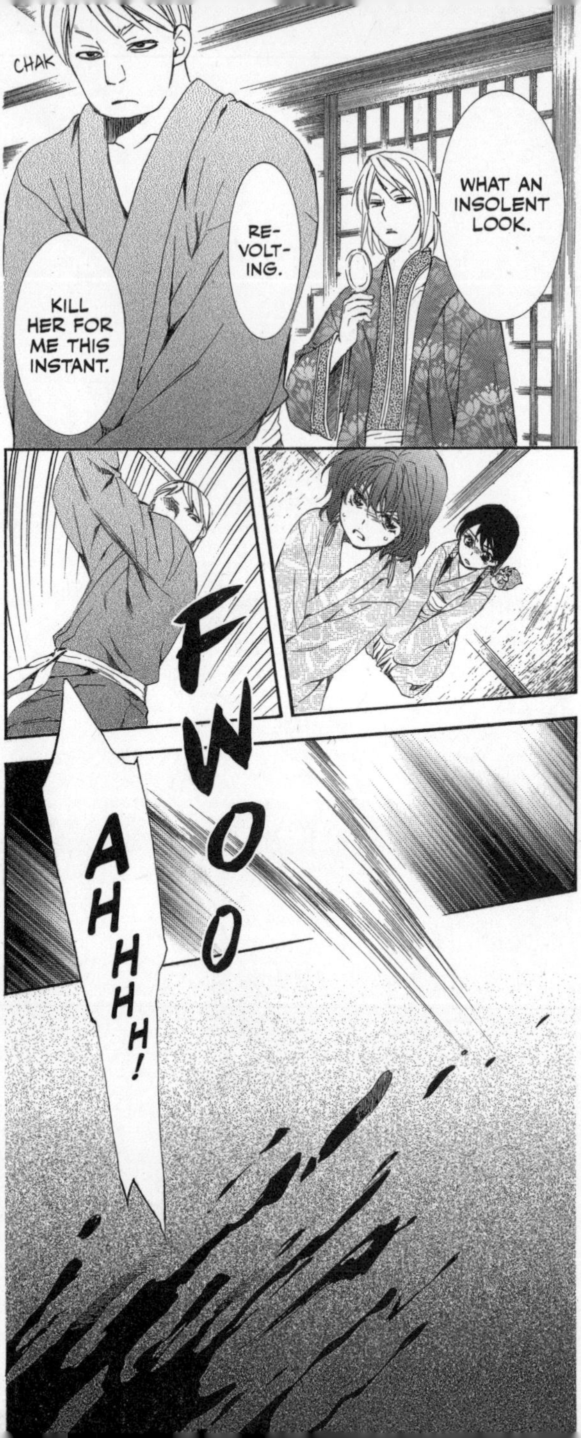
CHAK
WHAT AN INSOLENT LOOK.
RE-VOLTING.
KILL HER FOR ME THIS INSTANT.
FWOOO
AHHHH!

It's *Yona of the Dawn* volume 15! And this is Kusanagi—hello! Thank you to everyone who's stuck with us this long.

Because of your support, *Yona* is going to become an anime. The director and staff are very respectful of the source material and are creating a very faithful adaptation. I'm really looking forward to the final product. The art is incredibly cute.

I need to keep up the pace with the manga! Oh, and the cast from the CD drama is going to be performing in the anime, so I hope you'll watch Yona and her friends in motion!

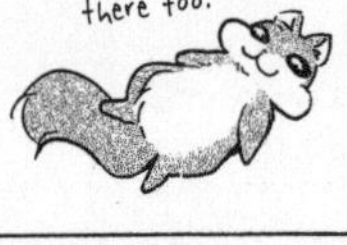
Pu-kyu will be there too.

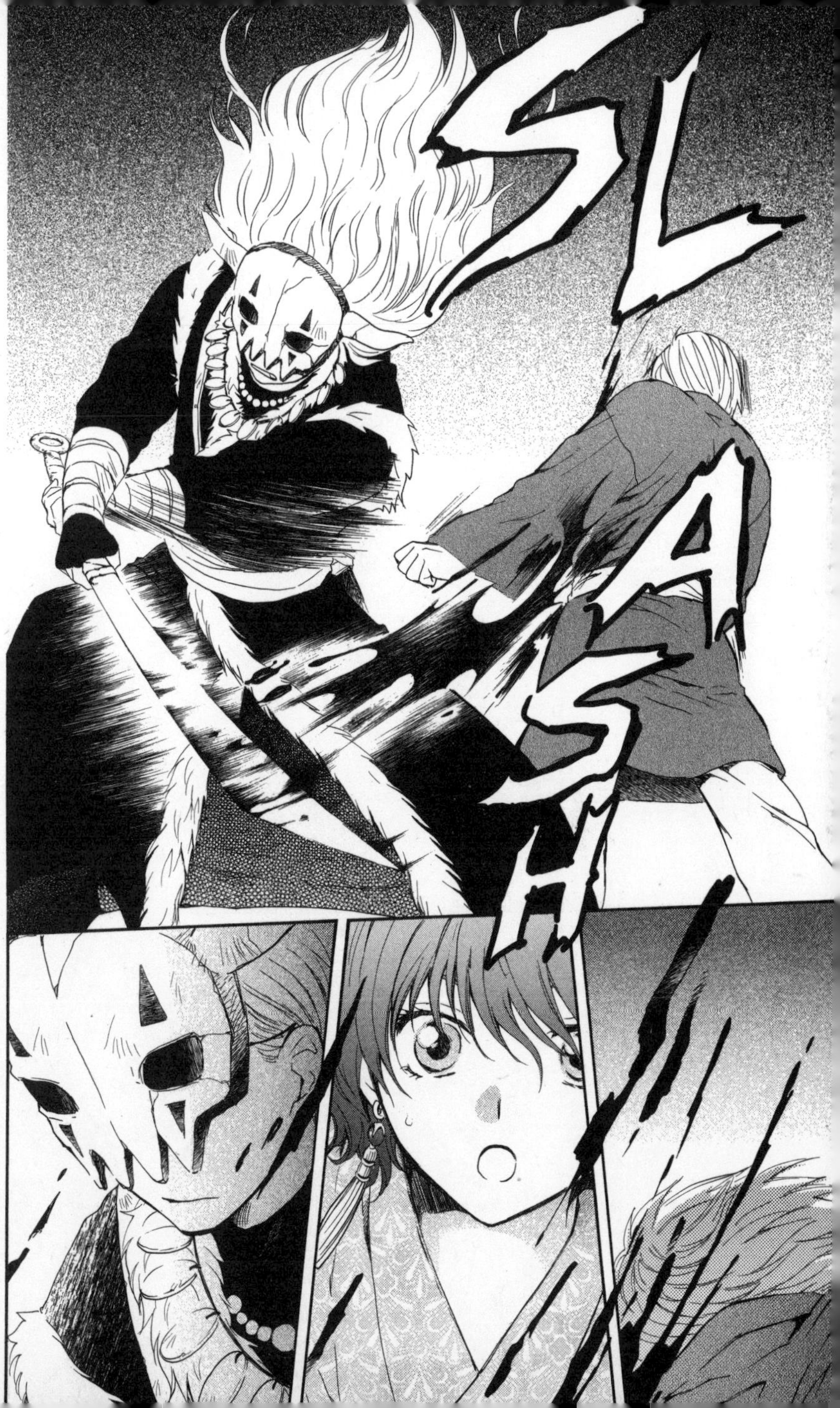
SLASH

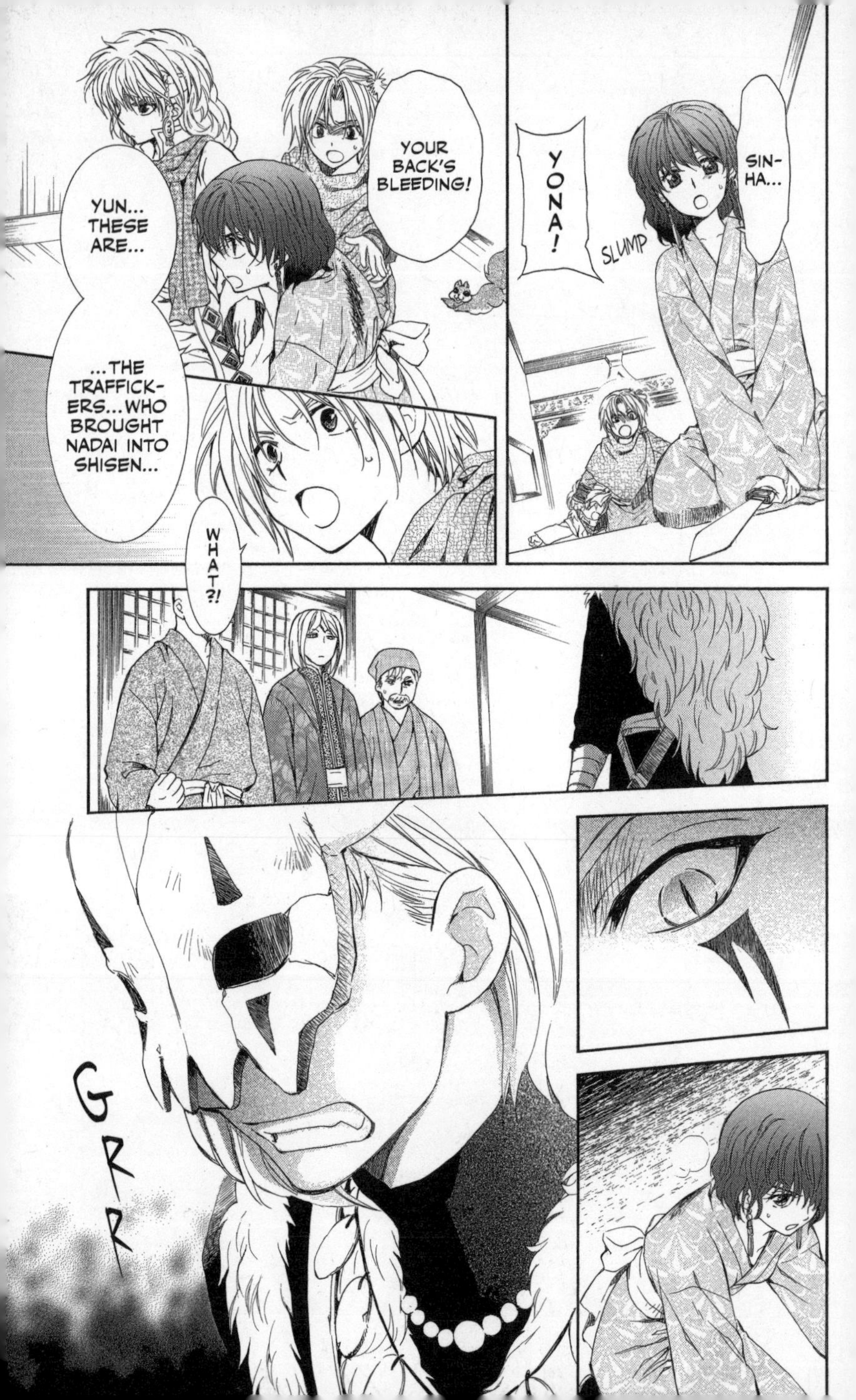
SIN-HA...
YONA!
SLUMP
YOUR BACK'S BLEEDING!
YUN... THESE ARE...
...THE TRAFFICK-ERS...WHO BROUGHT NADAI INTO SHISEN...
WHAT?!
GRRR

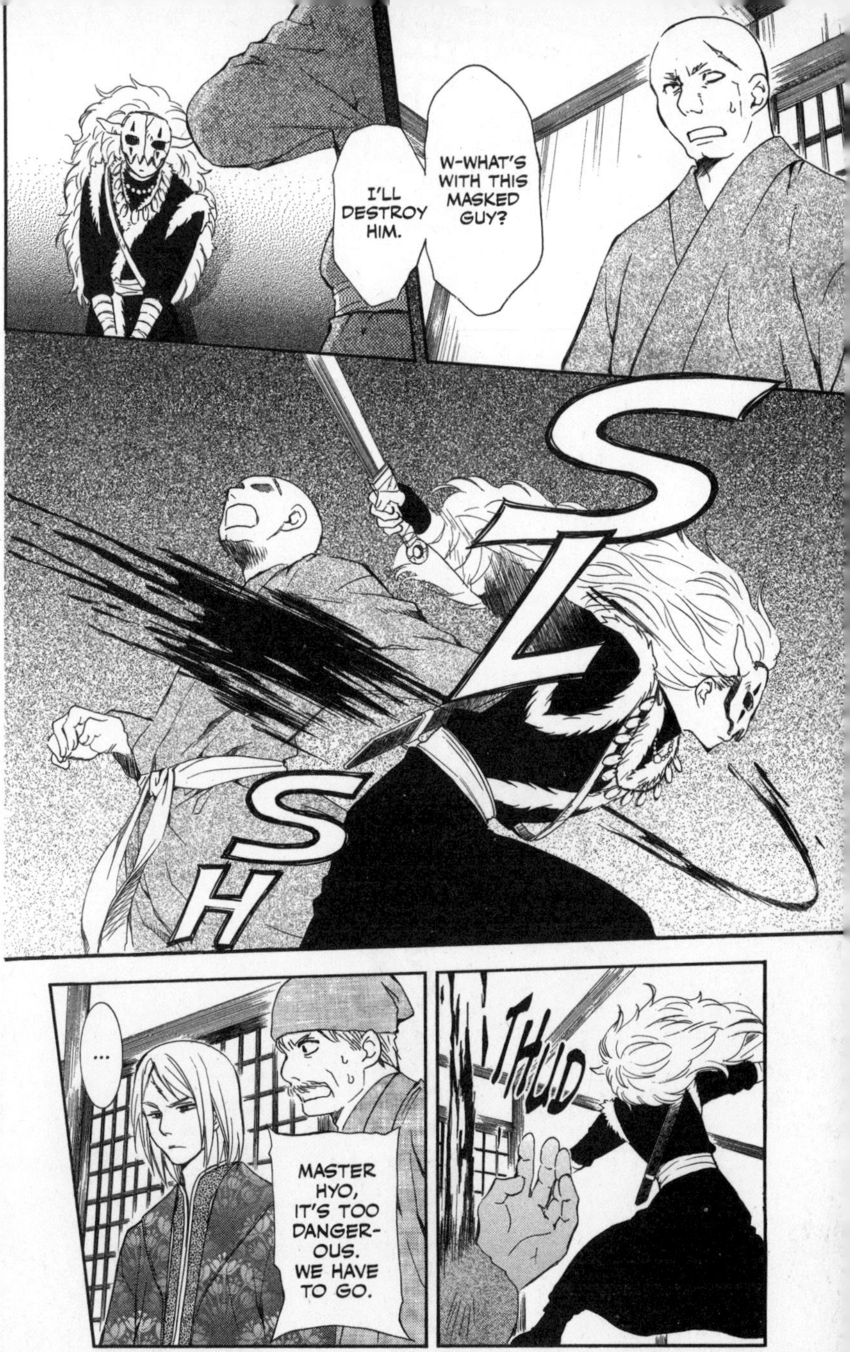
W-WHAT'S WITH THIS MASKED GUY?
I'LL DESTROY HIM.
THUD
...
MASTER HYO, IT'S TOO DANGER-OUS. WE HAVE TO GO.

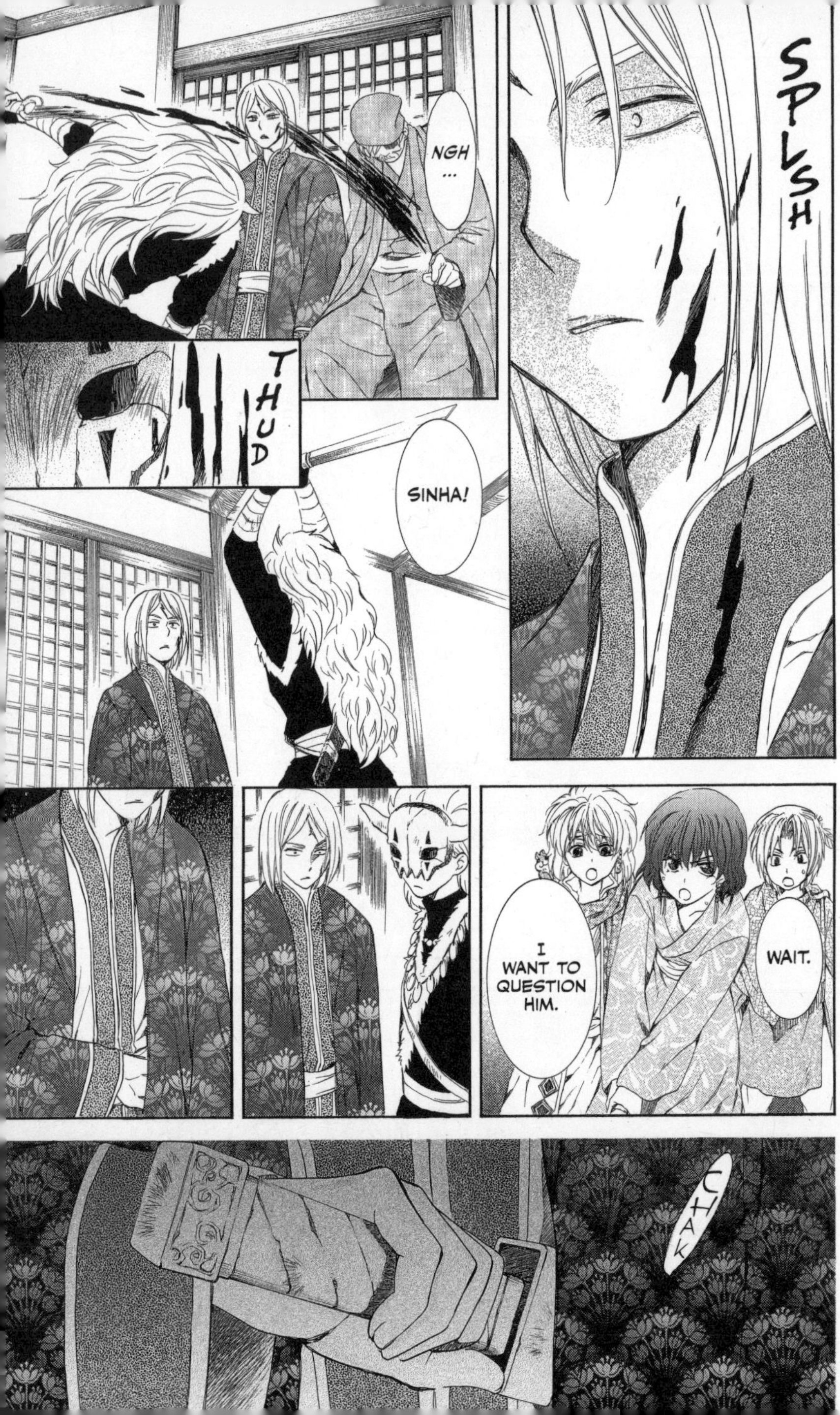
SPLSH
NGH ...
THUD
SINHA!
WAIT.
I WANT TO QUESTION HIM.
CHAK

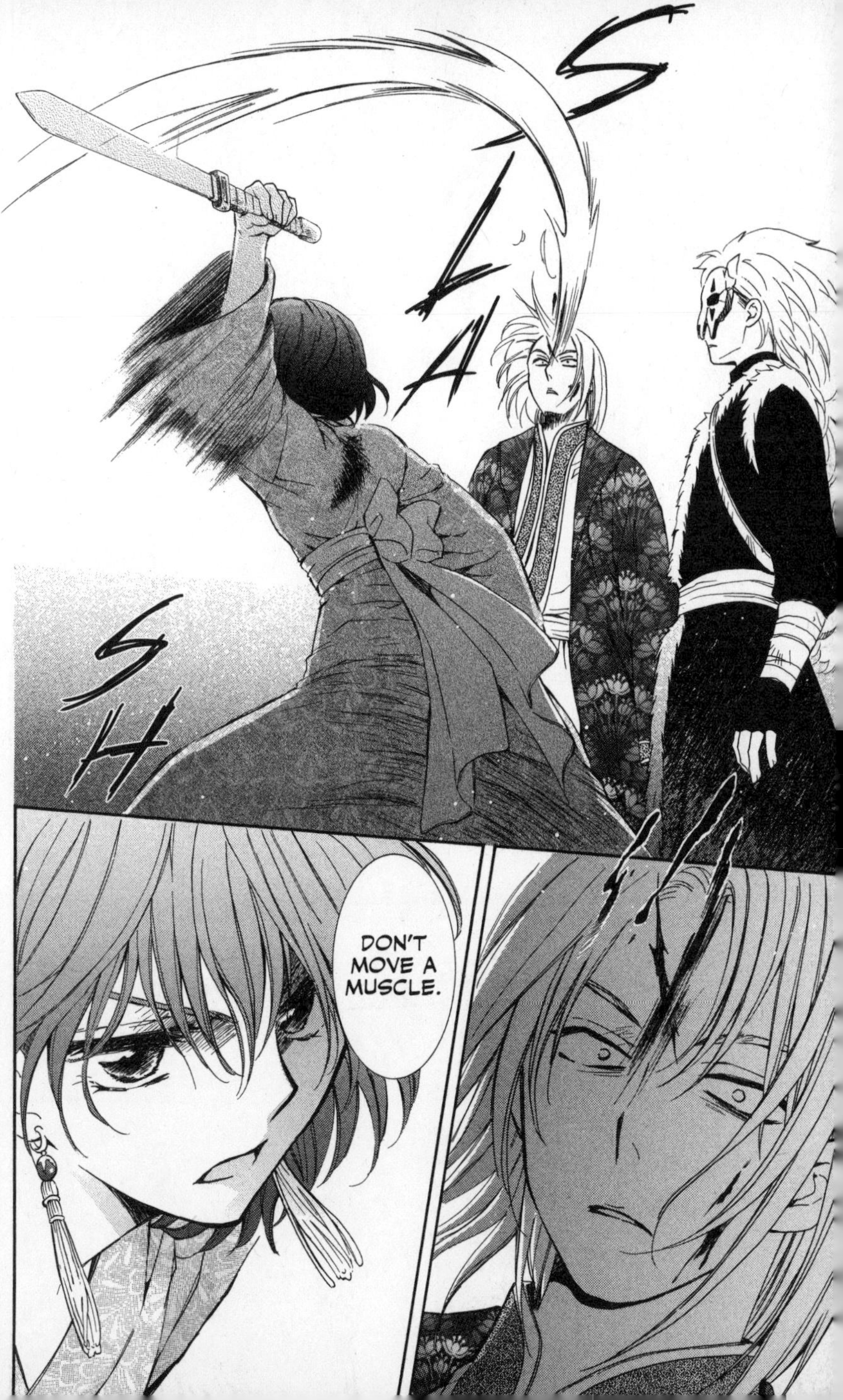
SLASH
SH
DON'T MOVE A MUSCLE.

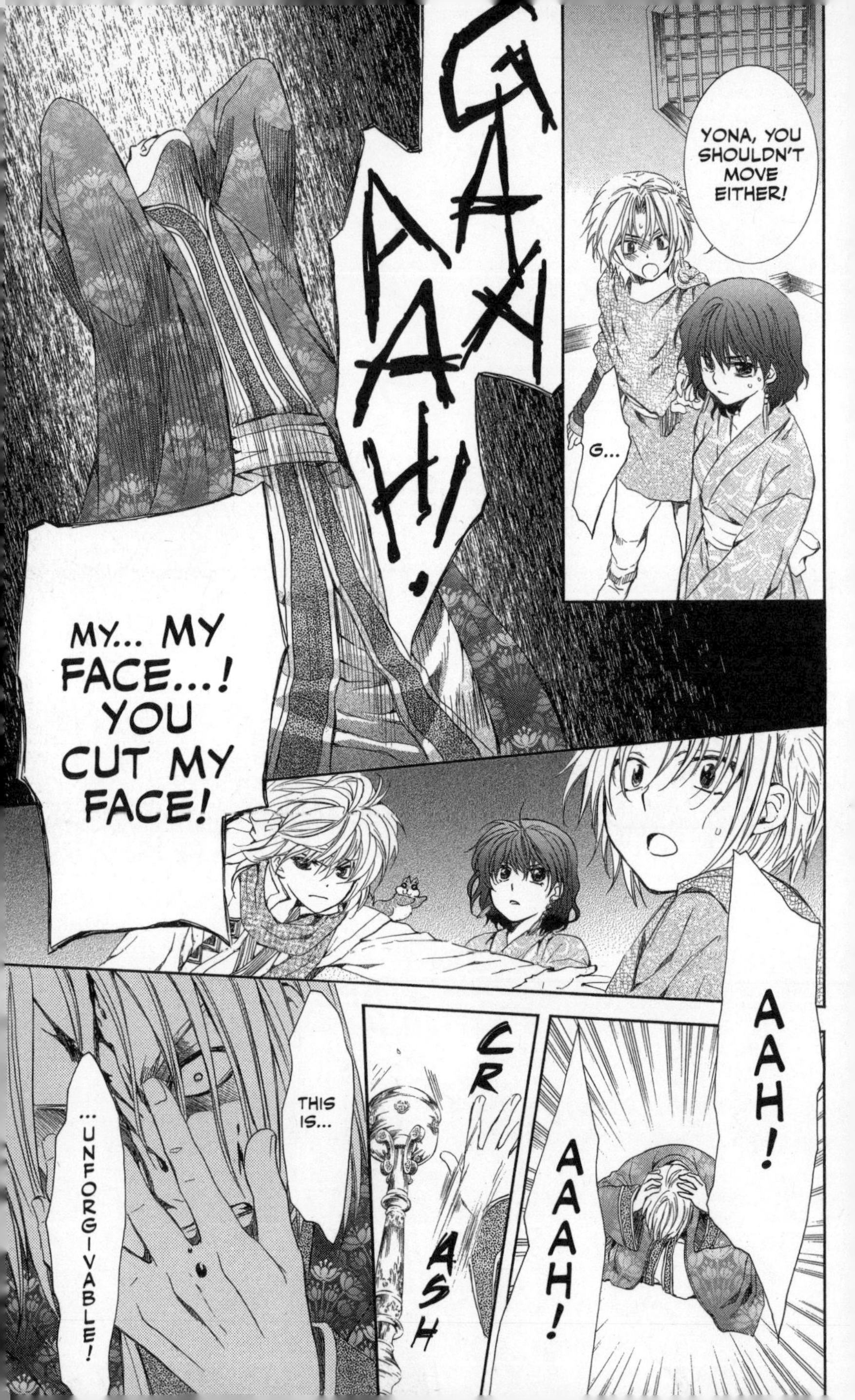

YONA, YOU SHOULDN'T MOVE EITHER!
G...
GAAAAH!
MY... MY FACE...! YOU CUT MY FACE!
AAH! AAAAH!
CRASH
THIS IS...
...UNFORGIVABLE!

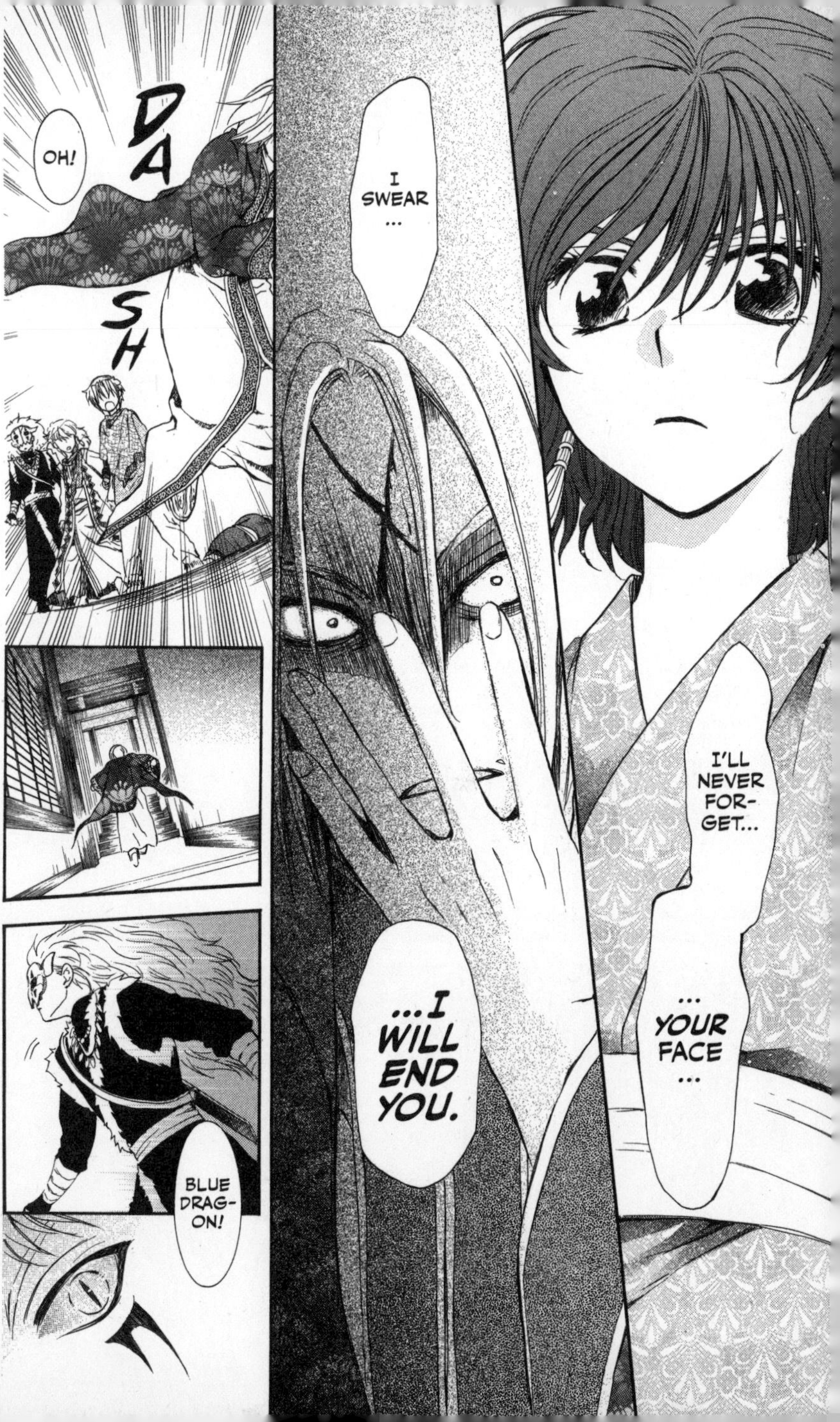
I'LL NEVER FOR-GET...
...YOUR FACE...
I SWEAR...
...I WILL END YOU.
DASH
OH!
BLUE DRAG-ON!

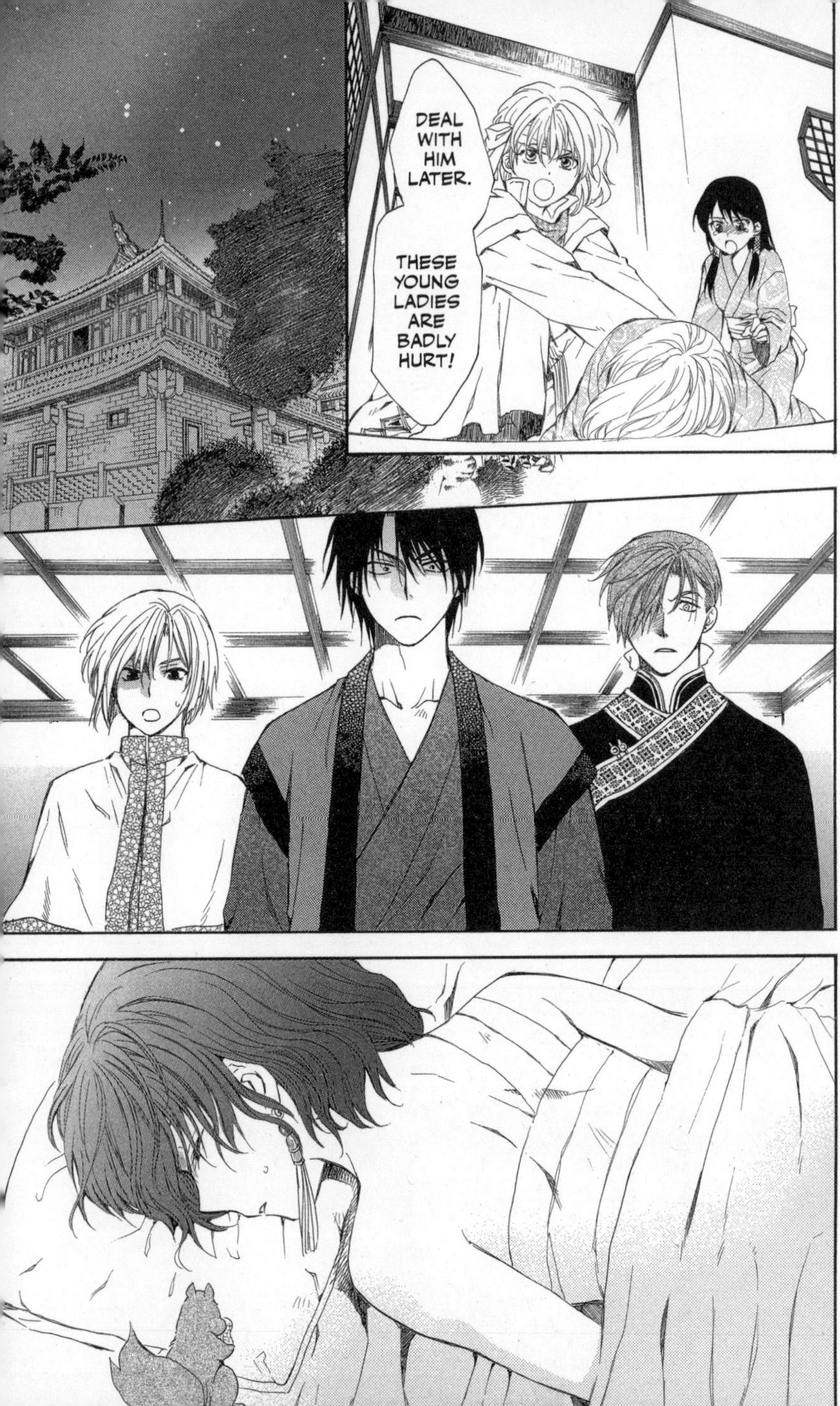
DEAL WITH HIM LATER.
THESE YOUNG LADIES ARE BADLY HURT!

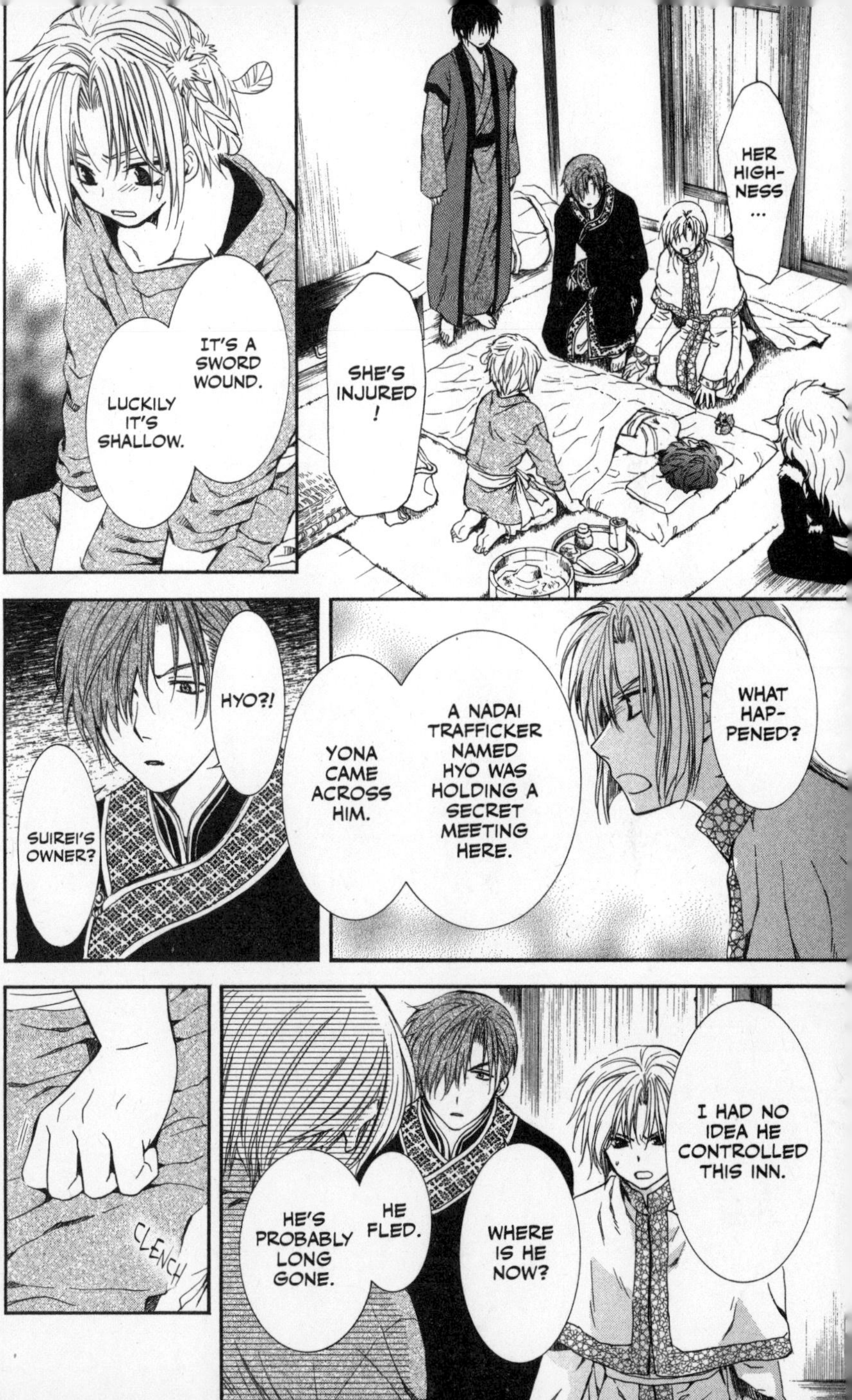
HER HIGH-NESS ...
SHE'S INJURED!
IT'S A SWORD WOUND.
LUCKILY IT'S SHALLOW.
WHAT HAP-PENED?
A NADAI TRAFFICKER NAMED HYO WAS HOLDING A SECRET MEETING HERE.
YONA CAME ACROSS HIM.
HYO?!
SUIREI'S OWNER?
I HAD NO IDEA HE CONTROLLED THIS INN.
WHERE IS HE NOW?
HE FLED.
HE'S PROBABLY LONG GONE.
CLENCH

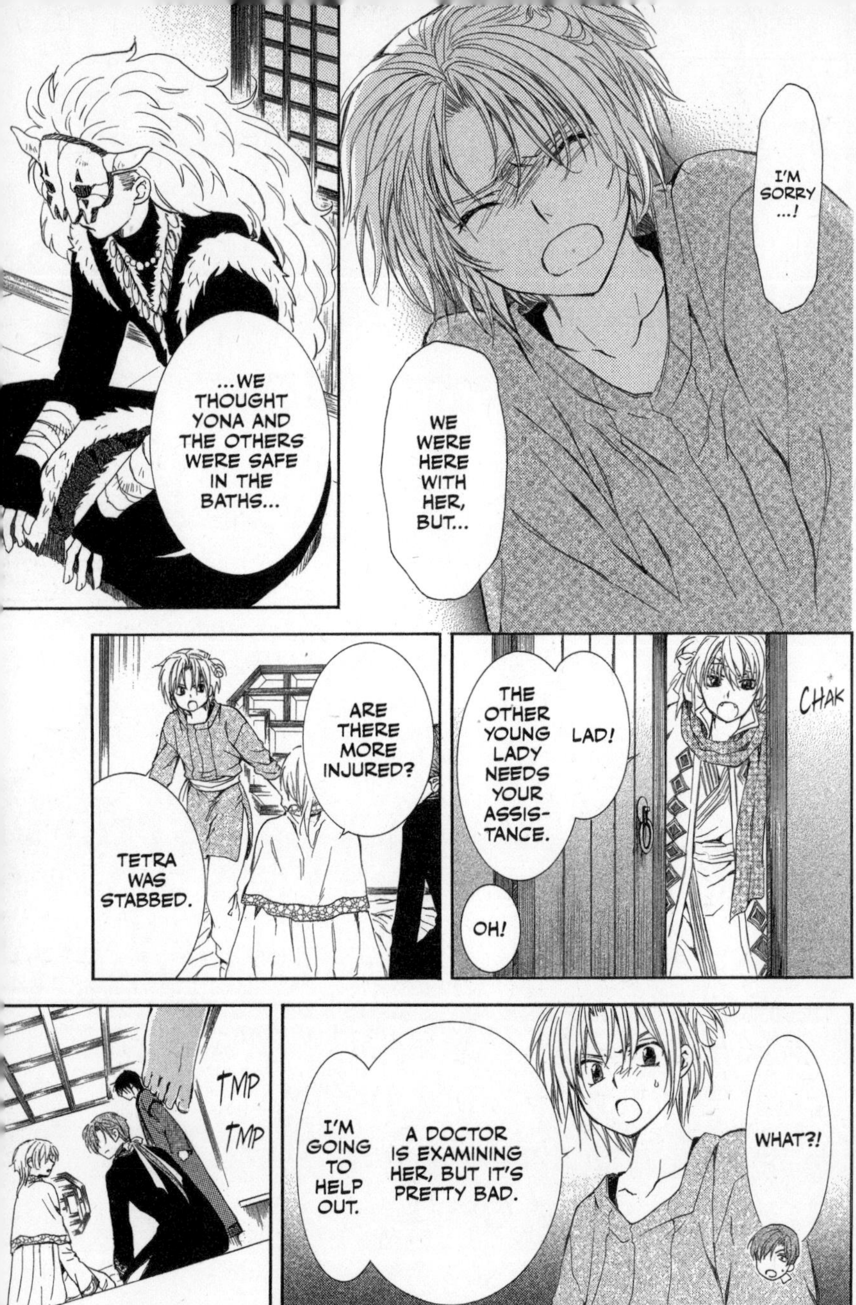
I'M SORRY ...!
WE WERE HERE WITH HER, BUT...
...WE THOUGHT YONA AND THE OTHERS WERE SAFE IN THE BATHS...
CHAK
LAD!
THE OTHER YOUNG LADY NEEDS YOUR ASSIS-TANCE.
OH!
ARE THERE MORE INJURED?
TETRA WAS STABBED.
WHAT?!
A DOCTOR IS EXAMINING HER, BUT IT'S PRETTY BAD.
I'M GOING TO HELP OUT.
TMP
TMP

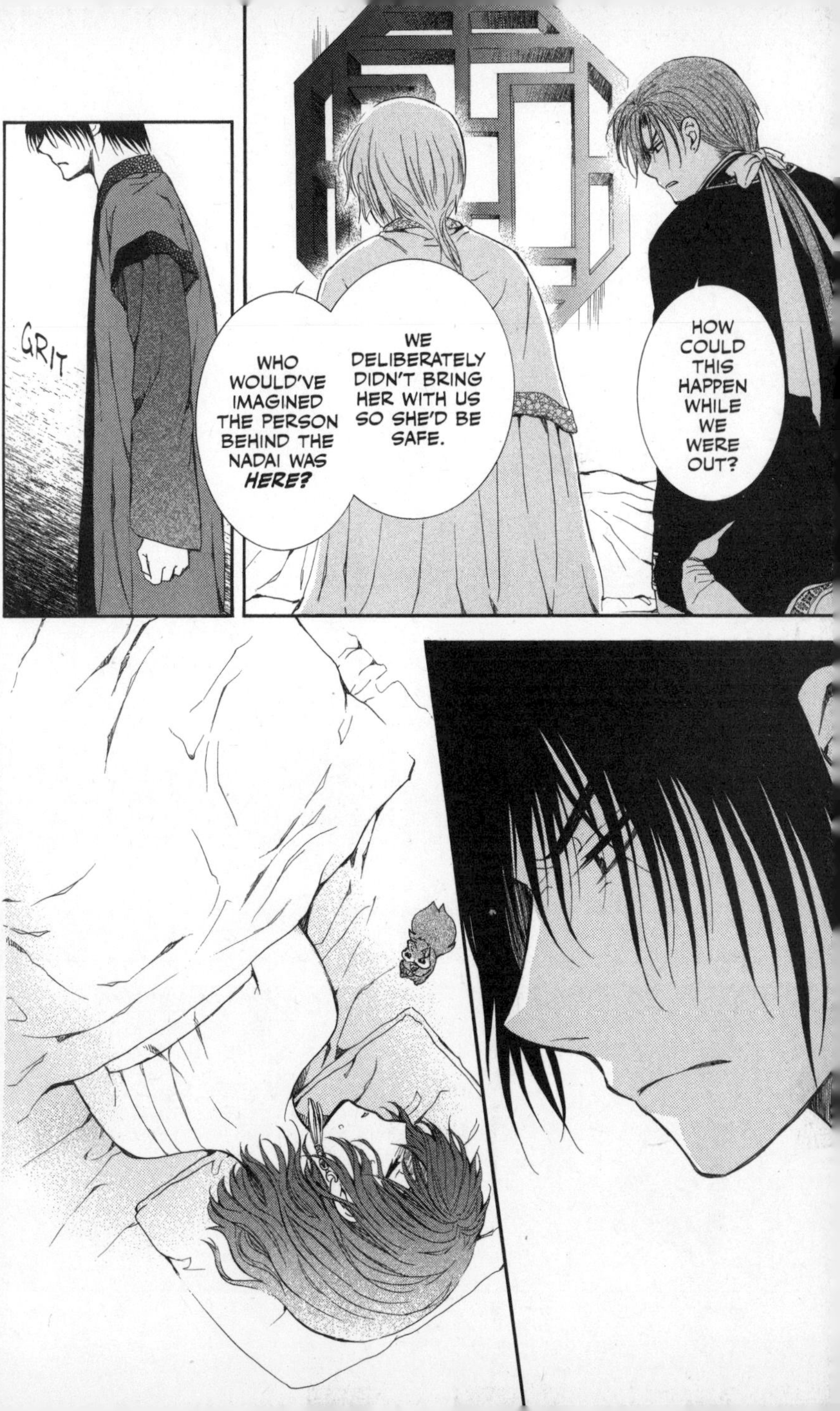
HOW COULD THIS HAPPEN WHILE WE WERE OUT?
WE DELIBERATELY DIDN'T BRING HER WITH US SO SHE'D BE SAFE.
WHO WOULD'VE IMAGINED THE PERSON BEHIND THE NADAI WAS *HERE?*
GRIT

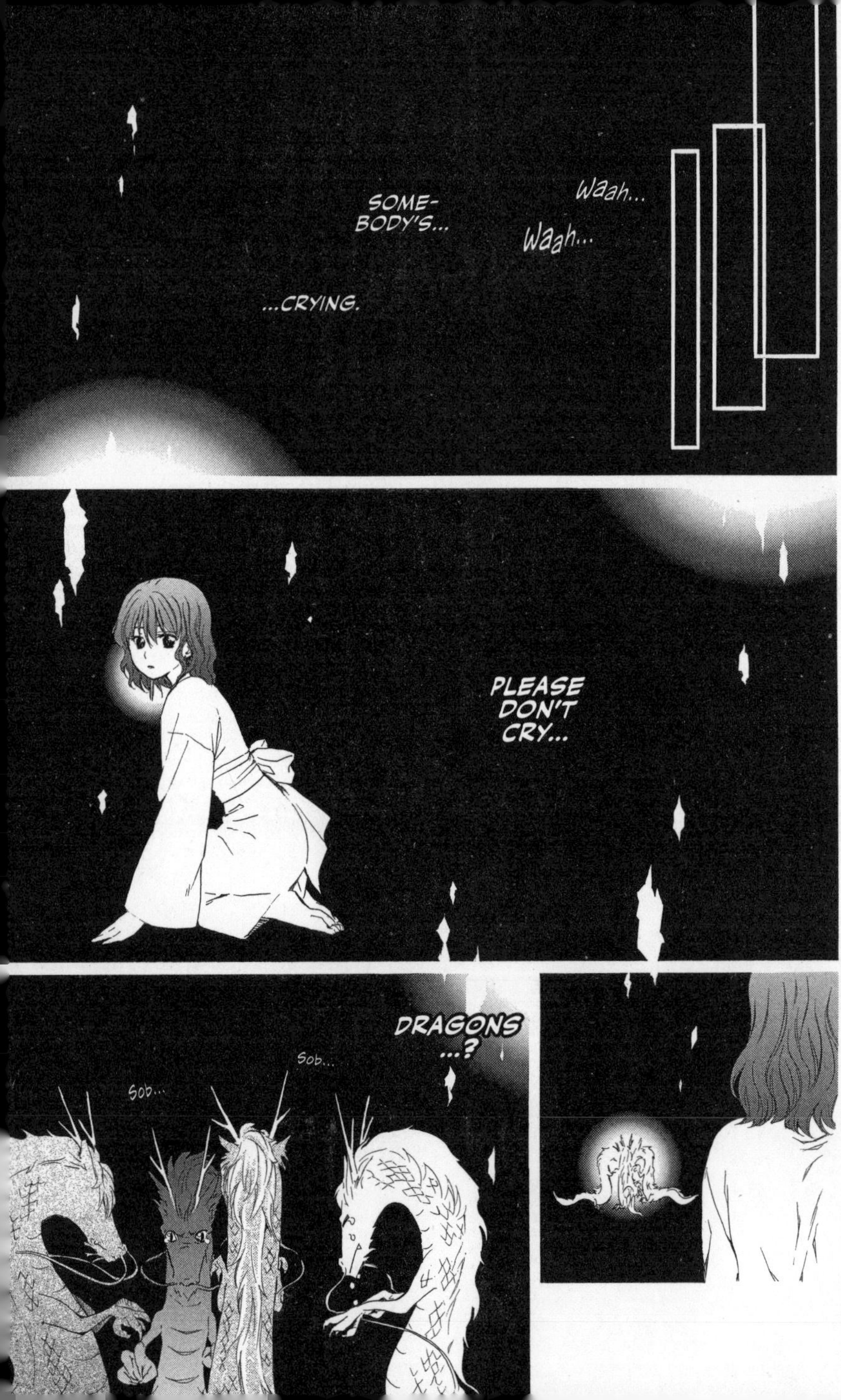
Waah...
Waah...
SOME-BODY'S...
...CRYING.
PLEASE DON'T CRY...
DRAGONS ...?
Sob...
Sob...

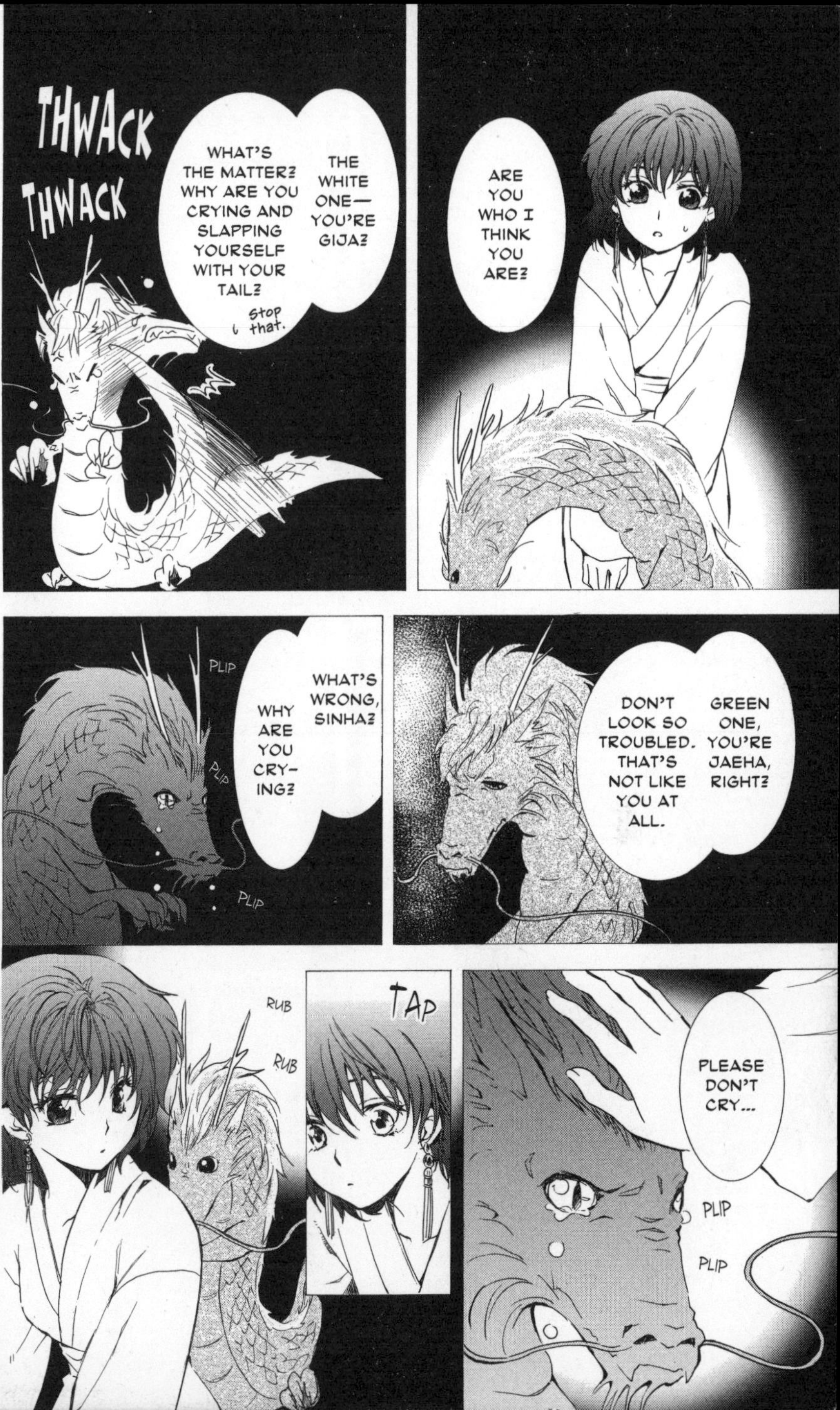
ARE YOU WHO I THINK YOU ARE?
THE WHITE ONE— YOU'RE GIJA?
WHAT'S THE MATTER? WHY ARE YOU CRYING AND SLAPPING YOURSELF WITH YOUR TAIL?
Stop that.
THWACK
THWACK
GREEN ONE, YOU'RE JAEHA, RIGHT?
DON'T LOOK SO TROUBLED. THAT'S NOT LIKE YOU AT ALL.
WHAT'S WRONG, SINHA?
WHY ARE YOU CRY-ING?
PLIP
PLIP
PLIP
PLEASE DON'T CRY...
PLIP
PLIP
TAP
RUB
RUB

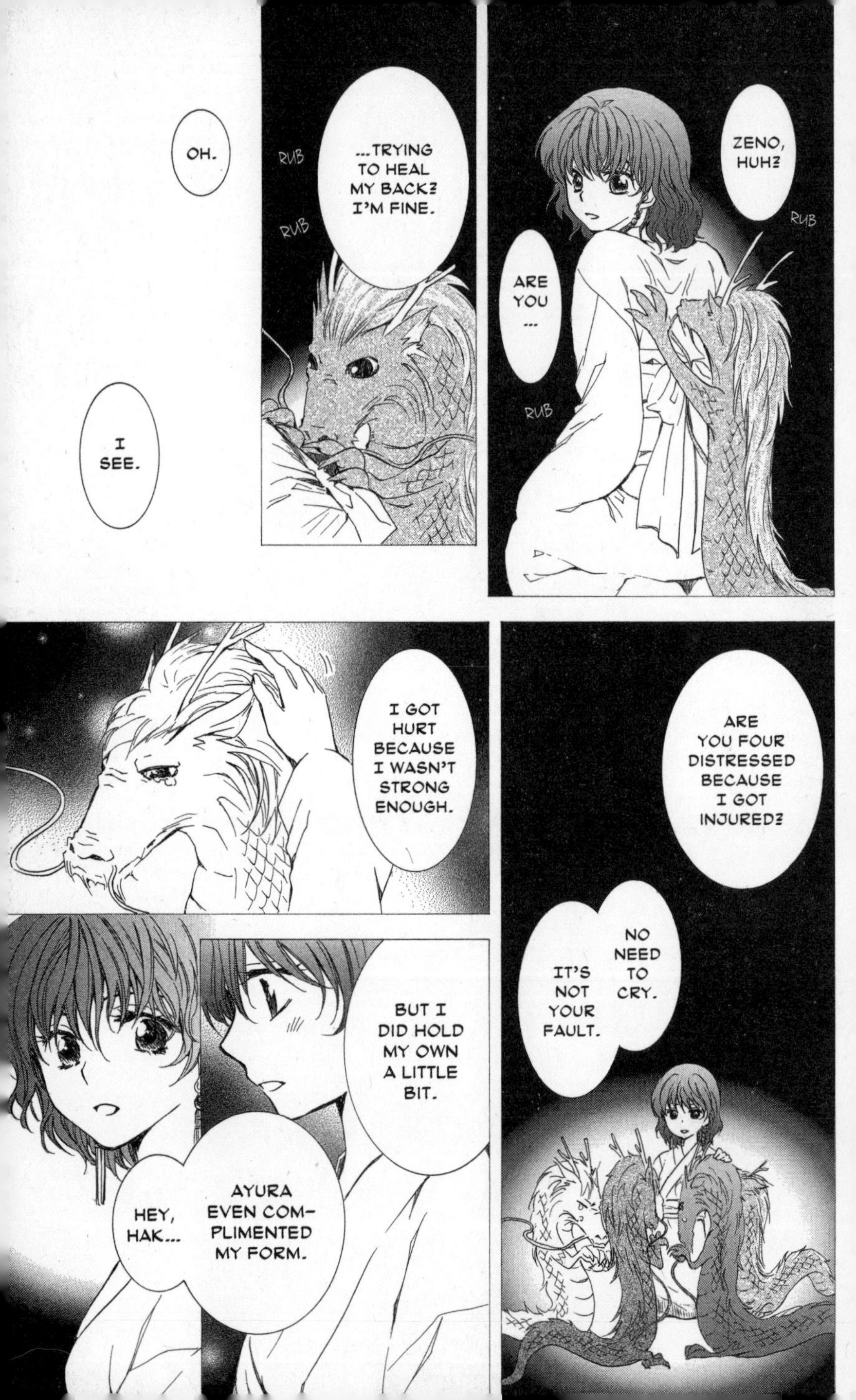
ZENO, HUH?
RUB
ARE YOU ...
RUB
...TRYING TO HEAL MY BACK? I'M FINE.
RUB
RUB
OH.
I SEE.
ARE YOU FOUR DISTRESSED BECAUSE I GOT INJURED?
NO NEED TO CRY.
IT'S NOT YOUR FAULT.
I GOT HURT BECAUSE I WASN'T STRONG ENOUGH.
BUT I DID HOLD MY OWN A LITTLE BIT.
AYURA EVEN COM-PLIMENTED MY FORM.
HEY, HAK...

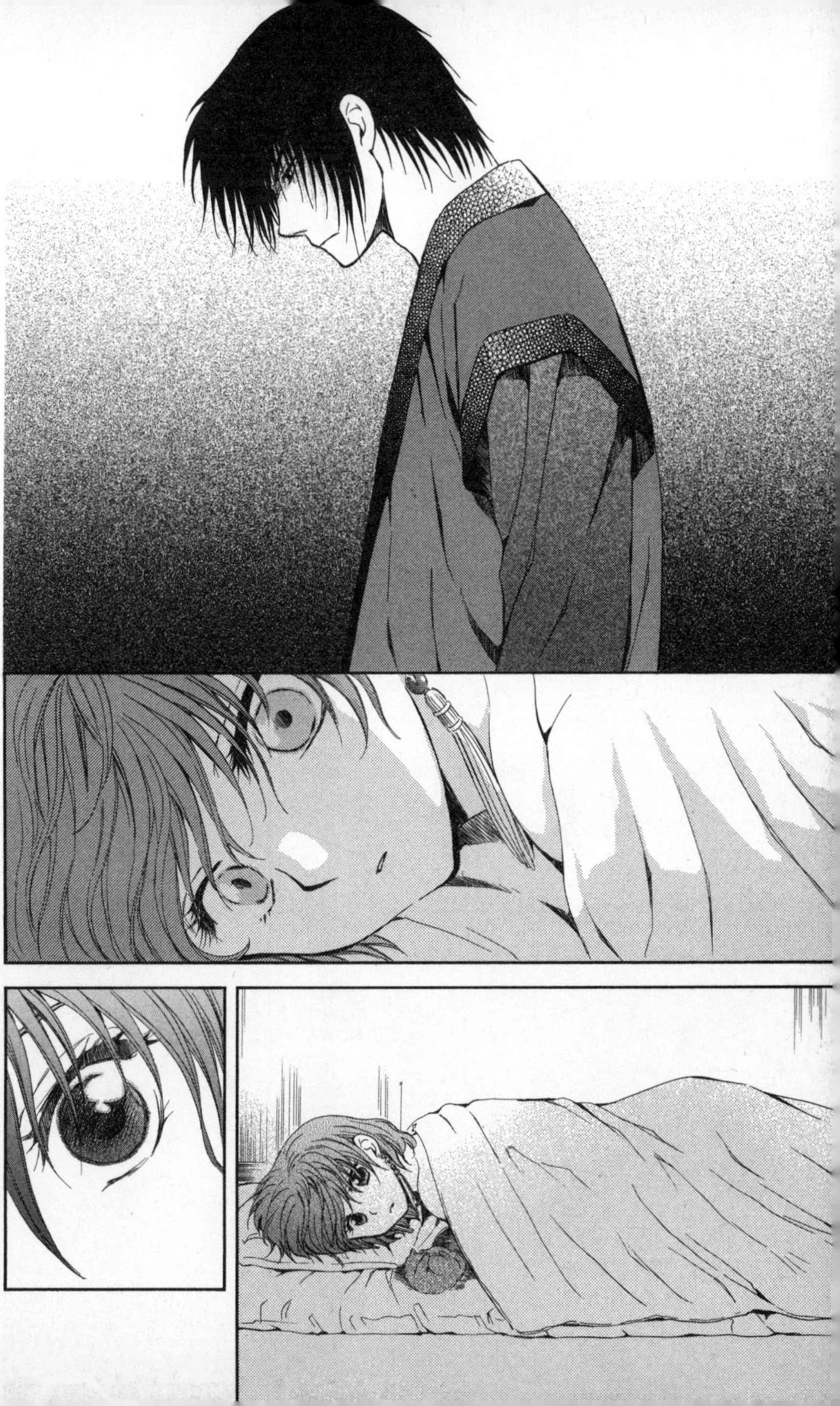

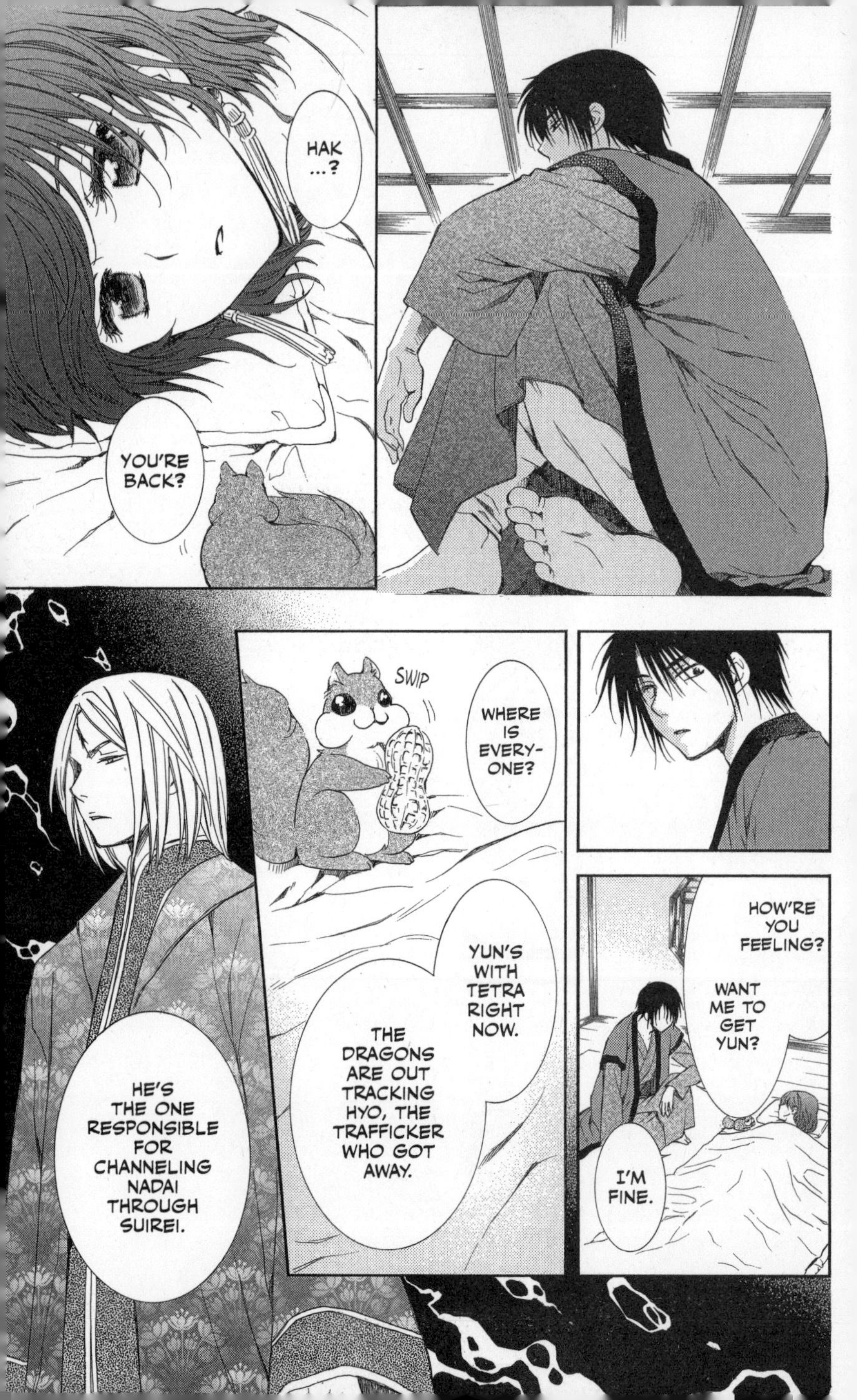
HAK ...?
YOU'RE BACK?
HOW'RE YOU FEELING?
WANT ME TO GET YUN?
I'M FINE.
WHERE IS EVERYONE?
SWIP
YUN'S WITH TETRA RIGHT NOW.
THE DRAGONS ARE OUT TRACKING HYO, THE TRAFFICKER WHO GOT AWAY.
HE'S THE ONE RESPONSIBLE FOR CHANNELING NADAI THROUGH SUIREI.

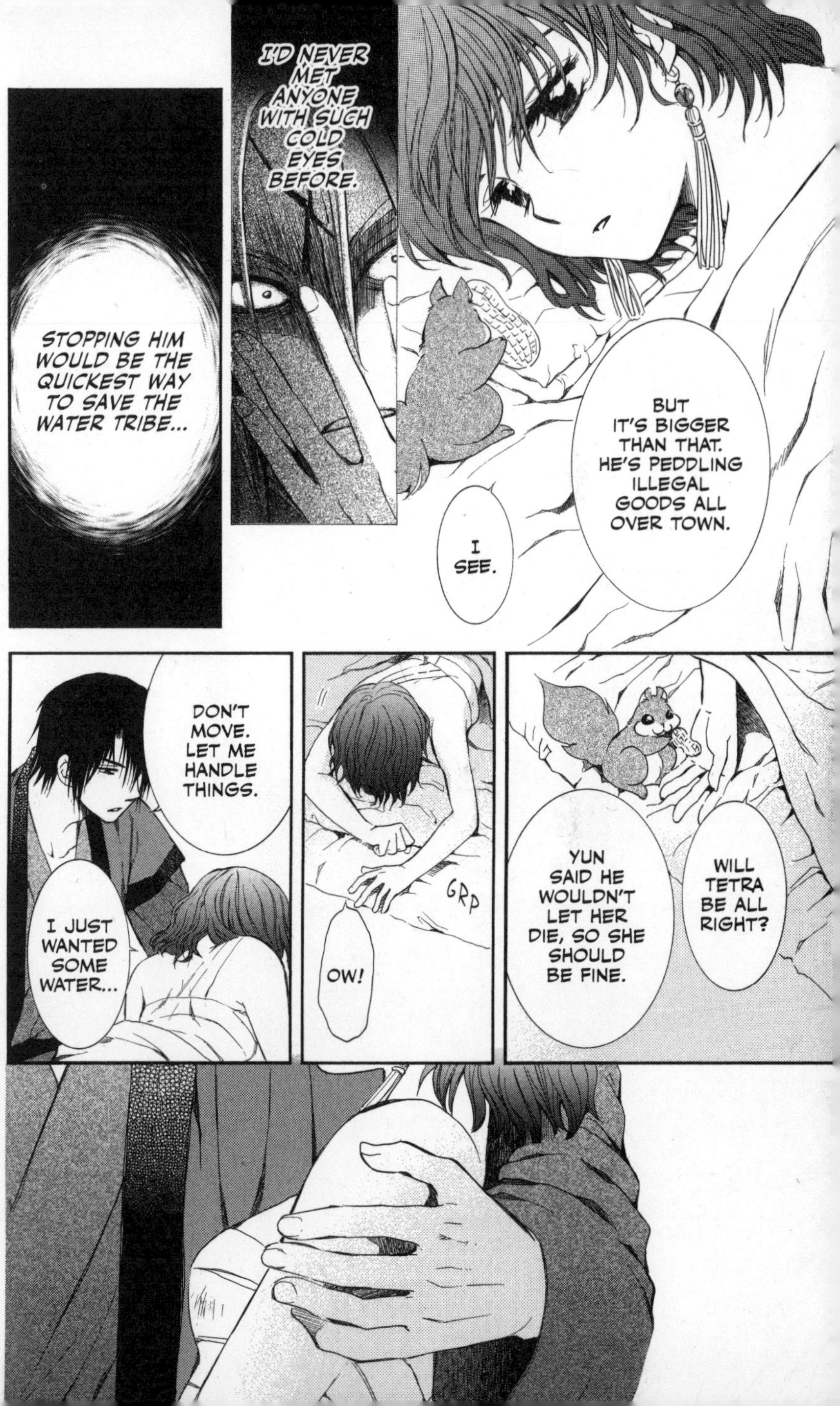
BUT IT'S BIGGER THAN THAT. HE'S PEDDLING ILLEGAL GOODS ALL OVER TOWN.
I SEE.
I'D NEVER MET ANYONE WITH SUCH COLD EYES BEFORE.
STOPPING HIM WOULD BE THE QUICKEST WAY TO SAVE THE WATER TRIBE...
WILL TETRA BE ALL RIGHT?
YUN SAID HE WOULDN'T LET HER DIE, SO SHE SHOULD BE FINE.
GRP
OW!
DON'T MOVE. LET ME HANDLE THINGS.
I JUST WANTED SOME WATER...

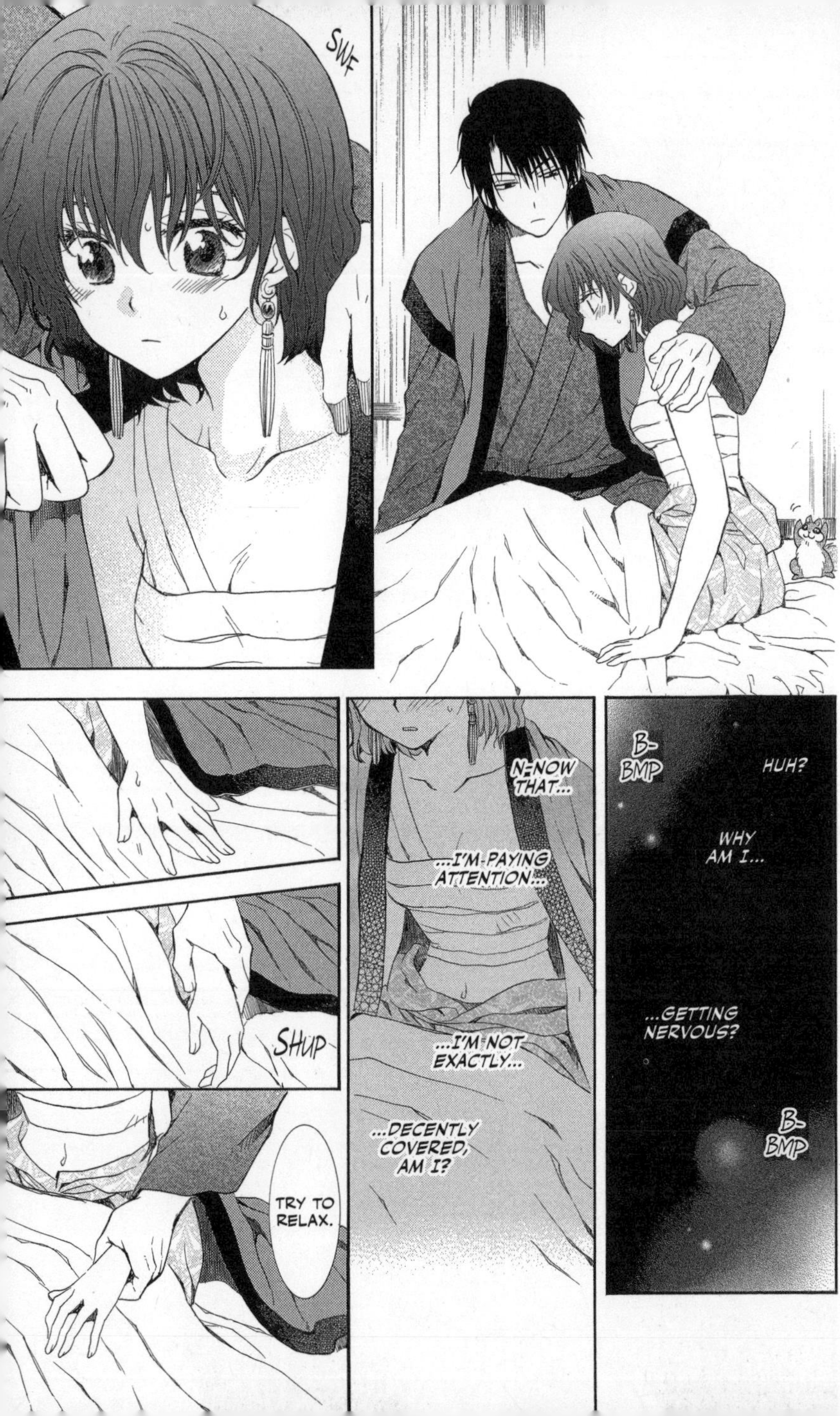
SWF
B-BMP
HUH?
WHY AM I...
...GETTING NERVOUS?
B-BMP
N-NOW THAT...
...I'M PAYING ATTENTION...
...I'M NOT EXACTLY...
...DECENTLY COVERED, AM I?
SHUP
TRY TO RELAX.

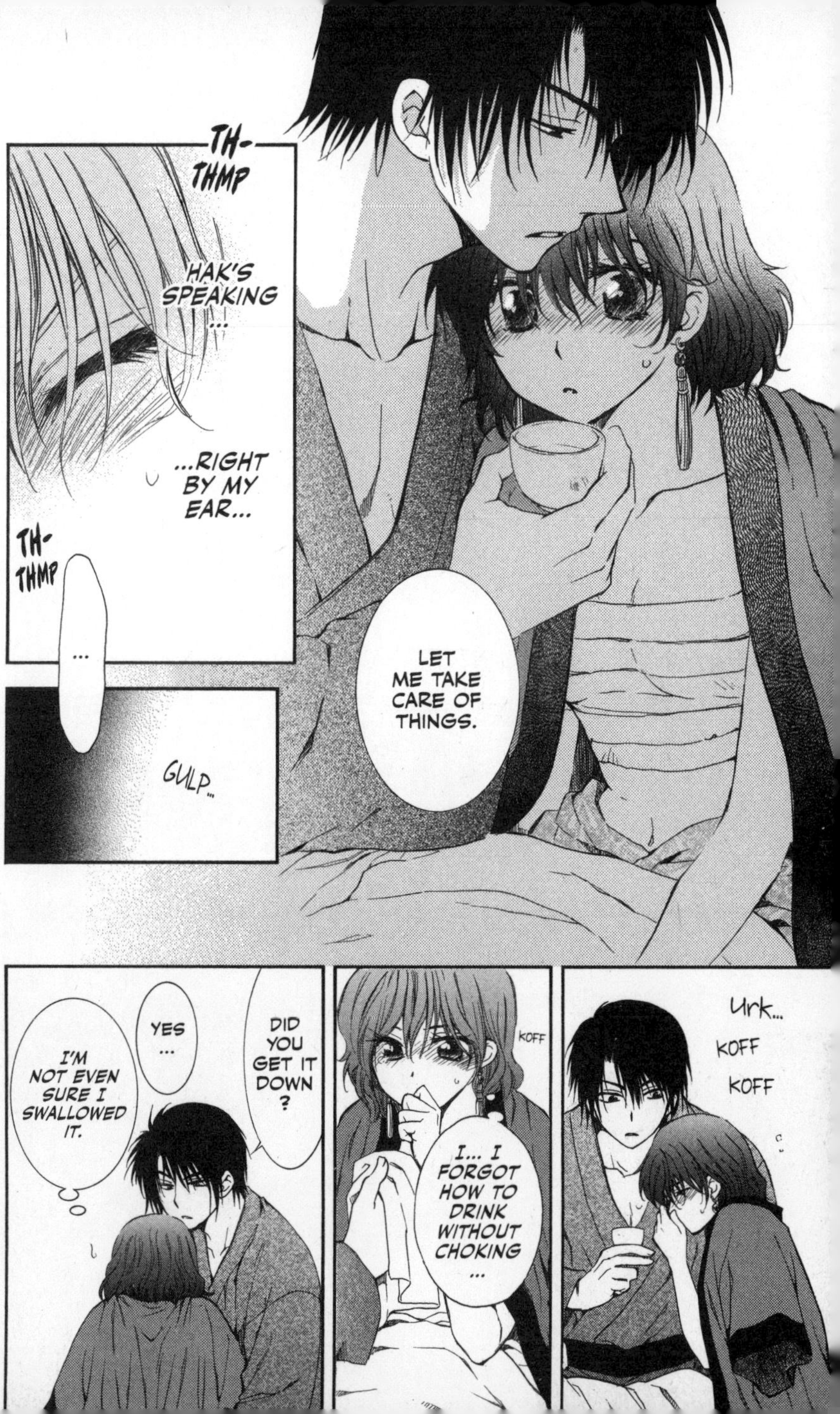
TH-THMP
LET ME TAKE CARE OF THINGS.
HAK'S SPEAKING...
...RIGHT BY MY EAR...
TH-THMP
...
GULP...
Urk...
KOFF
KOFF
KOFF
I... I FORGOT HOW TO DRINK WITHOUT CHOKING...
DID YOU GET IT DOWN?
YES...
I'M NOT EVEN SURE I SWALLOWED IT.

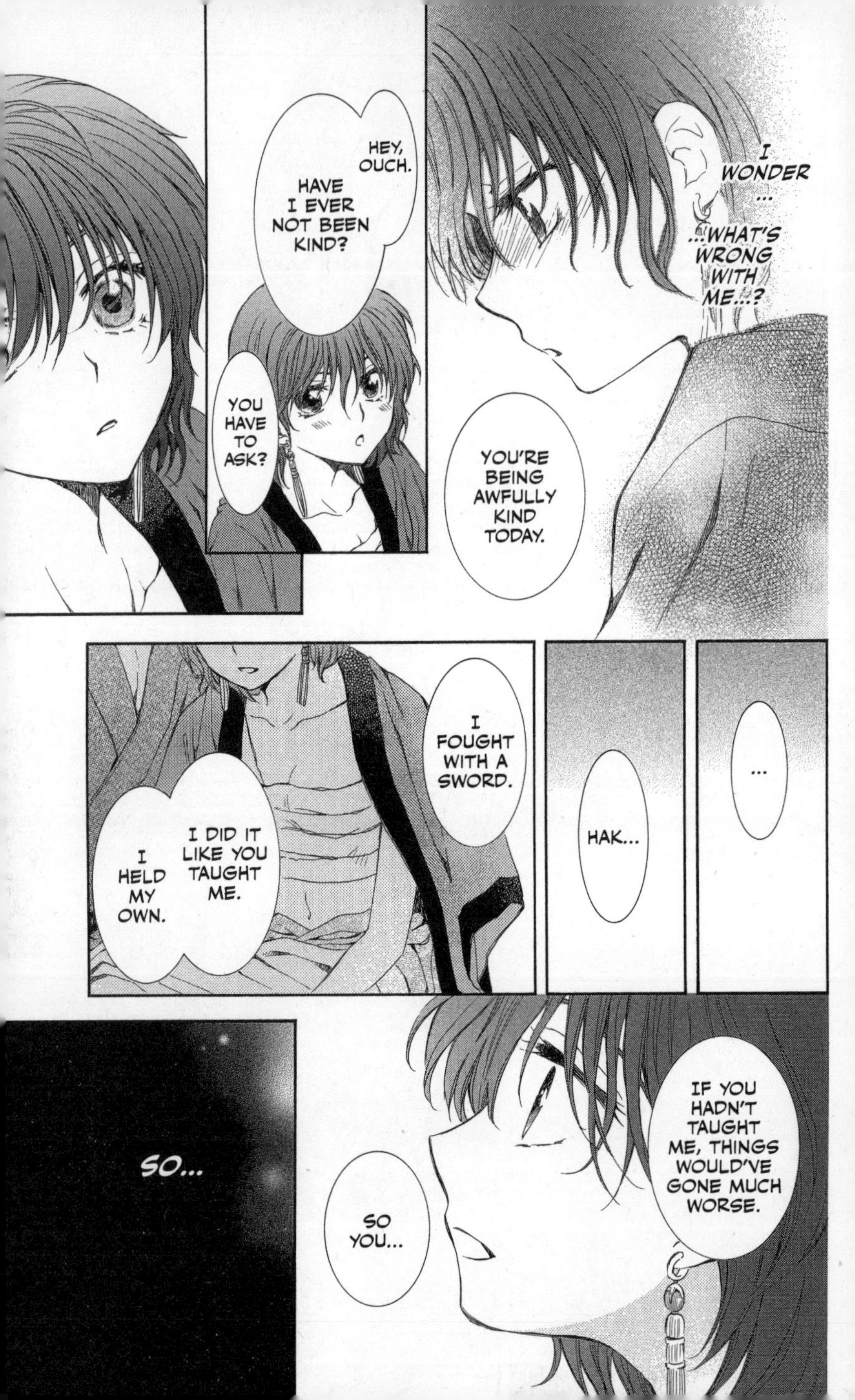

I WONDER ...
...WHAT'S WRONG WITH ME...?
YOU'RE BEING AWFULLY KIND TODAY.
HEY, OUCH.
HAVE I EVER NOT BEEN KIND?
YOU HAVE TO ASK?
...
HAK...
I FOUGHT WITH A SWORD.
I DID IT LIKE YOU TAUGHT ME.
I HELD MY OWN.
IF YOU HADN'T TAUGHT ME, THINGS WOULD'VE GONE MUCH WORSE.
SO YOU...
SO...

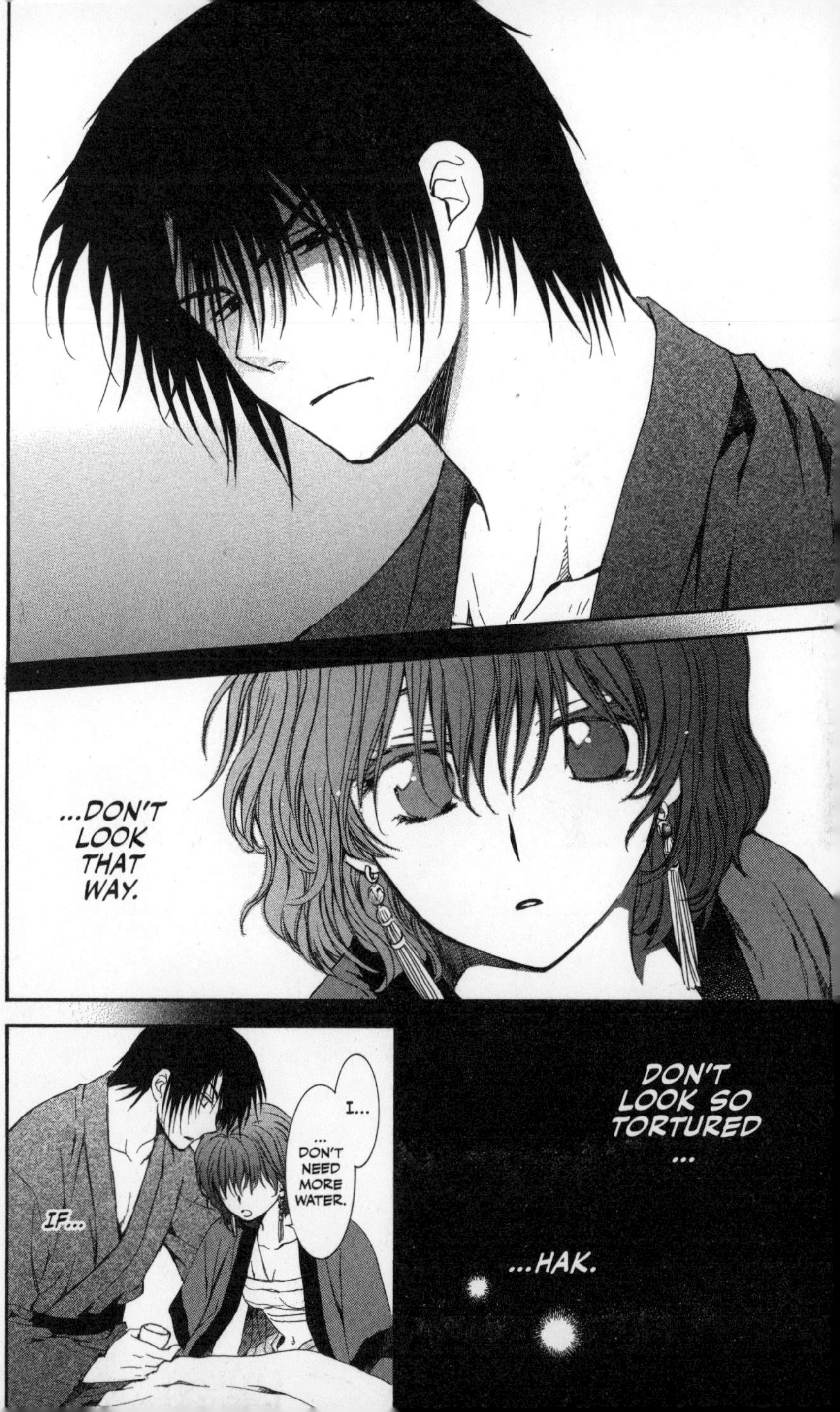
...DON'T LOOK THAT WAY.
DON'T LOOK SO TORTURED ...
...HAK.
I... ... DON'T NEED MORE WATER.
IF...

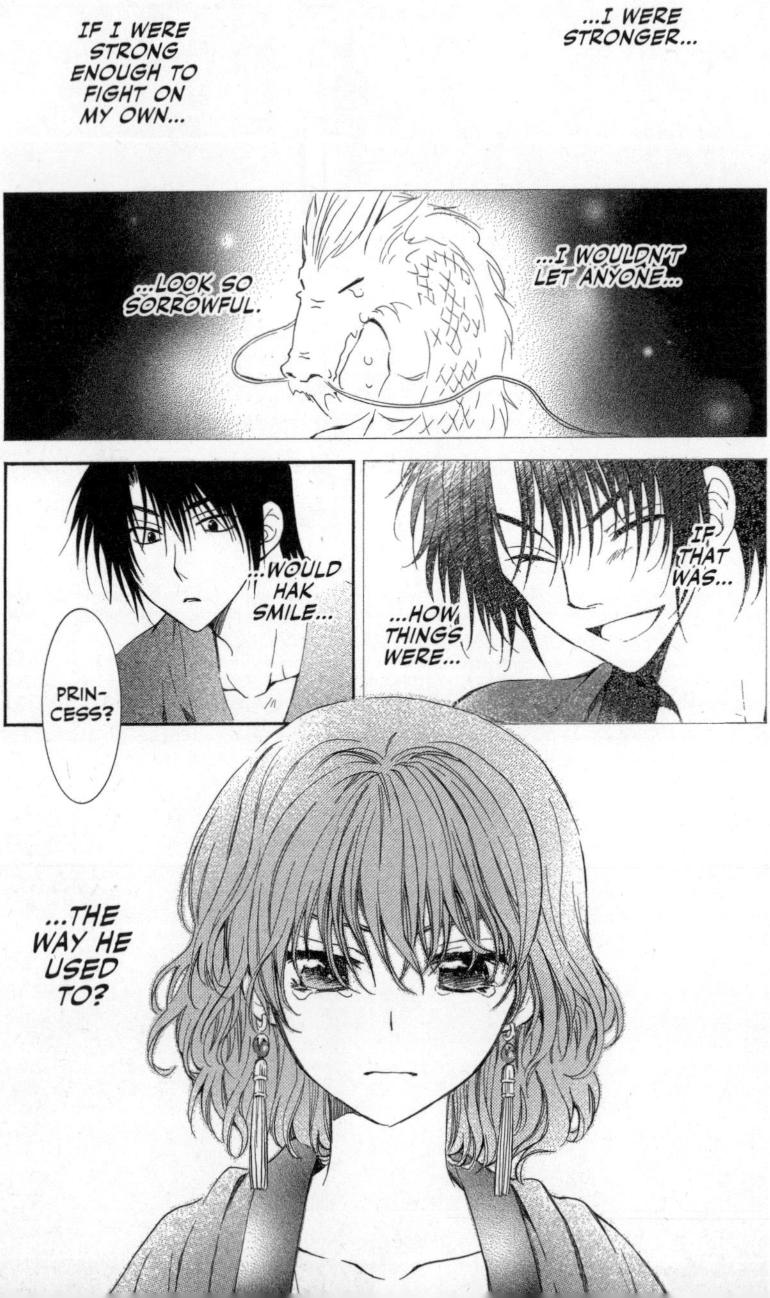
...I WERE STRONGER...
IF I WERE STRONG ENOUGH TO FIGHT ON MY OWN...
...I WOULDN'T LET ANYONE...
...LOOK SO SORROWFUL.
IF THAT WAS...
...HOW THINGS WERE...
...WOULD HAK SMILE...
PRIN-CESS?
...THE WAY HE USED TO?

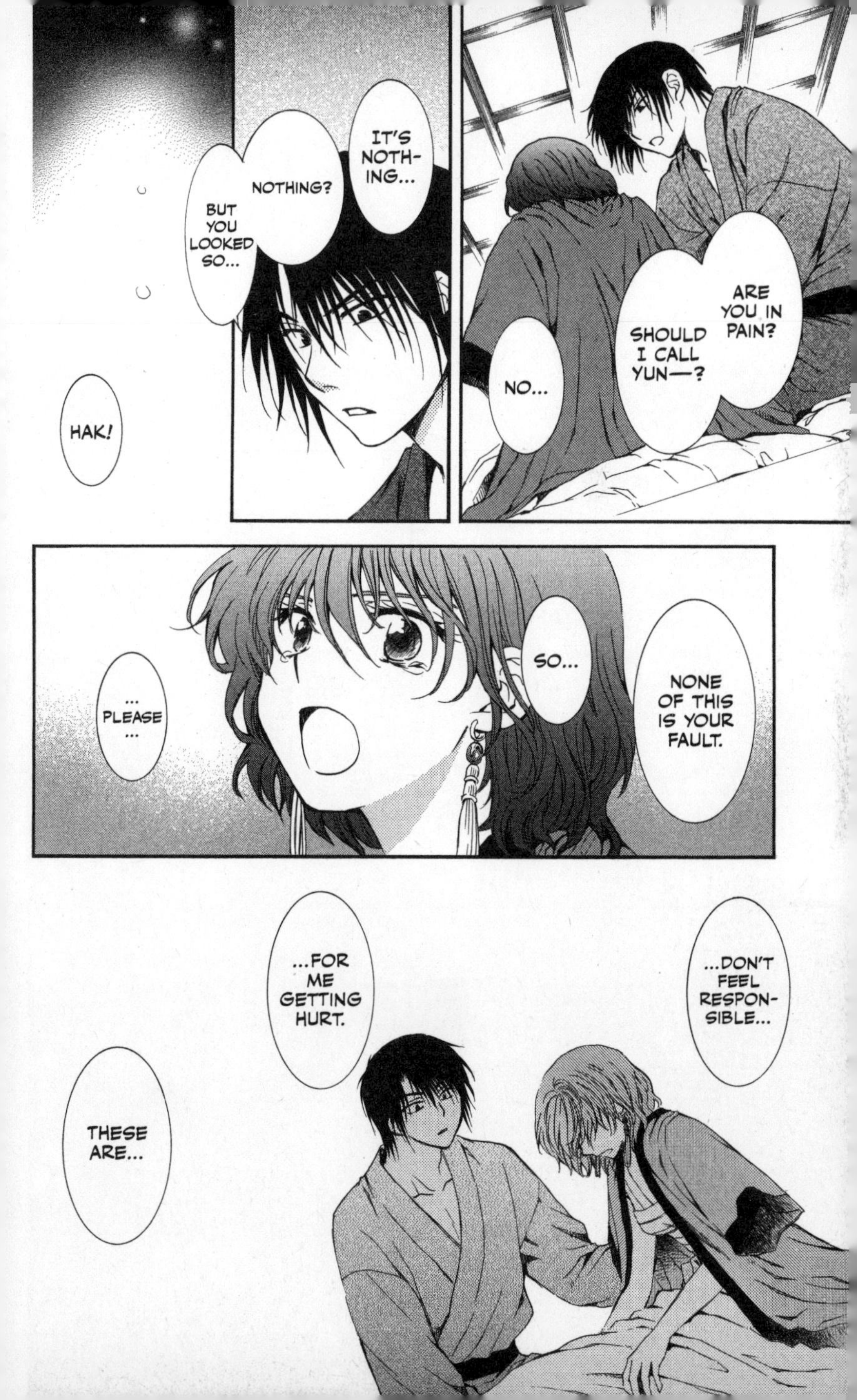
ARE YOU IN PAIN?
SHOULD I CALL YUN—?
NO...
IT'S NOTH-ING...
NOTHING?
BUT YOU LOOKED SO...
HAK!
NONE OF THIS IS YOUR FAULT.
SO...
...PLEASE...
...DON'T FEEL RESPON-SIBLE...
...FOR ME GETTING HURT.
THESE ARE...

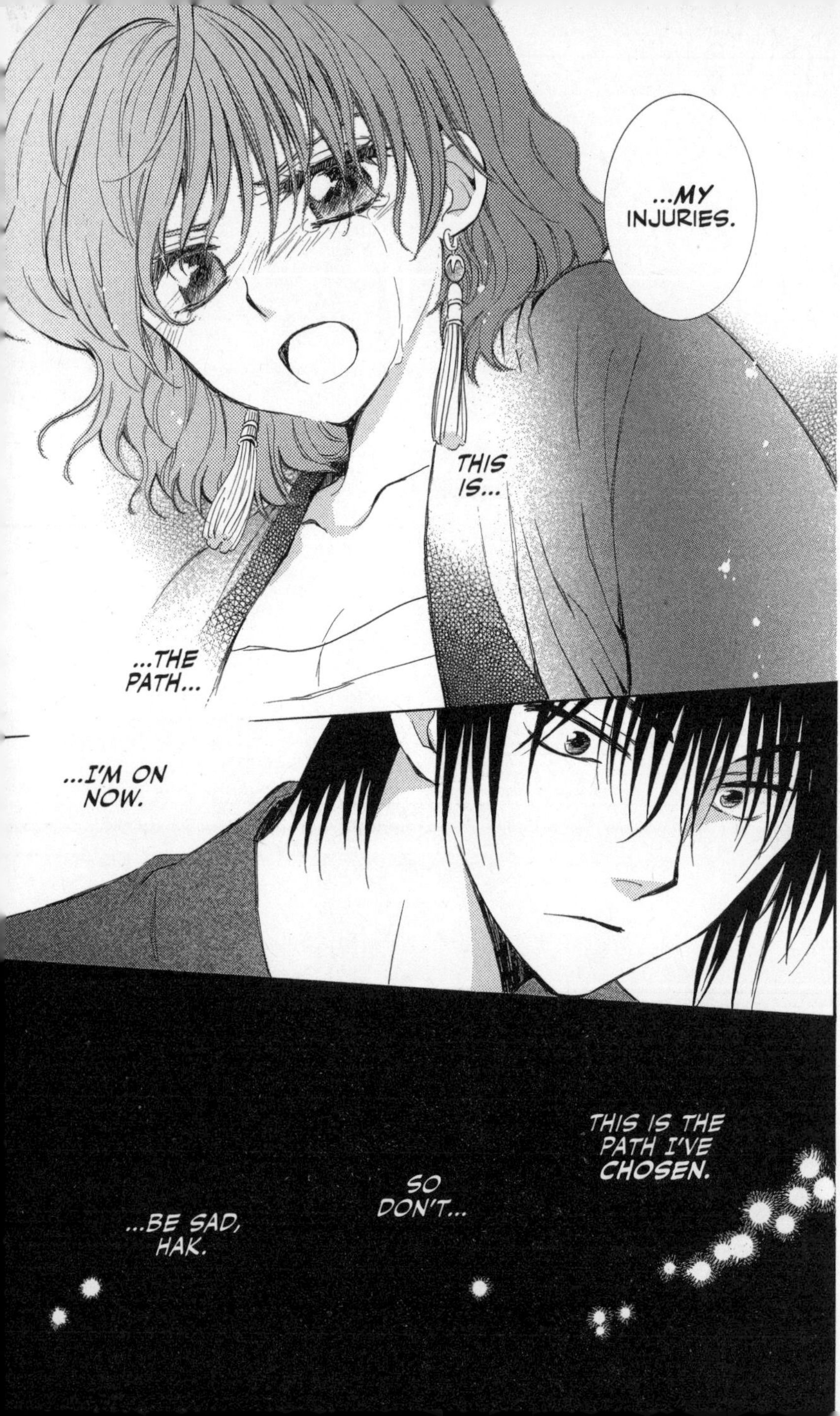
...MY INJURIES.
THIS IS...
...THE PATH...
...I'M ON NOW.
THIS IS THE PATH I'VE CHOSEN.
SO DON'T...
...BE SAD, HAK.

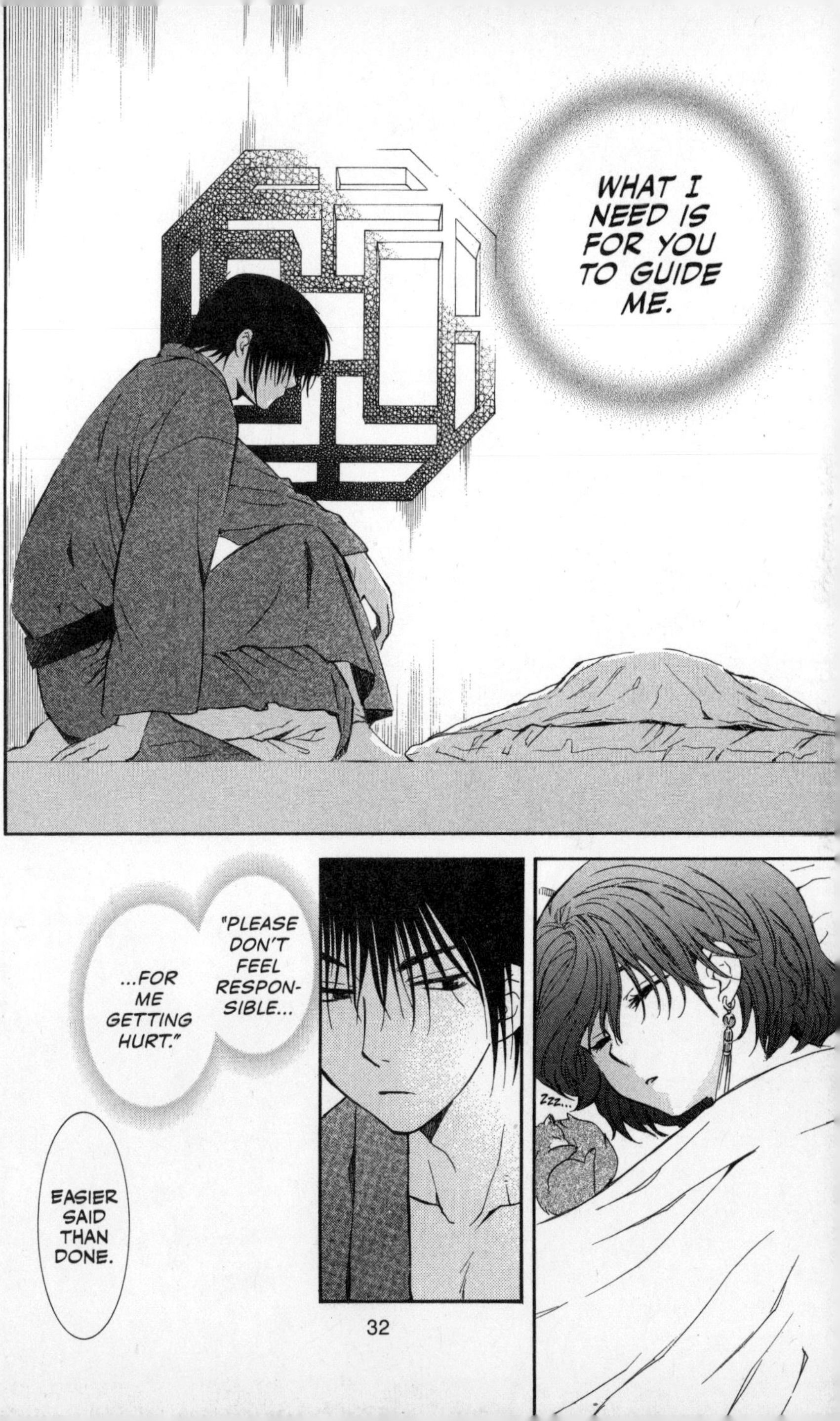
WHAT I NEED IS FOR YOU TO GUIDE ME.
Zzz...
"PLEASE DON'T FEEL RESPONSIBLE...
...FOR ME GETTING HURT."
EASIER SAID THAN DONE.

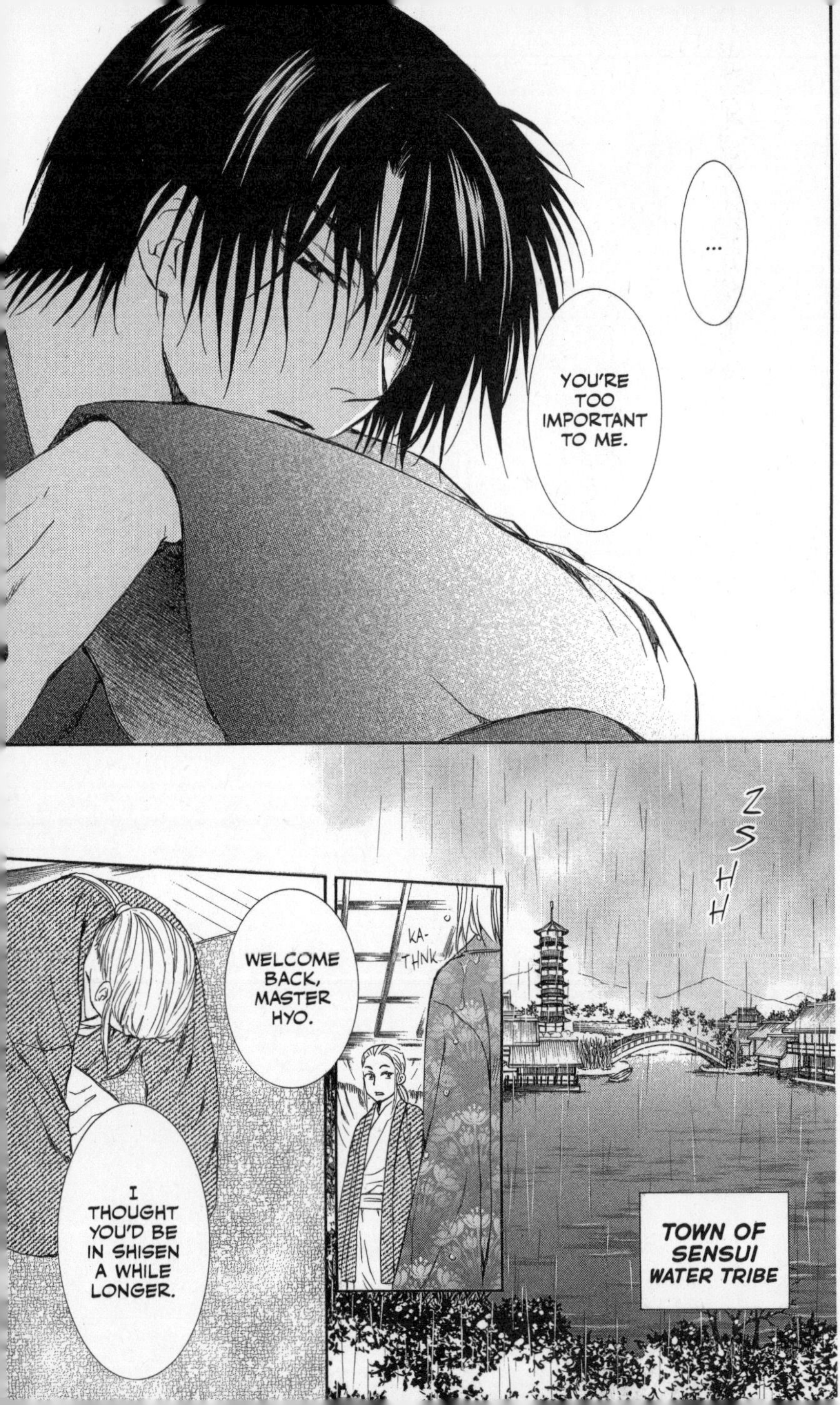
...
YOU'RE TOO IMPORTANT TO ME.
ZSHH
TOWN OF SENSUI WATER TRIBE
KA-THNK
WELCOME BACK, MASTER HYO.
I THOUGHT YOU'D BE IN SHISEN A WHILE LONGER.

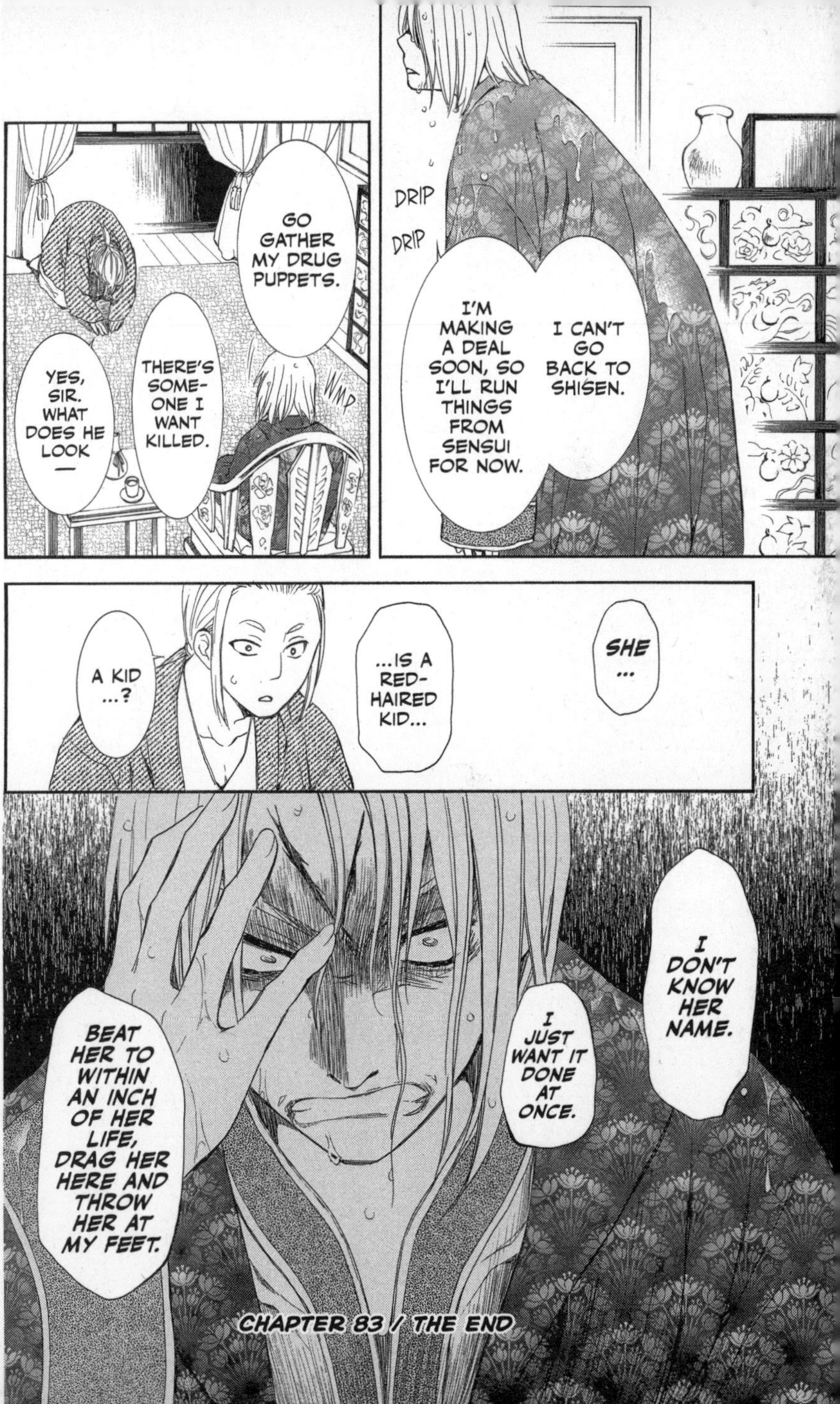
DRIP
DRIP
I CAN'T GO BACK TO SHISEN.
I'M MAKING A DEAL SOON, SO I'LL RUN THINGS FROM SENSUI FOR NOW.
GO GATHER MY DRUG PUPPETS.
WMP
THERE'S SOME-ONE I WANT KILLED.
YES, SIR. WHAT DOES HE LOOK—
SHE...
...IS A RED-HAIRED KID...
A KID...?
I DON'T KNOW HER NAME.
I JUST WANT IT DONE AT ONCE.
BEAT HER TO WITHIN AN INCH OF HER LIFE, DRAG HER HERE AND THROW HER AT MY FEET.
CHAPTER 83 / THE END

CHAPTER 84:
PARTING WAYS

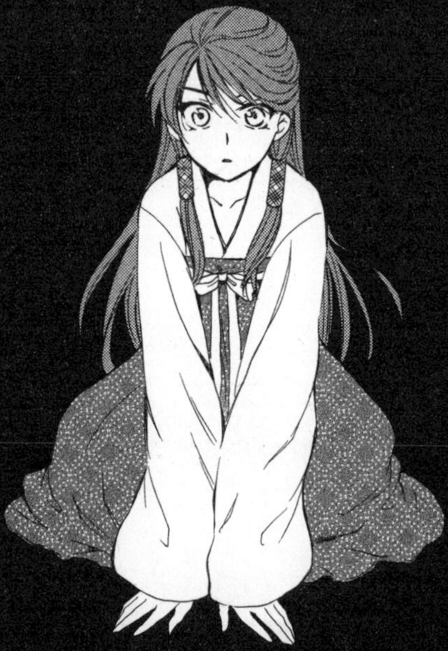

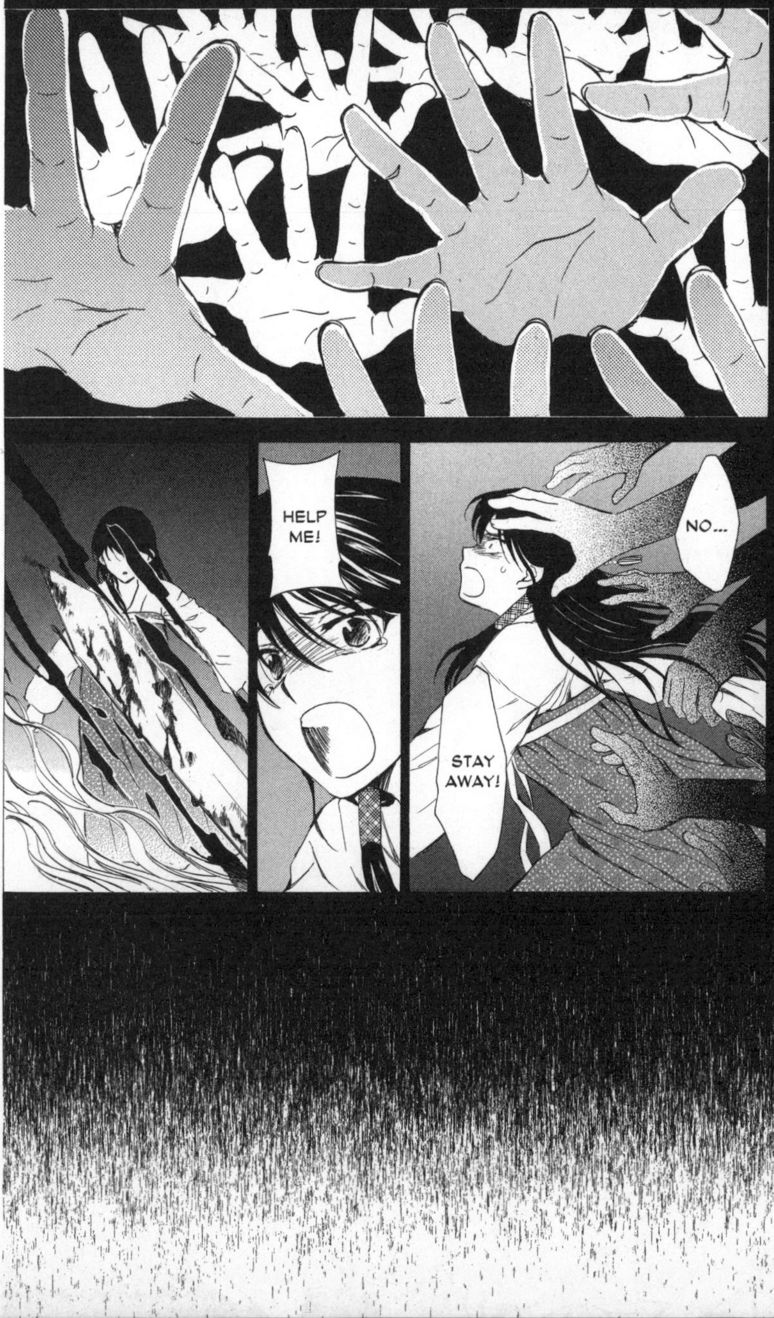
NO...
STAY AWAY!
HELP ME!

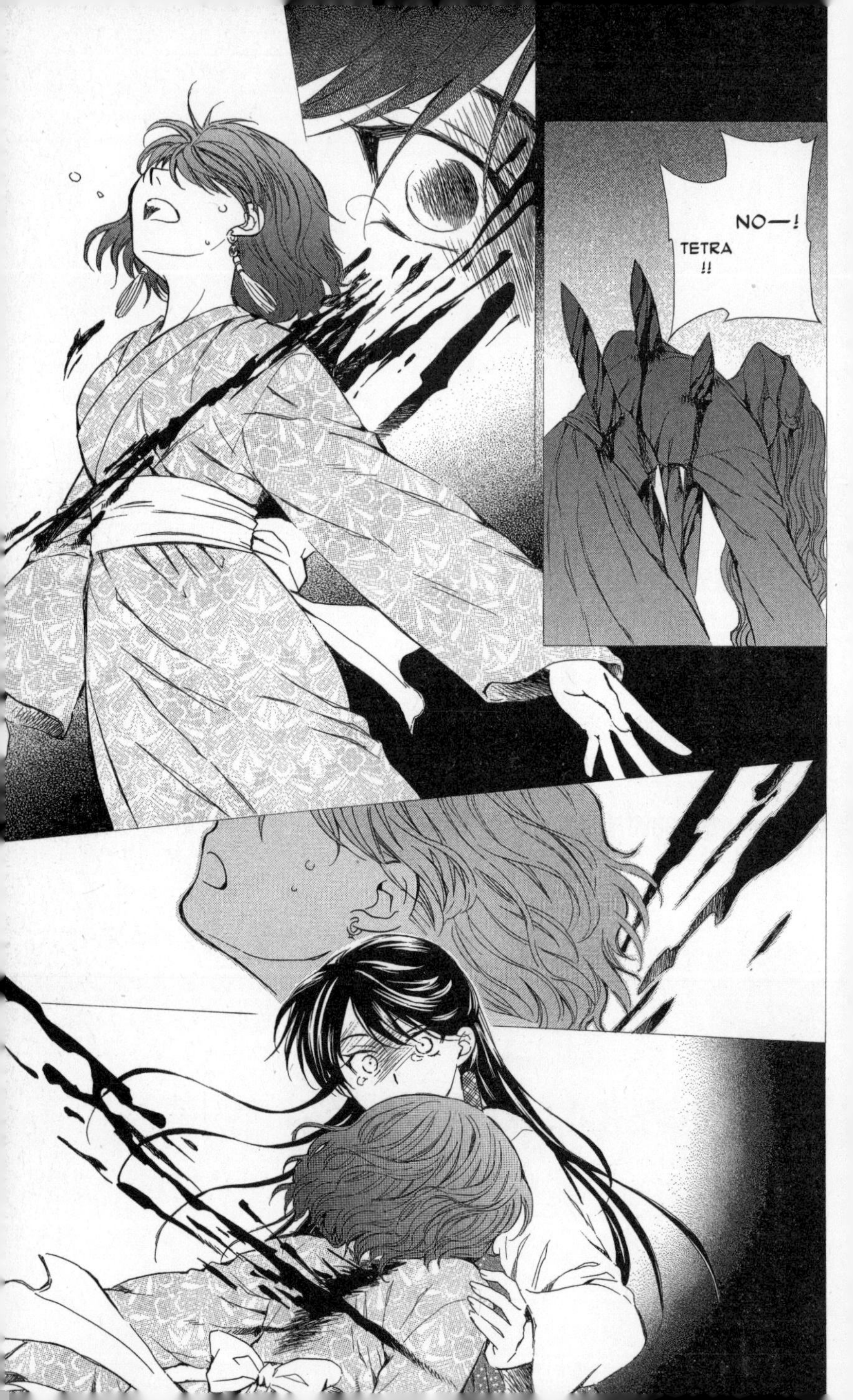
NO—!
TETRA !!

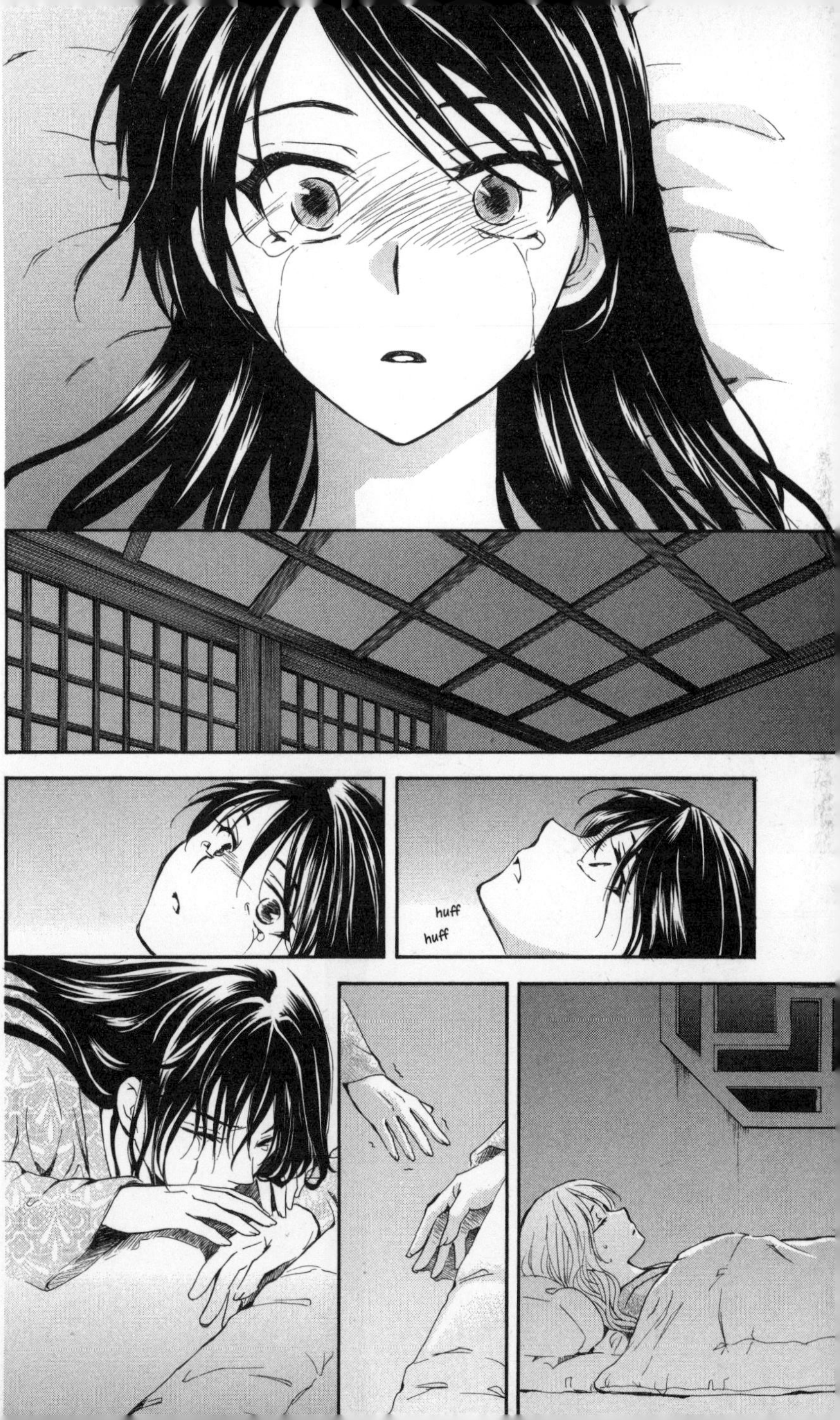
huff
huff

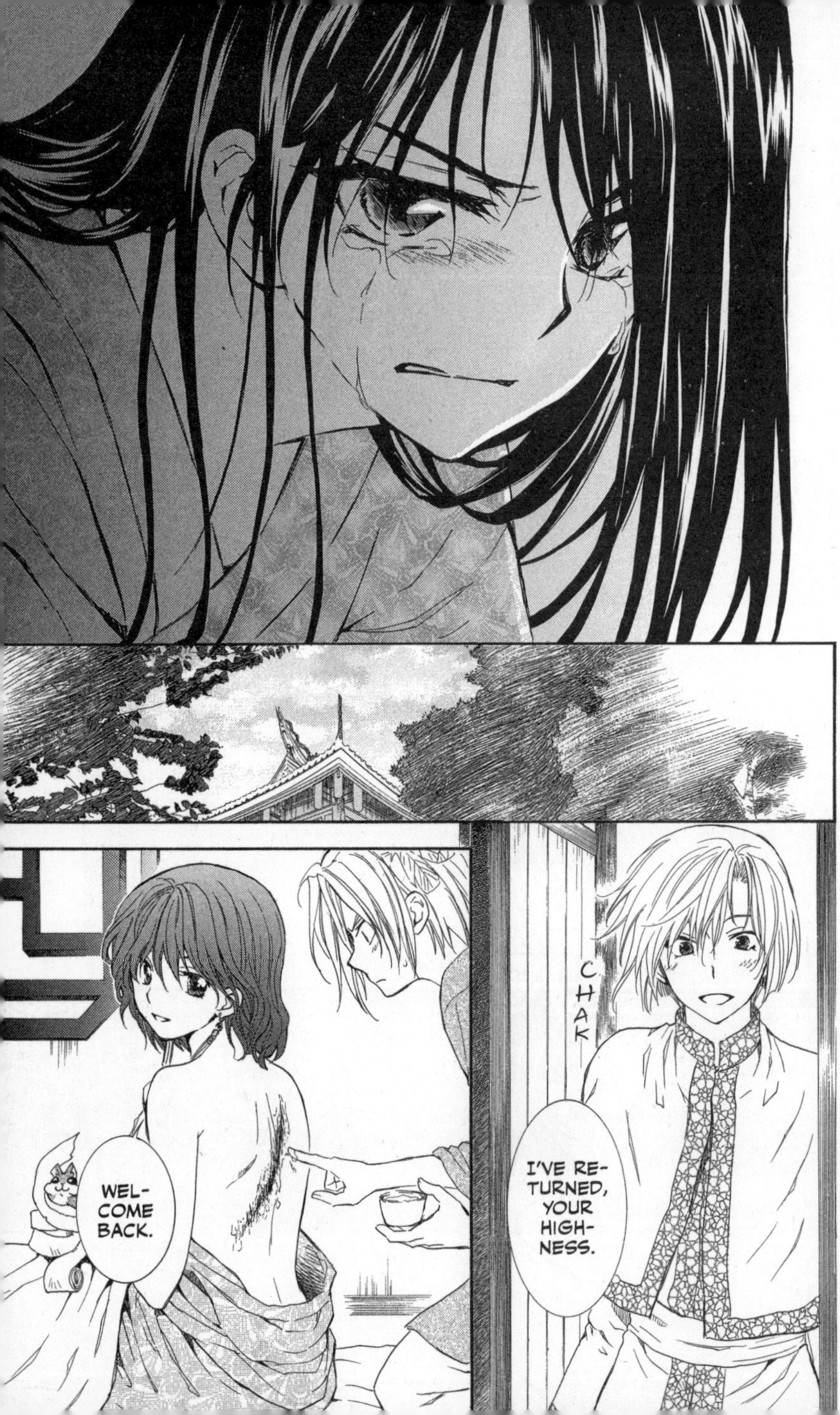
CHAK
I'VE RE-TURNED, YOUR HIGH-NESS.
WEL-COME BACK.

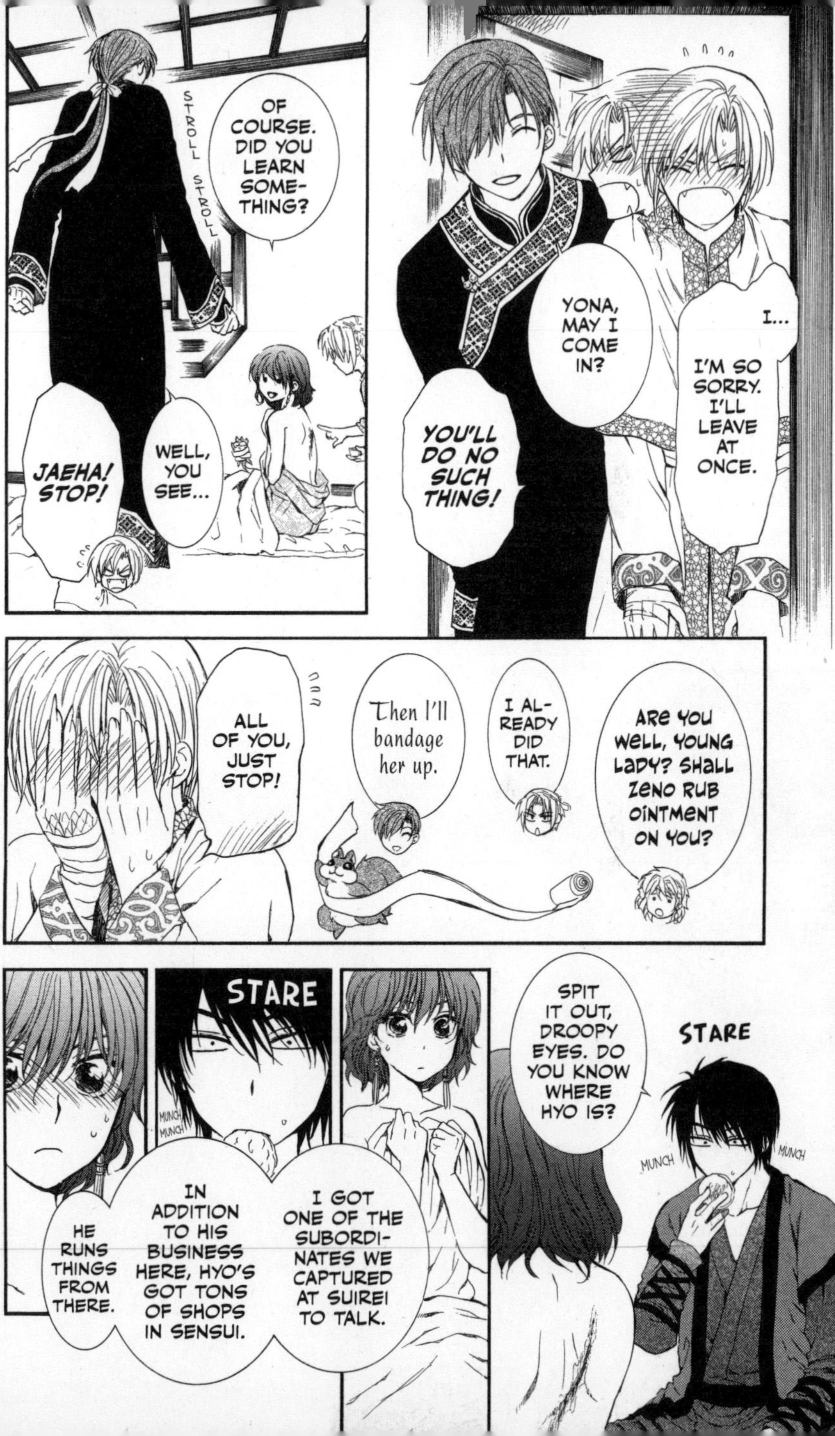
YONA, MAY I COME IN?
I...
I'M SO SORRY. I'LL LEAVE AT ONCE.
YOU'LL DO NO SUCH THING!
OF COURSE. DID YOU LEARN SOMETHING?
STROLL STROLL
WELL, YOU SEE...
JAEHA! STOP!
ARE YOU WELL, YOUNG LADY? SHALL ZENO RUB OINTMENT ON YOU?
I ALREADY DID THAT.
Then I'll bandage her up.
ALL OF YOU, JUST STOP!
STARE
SPIT IT OUT, DROOPY EYES. DO YOU KNOW WHERE HYO IS?
MUNCH
MUNCH
STARE
MUNCH MUNCH
I GOT ONE OF THE SUBORDINATES WE CAPTURED AT SUIREI TO TALK.
IN ADDITION TO HIS BUSINESS HERE, HYO'S GOT TONS OF SHOPS IN SENSUI.
HE RUNS THINGS FROM THERE.

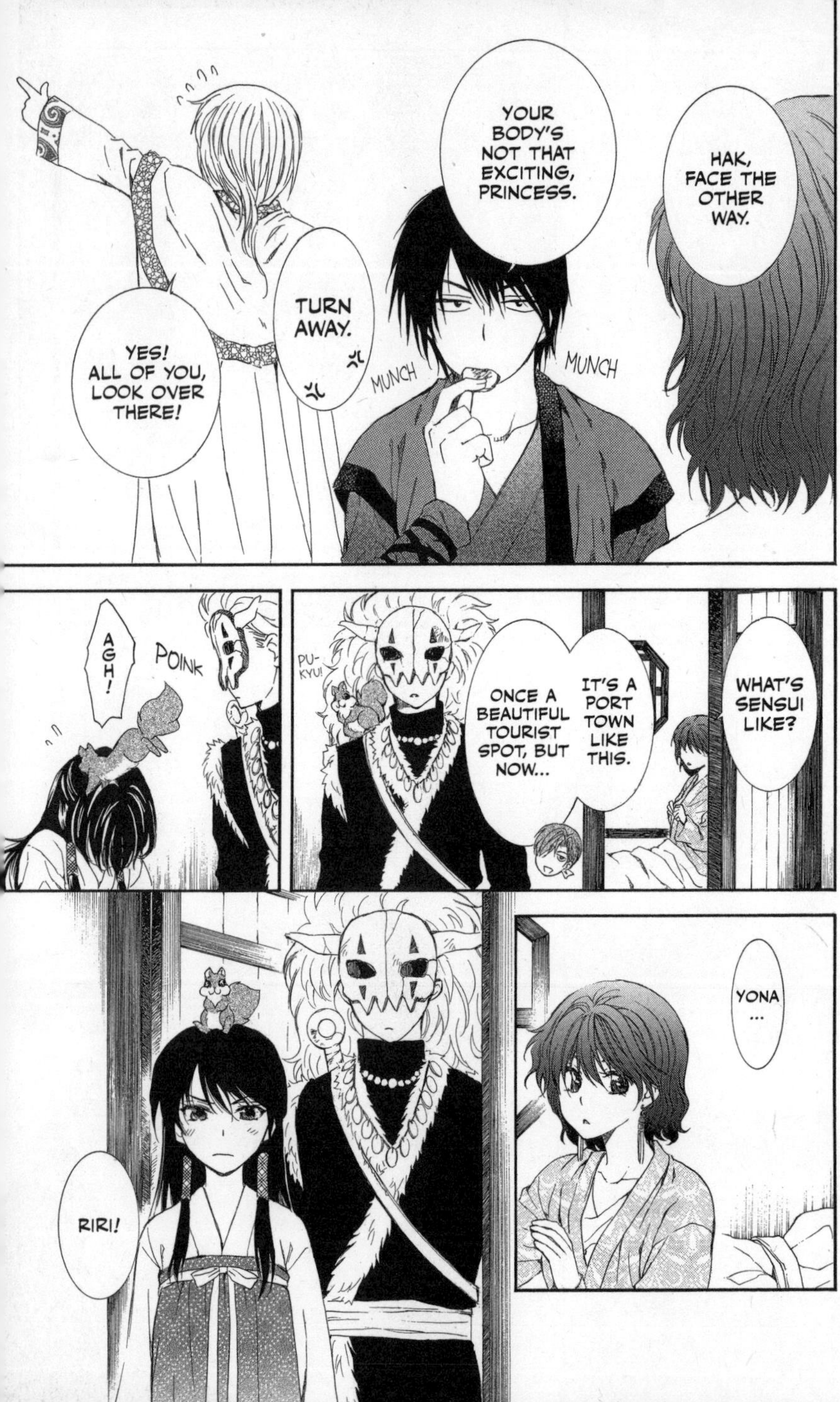
HAK, FACE THE OTHER WAY.
YOUR BODY'S NOT THAT EXCITING, PRINCESS.
MUNCH
MUNCH
TURN AWAY.
YES! ALL OF YOU, LOOK OVER THERE!
WHAT'S SENSUI LIKE?
IT'S A PORT TOWN LIKE THIS.
ONCE A BEAUTIFUL TOURIST SPOT, BUT NOW...
PU-KYU!
POINK
AGH!
YONA...
RIRI!

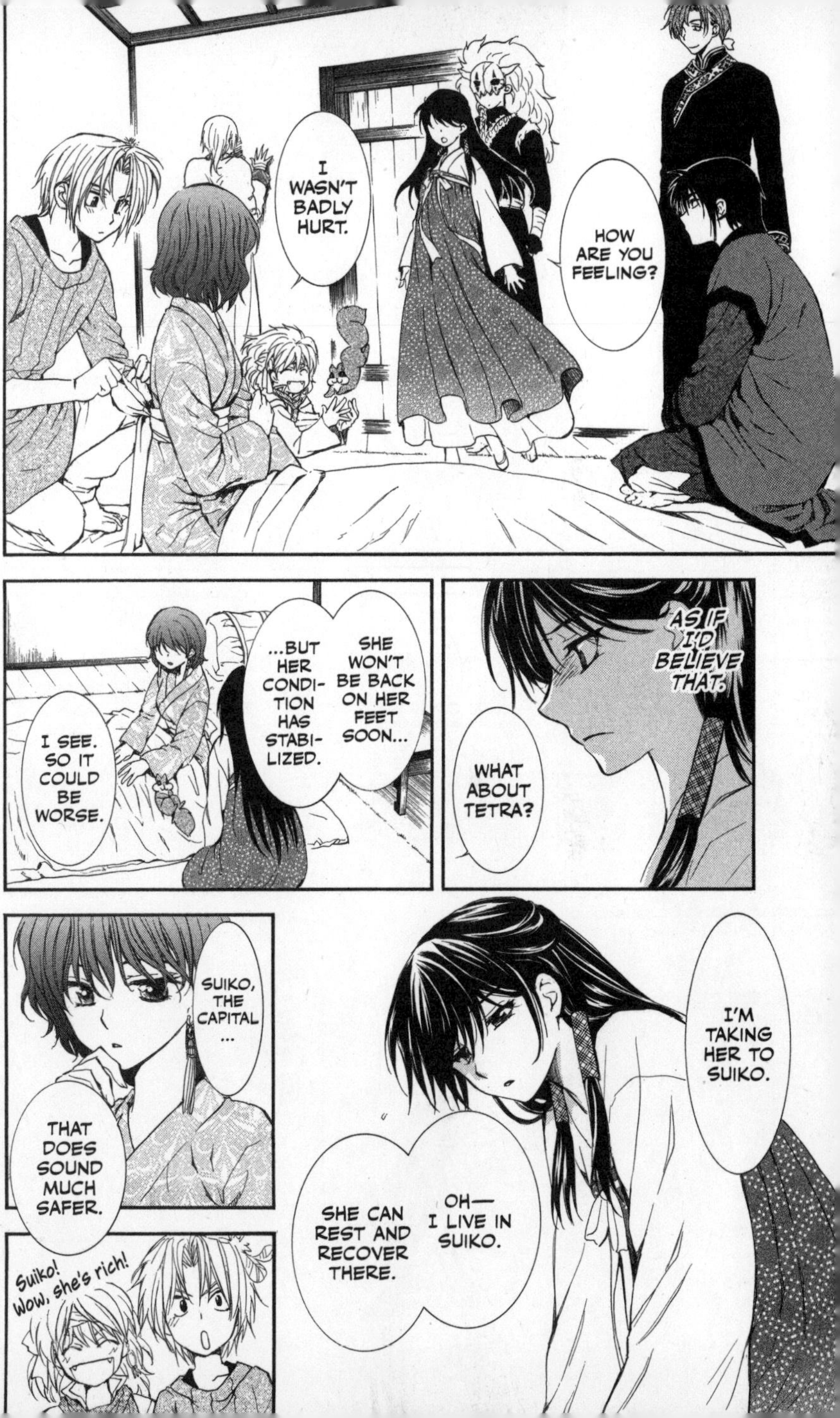
HOW ARE YOU FEELING?
I WASN'T BADLY HURT.
AS IF I'D BELIEVE THAT.
WHAT ABOUT TETRA?
SHE WON'T BE BACK ON HER FEET SOON...
...BUT HER CONDITION HAS STABILIZED.
I SEE. SO IT COULD BE WORSE.
I'M TAKING HER TO SUIKO.
OH— I LIVE IN SUIKO.
SHE CAN REST AND RECOVER THERE.
SUIKO, THE CAPITAL...
THAT DOES SOUND MUCH SAFER.
Suiko! Wow, she's rich!

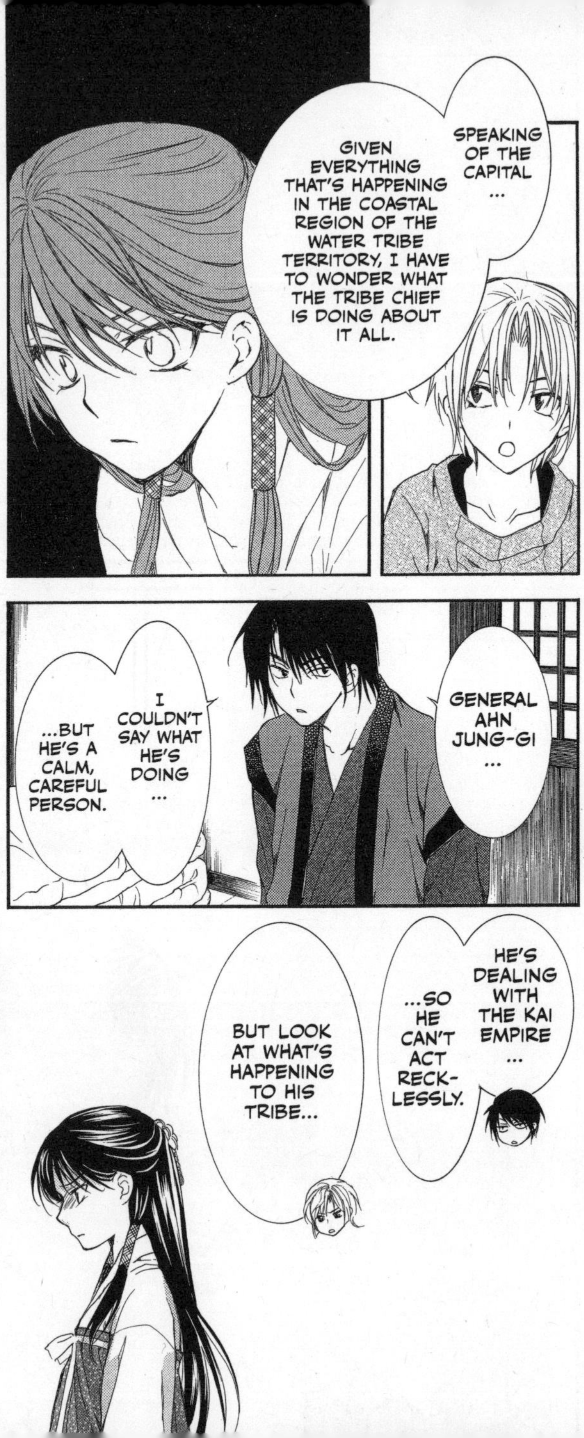
SPEAKING OF THE CAPITAL ...
GIVEN EVERYTHING THAT'S HAPPENING IN THE COASTAL REGION OF THE WATER TRIBE TERRITORY, I HAVE TO WONDER WHAT THE TRIBE CHIEF IS DOING ABOUT IT ALL.
GENERAL AHN JUNG-GI ...
I COULDN'T SAY WHAT HE'S DOING ...
...BUT HE'S A CALM, CAREFUL PERSON.
HE'S DEALING WITH THE KAI EMPIRE ...
...SO HE CAN'T ACT RECKLESSLY.
BUT LOOK AT WHAT'S HAPPENING TO HIS TRIBE...

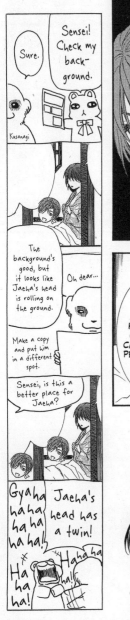

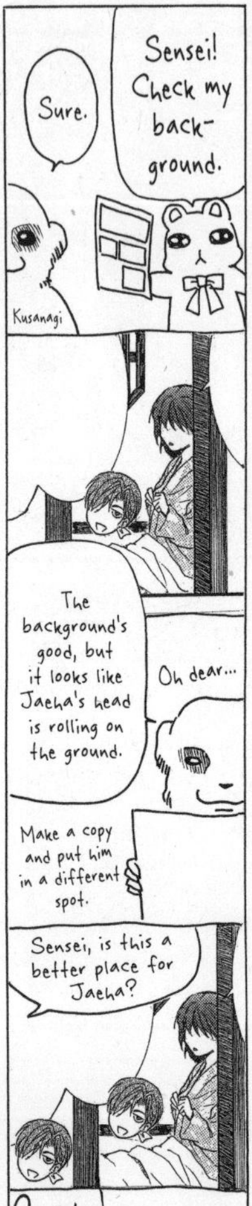
Sensei! Check my back-ground.
Sure.
Kusanagi
Oh dear...
The background's good, but it looks like Jaeha's head is rolling on the ground.
Make a copy and put him in a different spot.
Sensei, is this a better place for Jaeha?
Jaeha's head has a twin!
Gyahahahahahaha!
Hahaha!
Hahahaha!

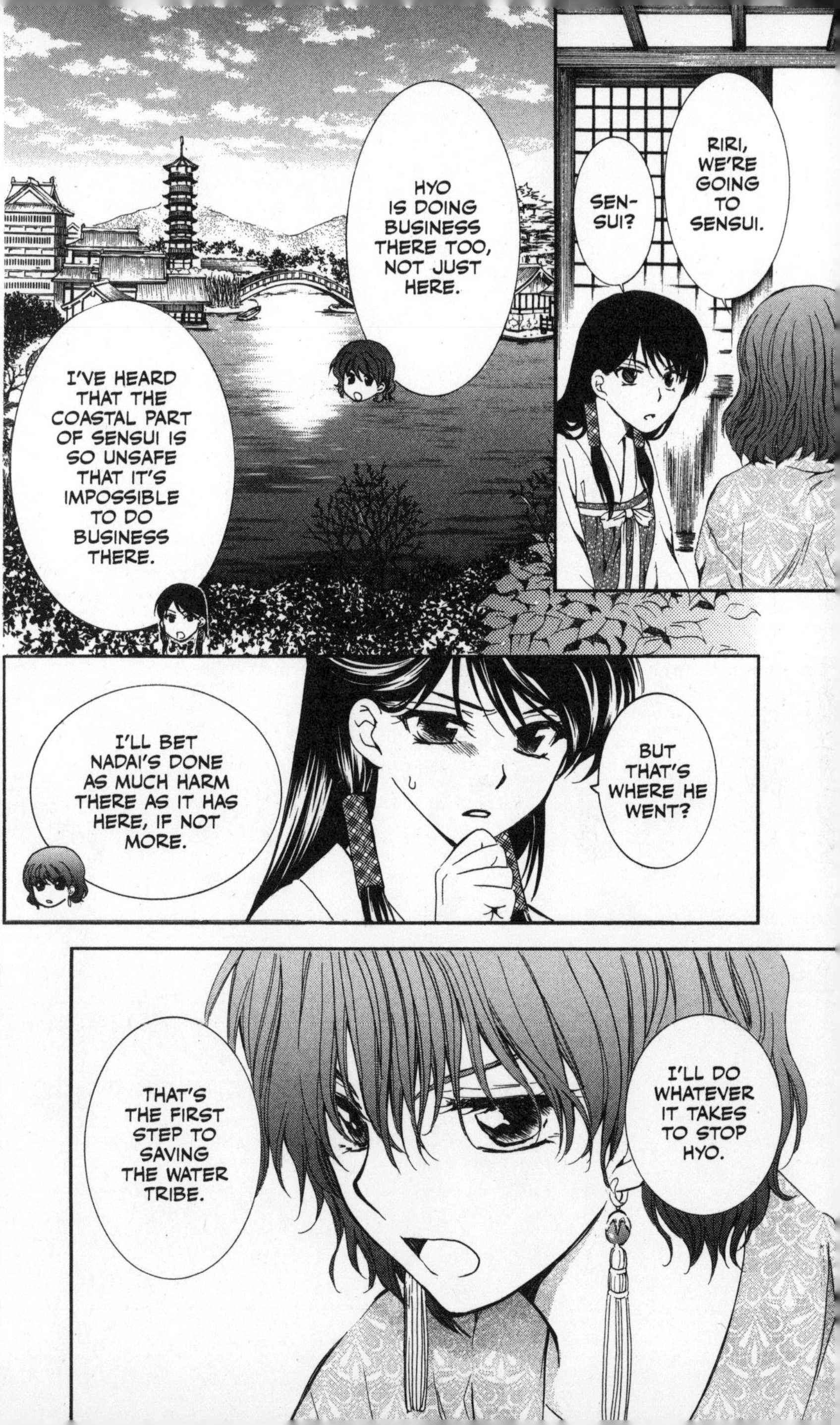
RIRI, WE'RE GOING TO SENSUI.
SEN-SUI?
HYO IS DOING BUSINESS THERE TOO, NOT JUST HERE.
I'VE HEARD THAT THE COASTAL PART OF SENSUI IS SO UNSAFE THAT IT'S IMPOSSIBLE TO DO BUSINESS THERE.
BUT THAT'S WHERE HE WENT?
I'LL BET NADAI'S DONE AS MUCH HARM THERE AS IT HAS HERE, IF NOT MORE.
I'LL DO WHATEVER IT TAKES TO STOP HYO.
THAT'S THE FIRST STEP TO SAVING THE WATER TRIBE.

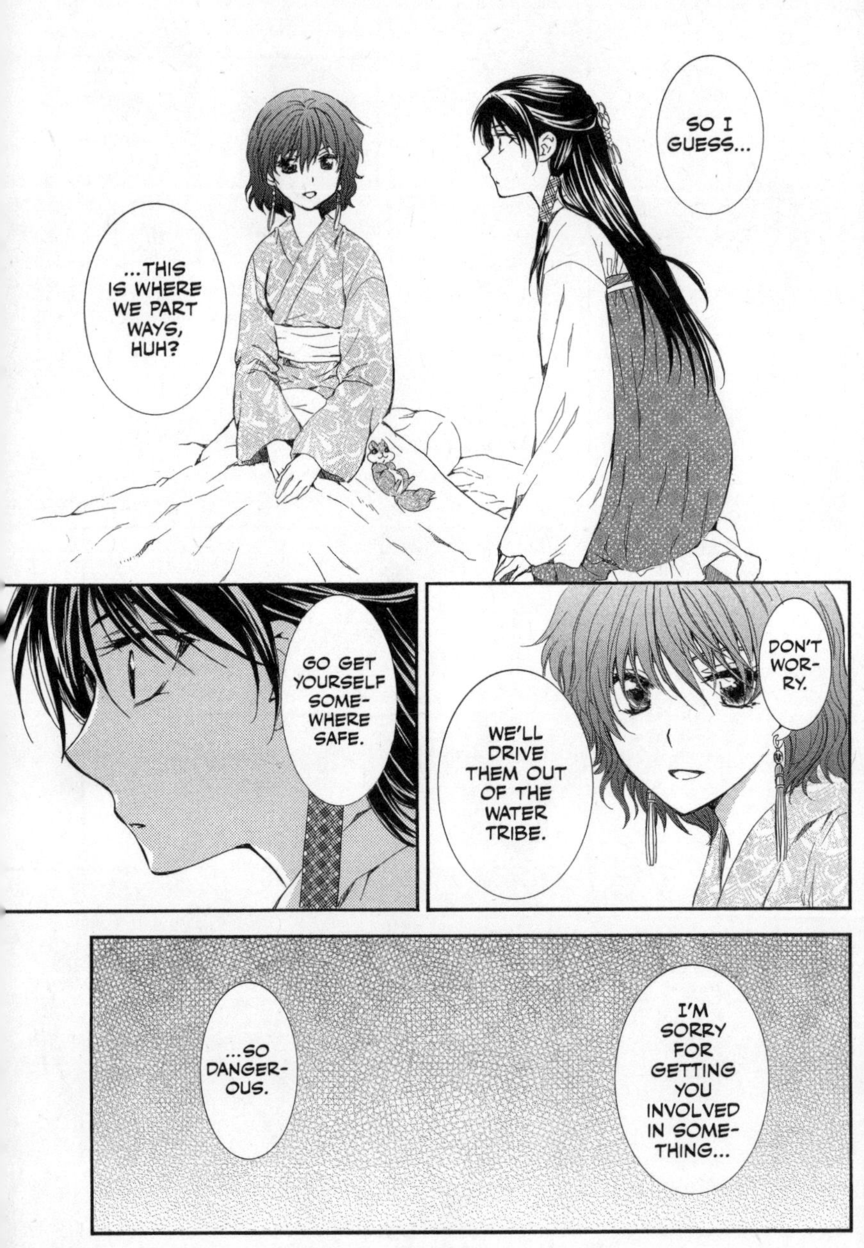
SO I GUESS...
...THIS IS WHERE WE PART WAYS, HUH?
DON'T WOR-RY.
WE'LL DRIVE THEM OUT OF THE WATER TRIBE.
GO GET YOURSELF SOME-WHERE SAFE.
I'M SORRY FOR GETTING YOU INVOLVED IN SOME-THING...
...SO DANGER-OUS.

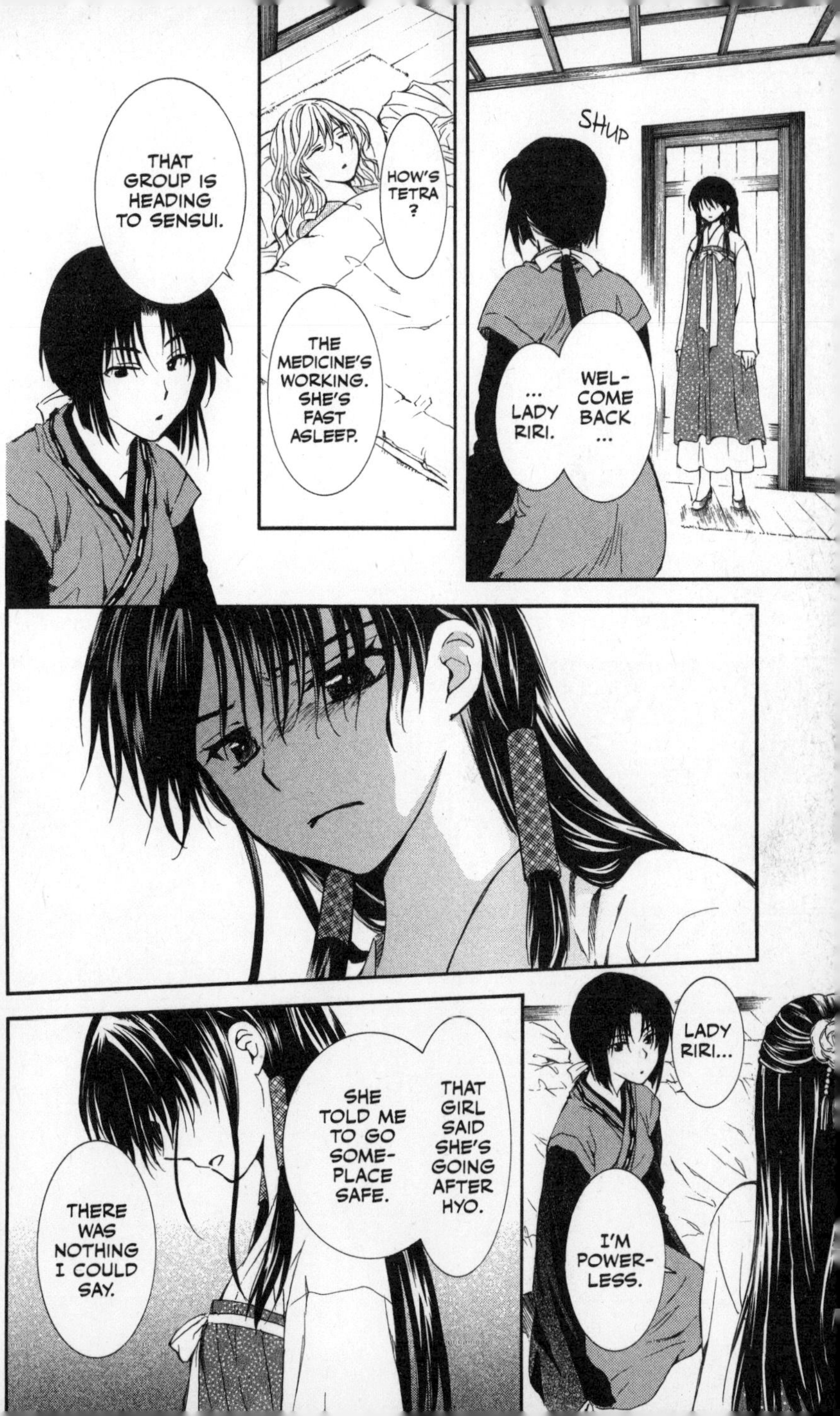
SHUP
WELCOME BACK...
...LADY RIRI.
HOW'S TETRA?
THE MEDICINE'S WORKING. SHE'S FAST ASLEEP.
THAT GROUP IS HEADING TO SENSUI.
LADY RIRI...
I'M POWERLESS.
THAT GIRL SAID SHE'S GOING AFTER HYO.
SHE TOLD ME TO GO SOMEPLACE SAFE.
THERE WAS NOTHING I COULD SAY.

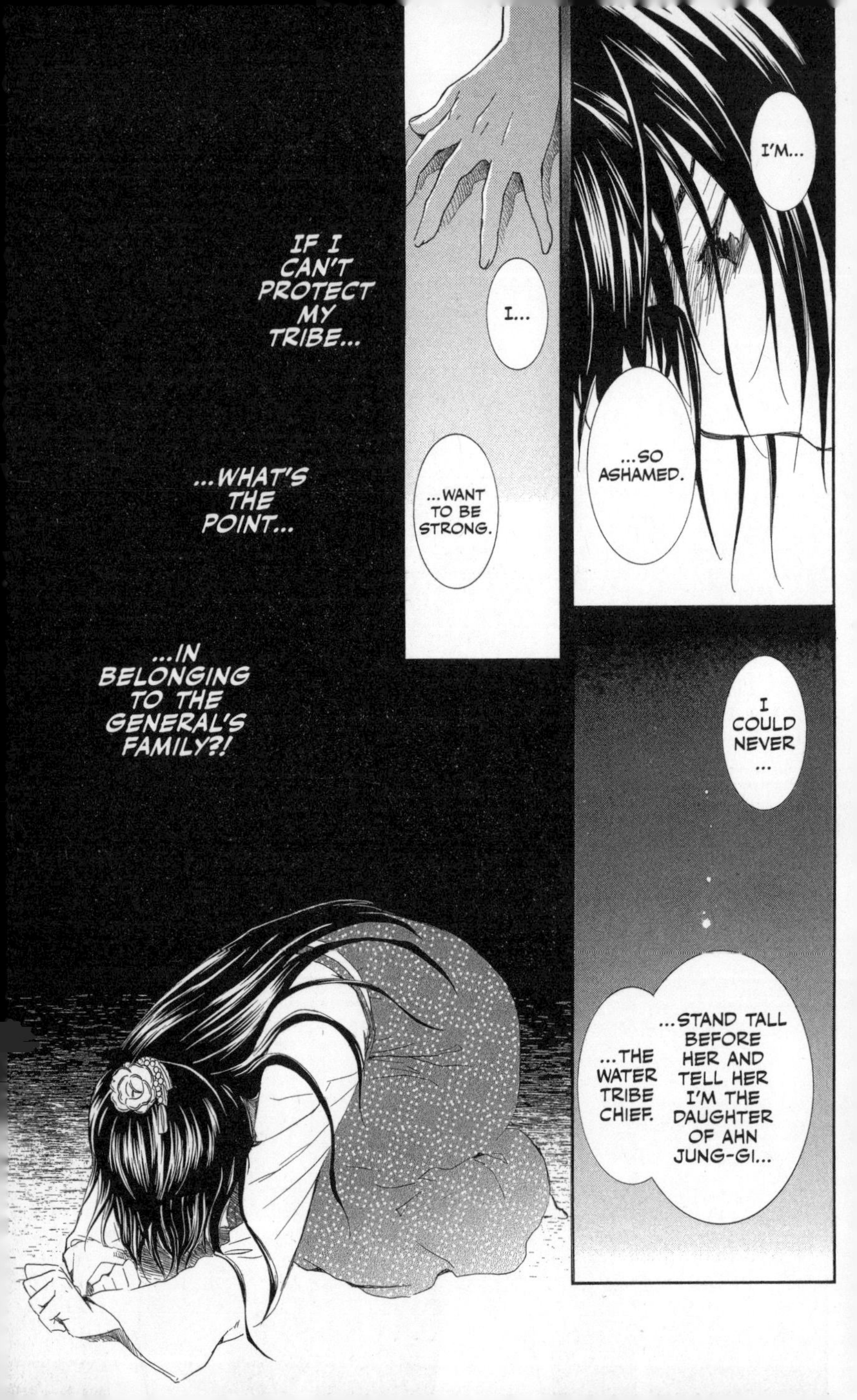
I'M...
...SO ASHAMED.
I...
...WANT TO BE STRONG.
I COULD NEVER...
...STAND TALL BEFORE HER AND TELL HER I'M THE DAUGHTER OF AHN JUNG-GI...
...THE WATER TRIBE CHIEF.
IF I CAN'T PROTECT MY TRIBE...
...WHAT'S THE POINT...
...IN BELONGING TO THE GENERAL'S FAMILY?!

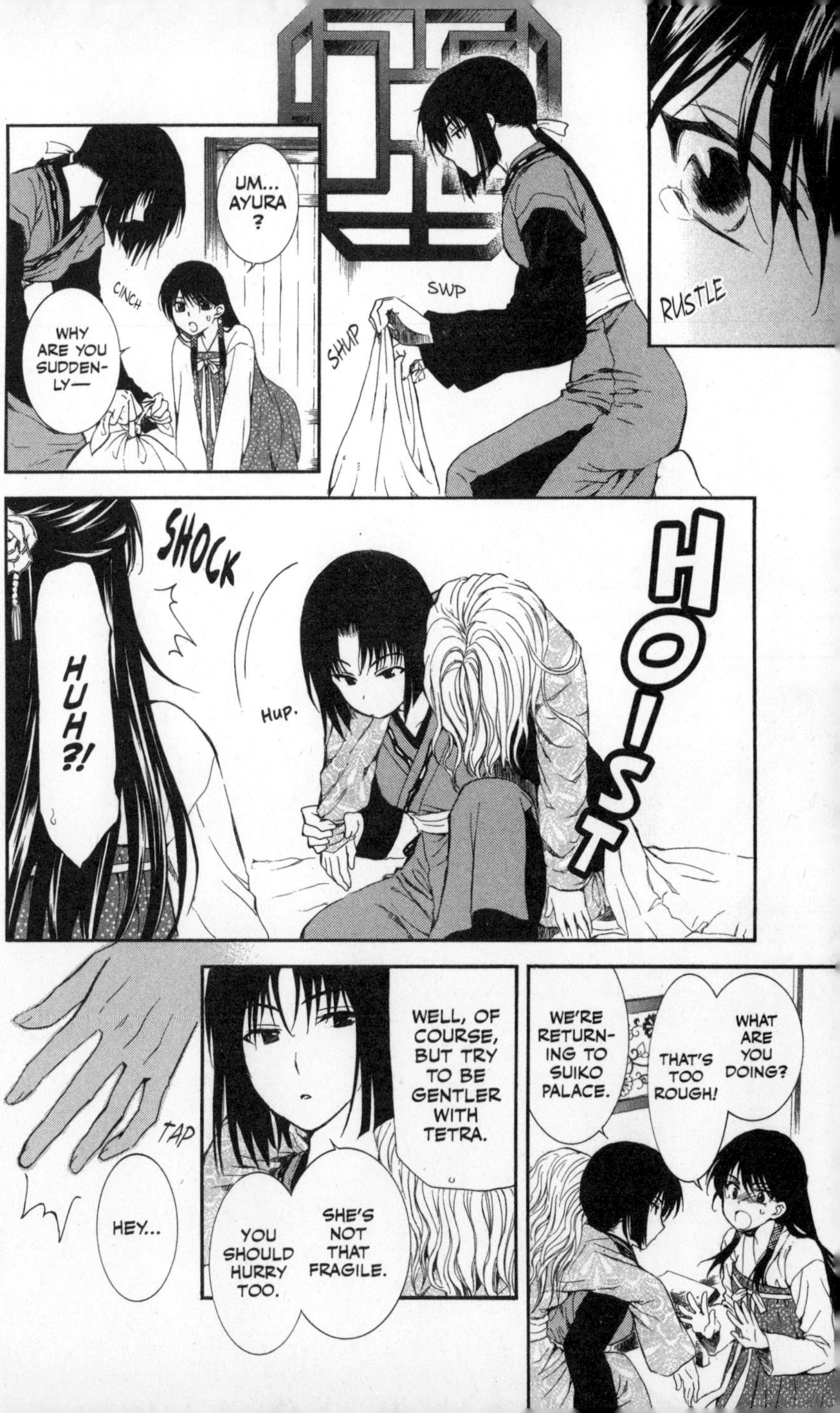
RUSTLE
SWP
SHUP
UM... AYURA?
CINCH
WHY ARE YOU SUDDENLY—
HOIST
Hup.
SHOCK
HUH?!
WHAT ARE YOU DOING?
THAT'S TOO ROUGH!
WE'RE RETURNING TO SUIKO PALACE.
WELL, OF COURSE, BUT TRY TO BE GENTLER WITH TETRA.
SHE'S NOT THAT FRAGILE.
YOU SHOULD HURRY TOO.
TAP
HEY...

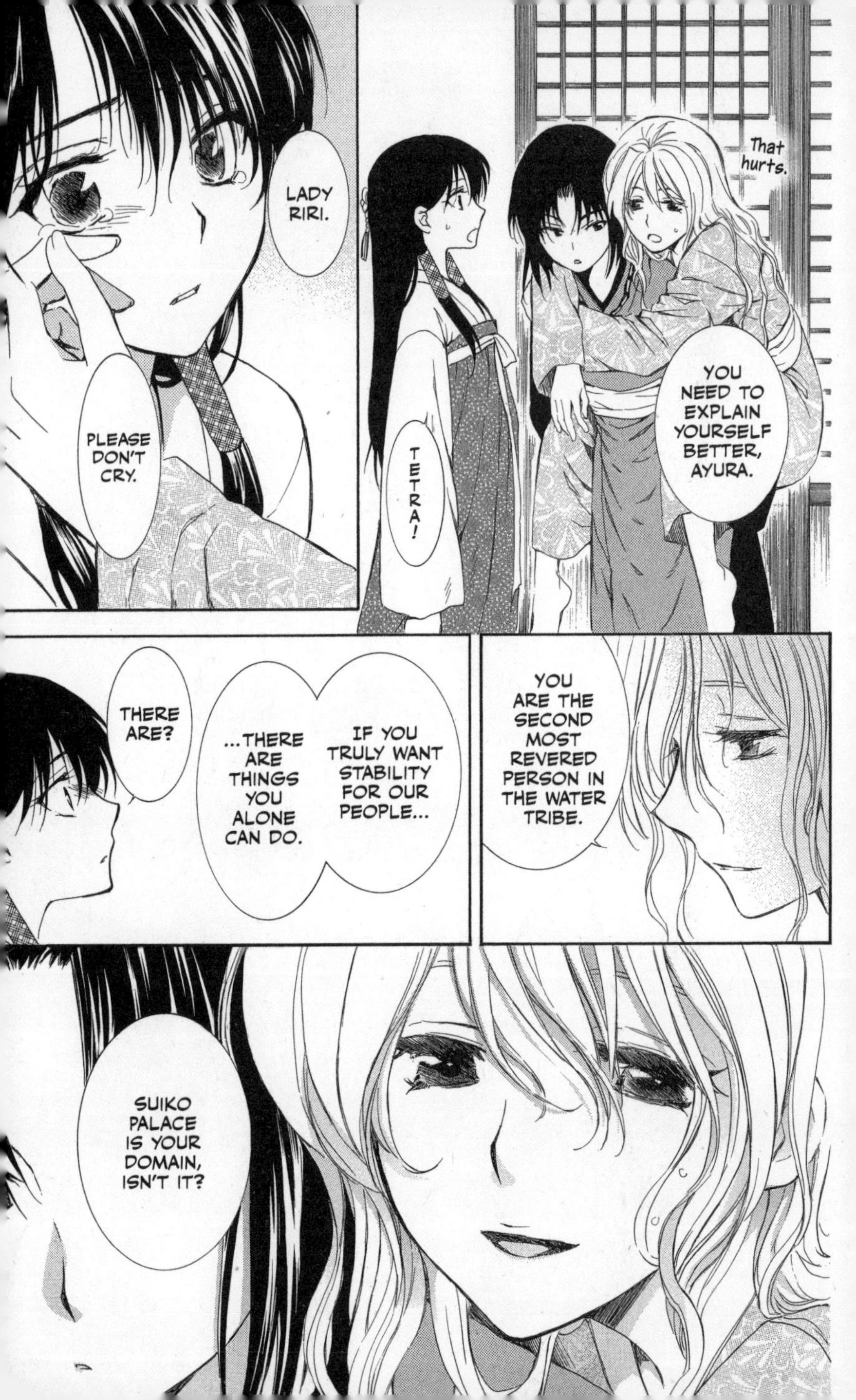
That hurts.
YOU NEED TO EXPLAIN YOURSELF BETTER, AYURA.
TETRA!
LADY RIRI.
PLEASE DON'T CRY.
YOU ARE THE SECOND MOST REVERED PERSON IN THE WATER TRIBE.
IF YOU TRULY WANT STABILITY FOR OUR PEOPLE...
...THERE ARE THINGS YOU ALONE CAN DO.
THERE ARE?
SUIKO PALACE IS YOUR DOMAIN, ISN'T IT?

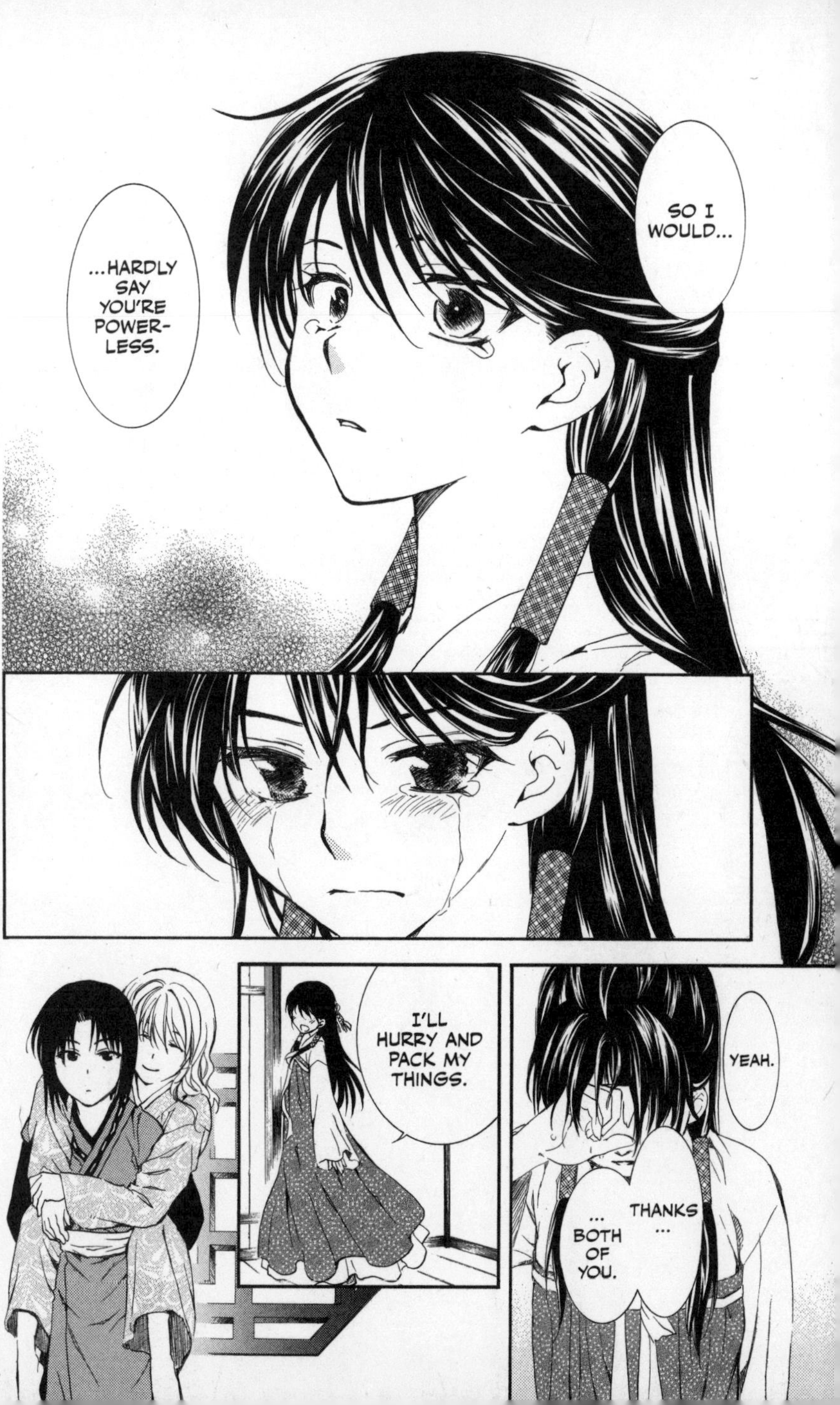
SO I WOULD...
...HARDLY SAY YOU'RE POWER-LESS.
YEAH.
THANKS...
...BOTH OF YOU.
I'LL HURRY AND PACK MY THINGS.

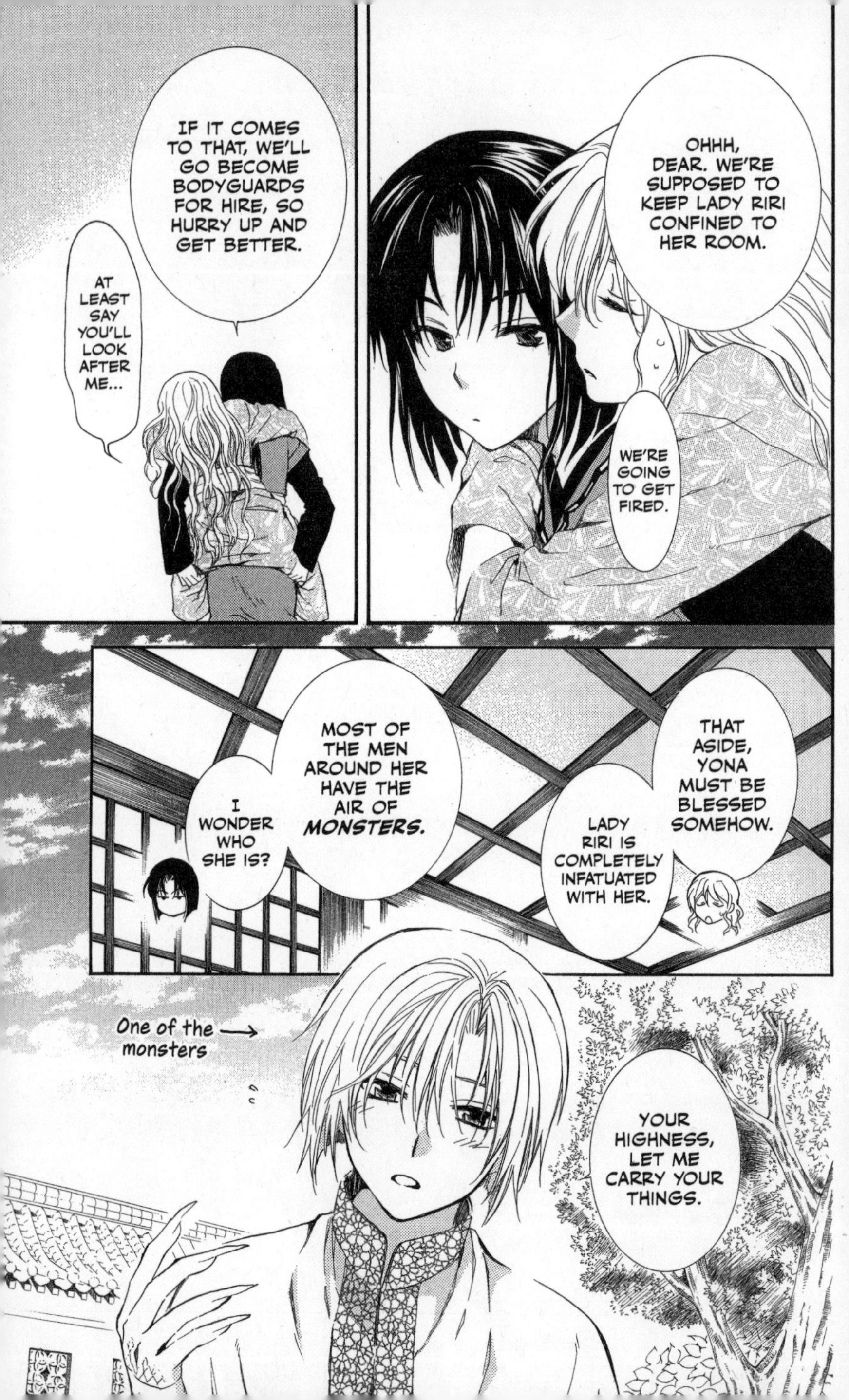
OHHH, DEAR. WE'RE SUPPOSED TO KEEP LADY RIRI CONFINED TO HER ROOM.
WE'RE GOING TO GET FIRED.
IF IT COMES TO THAT, WE'LL GO BECOME BODYGUARDS FOR HIRE, SO HURRY UP AND GET BETTER.
AT LEAST SAY YOU'LL LOOK AFTER ME...
THAT ASIDE, YONA MUST BE BLESSED SOMEHOW.
LADY RIRI IS COMPLETELY INFATUATED WITH HER.
MOST OF THE MEN AROUND HER HAVE THE AIR OF *MONSTERS.*
I WONDER WHO SHE IS?
YOUR HIGHNESS, LET ME CARRY YOUR THINGS.
One of the monsters →

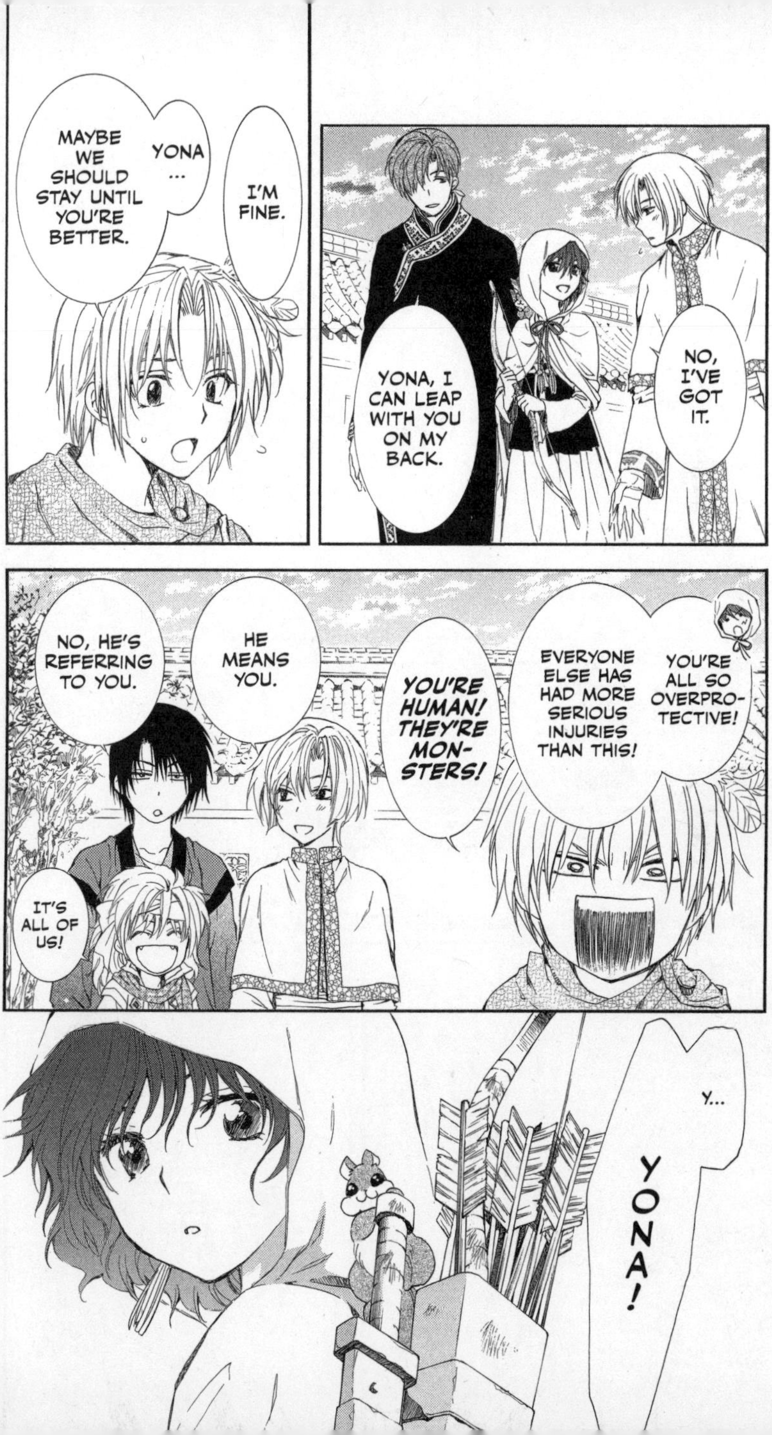
NO, I'VE GOT IT.
YONA, I CAN LEAP WITH YOU ON MY BACK.
I'M FINE.
YONA ...
MAYBE WE SHOULD STAY UNTIL YOU'RE BETTER.
YOU'RE ALL SO OVERPROTECTIVE!
EVERYONE ELSE HAS HAD MORE SERIOUS INJURIES THAN THIS!
YOU'RE HUMAN! THEY'RE MONSTERS!
HE MEANS YOU.
NO, HE'S REFERRING TO YOU.
IT'S ALL OF US!
Y...
YONA!

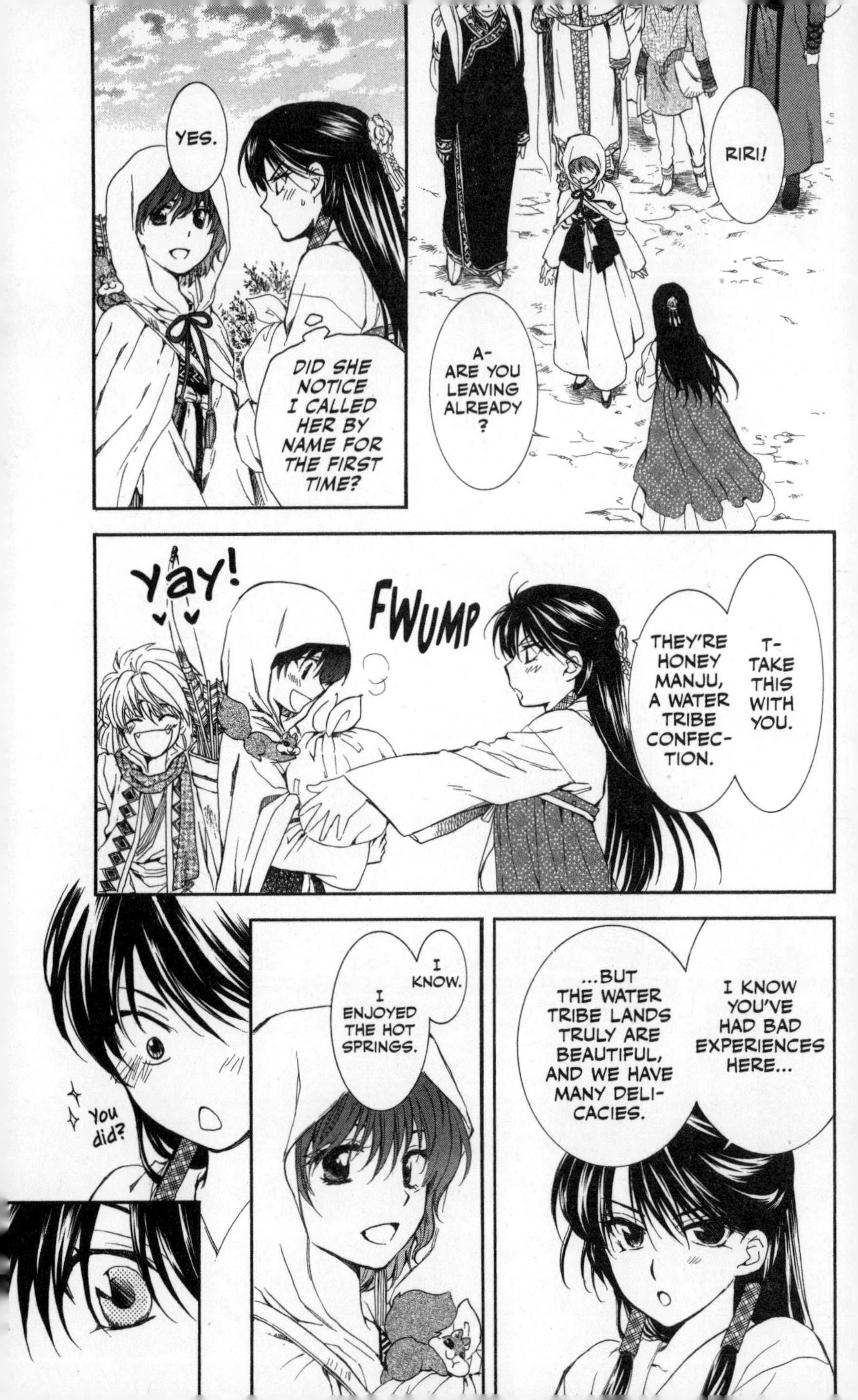
RIRI!
A- ARE YOU LEAVING ALREADY?
YES.
DID SHE NOTICE I CALLED HER BY NAME FOR THE FIRST TIME?
T- TAKE THIS WITH YOU.
THEY'RE HONEY MANJU, A WATER TRIBE CONFECTION.
FWUMP
Yay!
I KNOW YOU'VE HAD BAD EXPERIENCES HERE...
...BUT THE WATER TRIBE LANDS TRULY ARE BEAUTIFUL, AND WE HAVE MANY DELICACIES.
I KNOW.
I ENJOYED THE HOT SPRINGS.
You did?

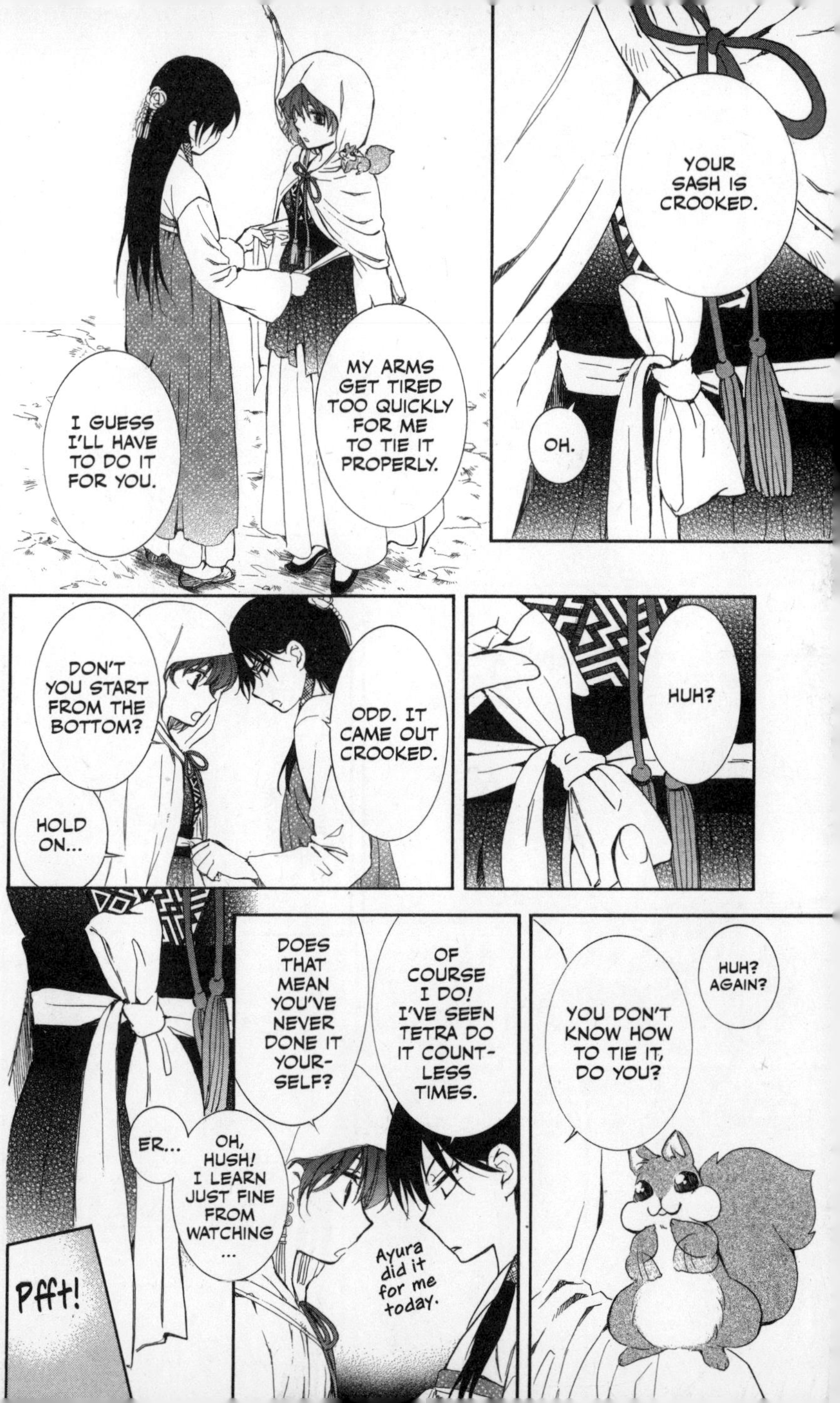
YOUR SASH IS CROOKED.
OH.
MY ARMS GET TIRED TOO QUICKLY FOR ME TO TIE IT PROPERLY.
I GUESS I'LL HAVE TO DO IT FOR YOU.
HUH?
ODD. IT CAME OUT CROOKED.
DON'T YOU START FROM THE BOTTOM?
HOLD ON...
HUH? AGAIN?
YOU DON'T KNOW HOW TO TIE IT, DO YOU?
OF COURSE I DO! I'VE SEEN TETRA DO IT COUNTLESS TIMES.
DOES THAT MEAN YOU'VE NEVER DONE IT YOURSELF?
Ayura did it for me today.
OH, HUSH! I LEARN JUST FINE FROM WATCHING...
ER...
Pfft!

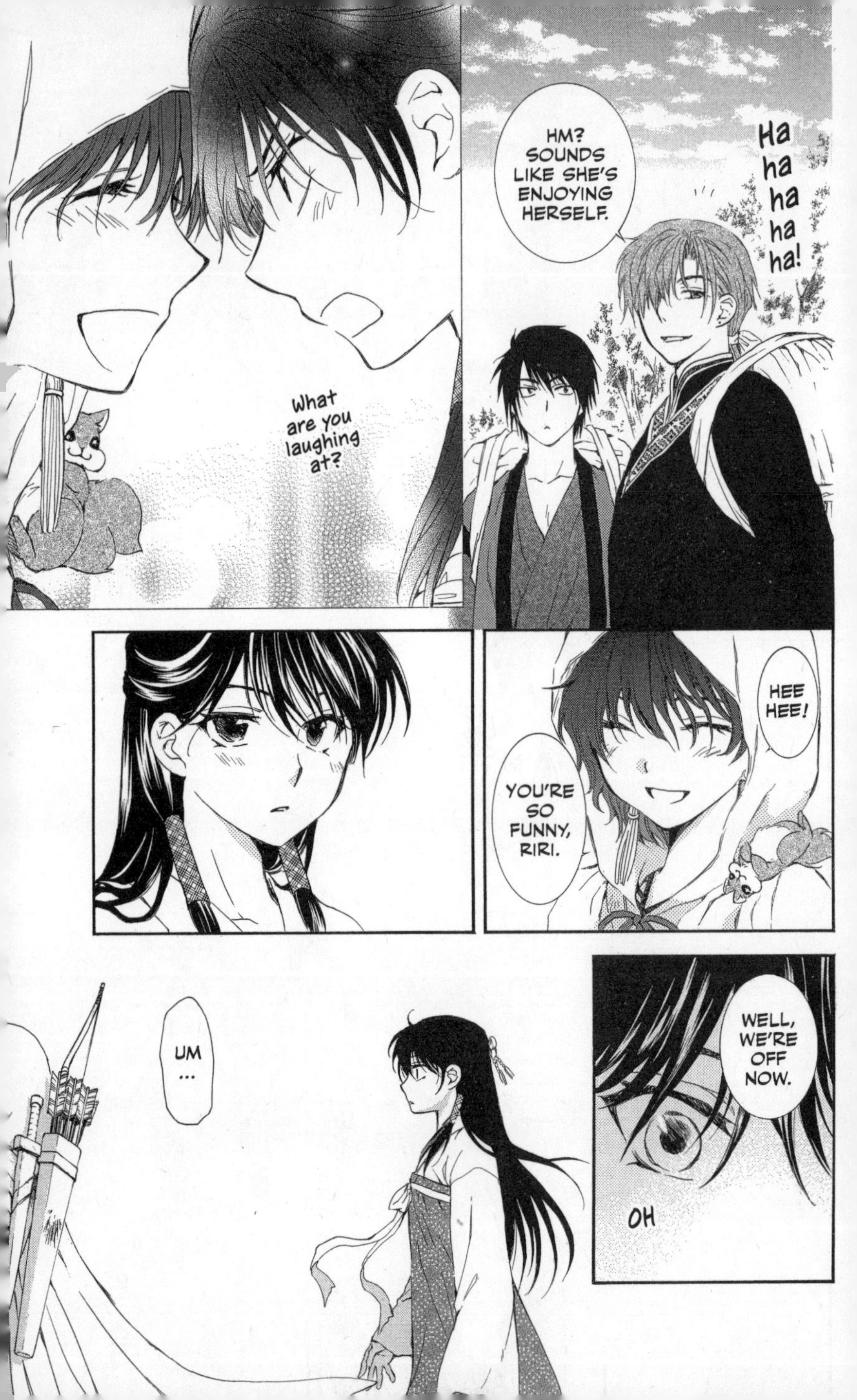
Ha ha ha ha ha!
HM? SOUNDS LIKE SHE'S ENJOYING HERSELF.
What are you laughing at?
HEE HEE!
YOU'RE SO FUNNY, RIRI.
WELL, WE'RE OFF NOW.
OH
UM ...

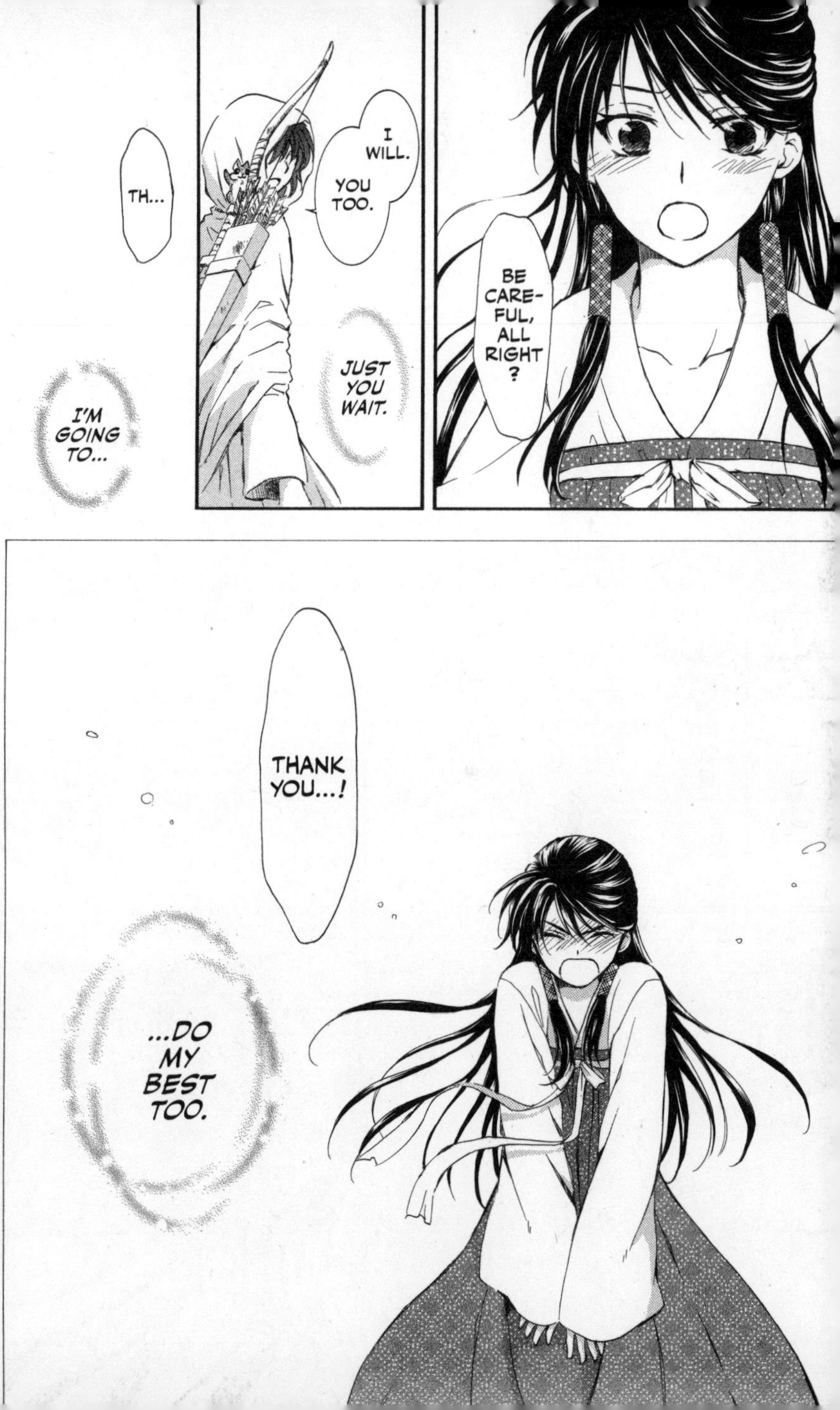
BE CARE-FUL, ALL RIGHT?
I WILL. YOU TOO.
JUST YOU WAIT.
TH...
I'M GOING TO...
THANK YOU...!
...DO MY BEST TOO.

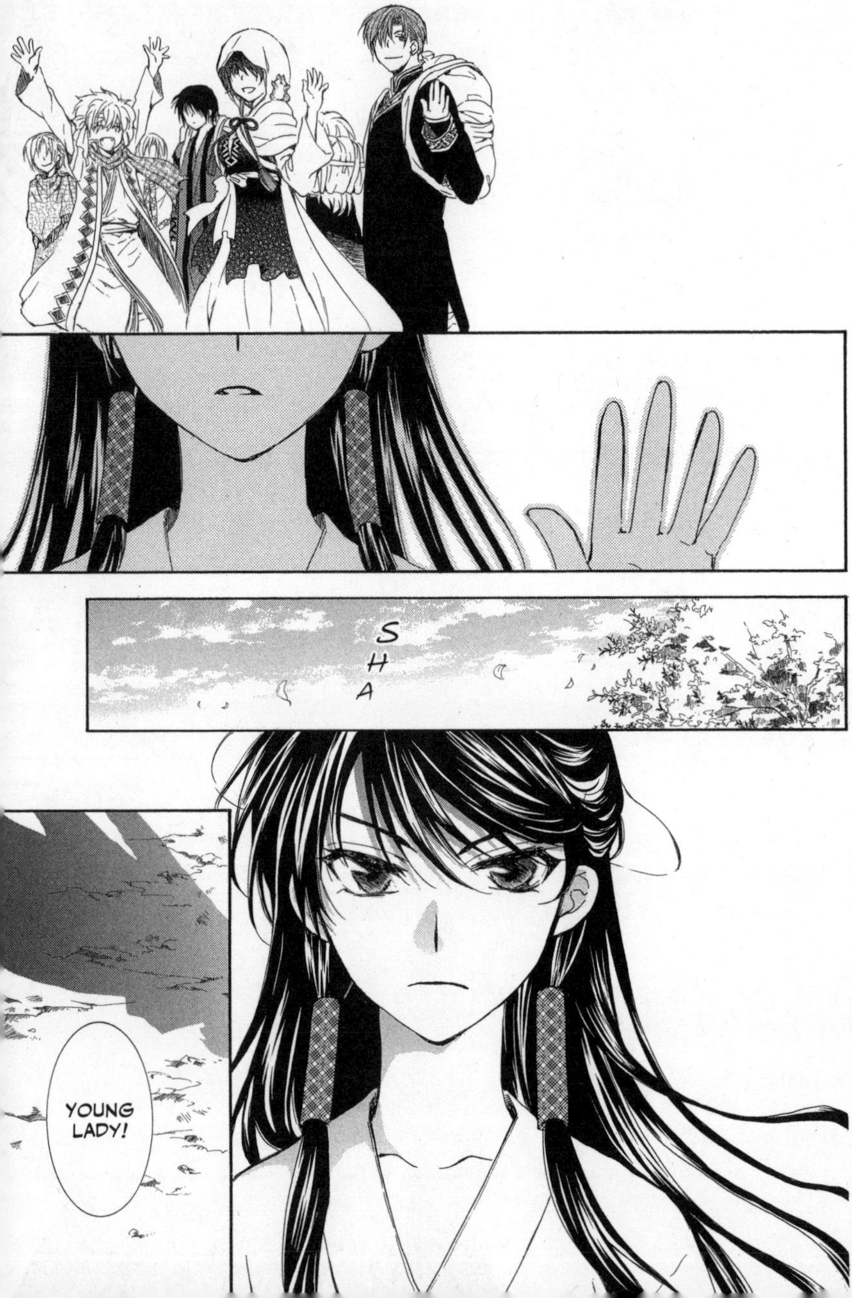
SHA
YOUNG LADY!

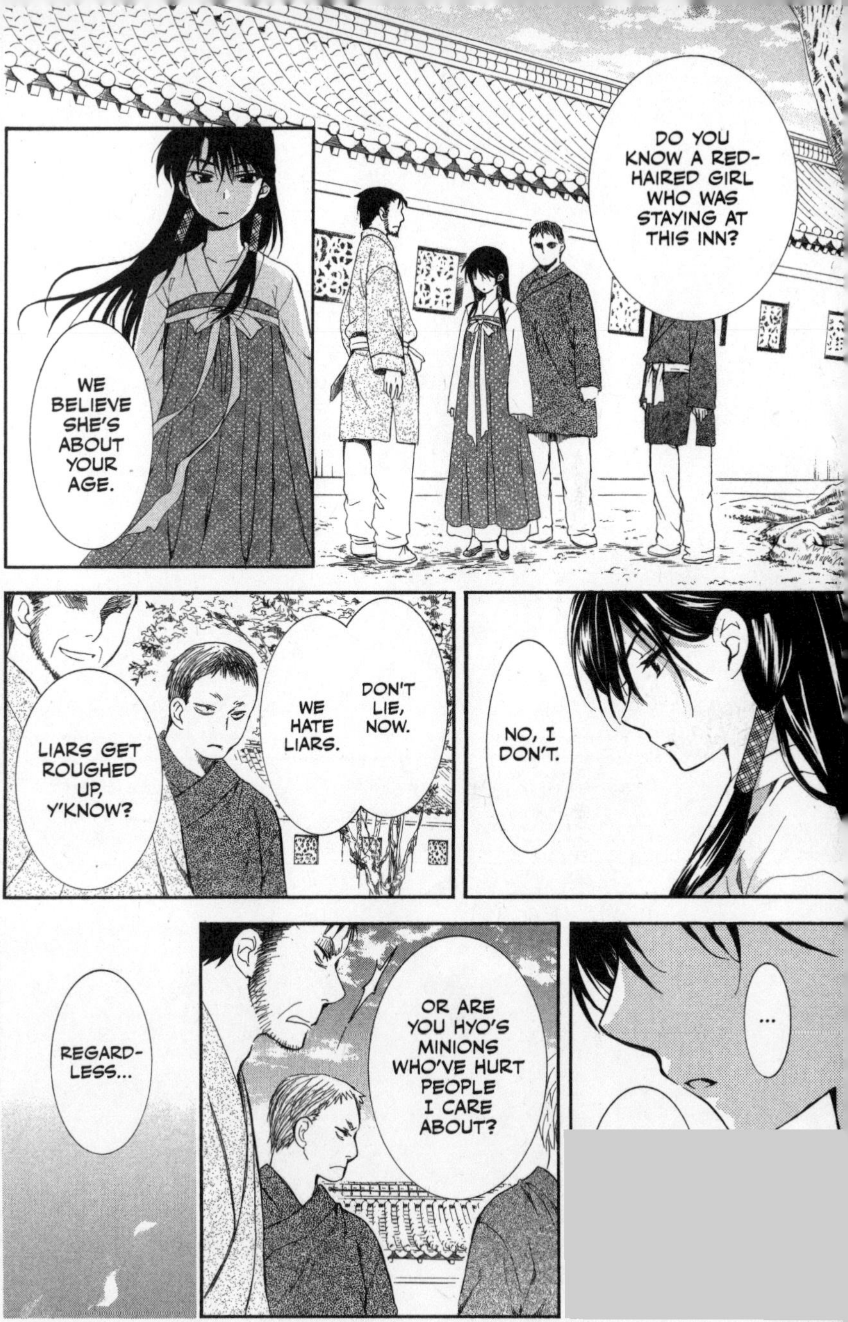
DO YOU KNOW A RED-HAIRED GIRL WHO WAS STAYING AT THIS INN?
WE BELIEVE SHE'S ABOUT YOUR AGE.
NO, I DON'T.
DON'T LIE, NOW.
WE HATE LIARS.
LIARS GET ROUGHED UP, Y'KNOW?
...
OR ARE YOU HYO'S MINIONS WHO'VE HURT PEOPLE I CARE ABOUT?
REGARDLESS...

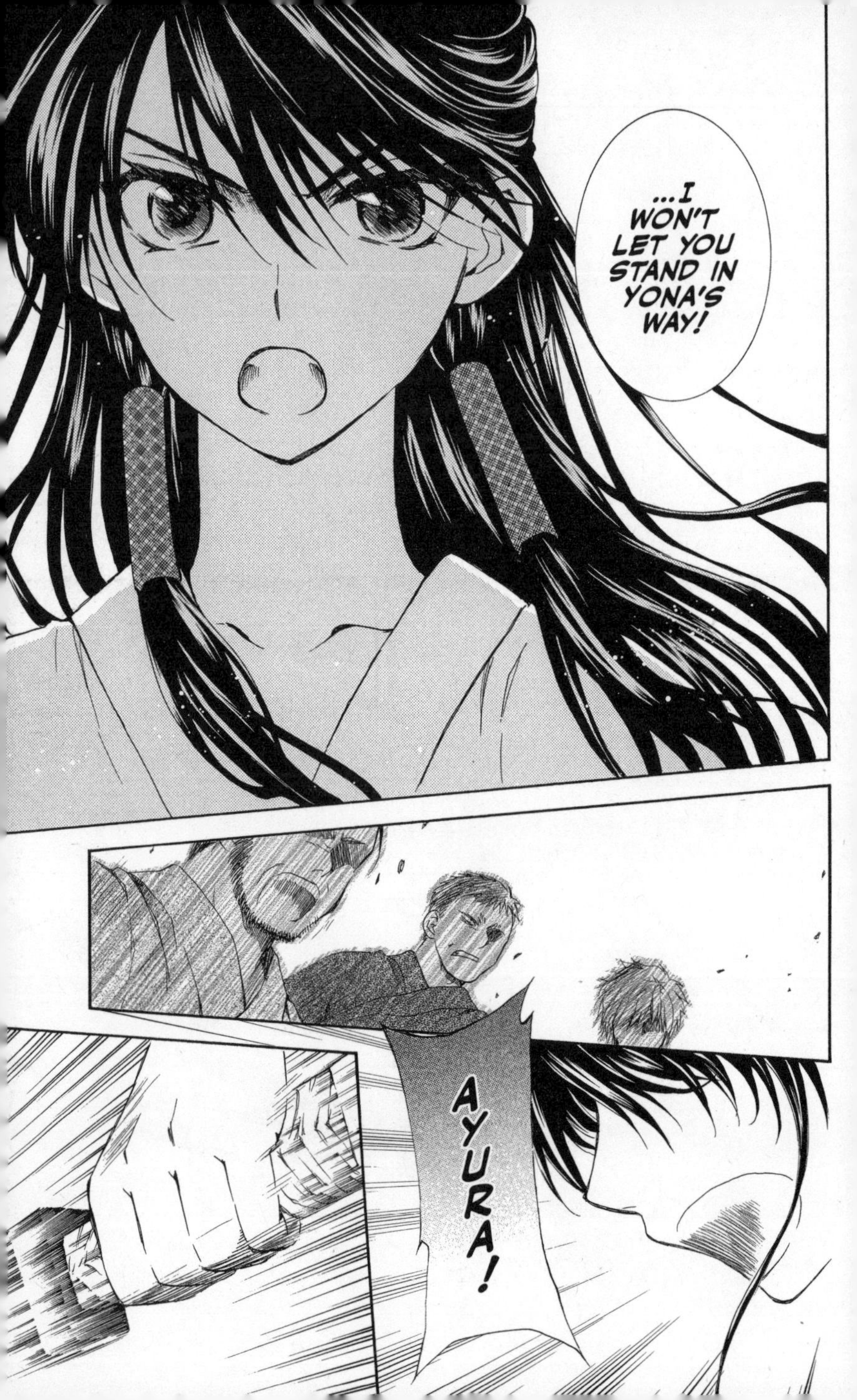
...I WON'T LET YOU STAND IN YONA'S WAY!
AYURA!

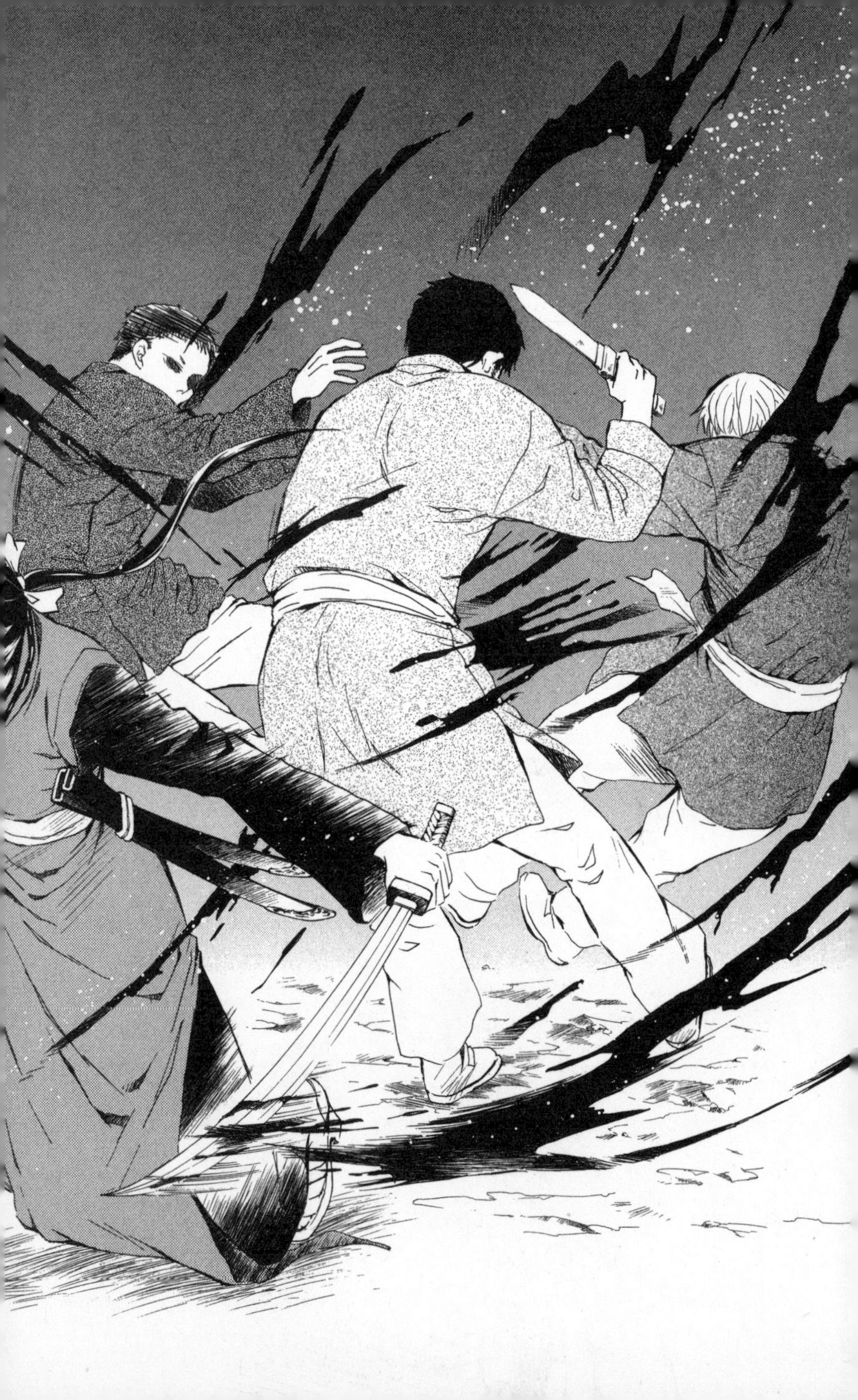

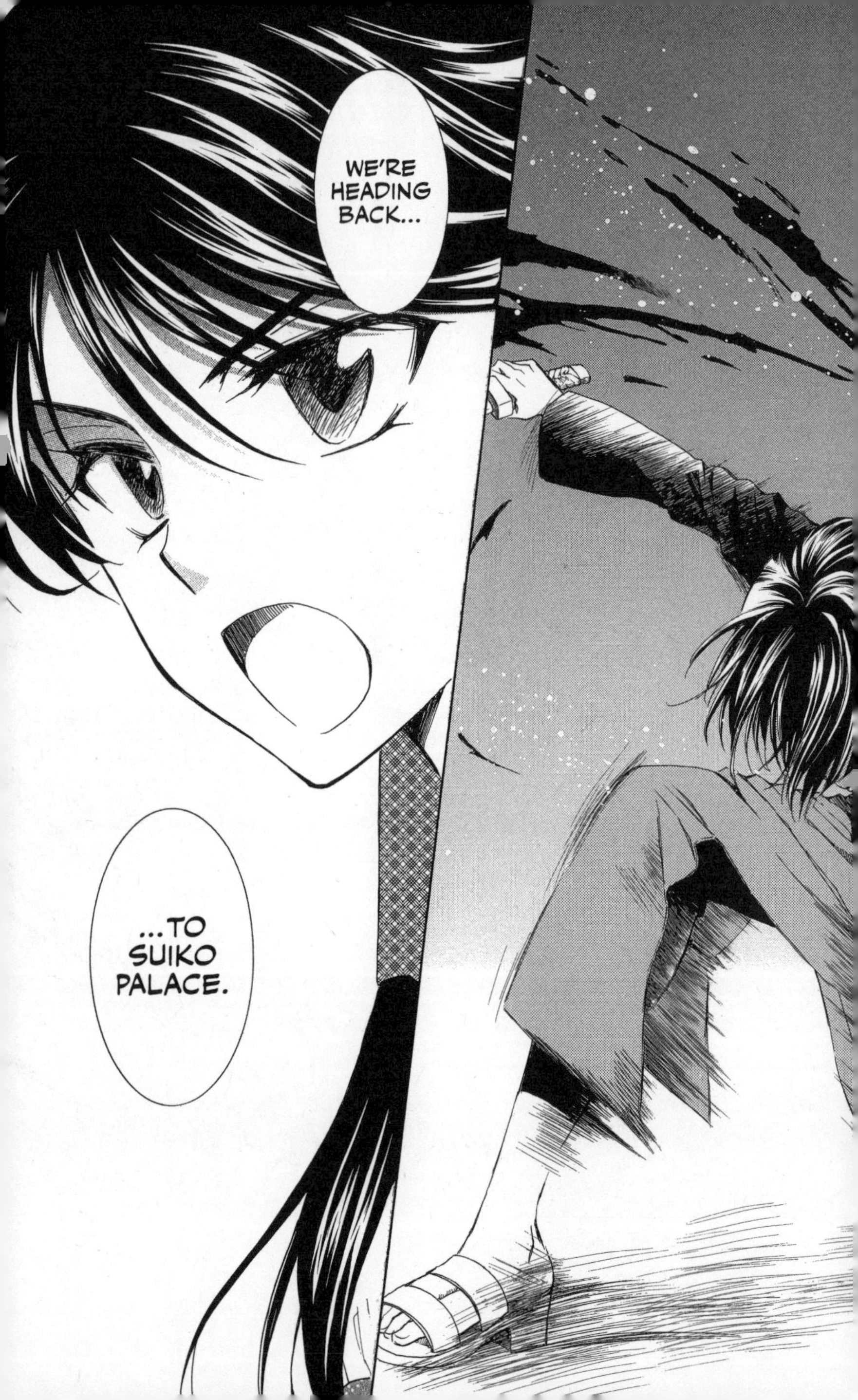
WE'RE HEADING BACK...
...TO SUIKO PALACE.

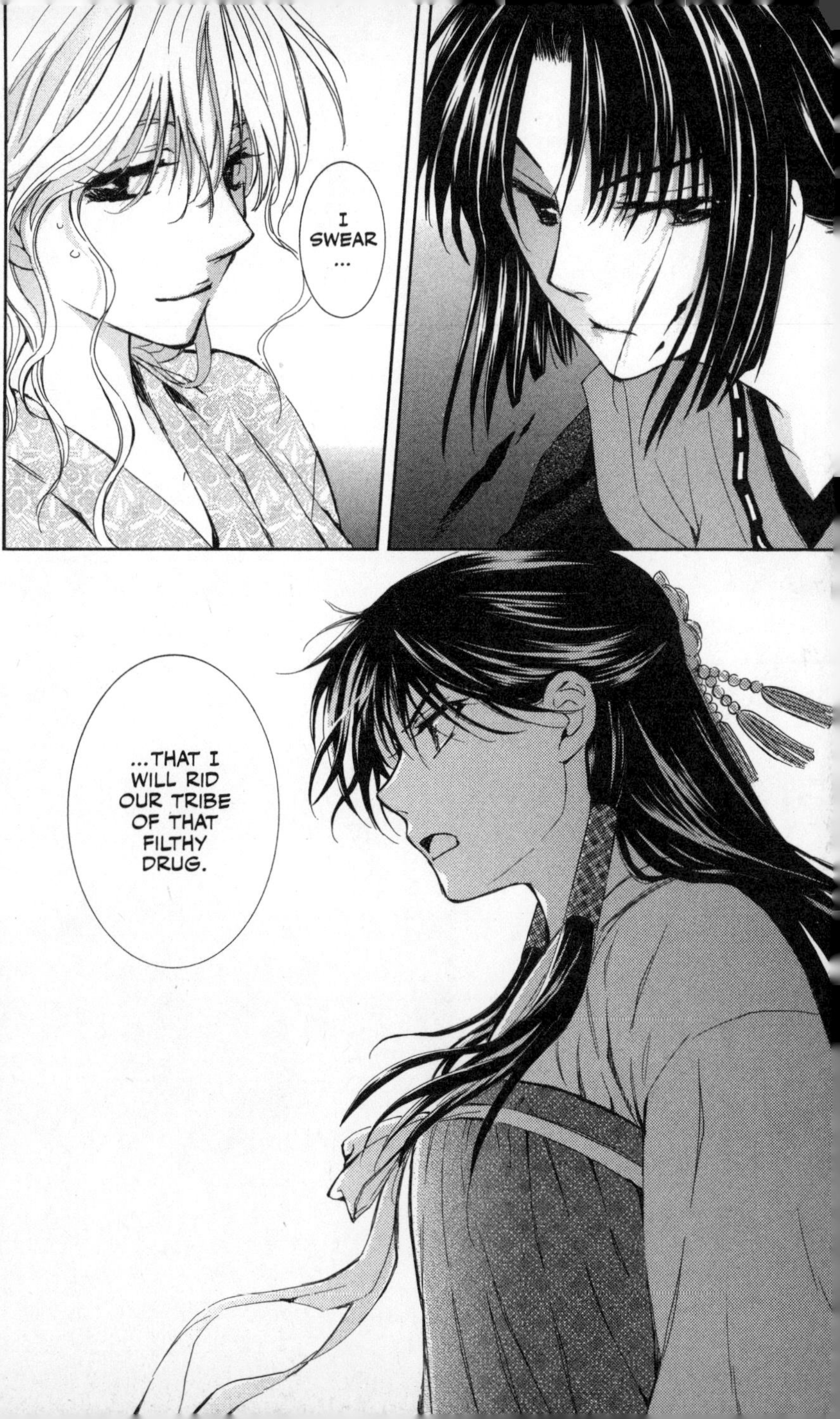
I SWEAR ...
...THAT I WILL RID OUR TRIBE OF THAT FILTHY DRUG.

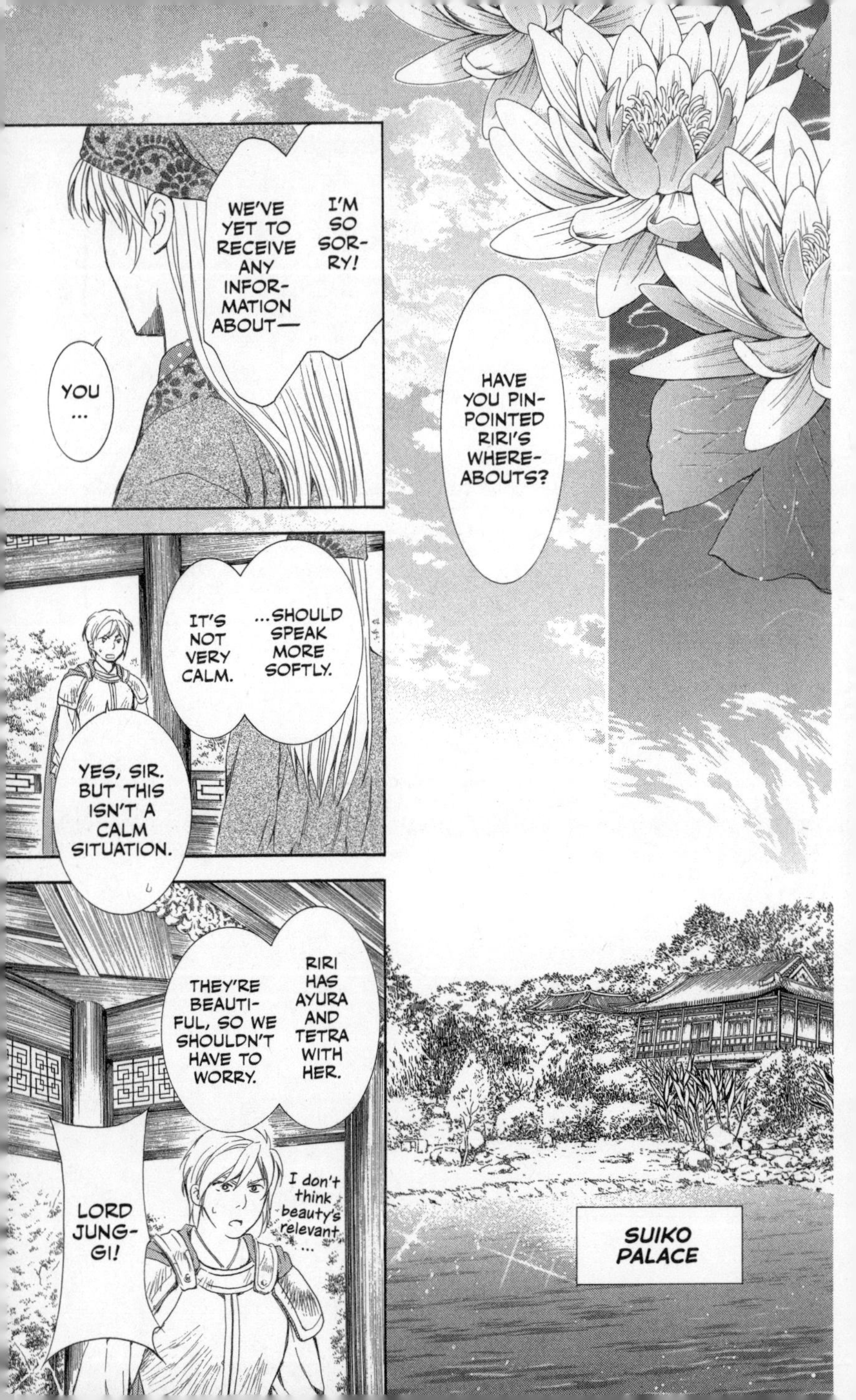
HAVE YOU PIN-POINTED RIRI'S WHERE-ABOUTS?
SUIKO PALACE
I'M SO SOR-RY!
WE'VE YET TO RECEIVE ANY INFOR-MATION ABOUT—
YOU ...
...SHOULD SPEAK MORE SOFTLY.
IT'S NOT VERY CALM.
YES, SIR. BUT THIS ISN'T A CALM SITUATION.
RIRI HAS AYURA AND TETRA WITH HER.
THEY'RE BEAUTI-FUL, SO WE SHOULDN'T HAVE TO WORRY.
I don't think beauty's relevant ...
LORD JUNG-GI!

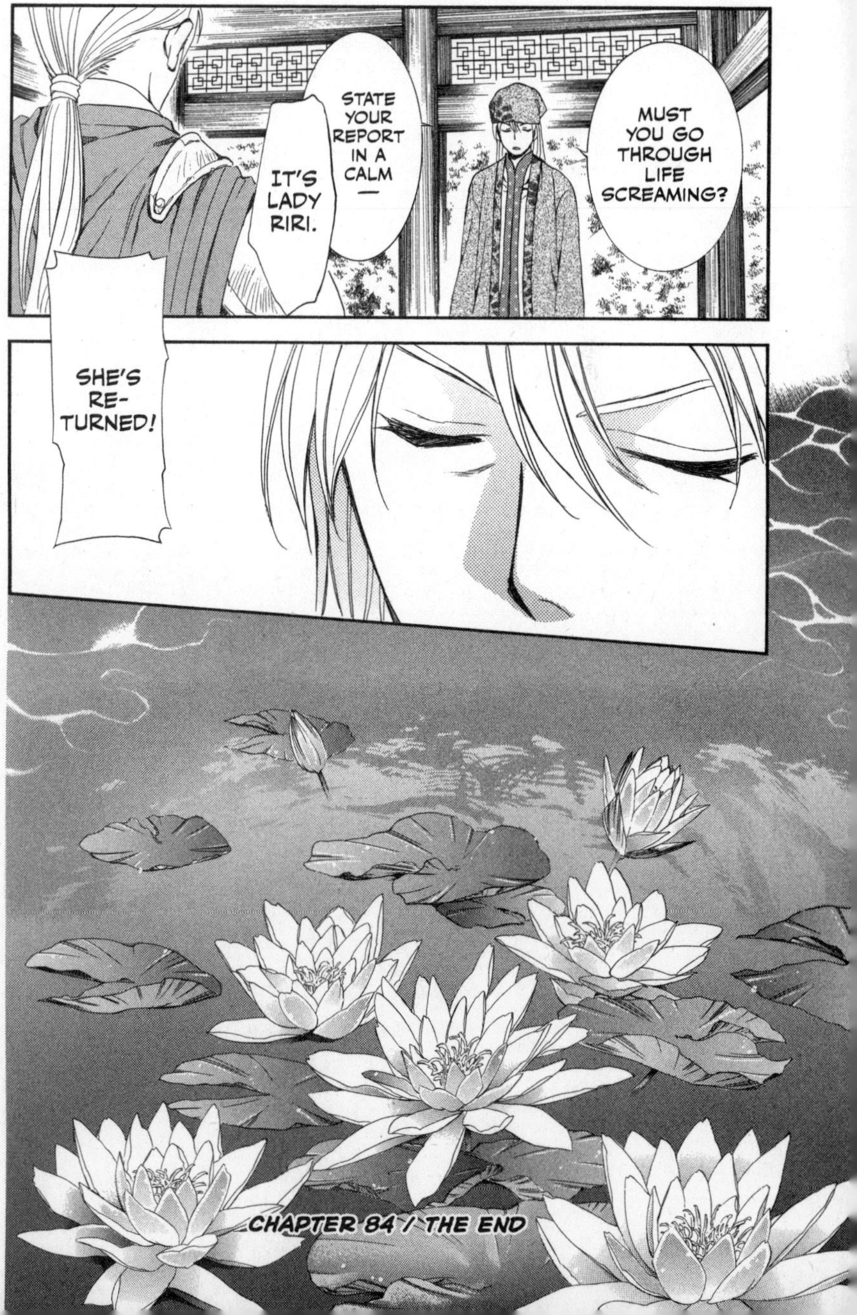
MUST YOU GO THROUGH LIFE SCREAMING?
STATE YOUR REPORT IN A CALM —
IT'S LADY RIRI.
SHE'S RE-TURNED!
CHAPTER 84 / THE END

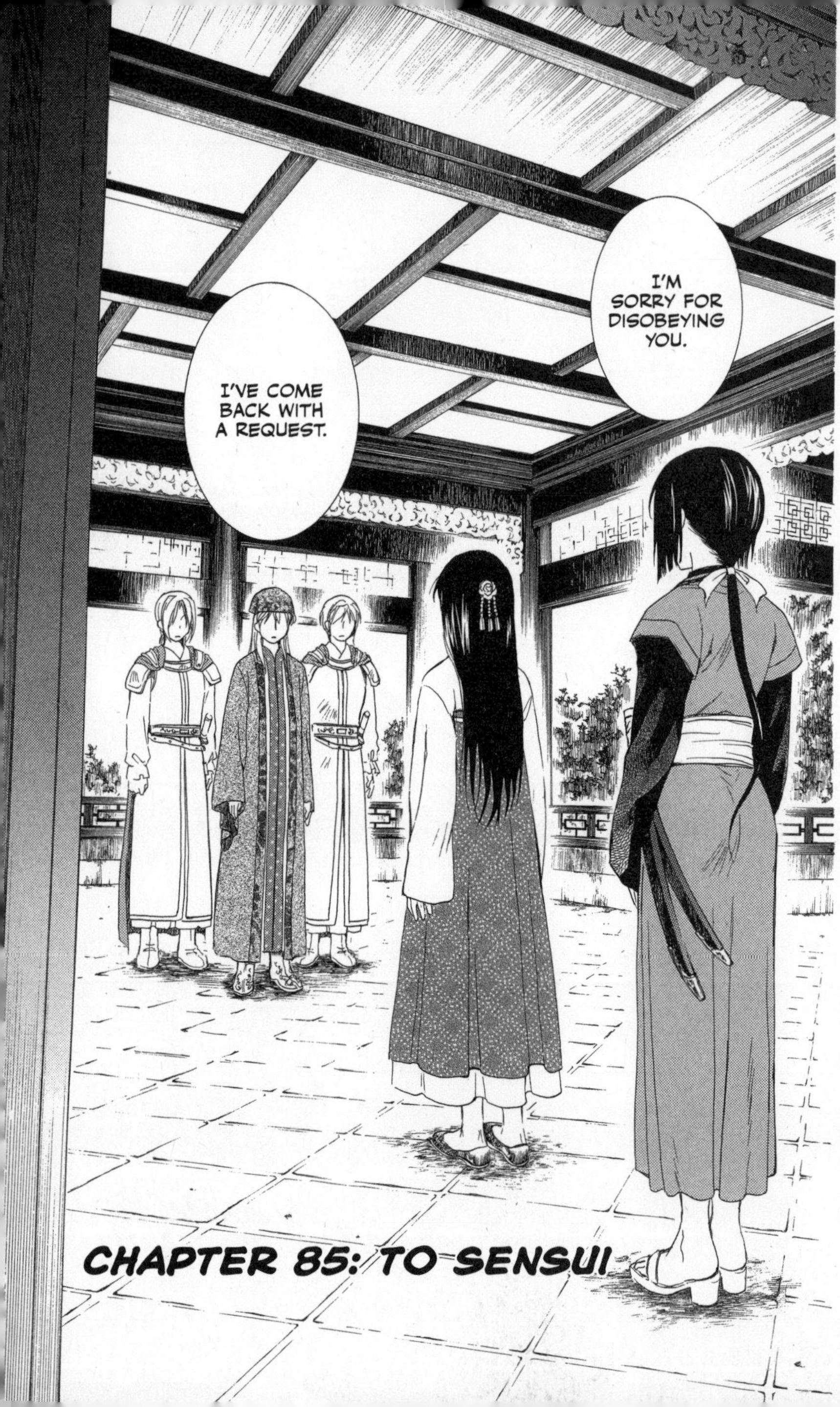
I'M SORRY FOR DISOBEYING YOU.
I'VE COME BACK WITH A REQUEST.
CHAPTER 85: TO SENSUI

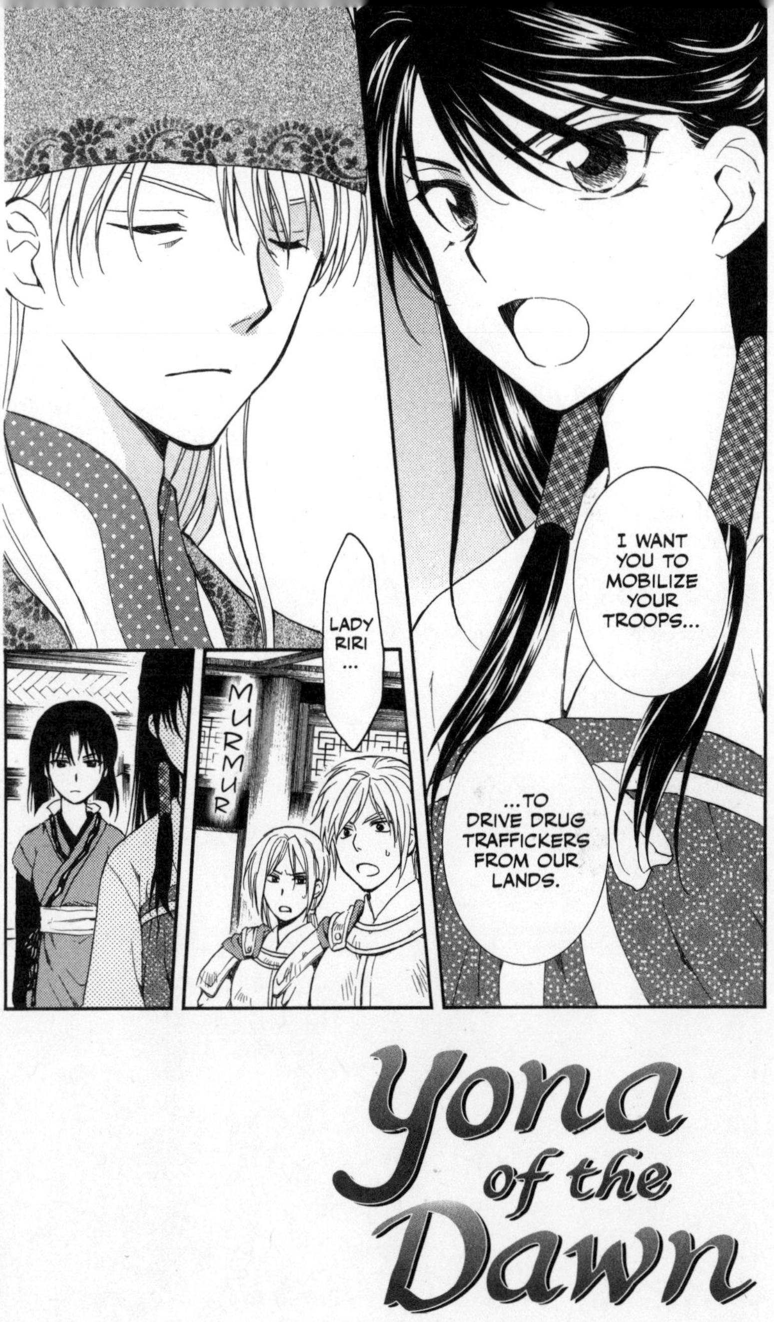

I WANT YOU TO MOBILIZE YOUR TROOPS...
...TO DRIVE DRUG TRAFFICKERS FROM OUR LANDS.
LADY RIRI...
MURMUR

Yona of the Dawn

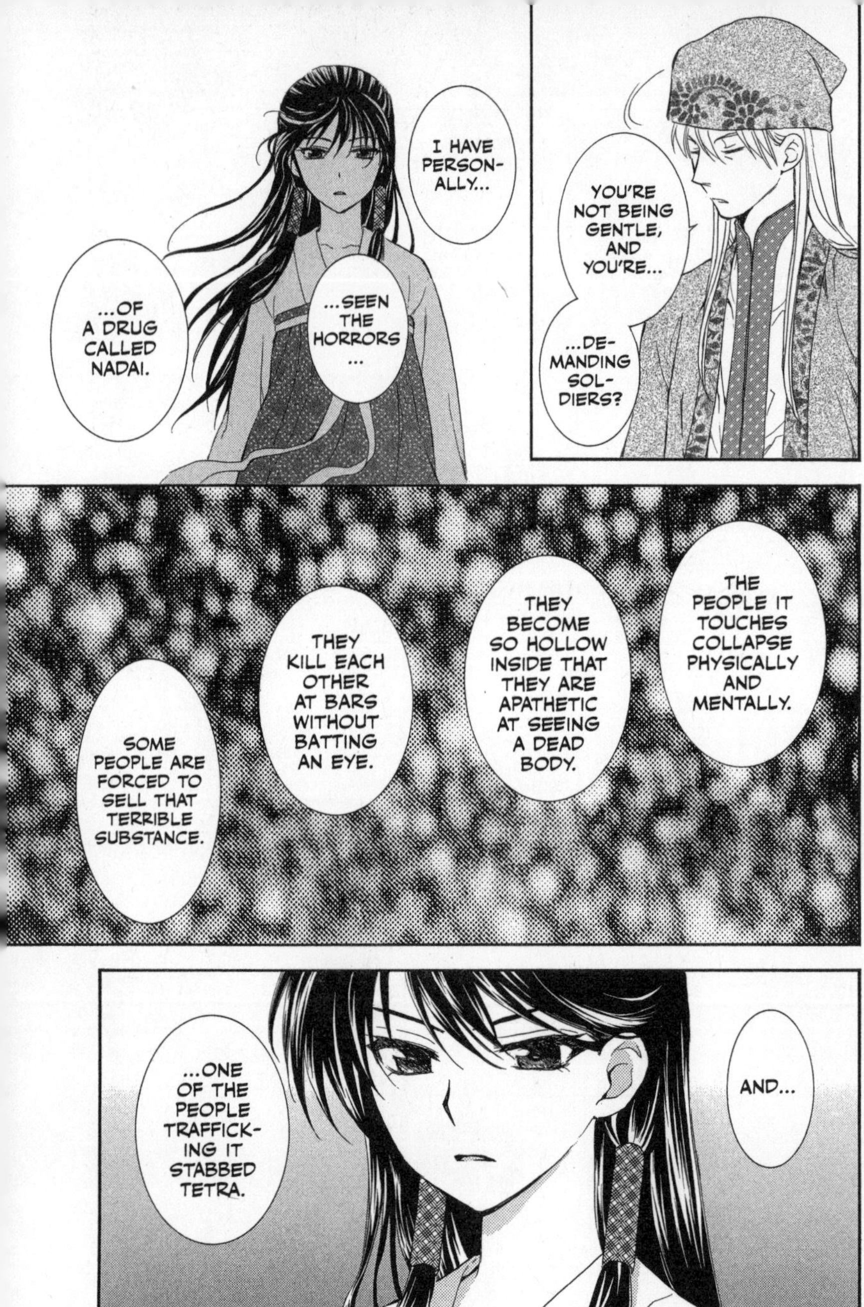
YOU'RE NOT BEING GENTLE, AND YOU'RE...
...DEMANDING SOLDIERS?
I HAVE PERSONALLY...
...SEEN THE HORRORS...
...OF A DRUG CALLED NADAI.
THE PEOPLE IT TOUCHES COLLAPSE PHYSICALLY AND MENTALLY.
THEY BECOME SO HOLLOW INSIDE THAT THEY ARE APATHETIC AT SEEING A DEAD BODY.
THEY KILL EACH OTHER AT BARS WITHOUT BATTING AN EYE.
SOME PEOPLE ARE FORCED TO SELL THAT TERRIBLE SUBSTANCE.
AND...
...ONE OF THE PEOPLE TRAFFICKING IT STABBED TETRA.

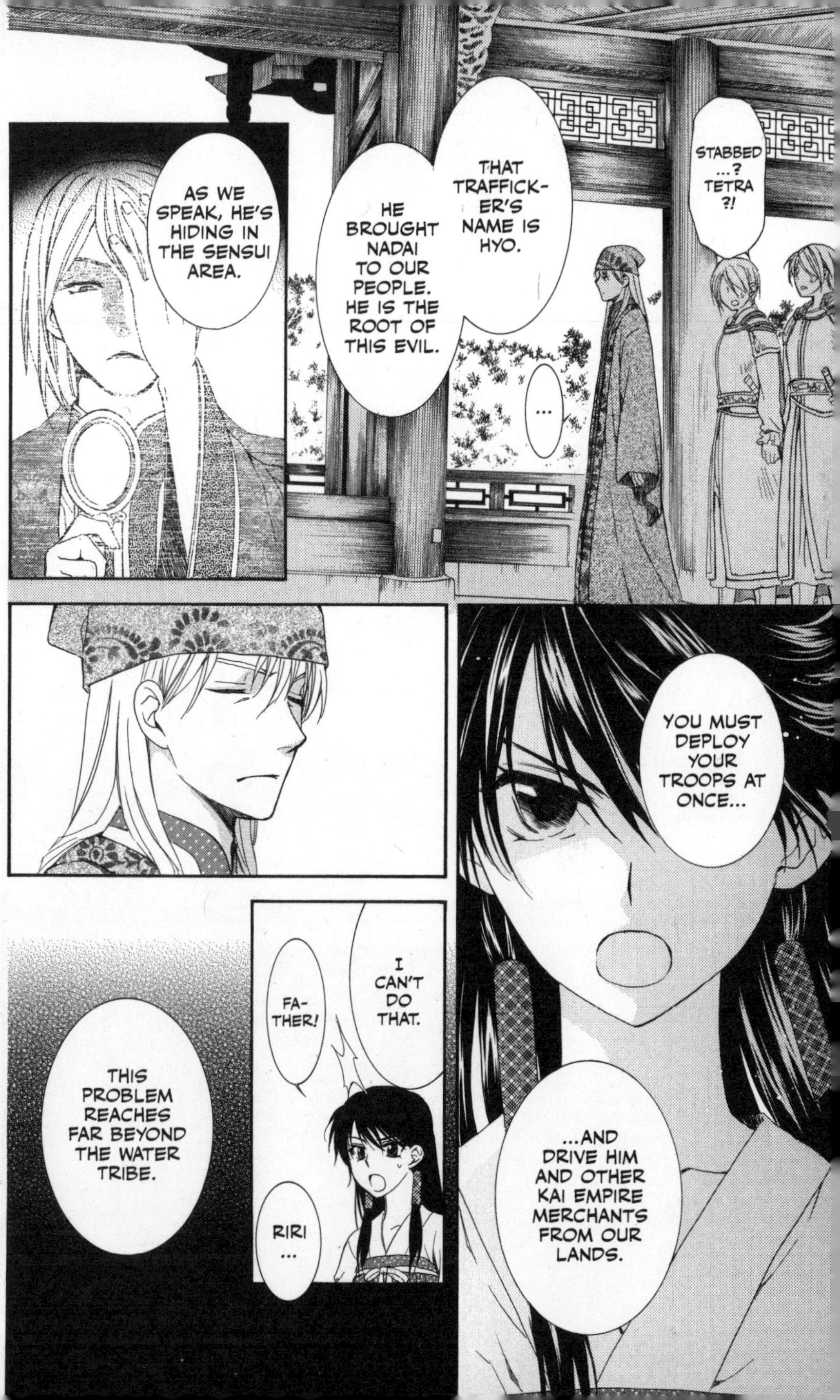
STABBED ...? TETRA ?!
THAT TRAFFICK-ER'S NAME IS HYO.
HE BROUGHT NADAI TO OUR PEOPLE. HE IS THE ROOT OF THIS EVIL.
...
AS WE SPEAK, HE'S HIDING IN THE SENSUI AREA.
YOU MUST DEPLOY YOUR TROOPS AT ONCE...
...AND DRIVE HIM AND OTHER KAI EMPIRE MERCHANTS FROM OUR LANDS.
I CAN'T DO THAT.
FA-THER!
RIRI ...
THIS PROBLEM REACHES FAR BEYOND THE WATER TRIBE.

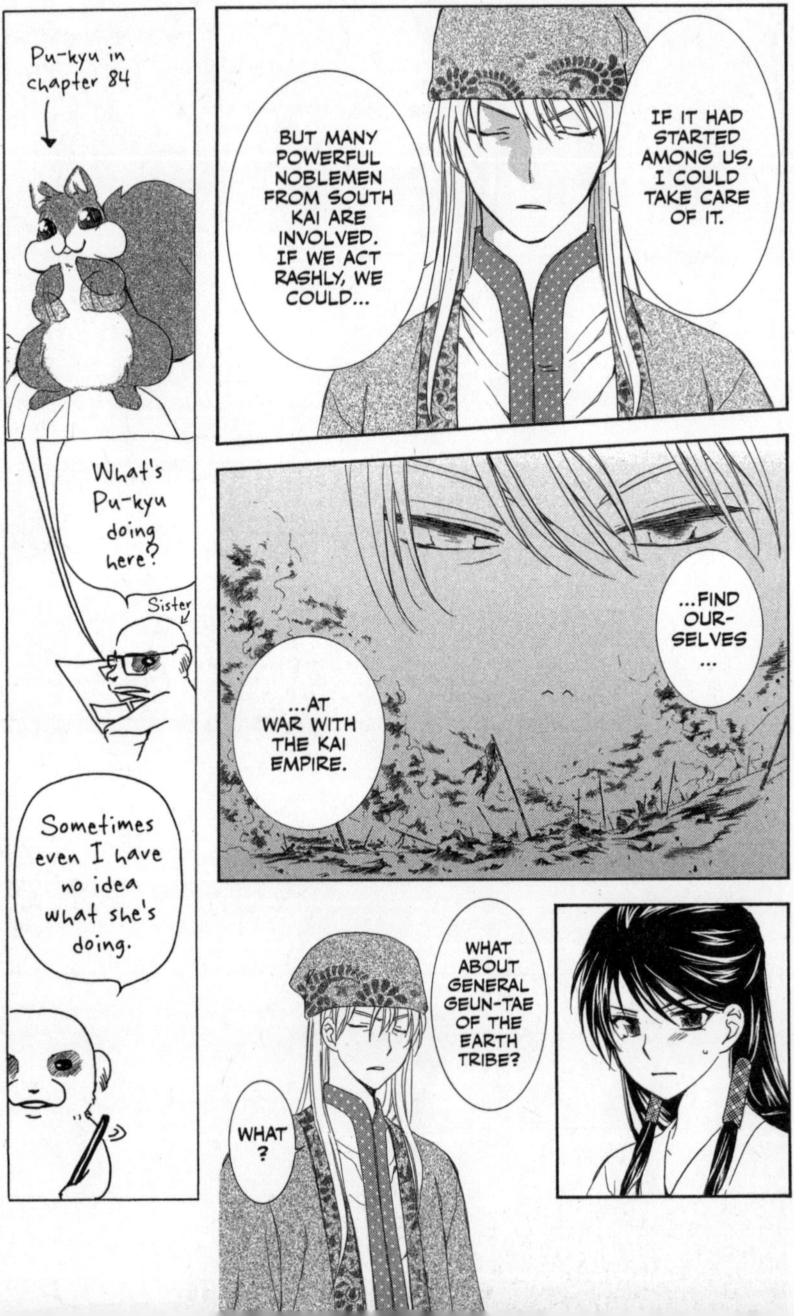
IF IT HAD STARTED AMONG US, I COULD TAKE CARE OF IT.
BUT MANY POWERFUL NOBLEMEN FROM SOUTH KAI ARE INVOLVED. IF WE ACT RASHLY, WE COULD...
...FIND OURSELVES...
...AT WAR WITH THE KAI EMPIRE.
WHAT ABOUT GENERAL GEUN-TAE OF THE EARTH TRIBE?
WHAT?
Pu-kyu in chapter 84
What's Pu-kyu doing here?
Sister
Sometimes even I have no idea what she's doing.

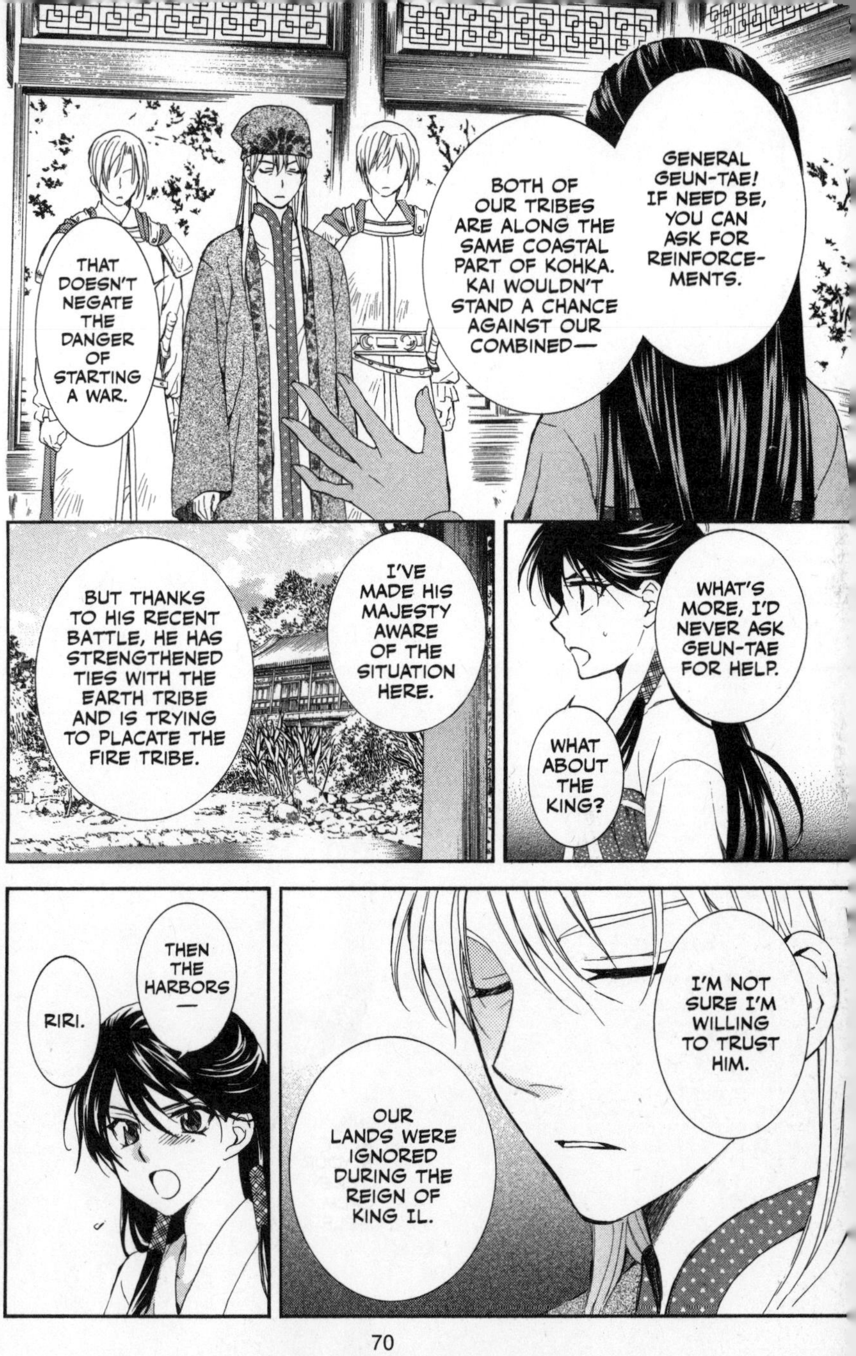
GENERAL GEUN-TAE! IF NEED BE, YOU CAN ASK FOR REINFORCEMENTS.
BOTH OF OUR TRIBES ARE ALONG THE SAME COASTAL PART OF KOHKA. KAI WOULDN'T STAND A CHANCE AGAINST OUR COMBINED—
THAT DOESN'T NEGATE THE DANGER OF STARTING A WAR.
WHAT'S MORE, I'D NEVER ASK GEUN-TAE FOR HELP.
WHAT ABOUT THE KING?
I'VE MADE HIS MAJESTY AWARE OF THE SITUATION HERE.
BUT THANKS TO HIS RECENT BATTLE, HE HAS STRENGTHENED TIES WITH THE EARTH TRIBE AND IS TRYING TO PLACATE THE FIRE TRIBE.
I'M NOT SURE I'M WILLING TO TRUST HIM.
OUR LANDS WERE IGNORED DURING THE REIGN OF KING IL.
THEN THE HARBORS—
RIRI.

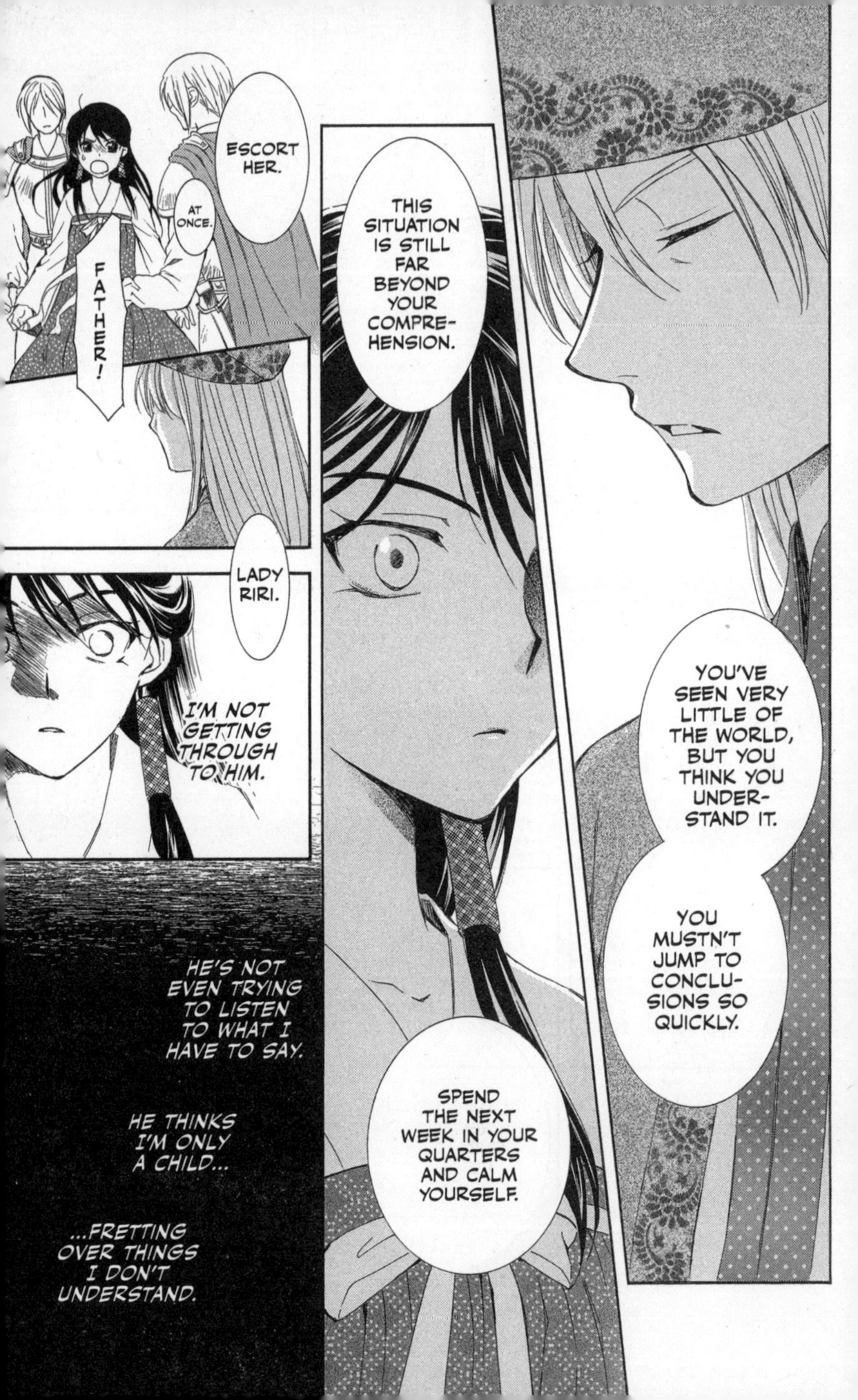
YOU'VE SEEN VERY LITTLE OF THE WORLD, BUT YOU THINK YOU UNDER-STAND IT.
YOU MUSTN'T JUMP TO CONCLU-SIONS SO QUICKLY.
THIS SITUATION IS STILL FAR BEYOND YOUR COMPRE-HENSION.
SPEND THE NEXT WEEK IN YOUR QUARTERS AND CALM YOURSELF.
ESCORT HER.
AT ONCE.
FATHER!
LADY RIRI.
I'M NOT GETTING THROUGH TO HIM.
HE'S NOT EVEN TRYING TO LISTEN TO WHAT I HAVE TO SAY.
HE THINKS I'M ONLY A CHILD...
...FRETTING OVER THINGS I DON'T UNDERSTAND.

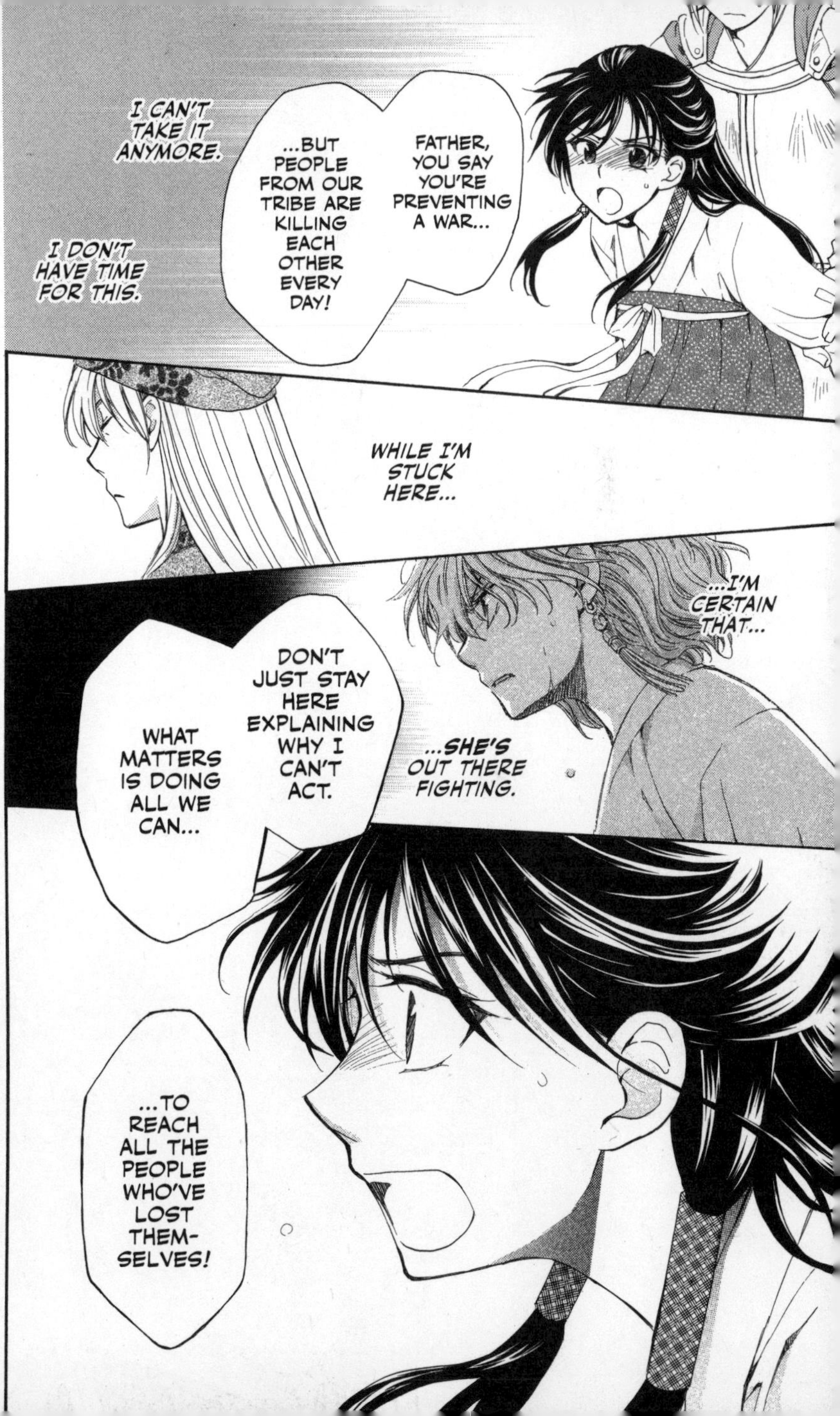
FATHER, YOU SAY YOU'RE PREVENTING A WAR...
...BUT PEOPLE FROM OUR TRIBE ARE KILLING EACH OTHER EVERY DAY!
I CAN'T TAKE IT ANYMORE.
I DON'T HAVE TIME FOR THIS.
WHILE I'M STUCK HERE...
...I'M CERTAIN THAT...
...SHE'S OUT THERE FIGHTING.
DON'T JUST STAY HERE EXPLAINING WHY I CAN'T ACT.
WHAT MATTERS IS DOING ALL WE CAN...
...TO REACH ALL THE PEOPLE WHO'VE LOST THEM-SELVES!

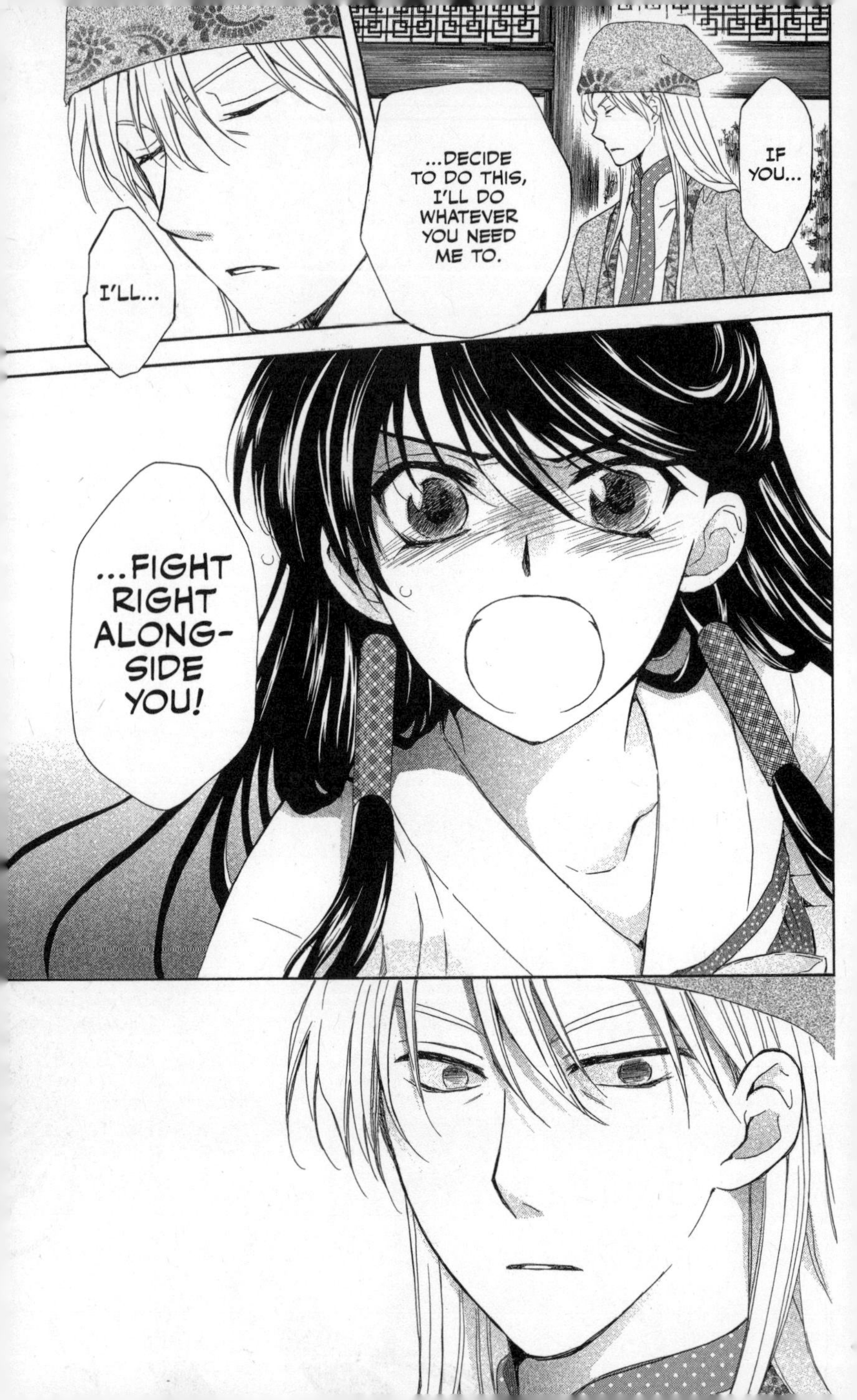
IF YOU...
...DECIDE TO DO THIS, I'LL DO WHATEVER YOU NEED ME TO.
I'LL...
...FIGHT RIGHT ALONG-SIDE YOU!

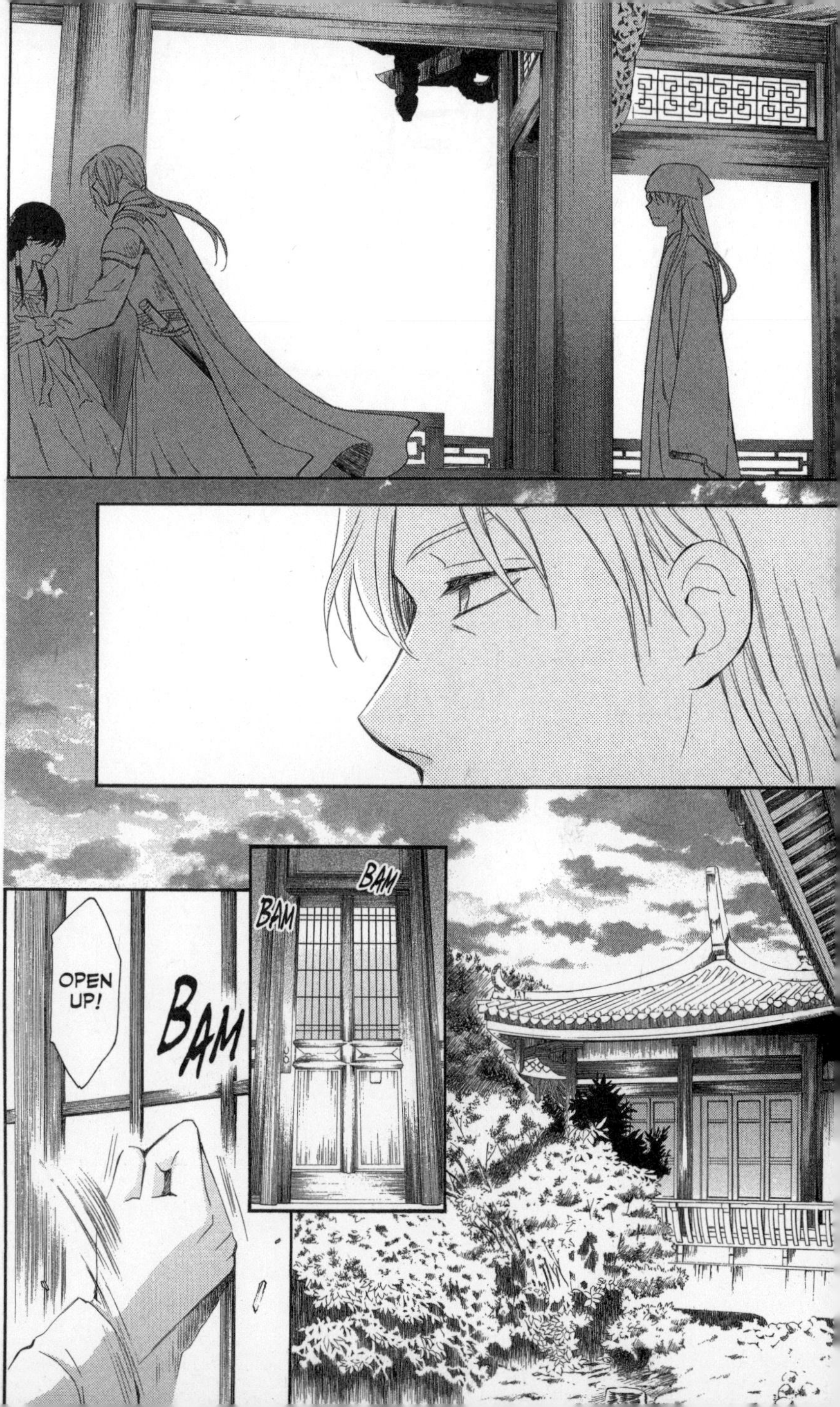
BAM
BAM
OPEN UP!
BAM

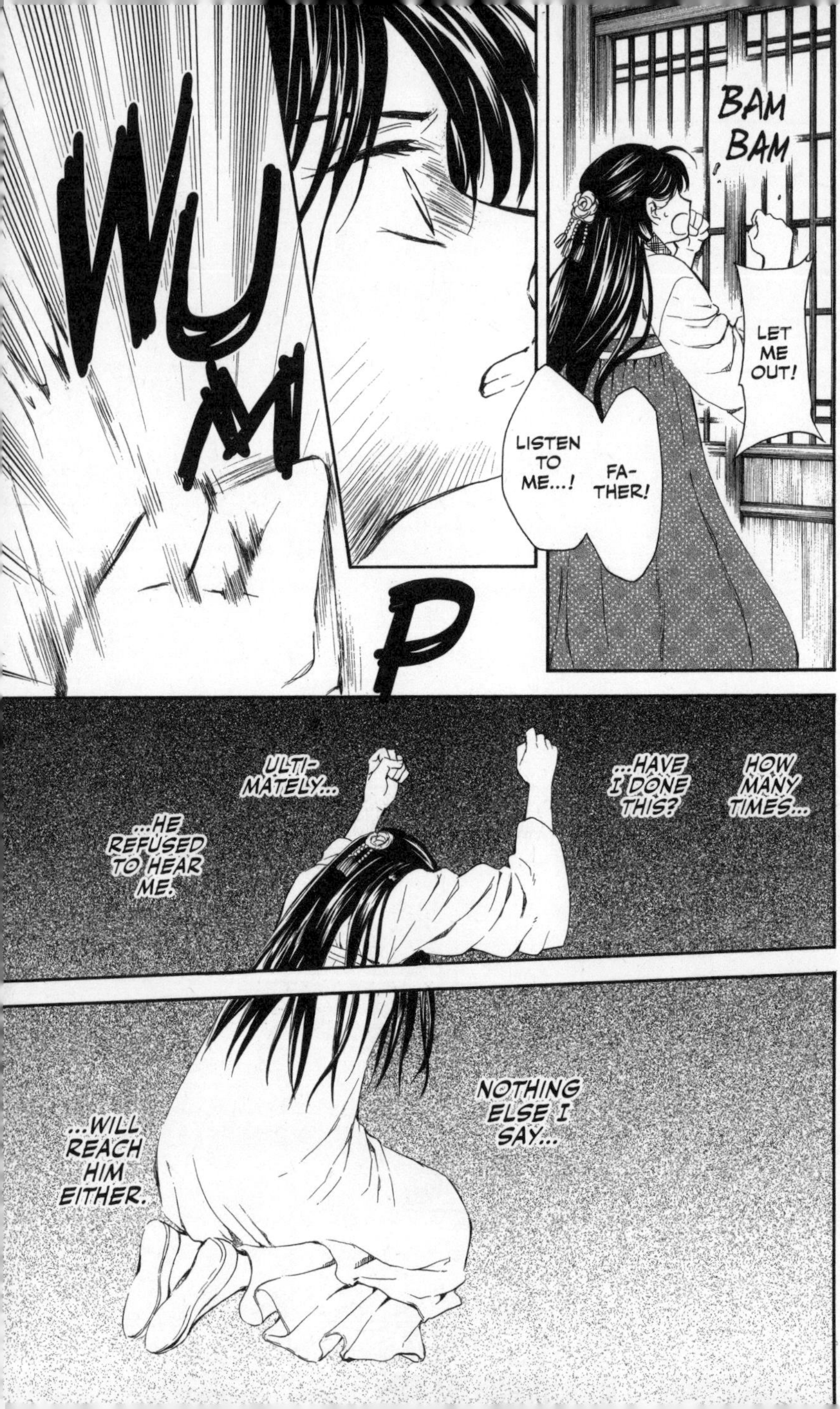
BAM BAM
LET ME OUT!
FA-THER!
LISTEN TO ME...!
WUMP
HOW MANY TIMES...
...HAVE I DONE THIS?
ULTI-MATELY...
...HE REFUSED TO HEAR ME.
NOTHING ELSE I SAY...
...WILL REACH HIM EITHER.

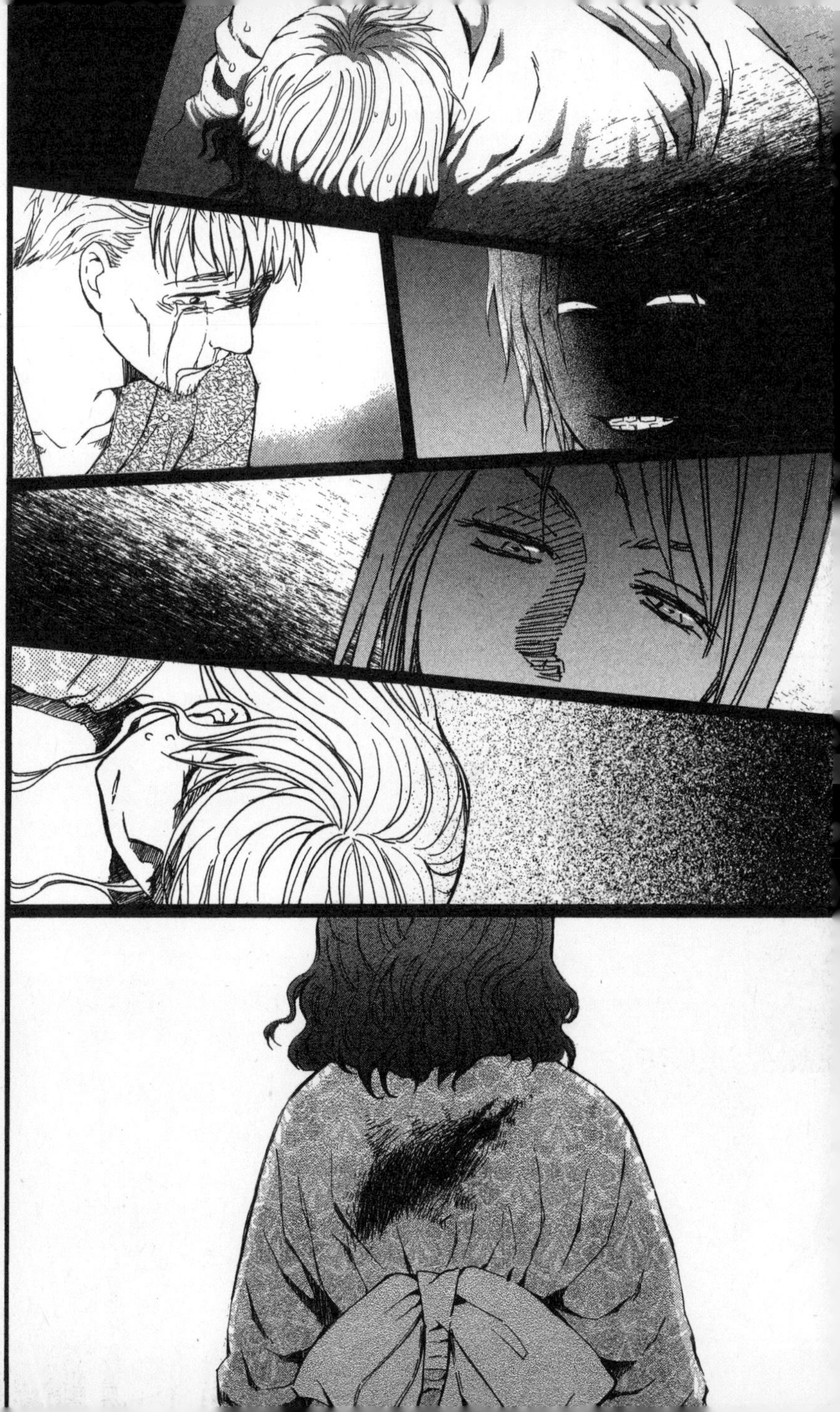

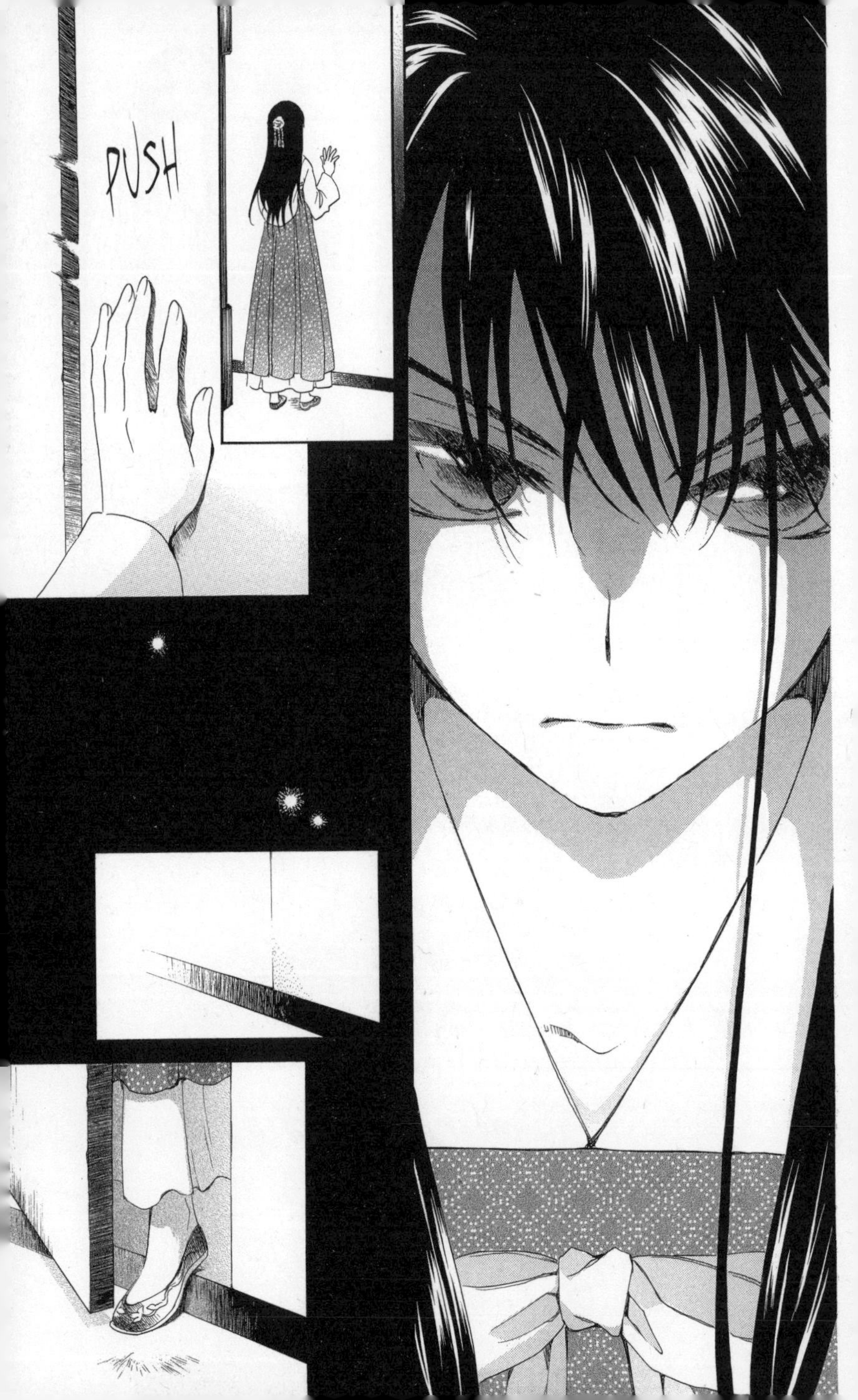
PUSH

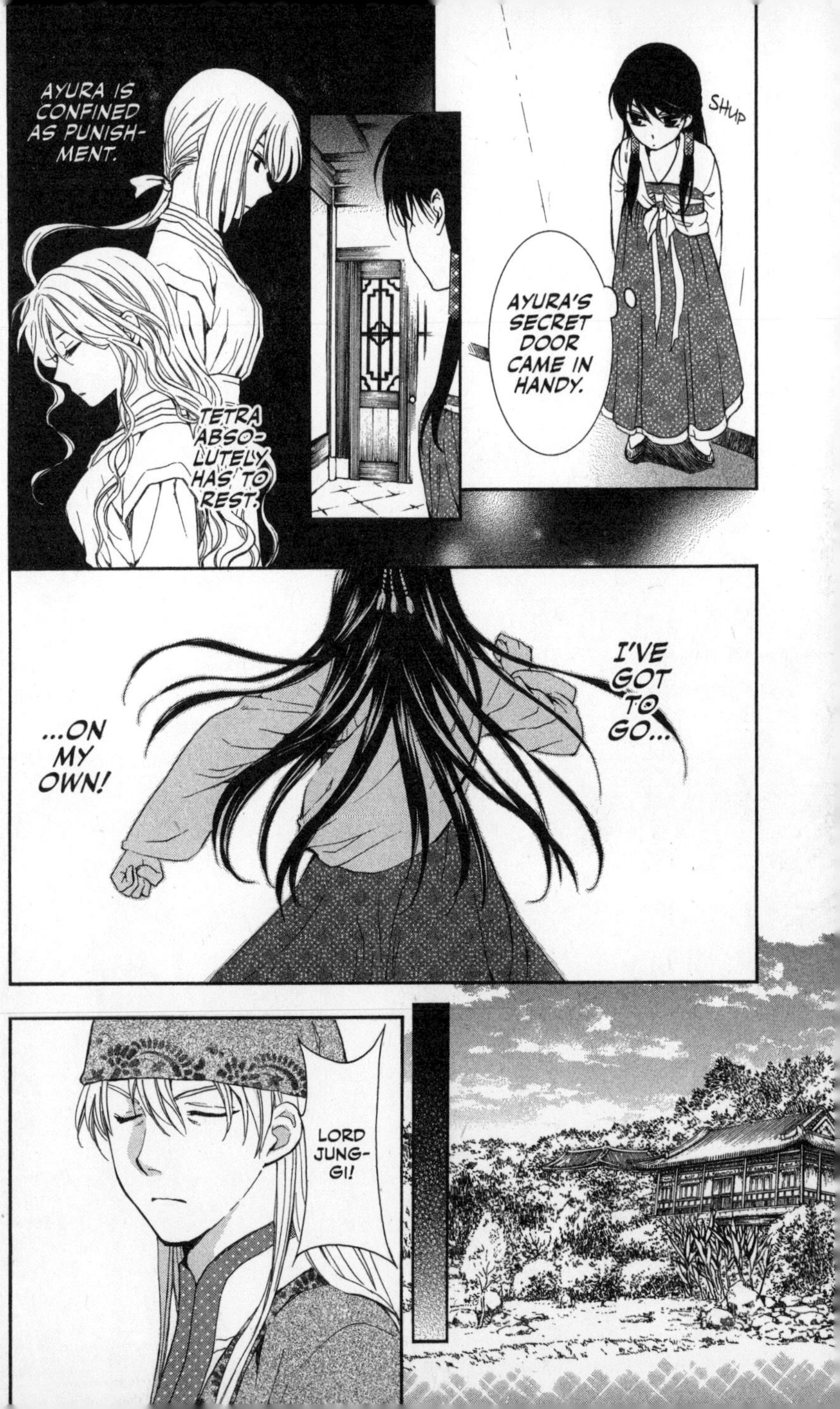
SHUP
AYURA'S SECRET DOOR CAME IN HANDY.
AYURA IS CONFINED AS PUNISHMENT.
TETRA ABSOLUTELY HAS TO REST.
I'VE GOT TO GO...
...ON MY OWN!
LORD JUNG-GI!

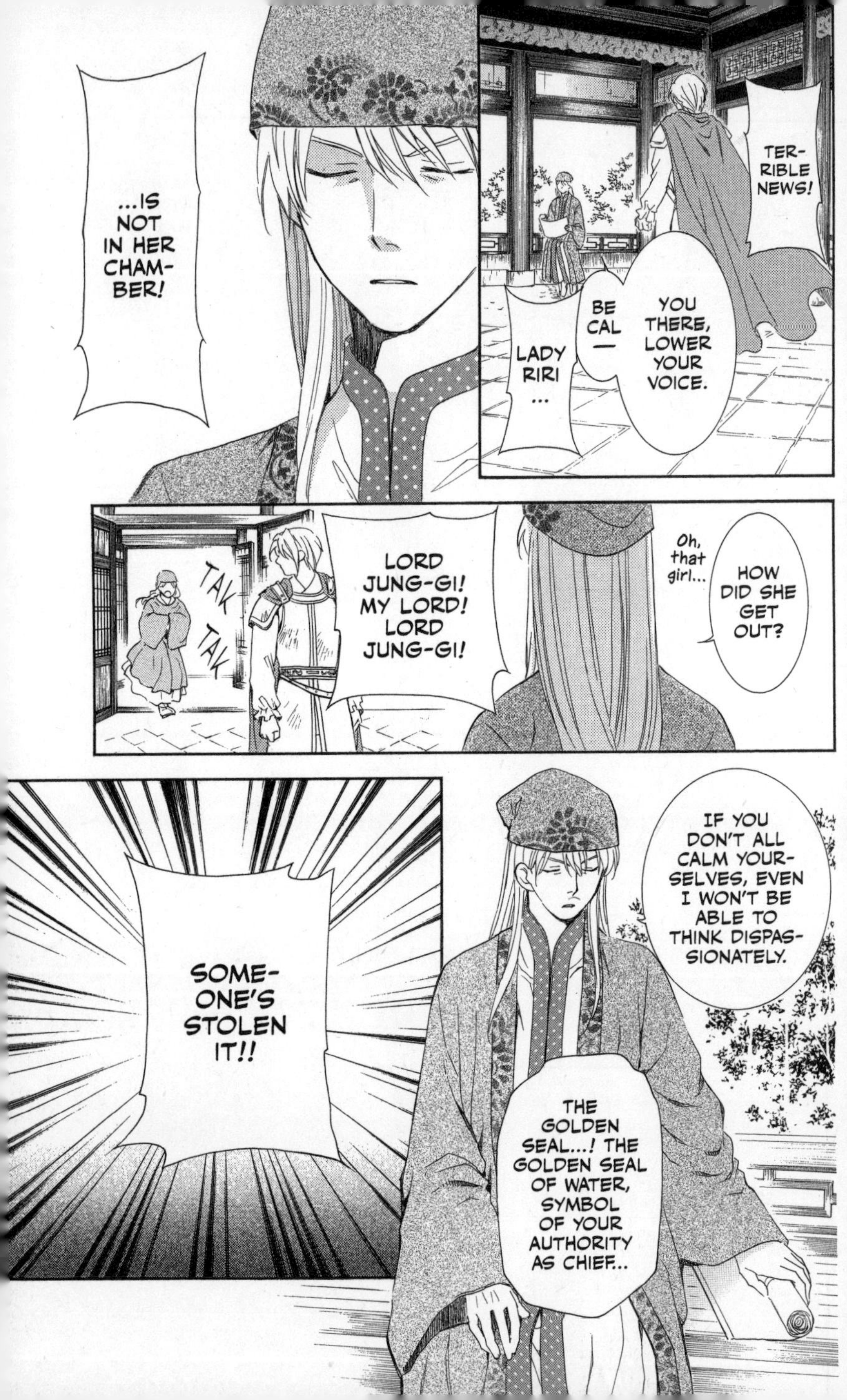
TER-RIBLE NEWS!
YOU THERE, LOWER YOUR VOICE.
BE CAL—
LADY RIRI...
...IS NOT IN HER CHAM-BER!
HOW DID SHE GET OUT?
Oh, that girl...
LORD JUNG-GI! MY LORD! LORD JUNG-GI!
TAK TAK
IF YOU DON'T ALL CALM YOUR-SELVES, EVEN I WON'T BE ABLE TO THINK DISPAS-SIONATELY.
THE GOLDEN SEAL...! THE GOLDEN SEAL OF WATER, SYMBOL OF YOUR AUTHORITY AS CHIEF...
SOME-ONE'S STOLEN IT!!

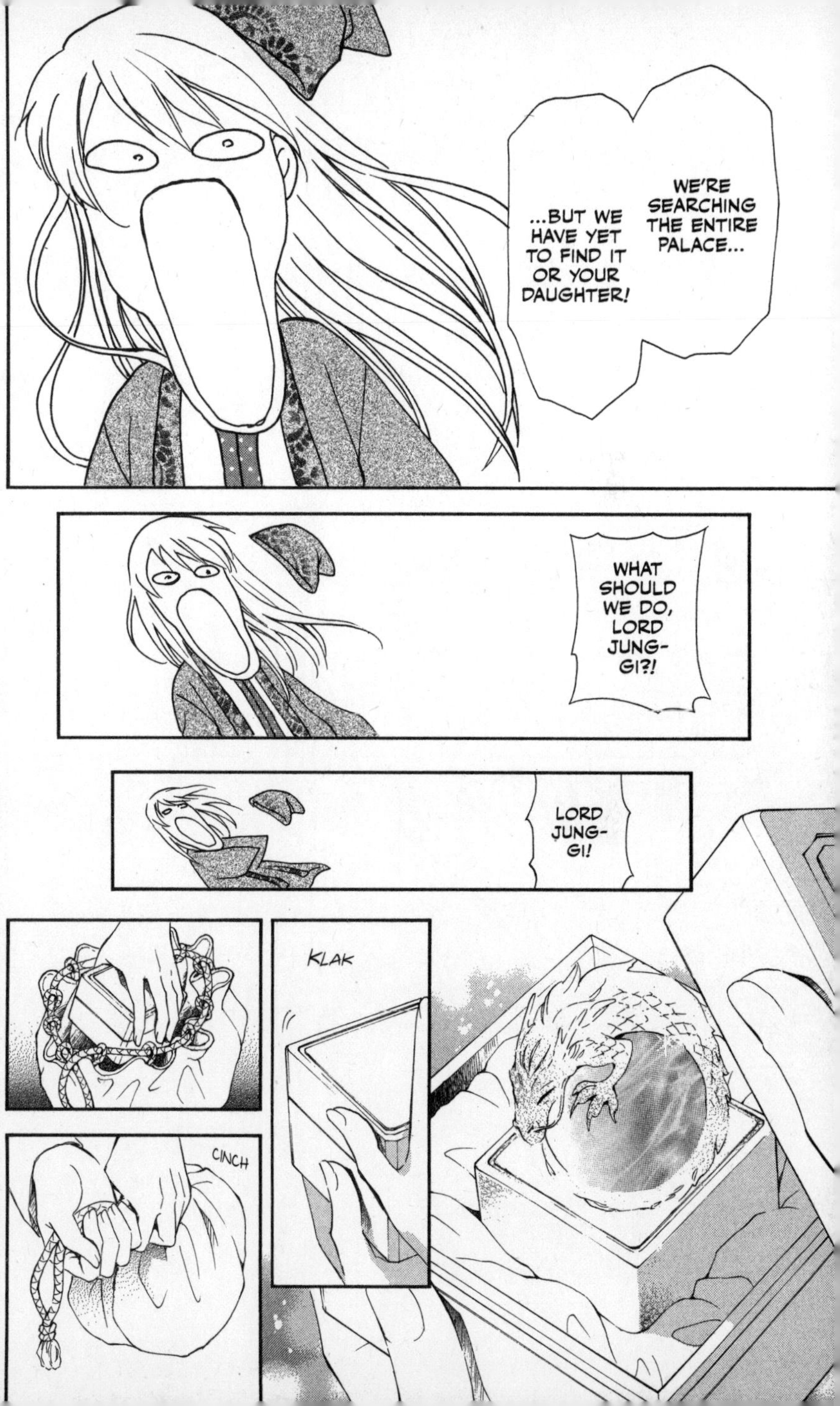
WE'RE SEARCHING THE ENTIRE PALACE...
...BUT WE HAVE YET TO FIND IT OR YOUR DAUGHTER!
WHAT SHOULD WE DO, LORD JUNG-GI?!
LORD JUNG-GI!
KLAK
CINCH

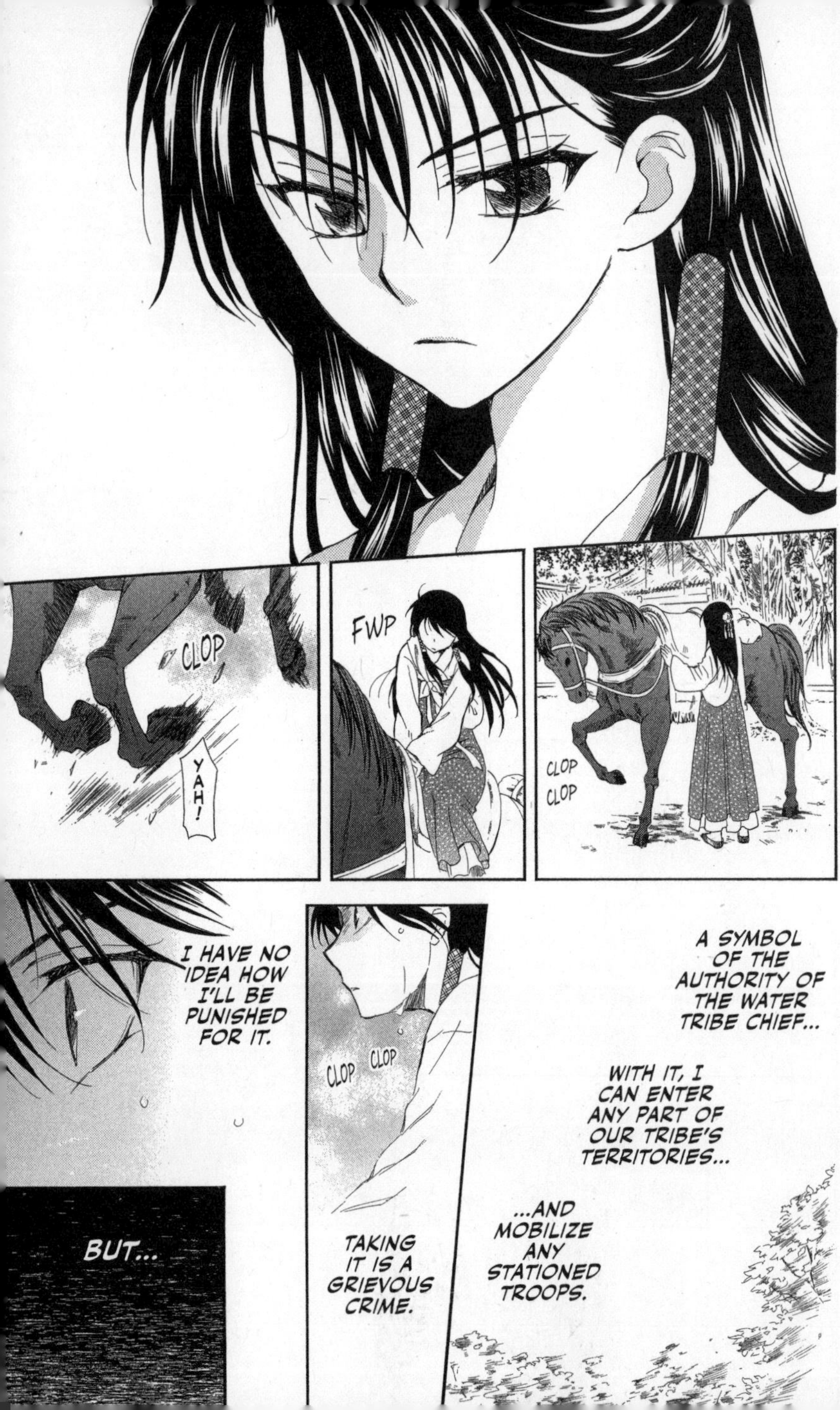
CLOP
CLOP
FWP
CLOP
YAH!
A SYMBOL OF THE AUTHORITY OF THE WATER TRIBE CHIEF...
WITH IT, I CAN ENTER ANY PART OF OUR TRIBE'S TERRITORIES...
...AND MOBILIZE ANY STATIONED TROOPS.
CLOP CLOP
TAKING IT IS A GRIEVOUS CRIME.
I HAVE NO IDEA HOW I'LL BE PUNISHED FOR IT.
BUT...

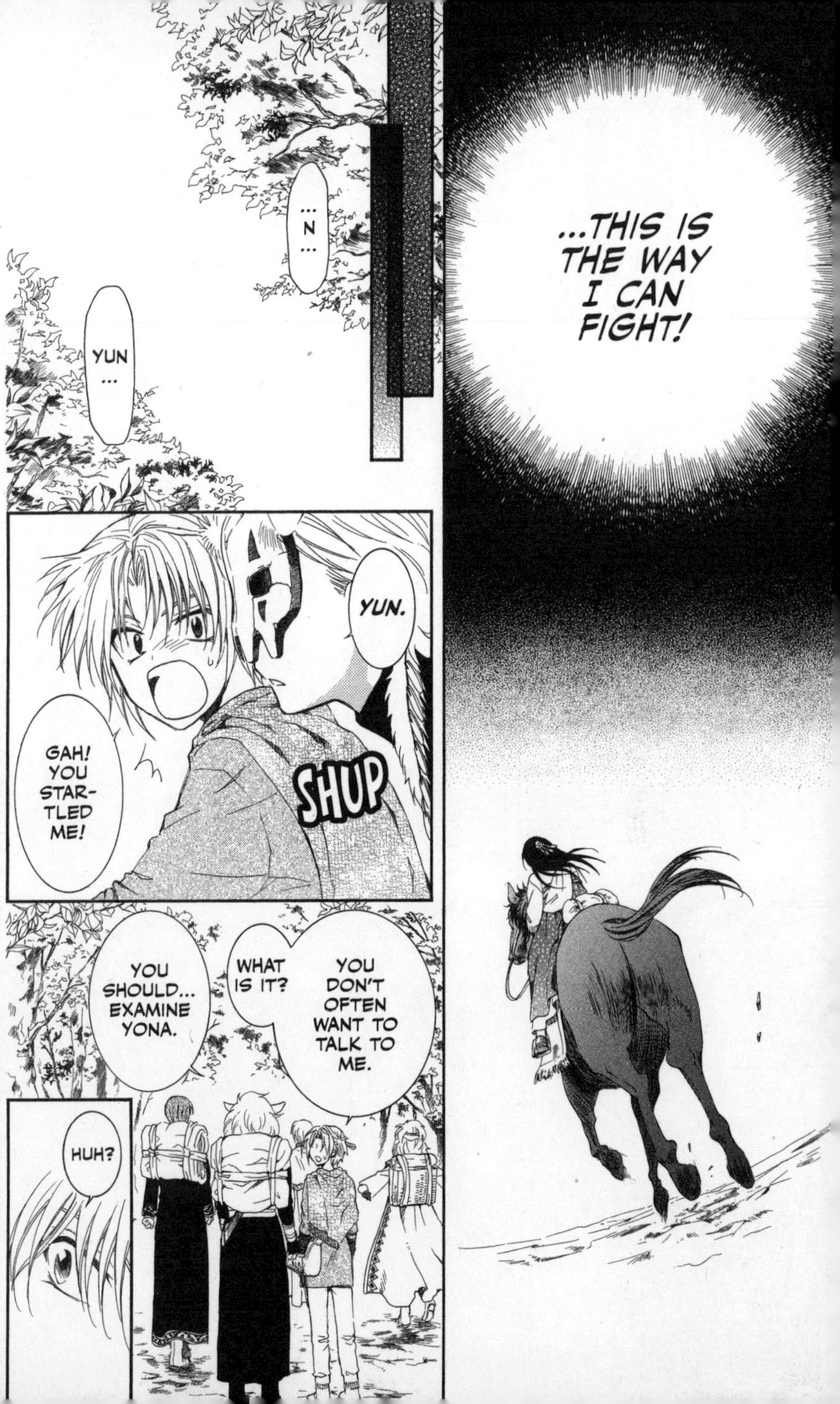
...THIS IS THE WAY I CAN FIGHT!
...N...
YUN...
YUN.
SHUP
GAH! YOU STAR-TLED ME!
WHAT IS IT?
YOU DON'T OFTEN WANT TO TALK TO ME.
YOU SHOULD... EXAMINE YONA.
HUH?

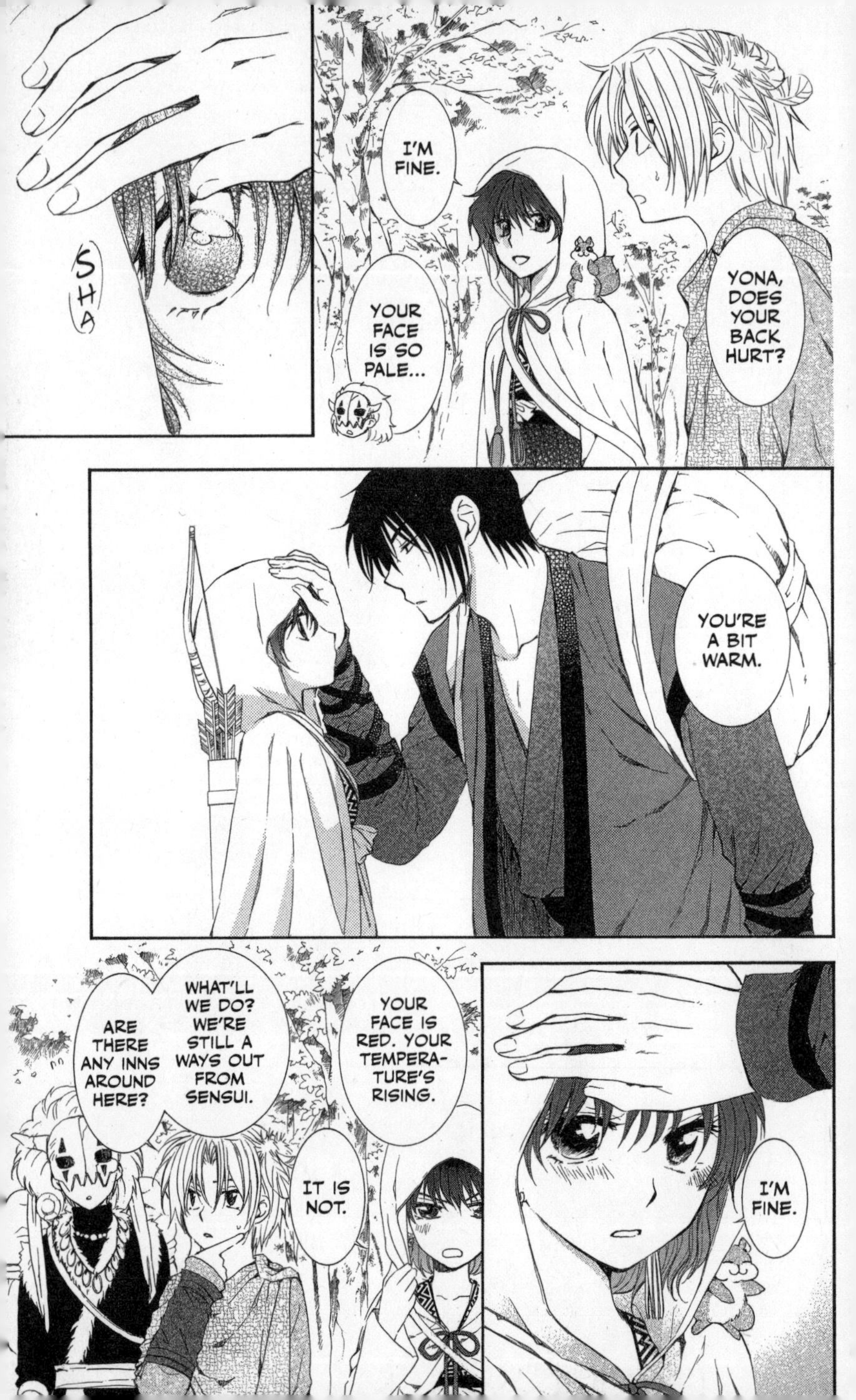
YONA, DOES YOUR BACK HURT?
I'M FINE.
YOUR FACE IS SO PALE...
SHA
YOU'RE A BIT WARM.
I'M FINE.
YOUR FACE IS RED. YOUR TEMPERA-TURE'S RISING.
IT IS NOT.
WHAT'LL WE DO? WE'RE STILL A WAYS OUT FROM SENSUI.
ARE THERE ANY INNS AROUND HERE?

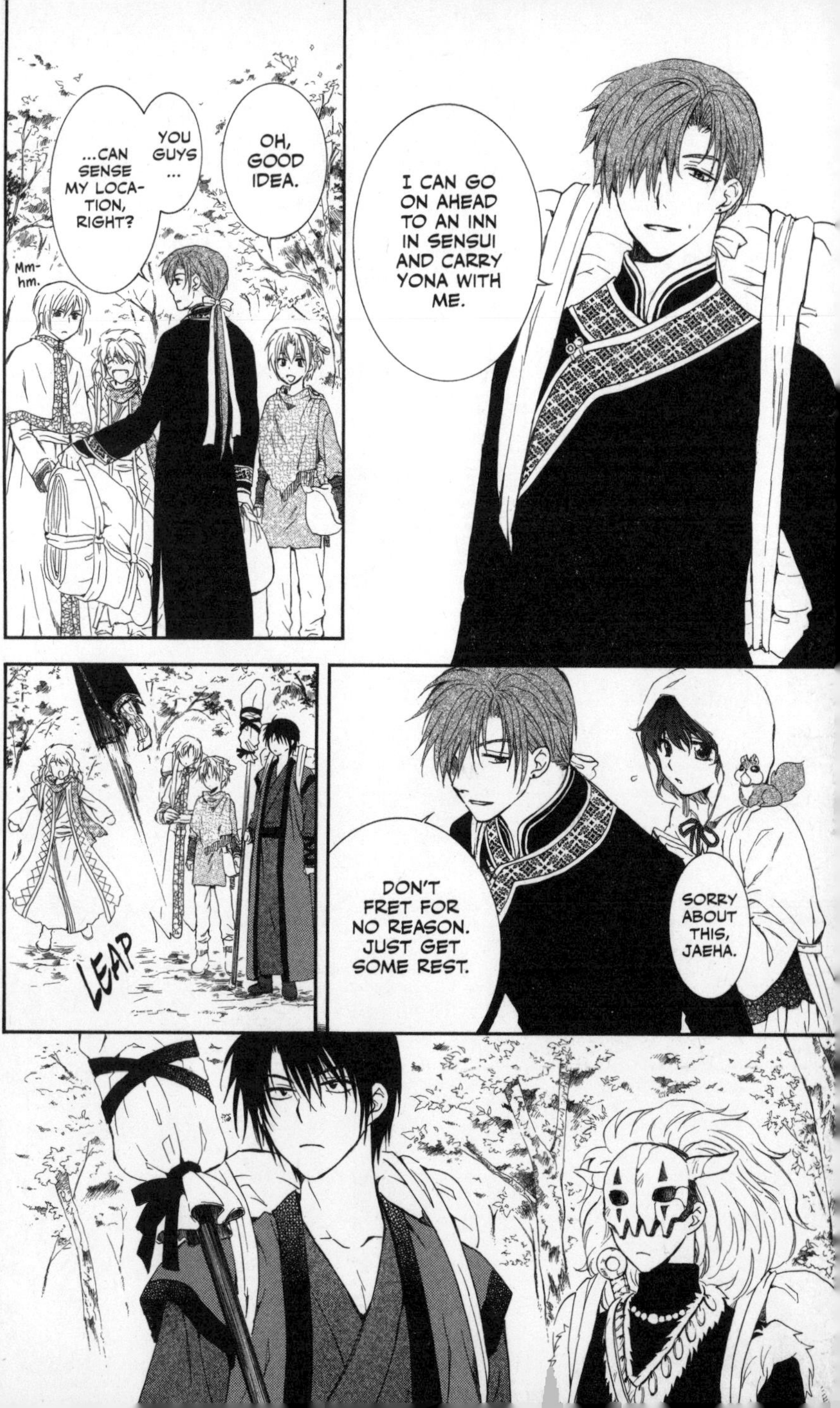
I CAN GO ON AHEAD TO AN INN IN SENSUI AND CARRY YONA WITH ME.
OH, GOOD IDEA.
YOU GUYS ...
...CAN SENSE MY LOCATION, RIGHT?
Mm-hm.
SORRY ABOUT THIS, JAEHA.
DON'T FRET FOR NO REASON. JUST GET SOME REST.
LEAP

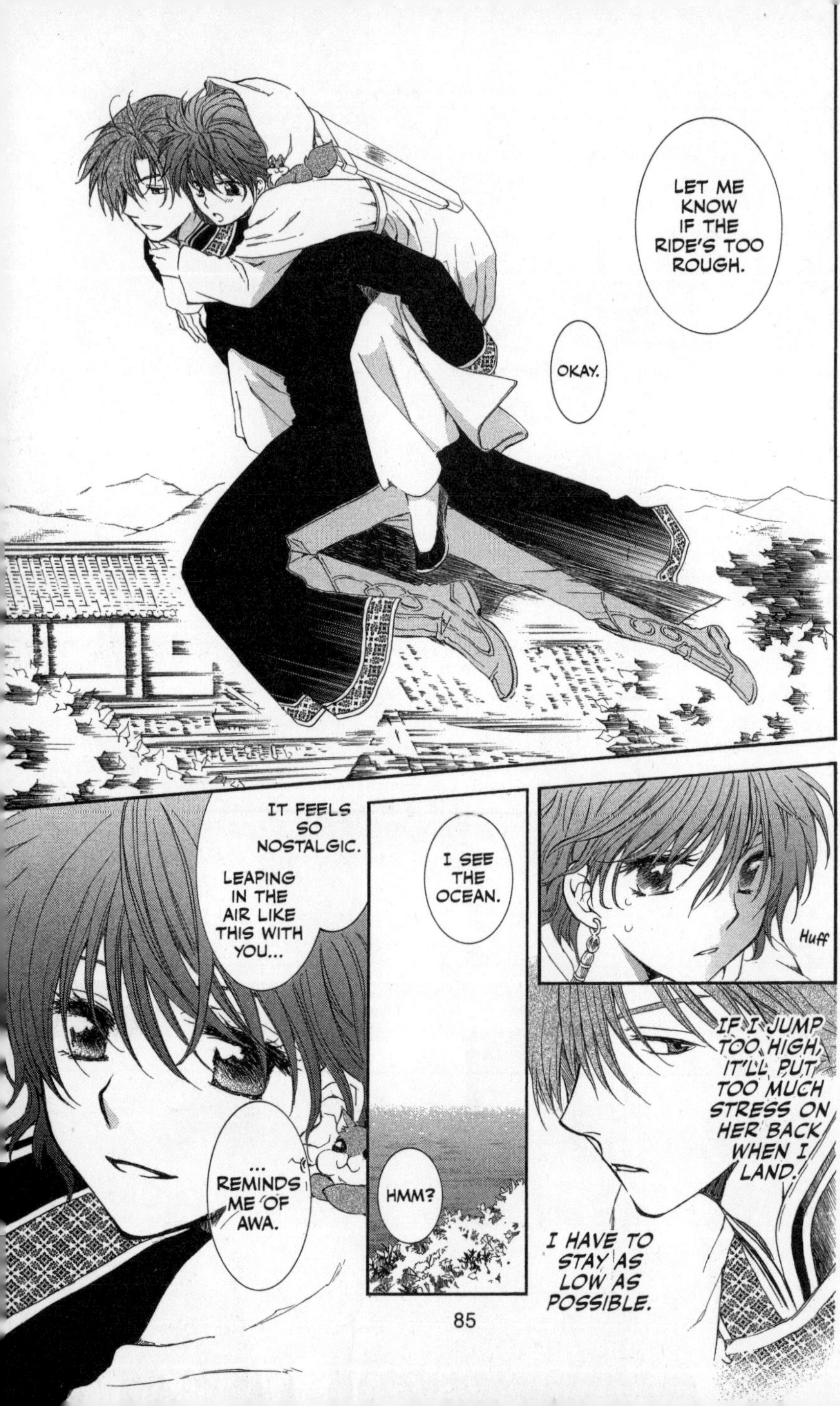
LET ME KNOW IF THE RIDE'S TOO ROUGH.
OKAY.
Huff
IF I JUMP TOO HIGH, IT'LL PUT TOO MUCH STRESS ON HER BACK WHEN I LAND.
I HAVE TO STAY AS LOW AS POSSIBLE.
I SEE THE OCEAN.
HMM?
IT FEELS SO NOSTALGIC.
LEAPING IN THE AIR LIKE THIS WITH YOU...
...REMINDS ME OF AWA.

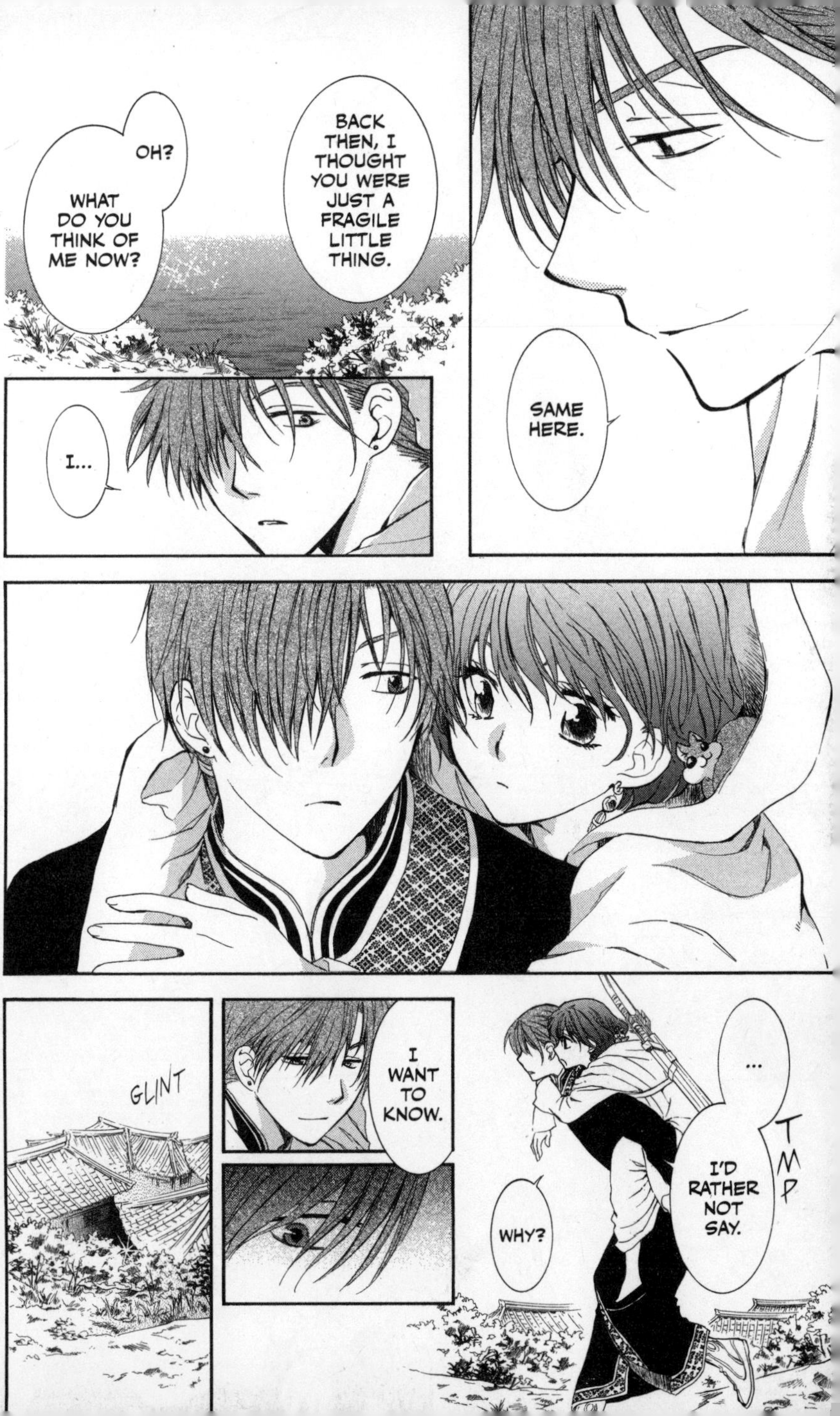
SAME HERE.
BACK THEN, I THOUGHT YOU WERE JUST A FRAGILE LITTLE THING.
OH?
WHAT DO YOU THINK OF ME NOW?
I...
...
I'D RATHER NOT SAY.
TMP
WHY?
I WANT TO KNOW.
GLINT

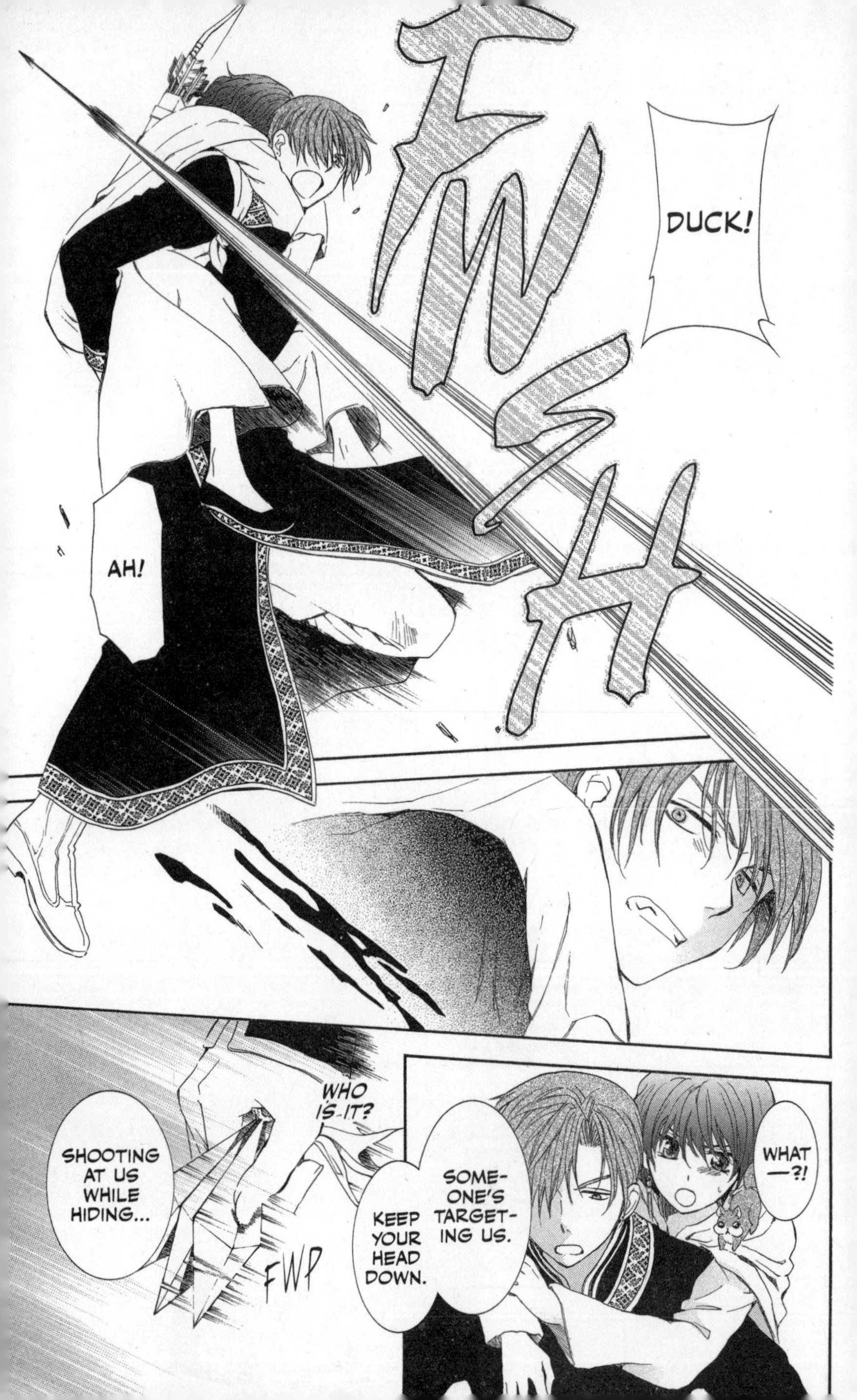
DUCK!
TWSHH
AH!
WHAT—?!
SOME-ONE'S TARGET-ING US.
KEEP YOUR HEAD DOWN.
WHO IS IT?
SHOOTING AT US WHILE HIDING...
FWP

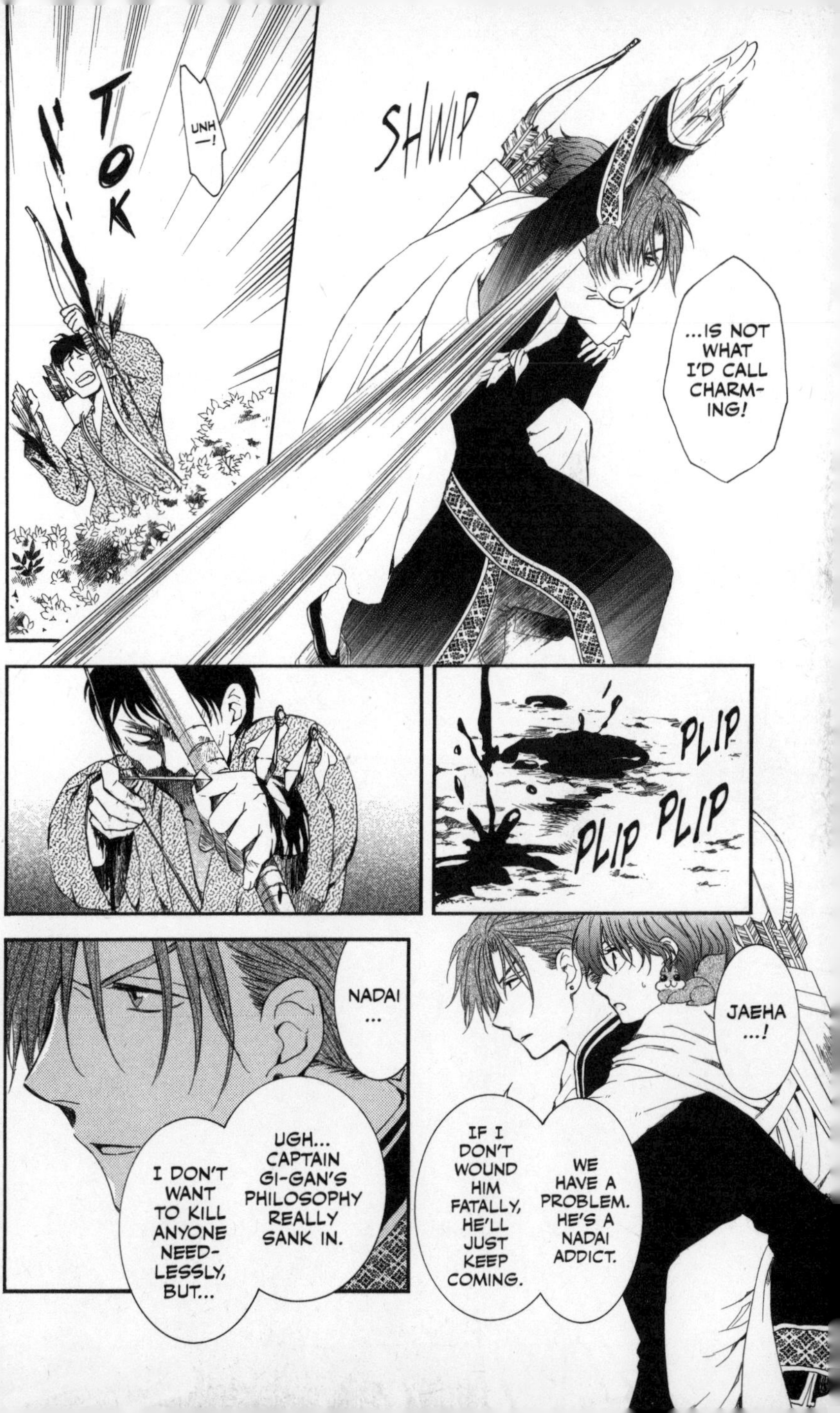
SHWIP
...IS NOT WHAT I'D CALL CHARM-ING!
UNH—!
TOK
PLIP
PLIP PLIP
JAEHA ...!
WE HAVE A PROBLEM. HE'S A NADAI ADDICT.
IF I DON'T WOUND HIM FATALLY, HE'LL JUST KEEP COMING.
NADAI ...
UGH... CAPTAIN GI-GAN'S PHILOSOPHY REALLY SANK IN.
I DON'T WANT TO KILL ANYONE NEED-LESSLY, BUT...

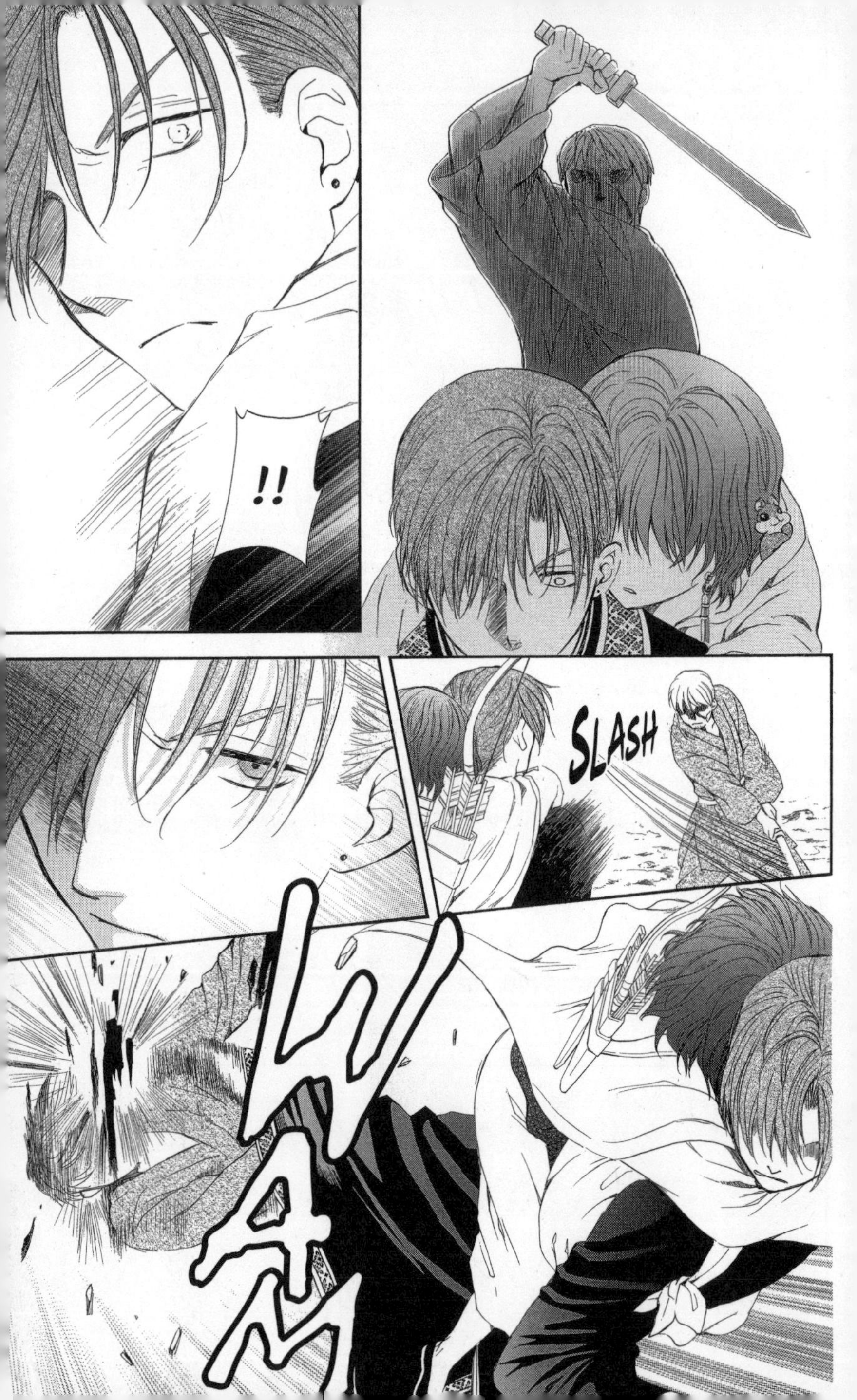
!!
SLASH
WAM

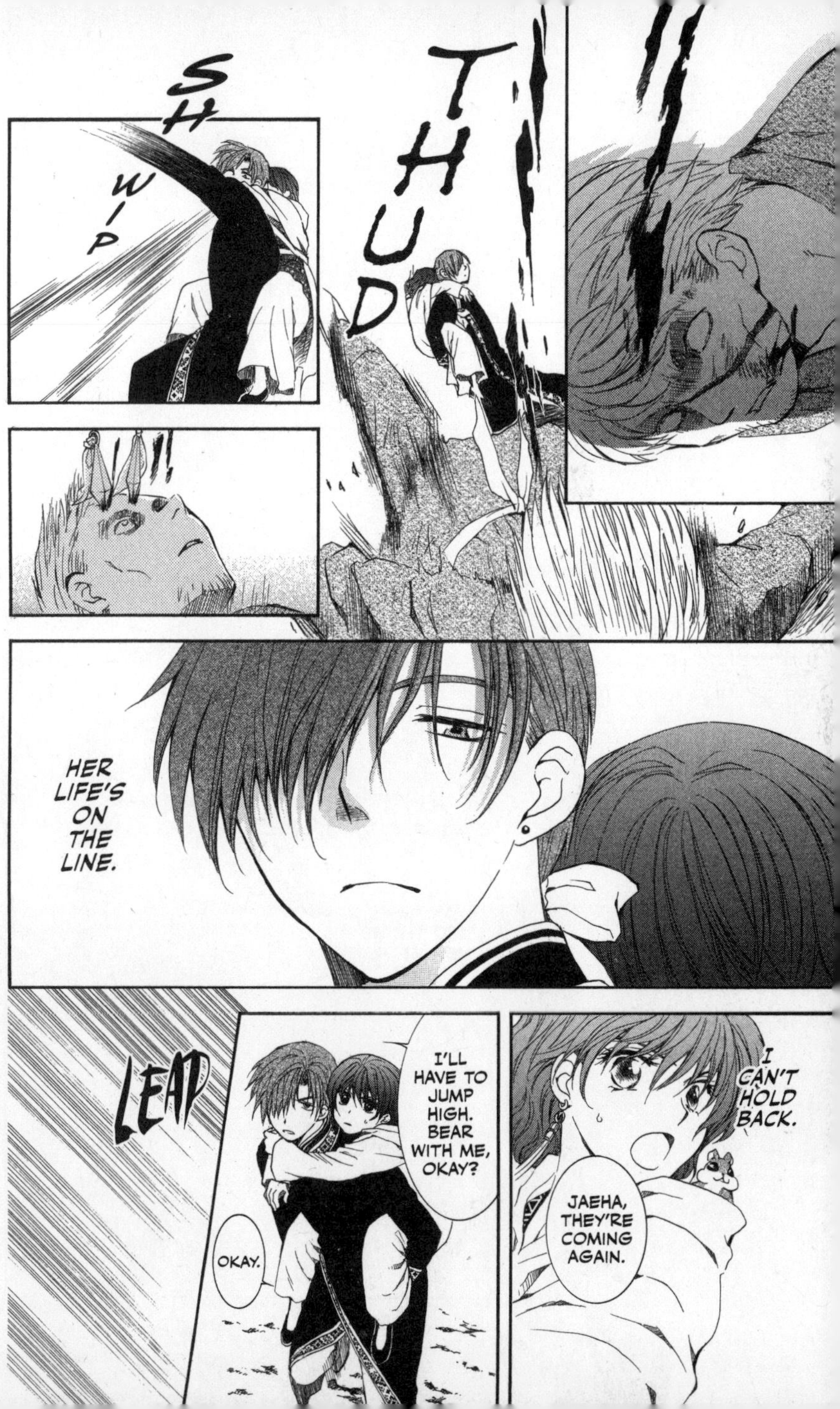
THUD
SHWIP
HER LIFE'S ON THE LINE.
I CAN'T HOLD BACK.
JAEHA, THEY'RE COMING AGAIN.
I'LL HAVE TO JUMP HIGH. BEAR WITH ME, OKAY?
OKAY.
LEAP

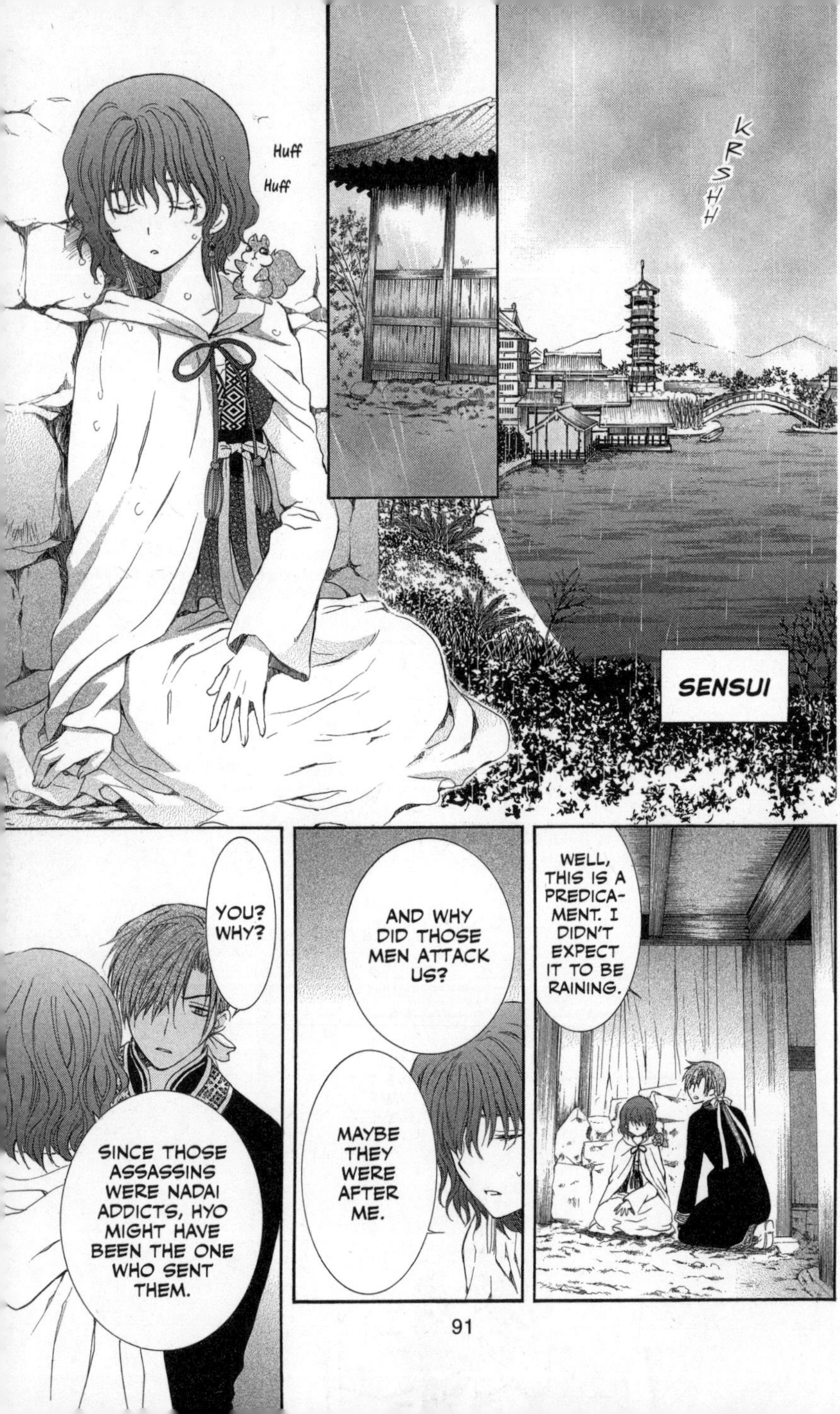
KRSHH
SENSUI
Huff
Huff
WELL, THIS IS A PREDICAMENT. I DIDN'T EXPECT IT TO BE RAINING.
AND WHY DID THOSE MEN ATTACK US?
MAYBE THEY WERE AFTER ME.
YOU? WHY?
SINCE THOSE ASSASSINS WERE NADAI ADDICTS, HYO MIGHT HAVE BEEN THE ONE WHO SENT THEM.

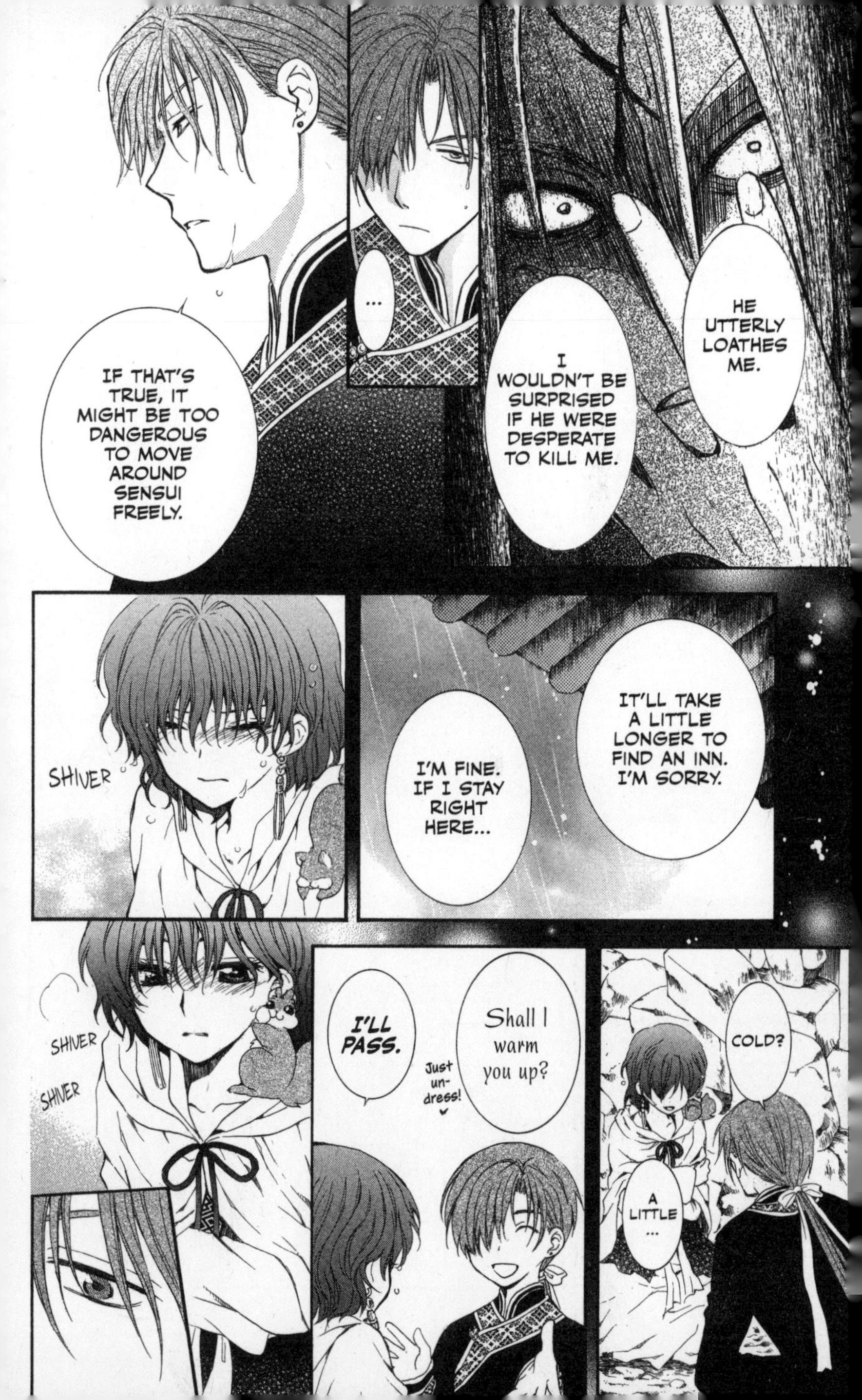
HE UTTERLY LOATHES ME.
I WOULDN'T BE SURPRISED IF HE WERE DESPERATE TO KILL ME.
...
IF THAT'S TRUE, IT MIGHT BE TOO DANGEROUS TO MOVE AROUND SENSUI FREELY.
IT'LL TAKE A LITTLE LONGER TO FIND AN INN. I'M SORRY.
I'M FINE. IF I STAY RIGHT HERE...
SHIVER
COLD?
A LITTLE...
Shall I warm you up?
Just un-dress!
I'LL PASS.
SHIVER
SHIVER

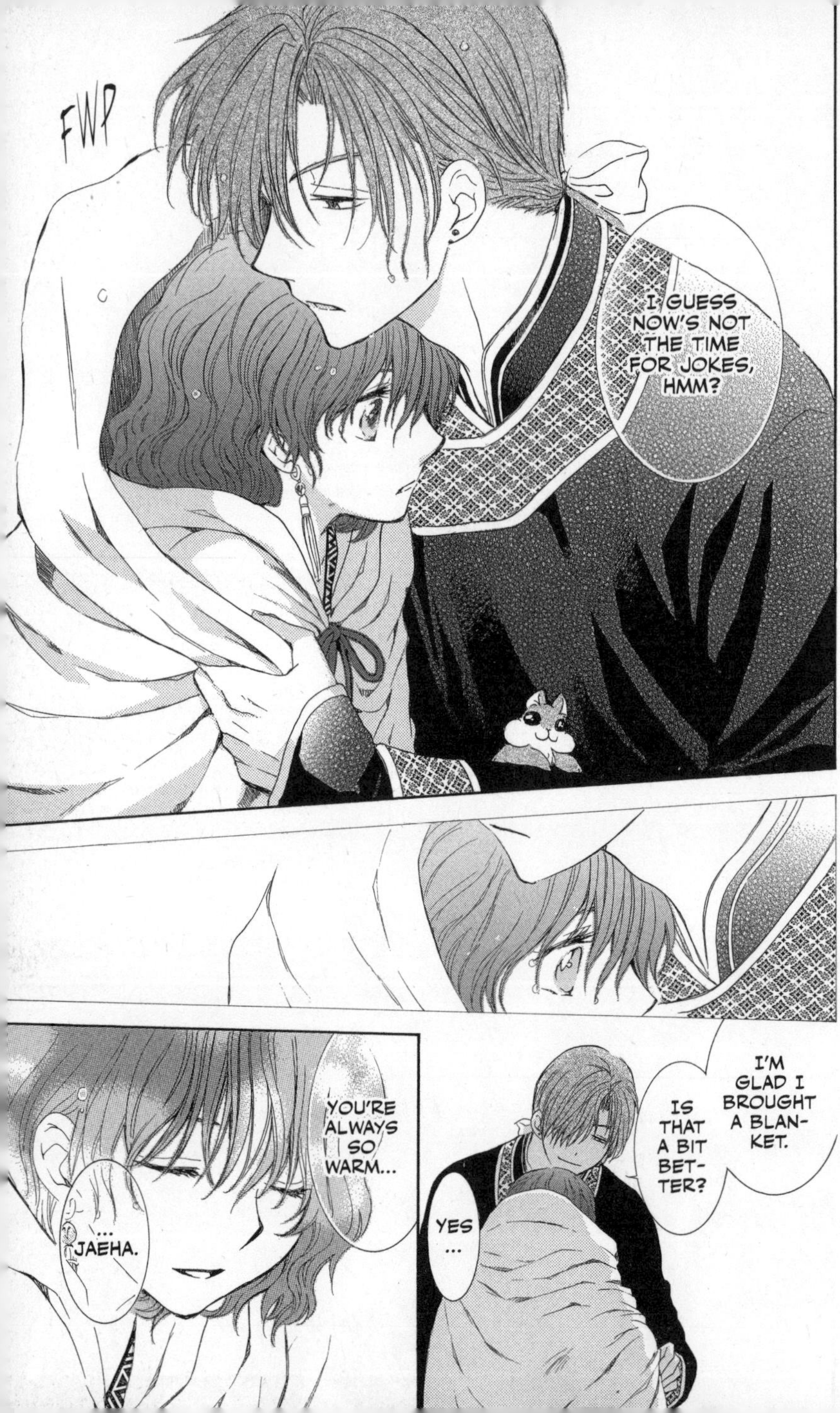
FWP
I GUESS NOW'S NOT THE TIME FOR JOKES, HMM?
I'M GLAD I BROUGHT A BLAN-KET.
IS THAT A BIT BET-TER?
YES...
YOU'RE ALWAYS SO WARM...
...JAEHA.

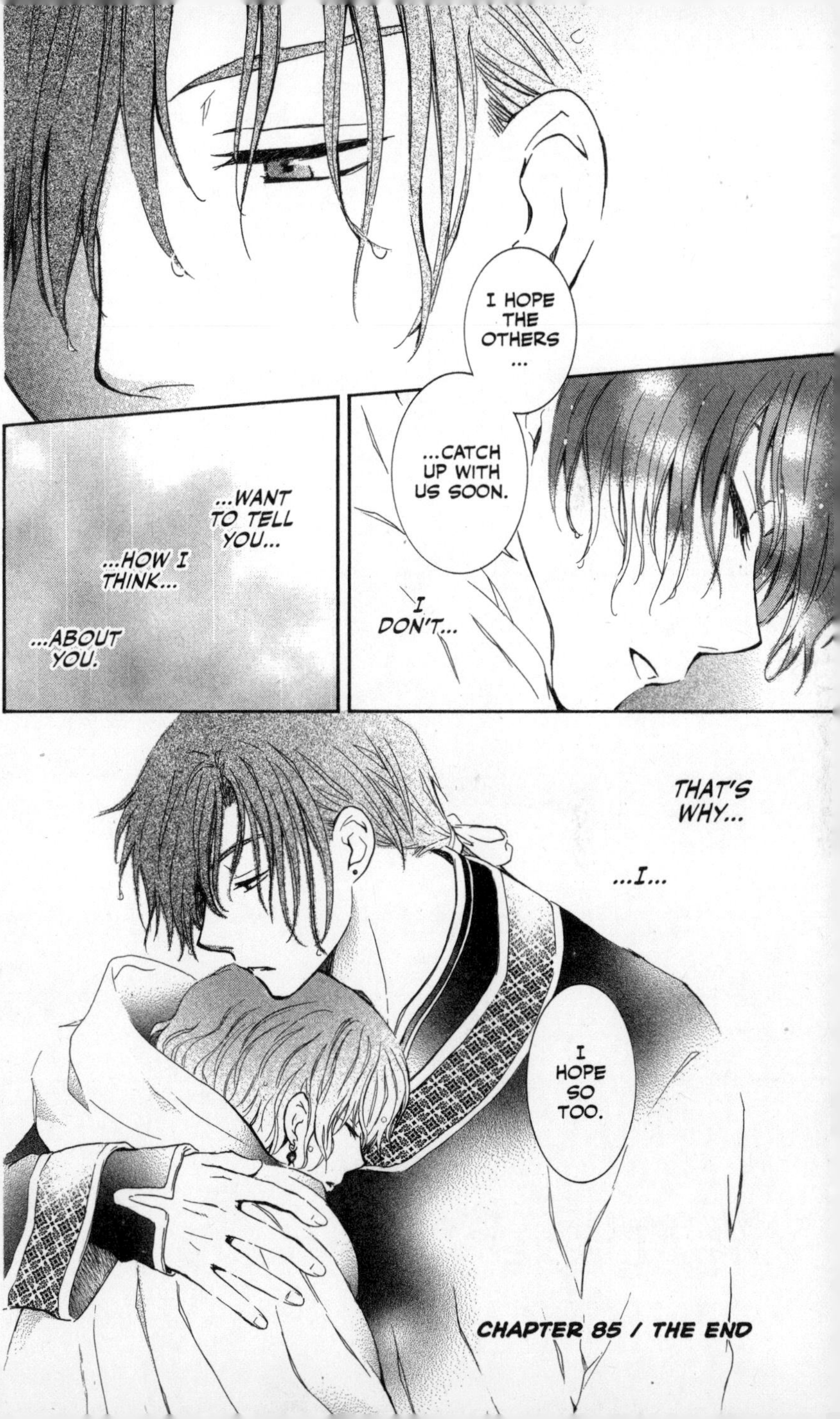
I HOPE THE OTHERS ...
...CATCH UP WITH US SOON.
I DON'T...
...WANT TO TELL YOU...
...HOW I THINK...
...ABOUT YOU.
THAT'S WHY...
...I...
I HOPE SO TOO.
CHAPTER 85 / THE END

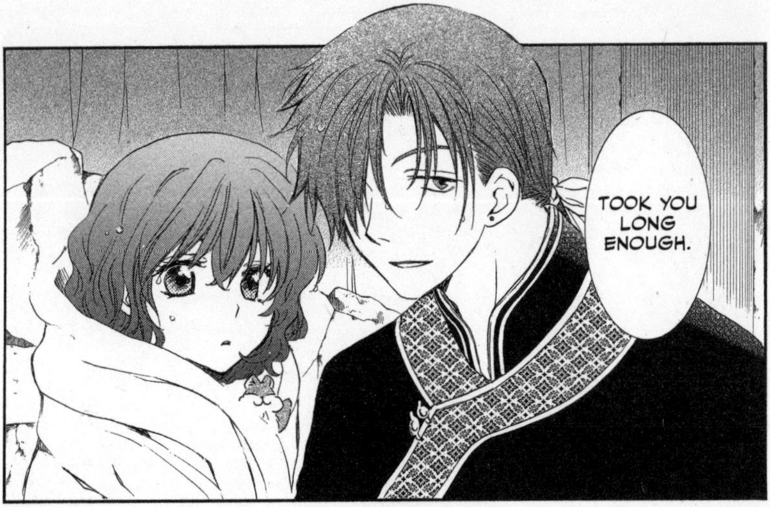
TOOK YOU LONG ENOUGH.

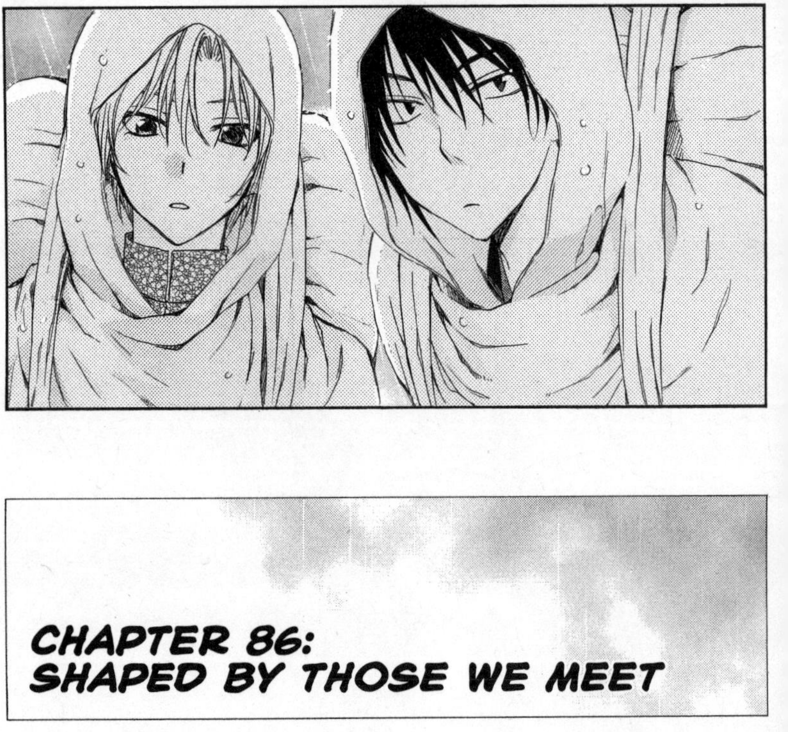

CHAPTER 86: SHAPED BY THOSE WE MEET

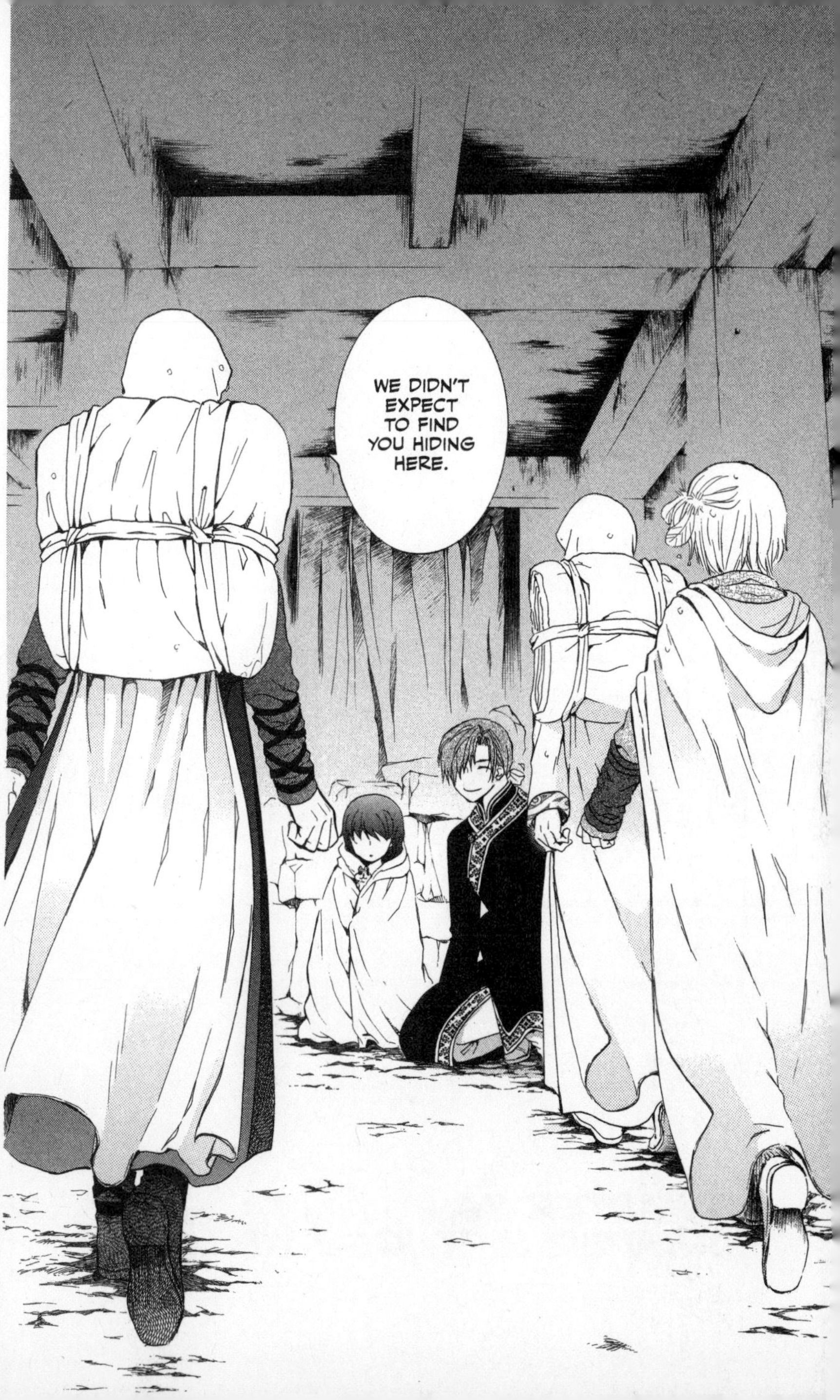
WE DIDN'T EXPECT TO FIND YOU HIDING HERE.

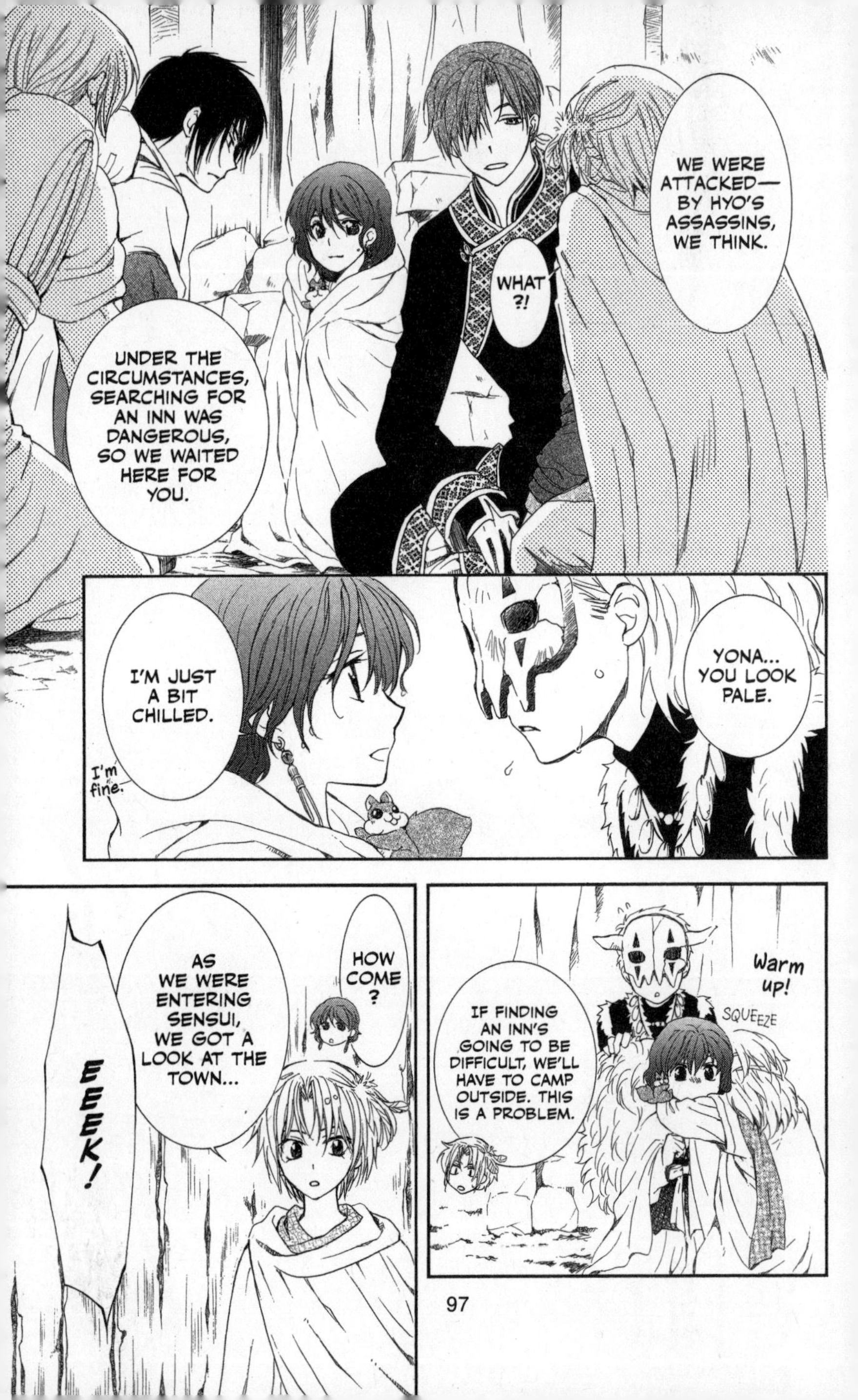
WE WERE ATTACKED— BY HYO'S ASSASSINS, WE THINK.
WHAT?!
UNDER THE CIRCUMSTANCES, SEARCHING FOR AN INN WAS DANGEROUS, SO WE WAITED HERE FOR YOU.
YONA... YOU LOOK PALE.
I'M JUST A BIT CHILLED.
I'm fine.
Warm up!
SQUEEZE
IF FINDING AN INN'S GOING TO BE DIFFICULT, WE'LL HAVE TO CAMP OUTSIDE. THIS IS A PROBLEM.
HOW COME?
AS WE WERE ENTERING SENSUI, WE GOT A LOOK AT THE TOWN...
EEEK!

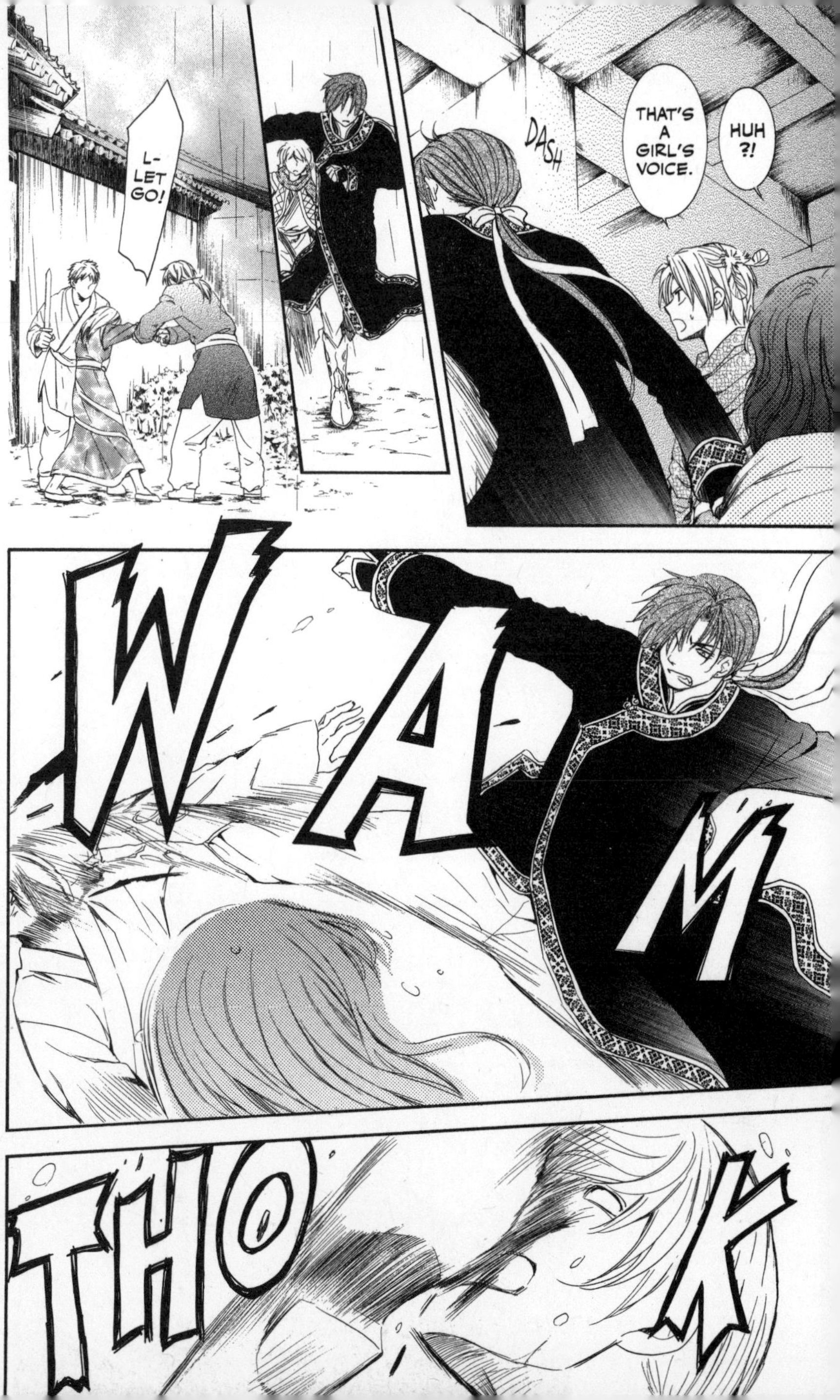
HUH ?!
THAT'S A GIRL'S VOICE.
DASH
L- LET GO!
WAM
THOK

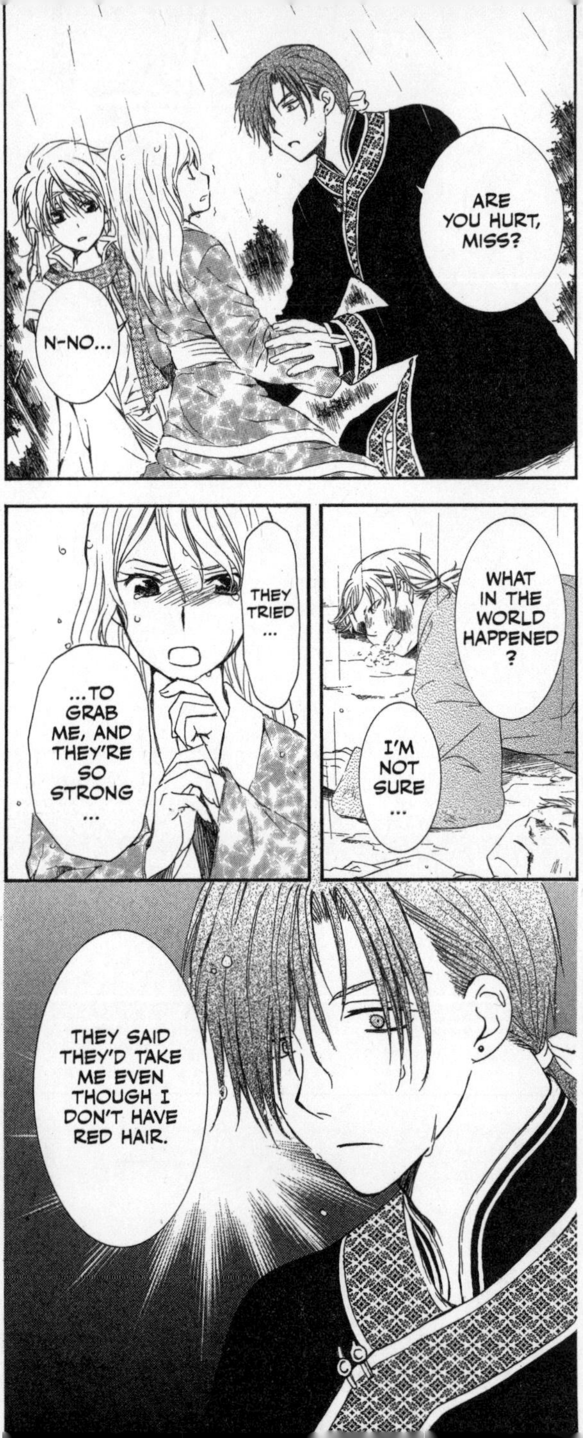
ARE YOU HURT, MISS?
N-NO...
WHAT IN THE WORLD HAPPENED?
I'M NOT SURE...
THEY TRIED...
...TO GRAB ME, AND THEY'RE SO STRONG...
THEY SAID THEY'D TAKE ME EVEN THOUGH I DON'T HAVE RED HAIR.

For volume 15 I've put together a special edition that includes a CD! The CD contains chapter 41 ("Dragon, Human or Both?") from volume 7 and chapter 76 ("Drifters' Market") from volume 13. You'll be surprised to hear that Yona's entire group is included! Hiro Shimono, who plays Zeno, makes his first appearance.

It's a comedy, so even Sinha talks a lot. It's so lively and fun! Some lines are original to this CD. Gija does a lot of ad-libbing. (Hee!) Also, something amazing happens during the conversation with the cast, so I hope you get ahold of the CD and listen to it over and over.

You can hear Pu-kyu say her name!

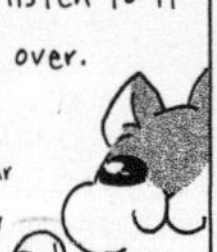
Pu!

I even wrote about what happened during the recording.

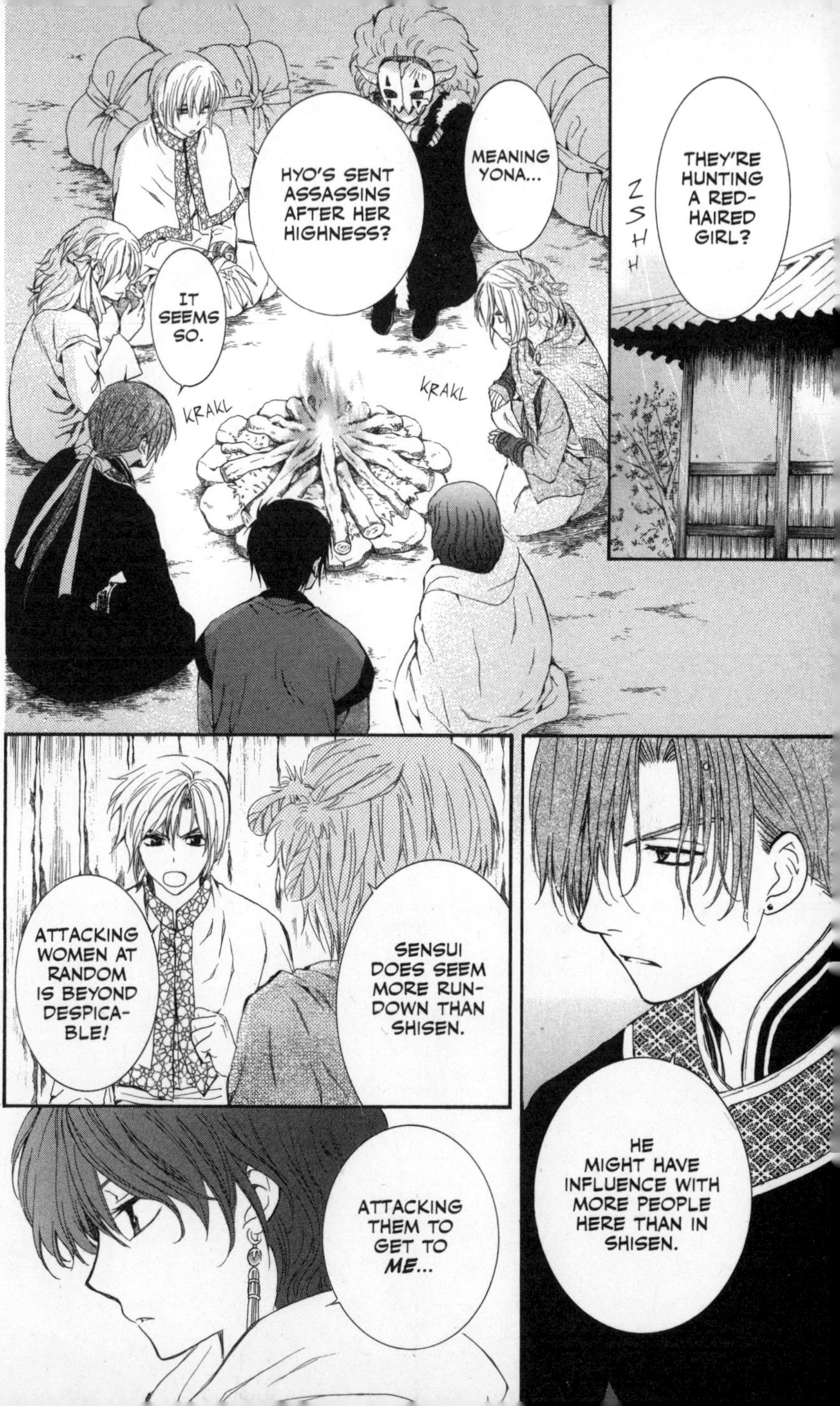
ZSHH
THEY'RE HUNTING A RED-HAIRED GIRL?
MEANING YONA...
HYO'S SENT ASSASSINS AFTER HER HIGHNESS?
IT SEEMS SO.
KRAKL
KRAKL
HE MIGHT HAVE INFLUENCE WITH MORE PEOPLE HERE THAN IN SHISEN.
SENSUI DOES SEEM MORE RUN-DOWN THAN SHISEN.
ATTACKING WOMEN AT RANDOM IS BEYOND DESPICA-BLE!
ATTACKING THEM TO GET TO *ME*...

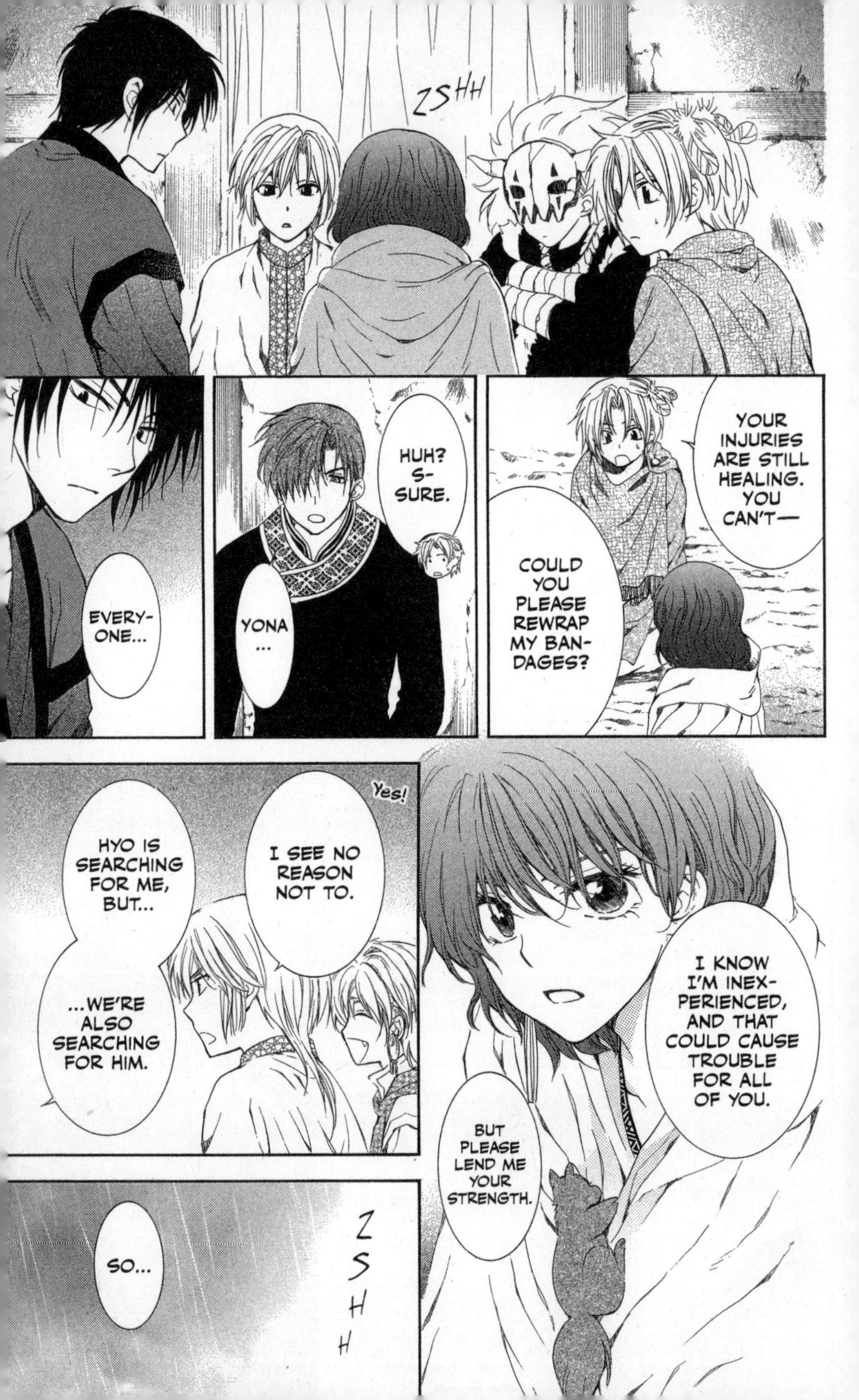

ZSHH
YOUR INJURIES ARE STILL HEALING. YOU CAN'T—
COULD YOU PLEASE REWRAP MY BANDAGES?
HUH? S-SURE.
YONA ...
EVERY-ONE...
I KNOW I'M INEXPERIENCED, AND THAT COULD CAUSE TROUBLE FOR ALL OF YOU.
BUT PLEASE LEND ME YOUR STRENGTH.
Yes!
I SEE NO REASON NOT TO.
HYO IS SEARCHING FOR ME, BUT...
...WE'RE ALSO SEARCHING FOR HIM.
ZSHH
SO...

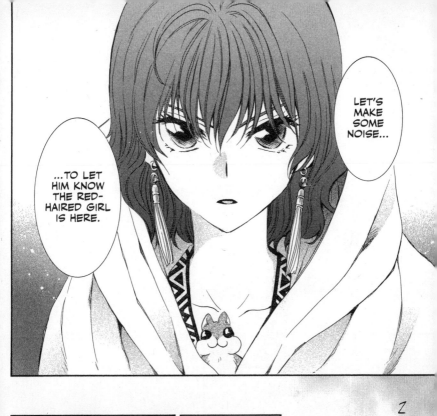

LET'S MAKE SOME NOISE...

...TO LET HIM KNOW THE RED-HAIRED GIRL IS HERE.

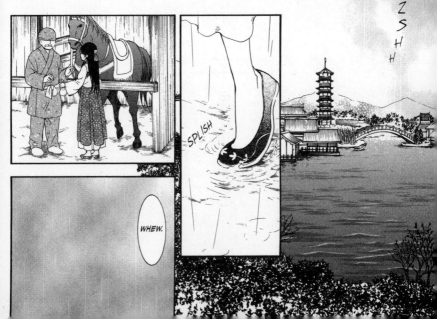

Z S H H

SPLISH

WHEW.

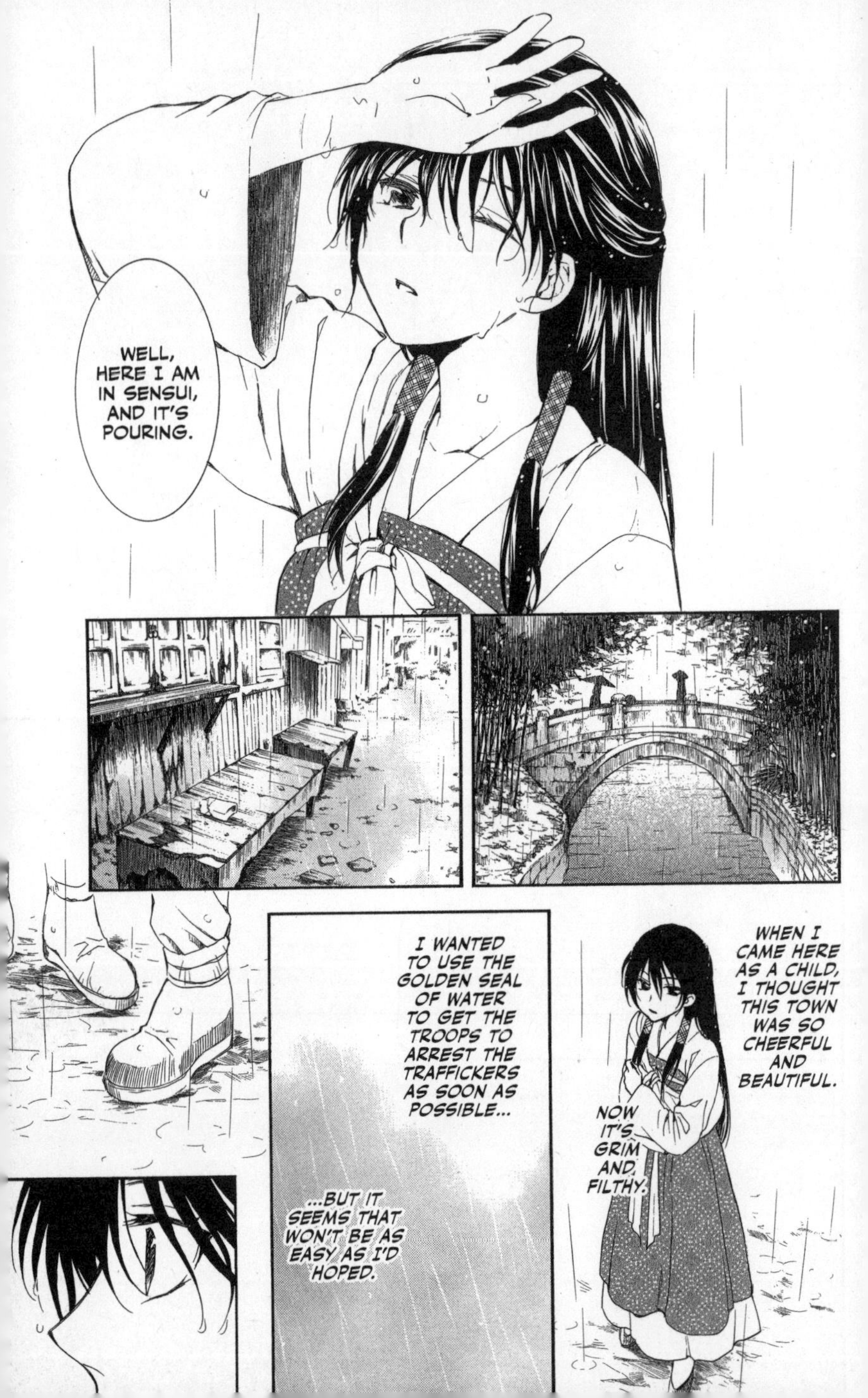
WELL, HERE I AM IN SENSUI, AND IT'S POURING.
WHEN I CAME HERE AS A CHILD, I THOUGHT THIS TOWN WAS SO CHEERFUL AND BEAUTIFUL.
NOW IT'S GRIM AND FILTHY.
I WANTED TO USE THE GOLDEN SEAL OF WATER TO GET THE TROOPS TO ARREST THE TRAFFICKERS AS SOON AS POSSIBLE...
...BUT IT SEEMS THAT WON'T BE AS EASY AS I'D HOPED.

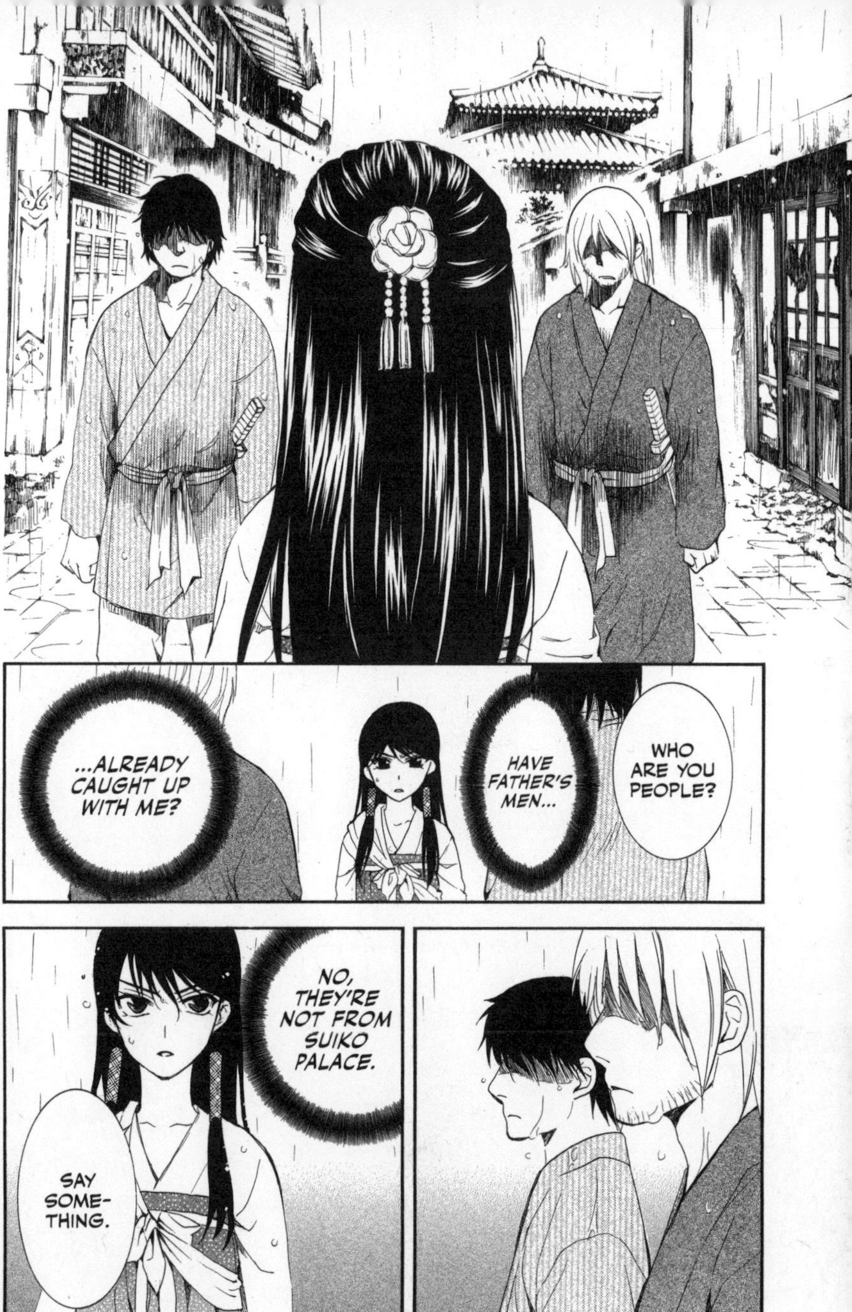
WHO ARE YOU PEOPLE?
HAVE FATHER'S MEN...
...ALREADY CAUGHT UP WITH ME?
NO, THEY'RE NOT FROM SUIKO PALACE.
SAY SOME-THING.

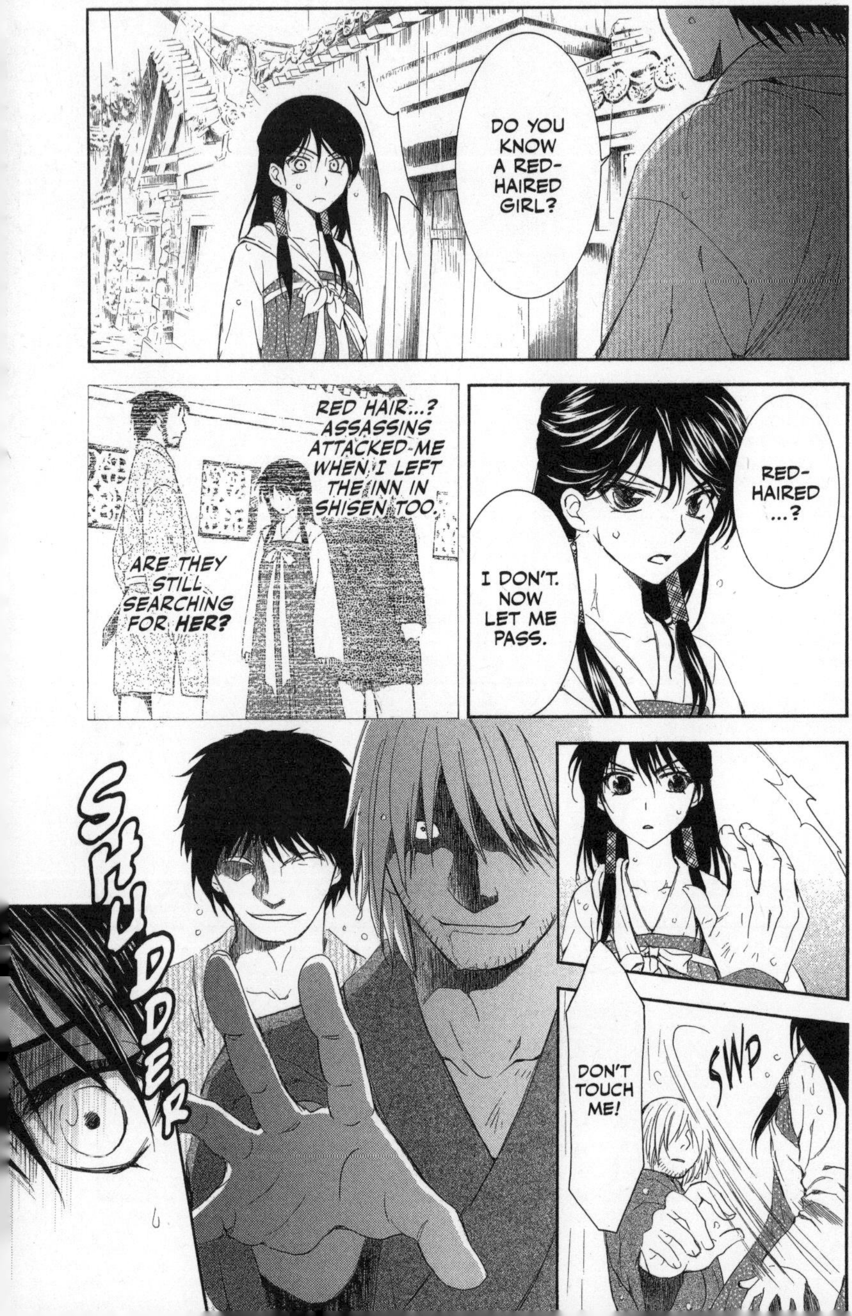
DO YOU KNOW A RED-HAIRED GIRL?
RED-HAIRED ...?
I DON'T. NOW LET ME PASS.
RED HAIR...? ASSASSINS ATTACKED ME WHEN I LEFT THE INN IN SHISEN TOO.
ARE THEY STILL SEARCHING FOR HER?
SHUDDER
DON'T TOUCH ME!
SWP

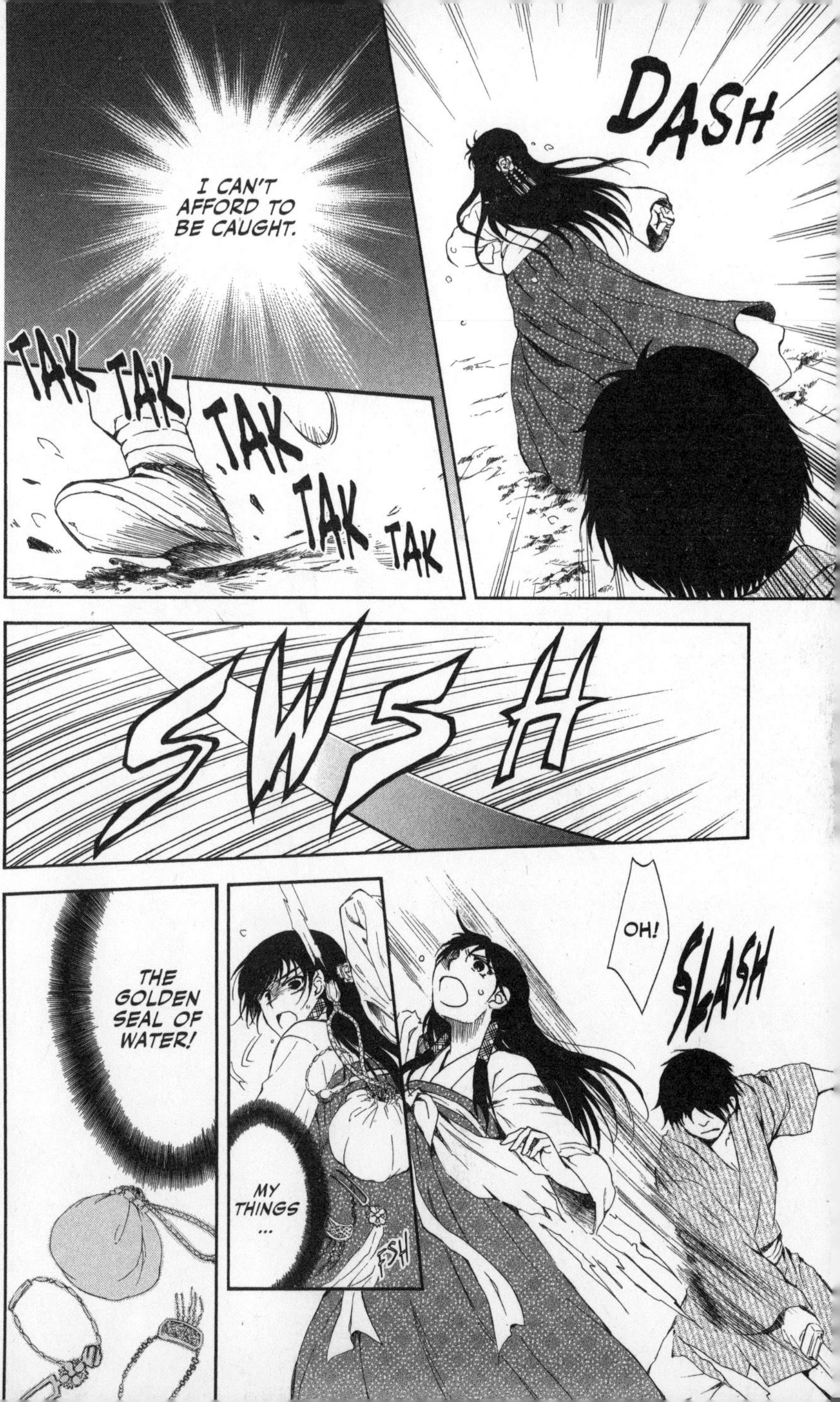
DASH
I CAN'T AFFORD TO BE CAUGHT.
TAK TAK TAK TAK TAK
SWSH
SLASH
OH!
FSH
MY THINGS ...
THE GOLDEN SEAL OF WATER!

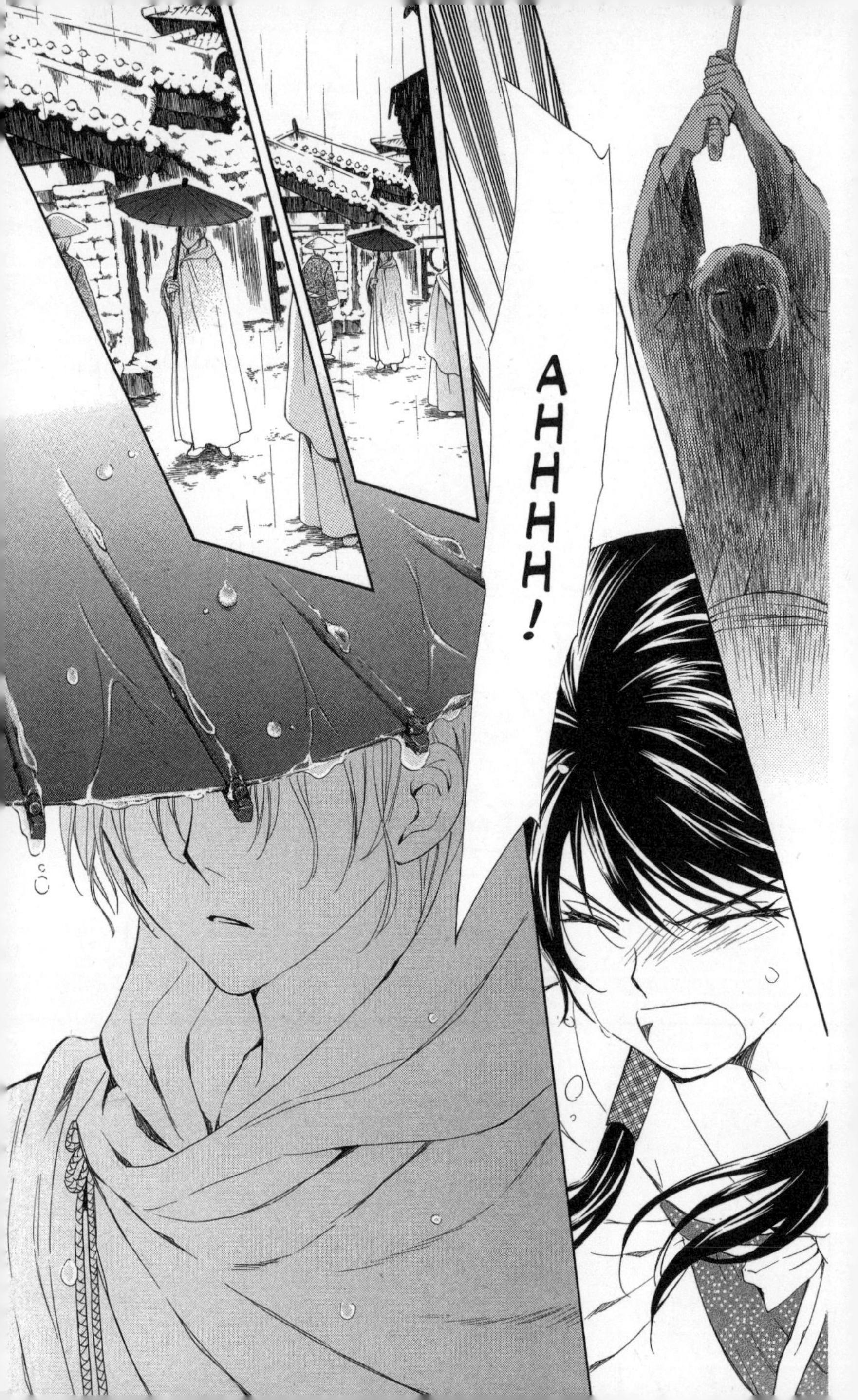
AHHHH!

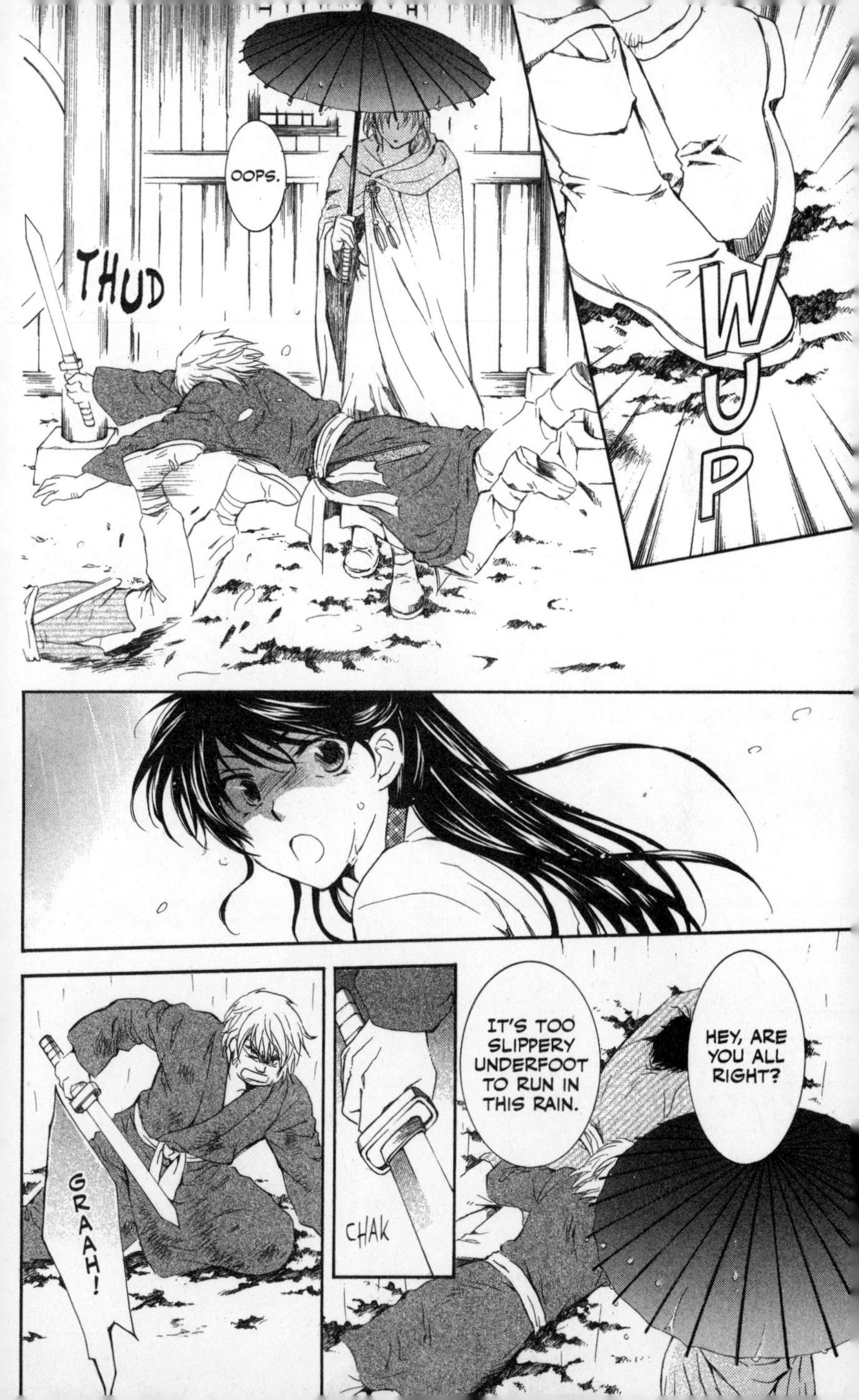
WUP
OOPS.
THUD
HEY, ARE YOU ALL RIGHT?
IT'S TOO SLIPPERY UNDERFOOT TO RUN IN THIS RAIN.
CHAK
GRAAH!

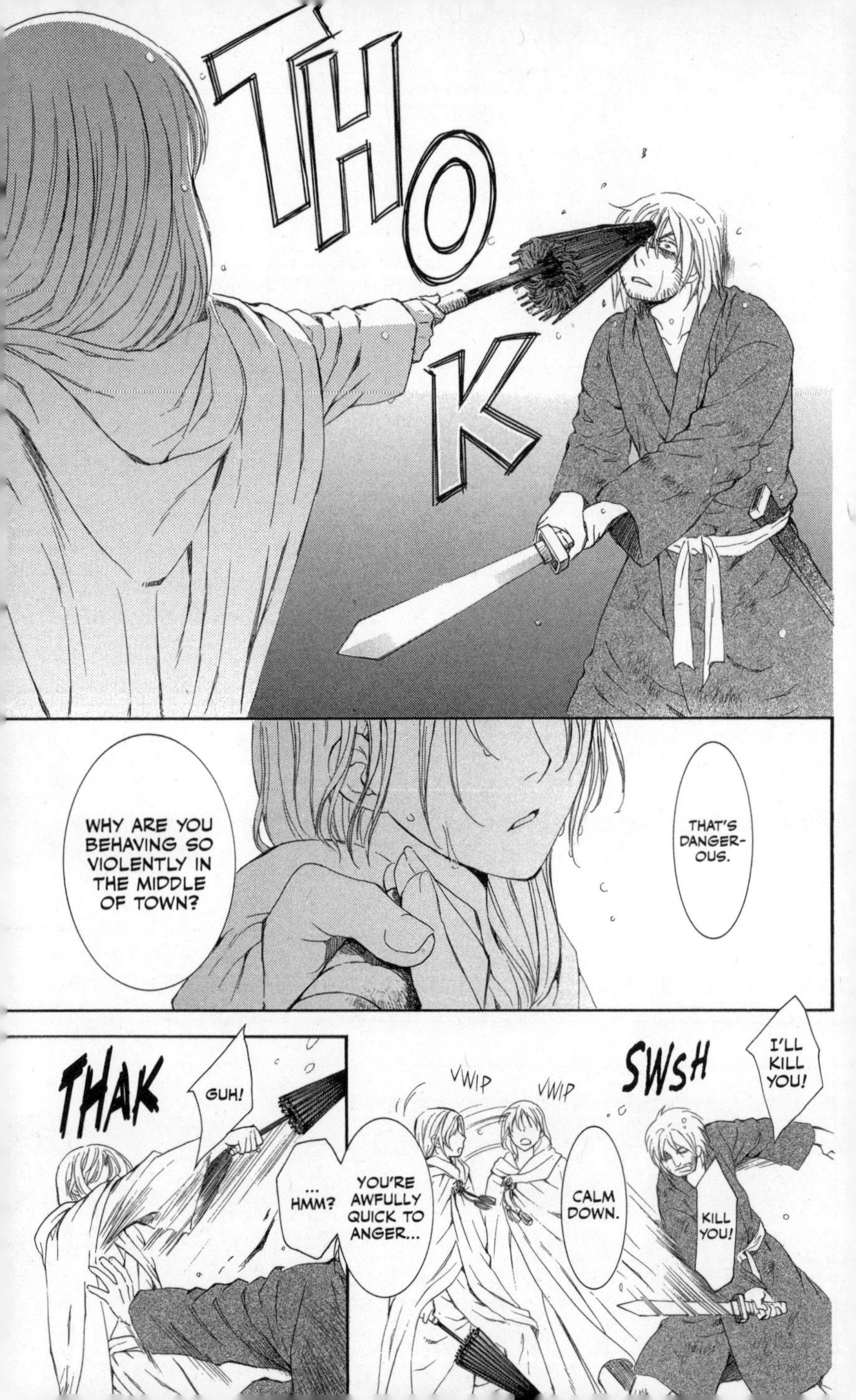
THOK
THAT'S DANGER-OUS.
WHY ARE YOU BEHAVING SO VIOLENTLY IN THE MIDDLE OF TOWN?
I'LL KILL YOU!
SWSH
KILL YOU!
CALM DOWN.
VWIP
VWIP
YOU'RE AWFULLY QUICK TO ANGER...
... HMM?
GUH!
THAK

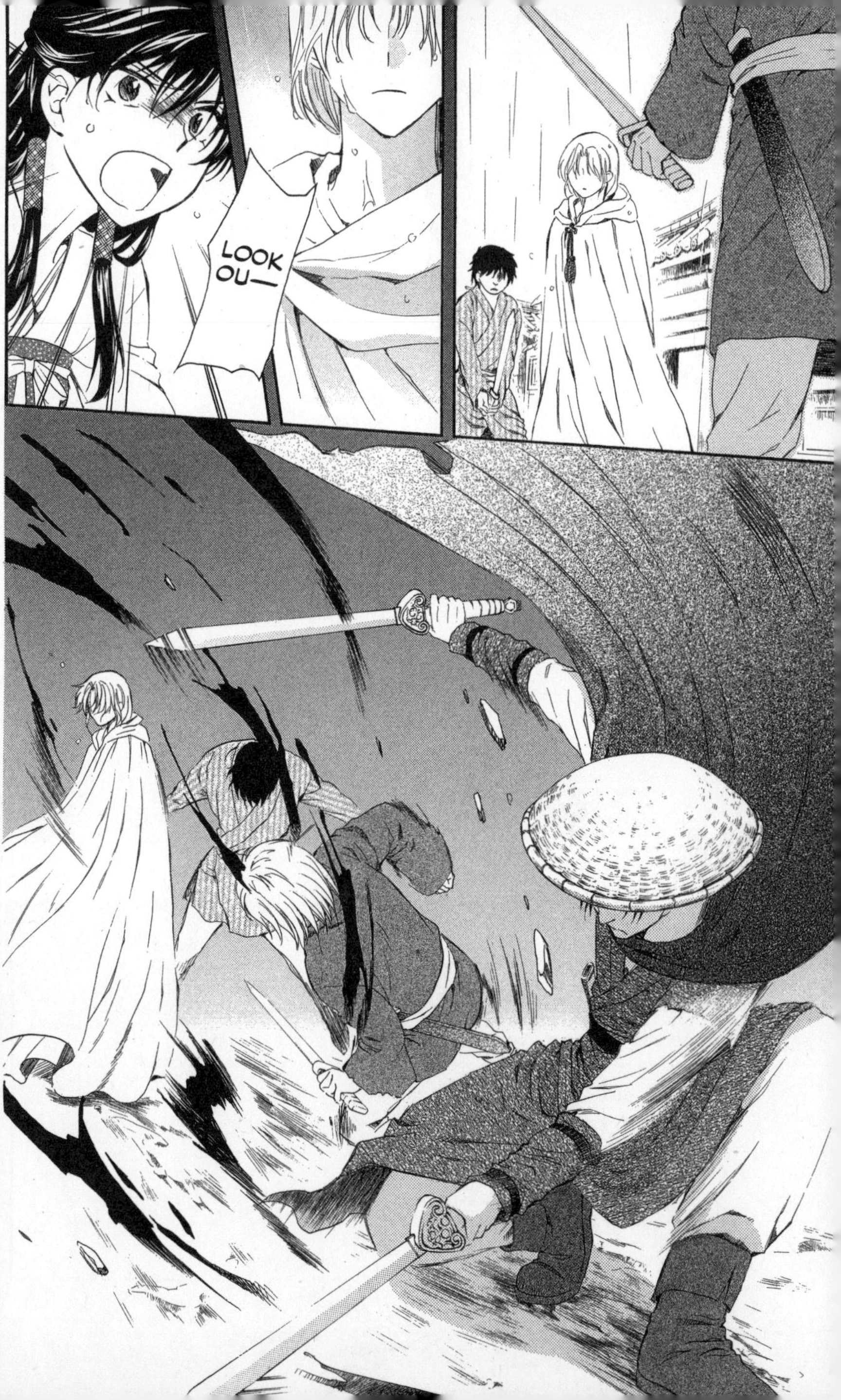
LOOK OU—

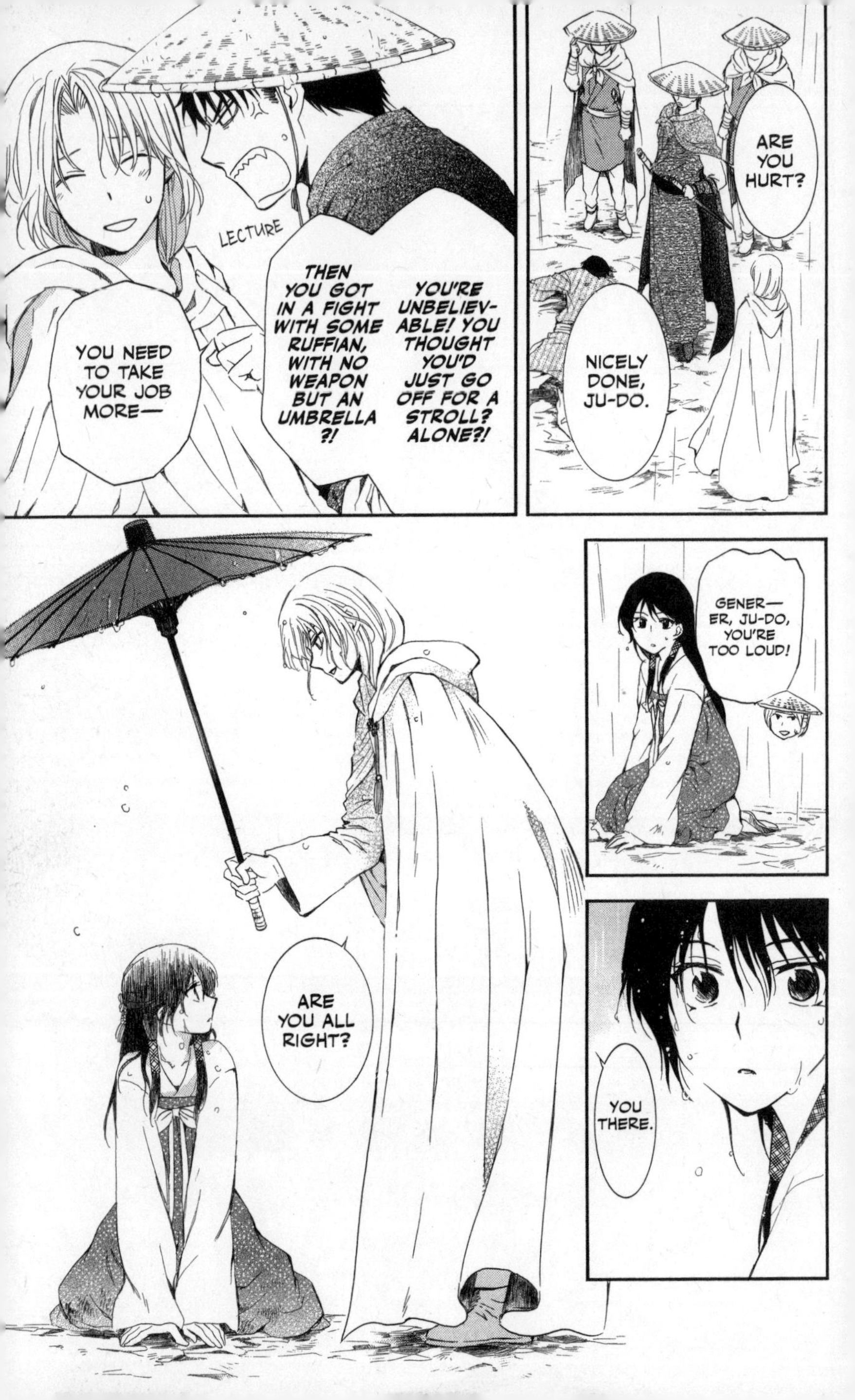
ARE YOU HURT?
NICELY DONE, JU-DO.
YOU'RE UNBELIEV-ABLE! YOU THOUGHT YOU'D JUST GO OFF FOR A STROLL? ALONE?!
THEN YOU GOT IN A FIGHT WITH SOME RUFFIAN, WITH NO WEAPON BUT AN UMBRELLA?!
LECTURE
YOU NEED TO TAKE YOUR JOB MORE—
GENER— ER, JU-DO, YOU'RE TOO LOUD!
YOU THERE.
ARE YOU ALL RIGHT?

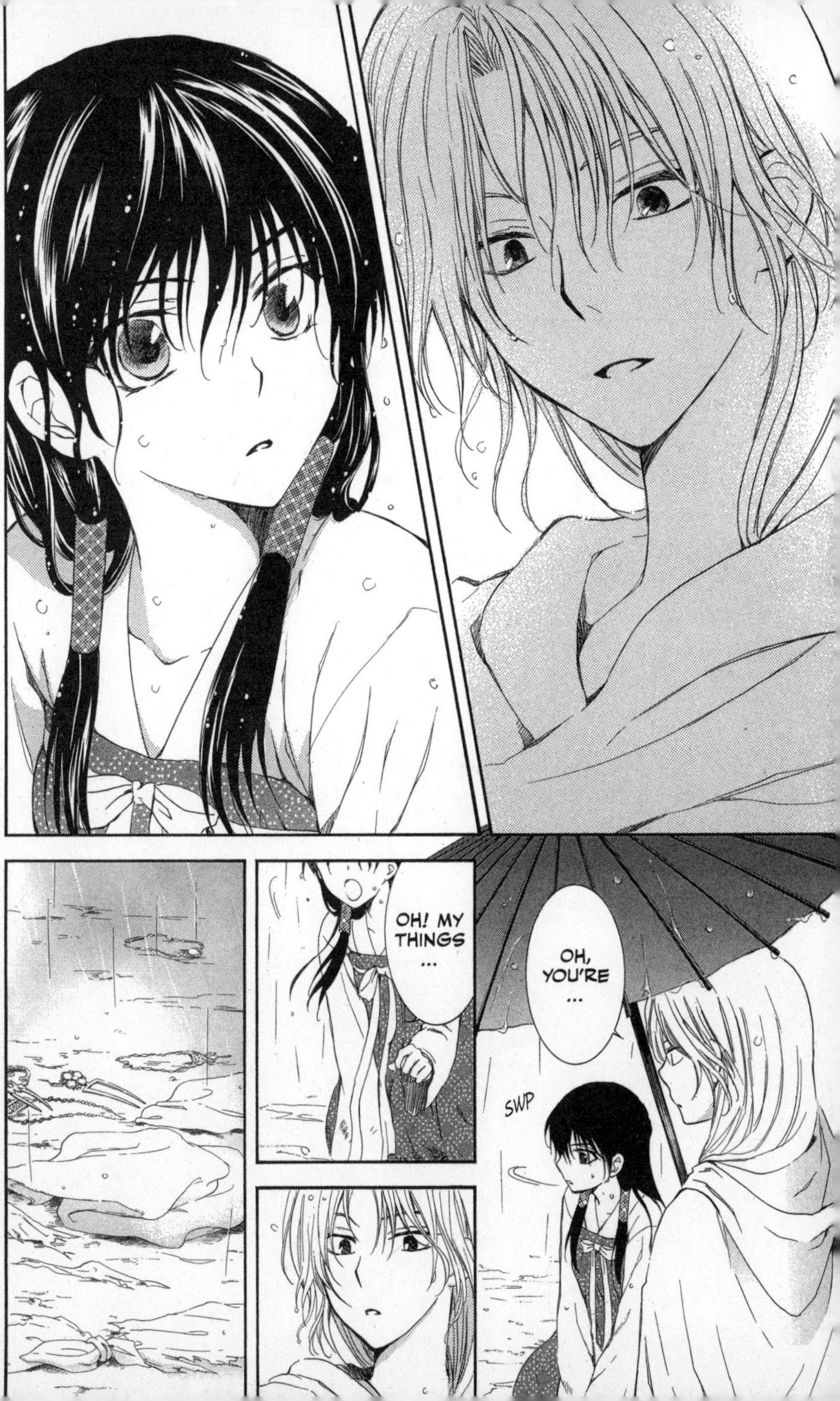
OH, YOU'RE ...
SWP
OH! MY THINGS ...

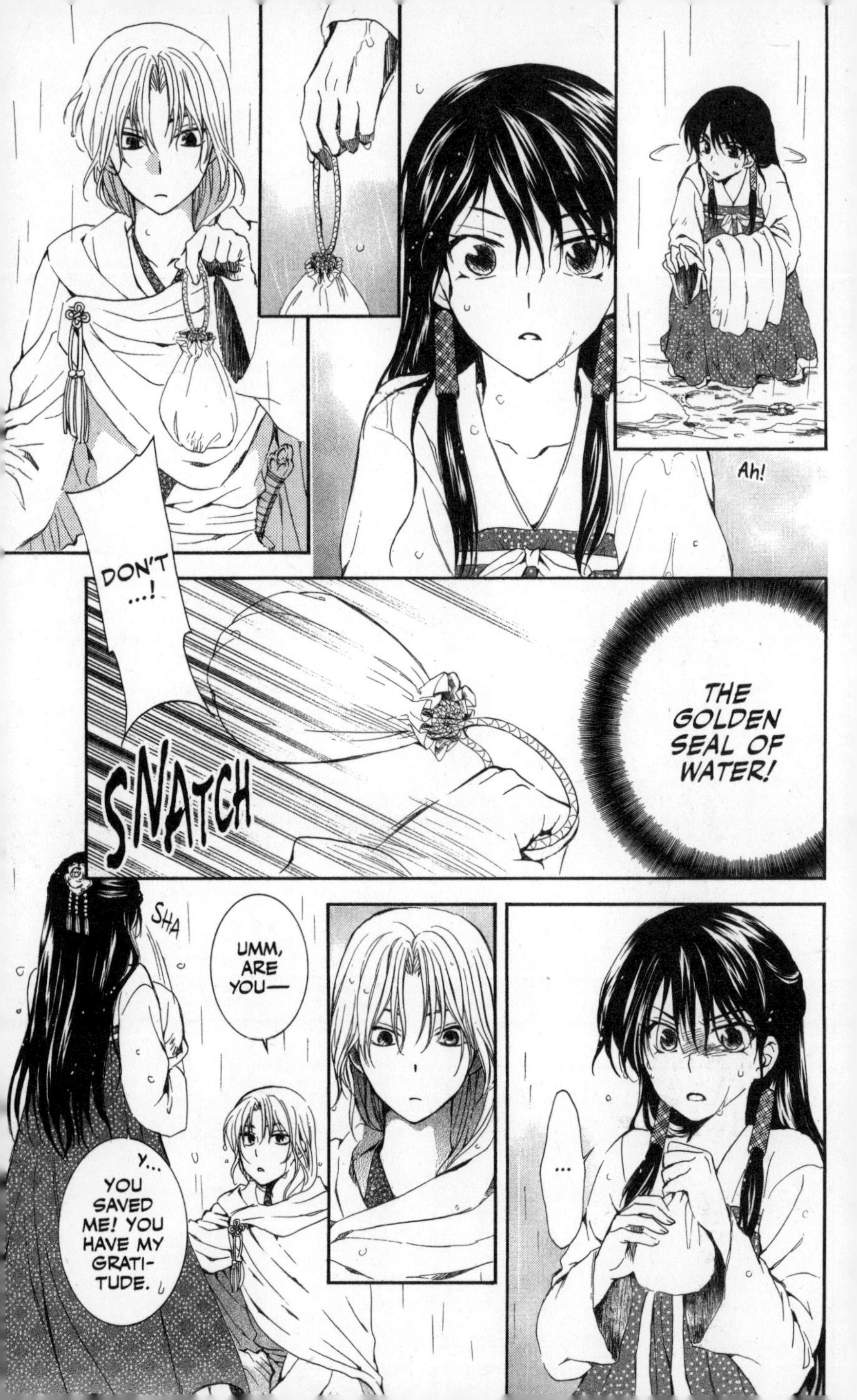
Ah!
DON'T ...!
THE GOLDEN SEAL OF WATER!
SNATCH
...
UMM, ARE YOU—
SHA
Y... YOU SAVED ME! YOU HAVE MY GRATI- TUDE.

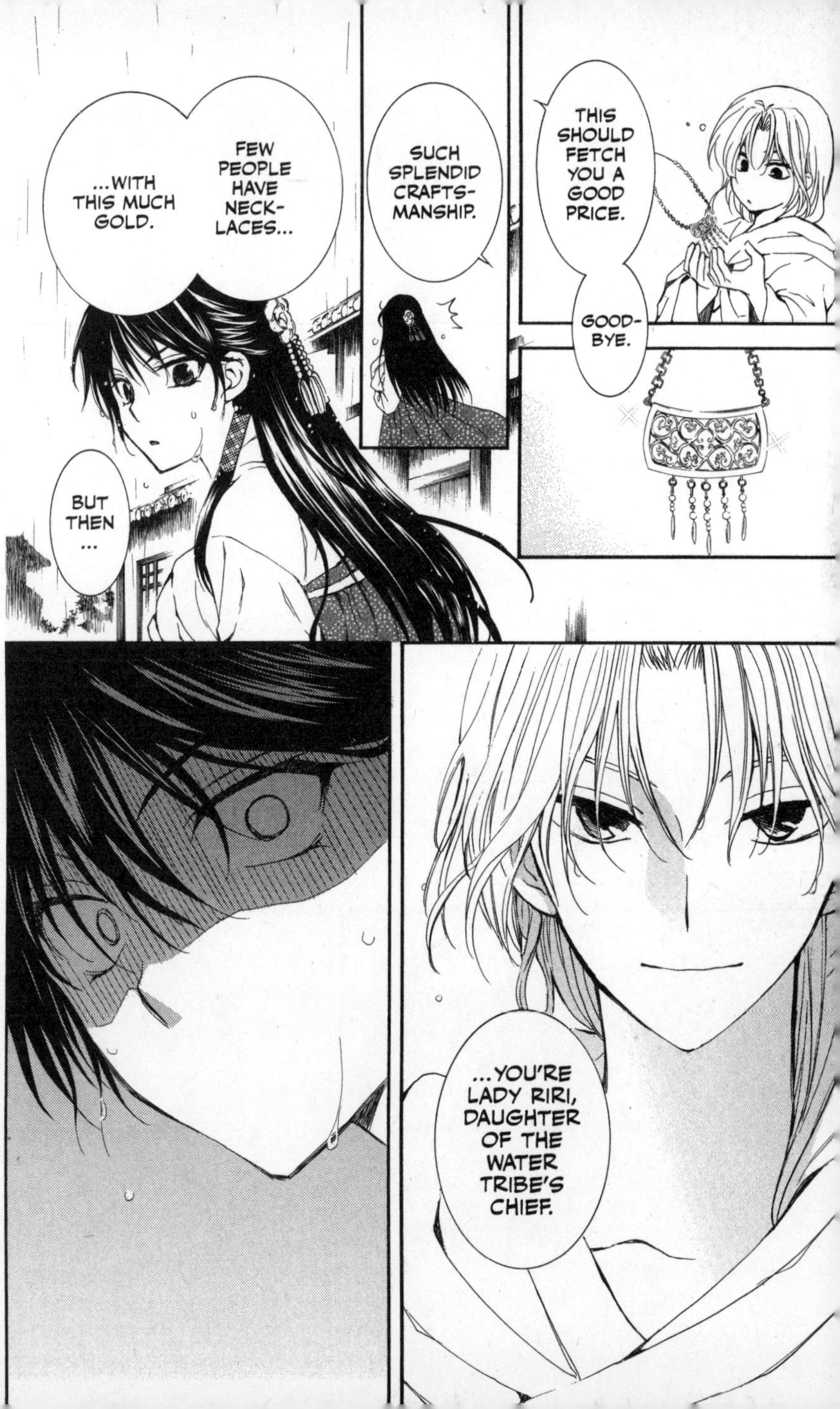
THIS SHOULD FETCH YOU A GOOD PRICE.
GOOD-BYE.
SUCH SPLENDID CRAFTSMANSHIP.
FEW PEOPLE HAVE NECKLACES...
...WITH THIS MUCH GOLD.
BUT THEN...
...YOU'RE LADY RIRI, DAUGHTER OF THE WATER TRIBE'S CHIEF.

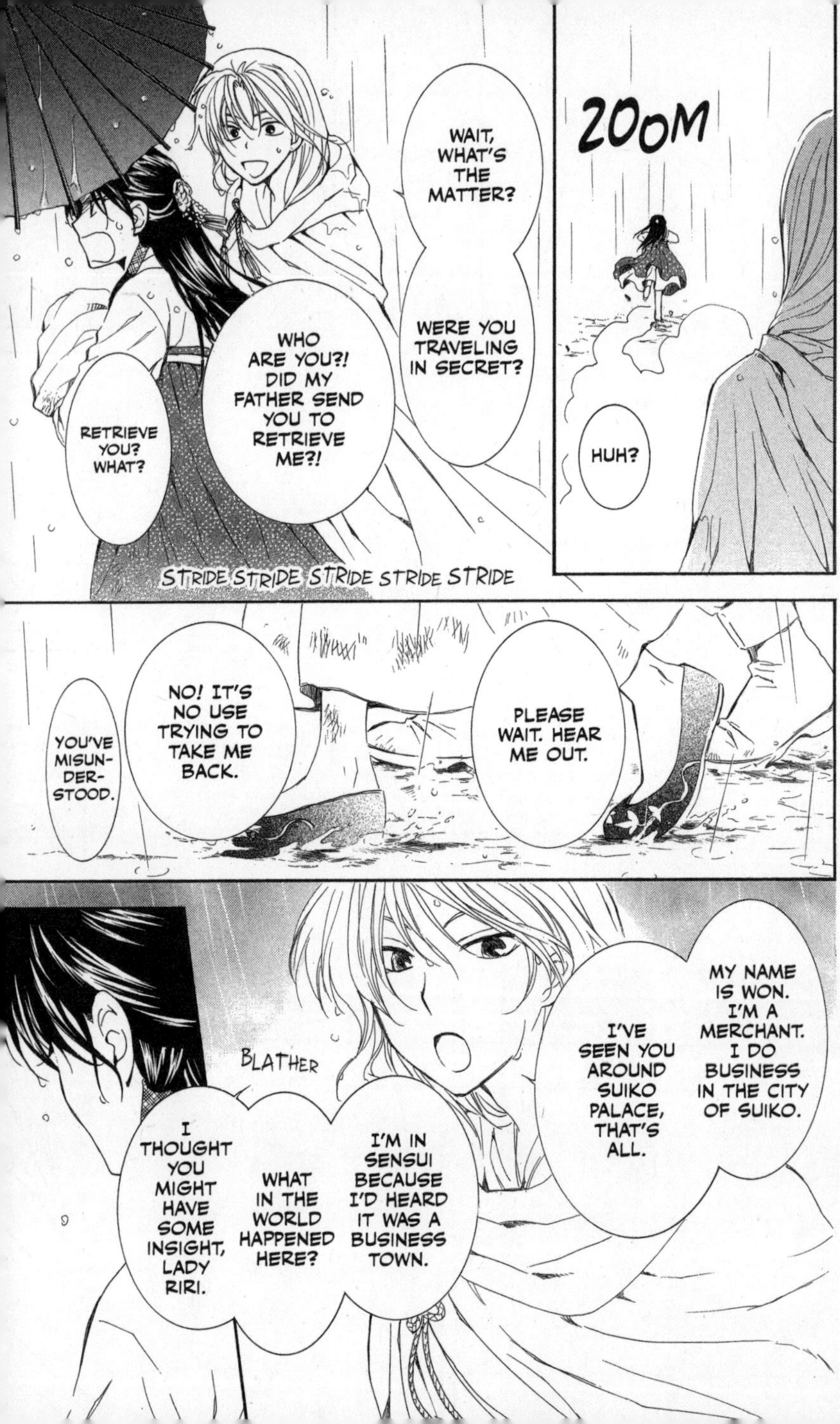
ZOOM
HUH?
WAIT, WHAT'S THE MATTER?
WERE YOU TRAVELING IN SECRET?
WHO ARE YOU?! DID MY FATHER SEND YOU TO RETRIEVE ME?!
RETRIEVE YOU? WHAT?
STRIDE STRIDE STRIDE STRIDE STRIDE
PLEASE WAIT. HEAR ME OUT.
NO! IT'S NO USE TRYING TO TAKE ME BACK.
YOU'VE MISUN-DER-STOOD.
MY NAME IS WON. I'M A MERCHANT. I DO BUSINESS IN THE CITY OF SUIKO.
I'VE SEEN YOU AROUND SUIKO PALACE, THAT'S ALL.
BLATHER
I'M IN SENSUI BECAUSE I'D HEARD IT WAS A BUSINESS TOWN.
WHAT IN THE WORLD HAPPENED HERE?
I THOUGHT YOU MIGHT HAVE SOME INSIGHT, LADY RIRI.

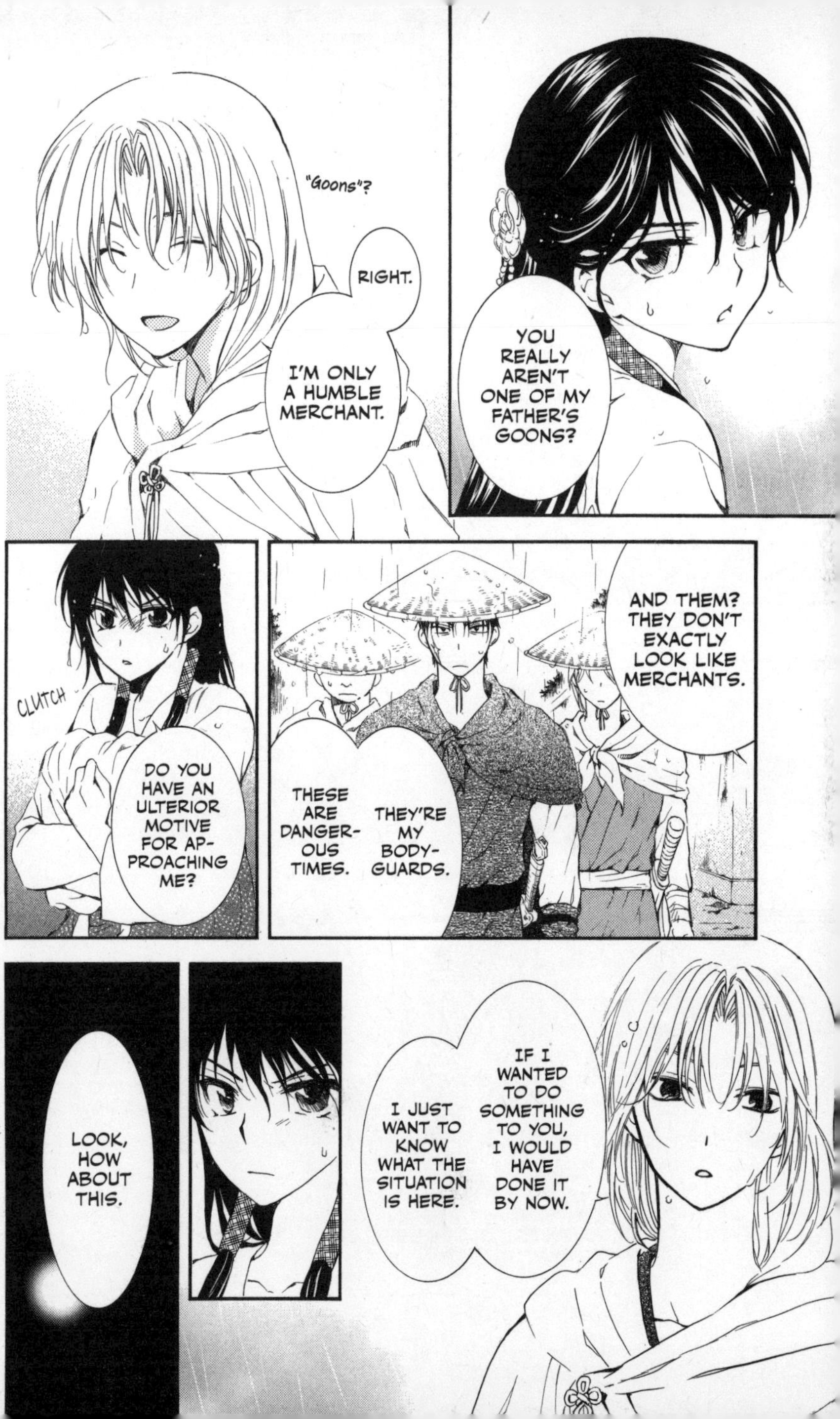
YOU REALLY AREN'T ONE OF MY FATHER'S GOONS?
"Goons"?
RIGHT.
I'M ONLY A HUMBLE MERCHANT.
AND THEM? THEY DON'T EXACTLY LOOK LIKE MERCHANTS.
THEY'RE MY BODY-GUARDS.
THESE ARE DANGER-OUS TIMES.
CLUTCH
DO YOU HAVE AN ULTERIOR MOTIVE FOR AP-PROACHING ME?
IF I WANTED TO DO SOMETHING TO YOU, I WOULD HAVE DONE IT BY NOW.
I JUST WANT TO KNOW WHAT THE SITUATION IS HERE.
LOOK, HOW ABOUT THIS.

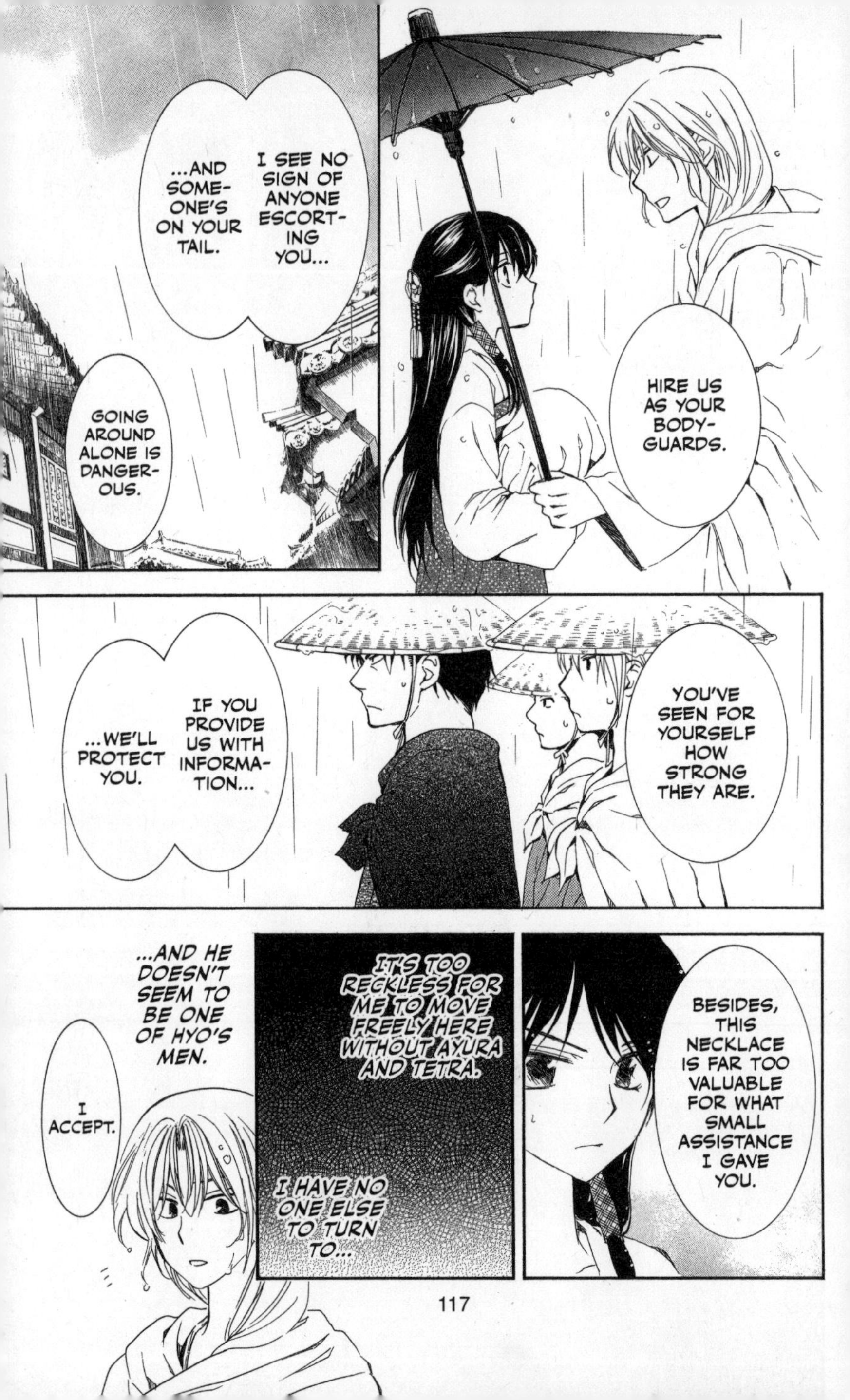
HIRE US AS YOUR BODY-GUARDS.
I SEE NO SIGN OF ANYONE ESCORT-ING YOU...
...AND SOME-ONE'S ON YOUR TAIL.
GOING AROUND ALONE IS DANGER-OUS.
YOU'VE SEEN FOR YOURSELF HOW STRONG THEY ARE.
IF YOU PROVIDE US WITH INFORMA-TION...
...WE'LL PROTECT YOU.
BESIDES, THIS NECKLACE IS FAR TOO VALUABLE FOR WHAT SMALL ASSISTANCE I GAVE YOU.
IT'S TOO RECKLESS FOR ME TO MOVE FREELY HERE WITHOUT AYURA AND TETRA.
I HAVE NO ONE ELSE TO TURN TO...
...AND HE DOESN'T SEEM TO BE ONE OF HYO'S MEN.
I ACCEPT.

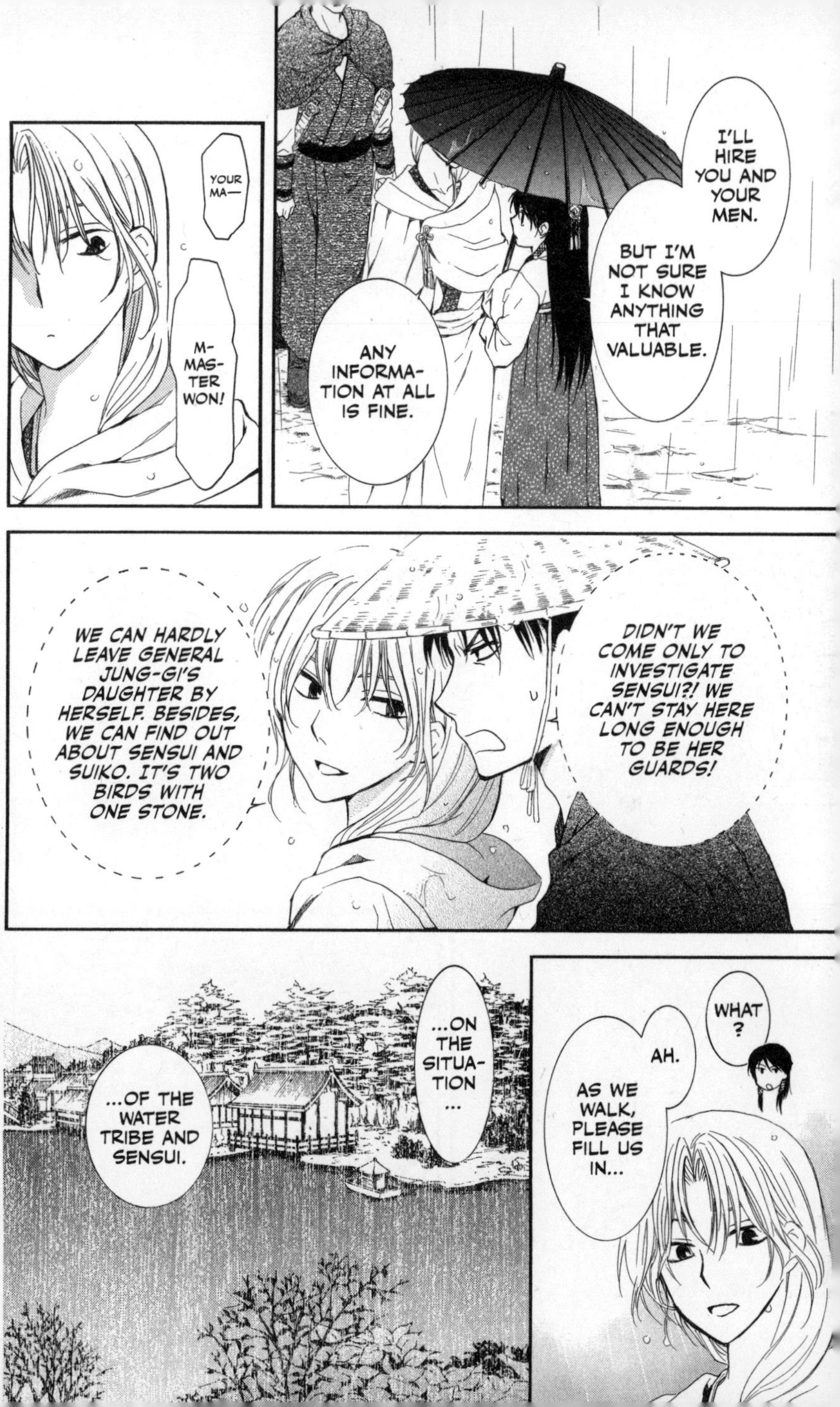
I'LL HIRE YOU AND YOUR MEN.
BUT I'M NOT SURE I KNOW ANYTHING THAT VALUABLE.
ANY INFORMATION AT ALL IS FINE.
YOUR MA—
M-MASTER WON!
DIDN'T WE COME ONLY TO INVESTIGATE SENSUI?! WE CAN'T STAY HERE LONG ENOUGH TO BE HER GUARDS!
WE CAN HARDLY LEAVE GENERAL JUNG-GI'S DAUGHTER BY HERSELF. BESIDES, WE CAN FIND OUT ABOUT SENSUI AND SUIKO. IT'S TWO BIRDS WITH ONE STONE.
WHAT?
AH.
AS WE WALK, PLEASE FILL US IN...
...ON THE SITUATION...
...OF THE WATER TRIBE AND SENSUI.

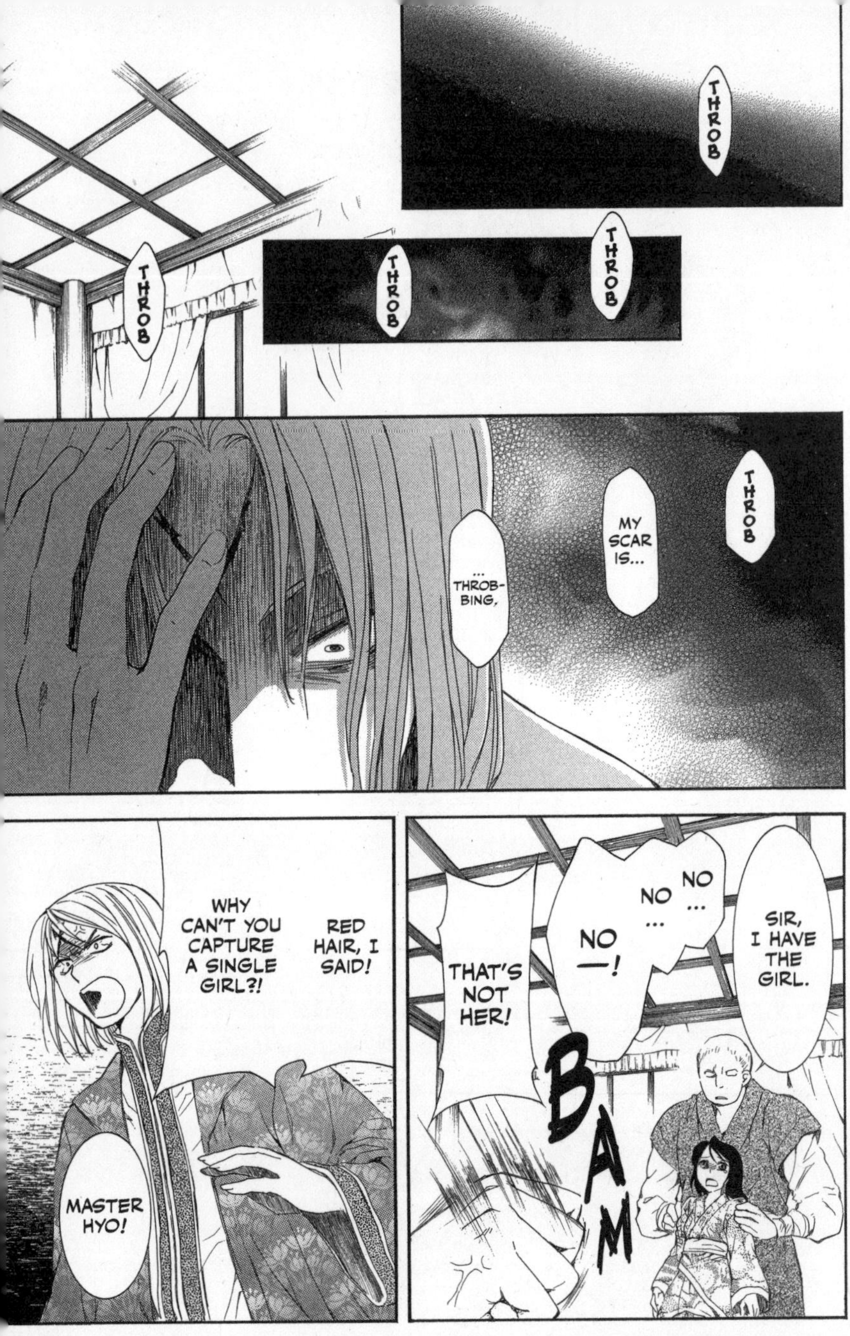
THROB
THROB
THROB
THROB
THROB
MY SCAR IS...
...THROBBING,
SIR, I HAVE THE GIRL.
NO...
NO...
NO—!
THAT'S NOT HER!
BAM
RED HAIR, I SAID!
WHY CAN'T YOU CAPTURE A SINGLE GIRL?!
MASTER HYO!

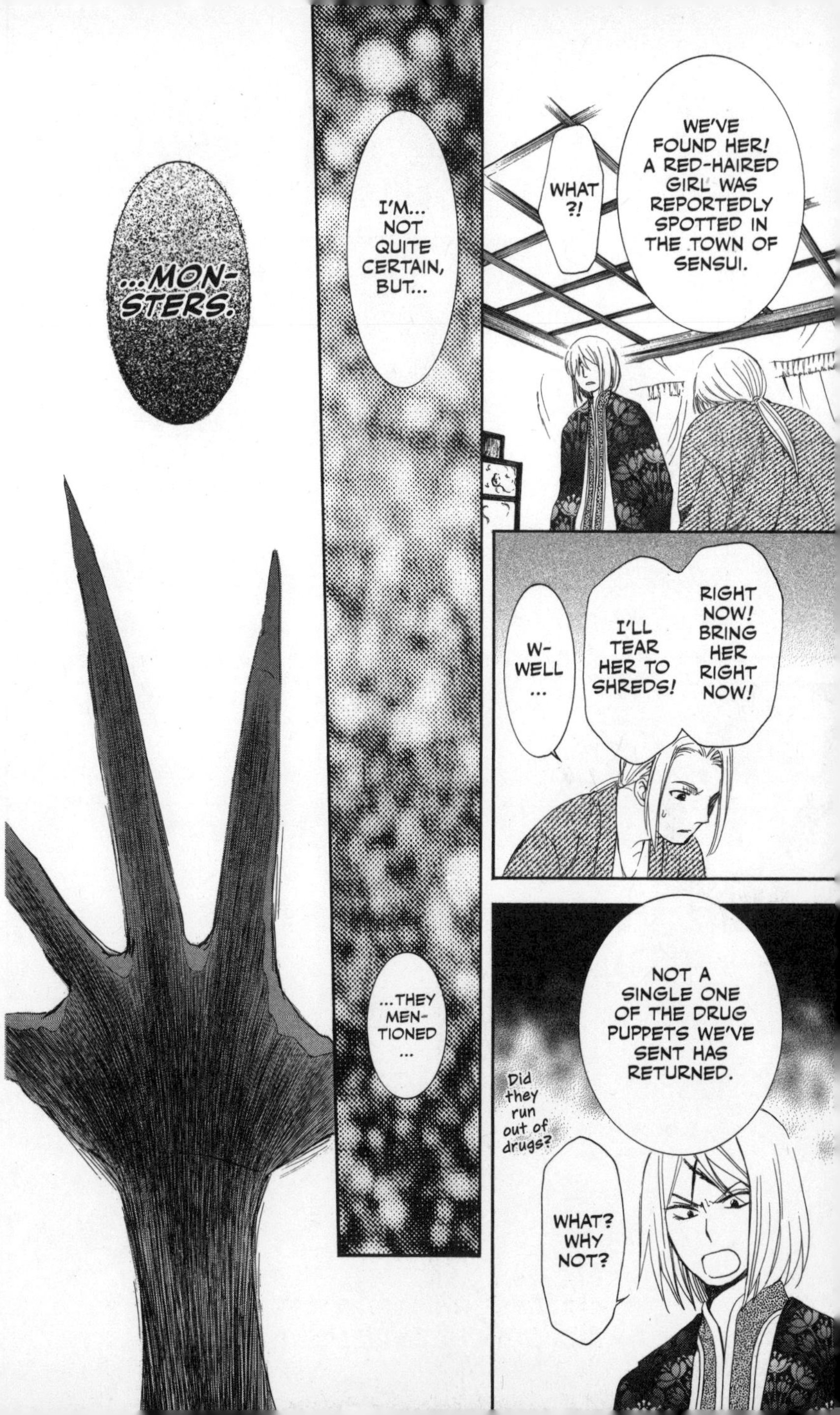
WE'VE FOUND HER! A RED-HAIRED GIRL WAS REPORTEDLY SPOTTED IN THE TOWN OF SENSUI.
WHAT?!
RIGHT NOW! BRING HER RIGHT NOW!
I'LL TEAR HER TO SHREDS!
W-WELL...
NOT A SINGLE ONE OF THE DRUG PUPPETS WE'VE SENT HAS RETURNED.
Did they run out of drugs?
WHAT? WHY NOT?
I'M... NOT QUITE CERTAIN, BUT...
...THEY MENTIONED...
...MONSTERS.

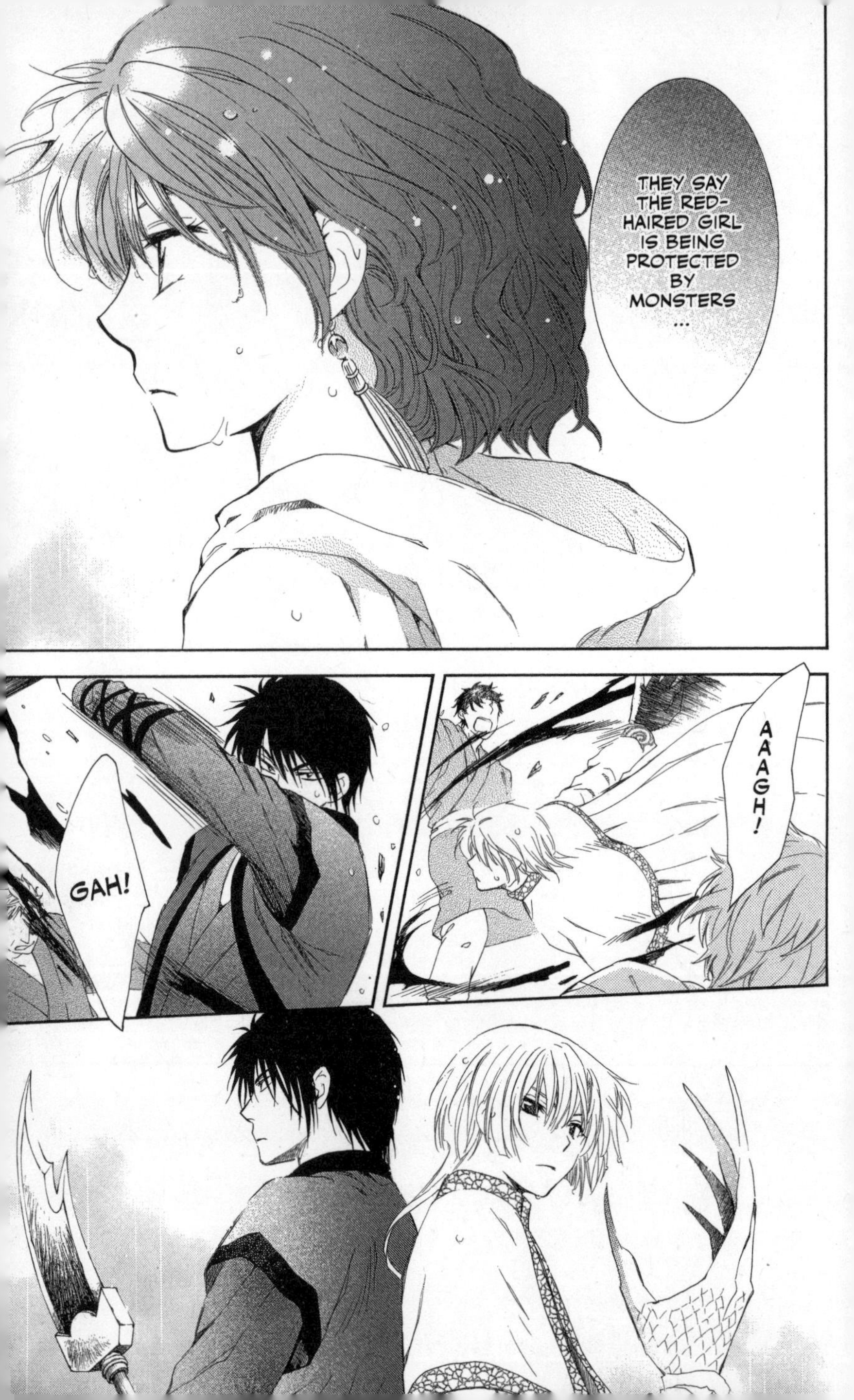
THEY SAY THE RED-HAIRED GIRL IS BEING PROTECTED BY MONSTERS...
AAAGH!
GAH!

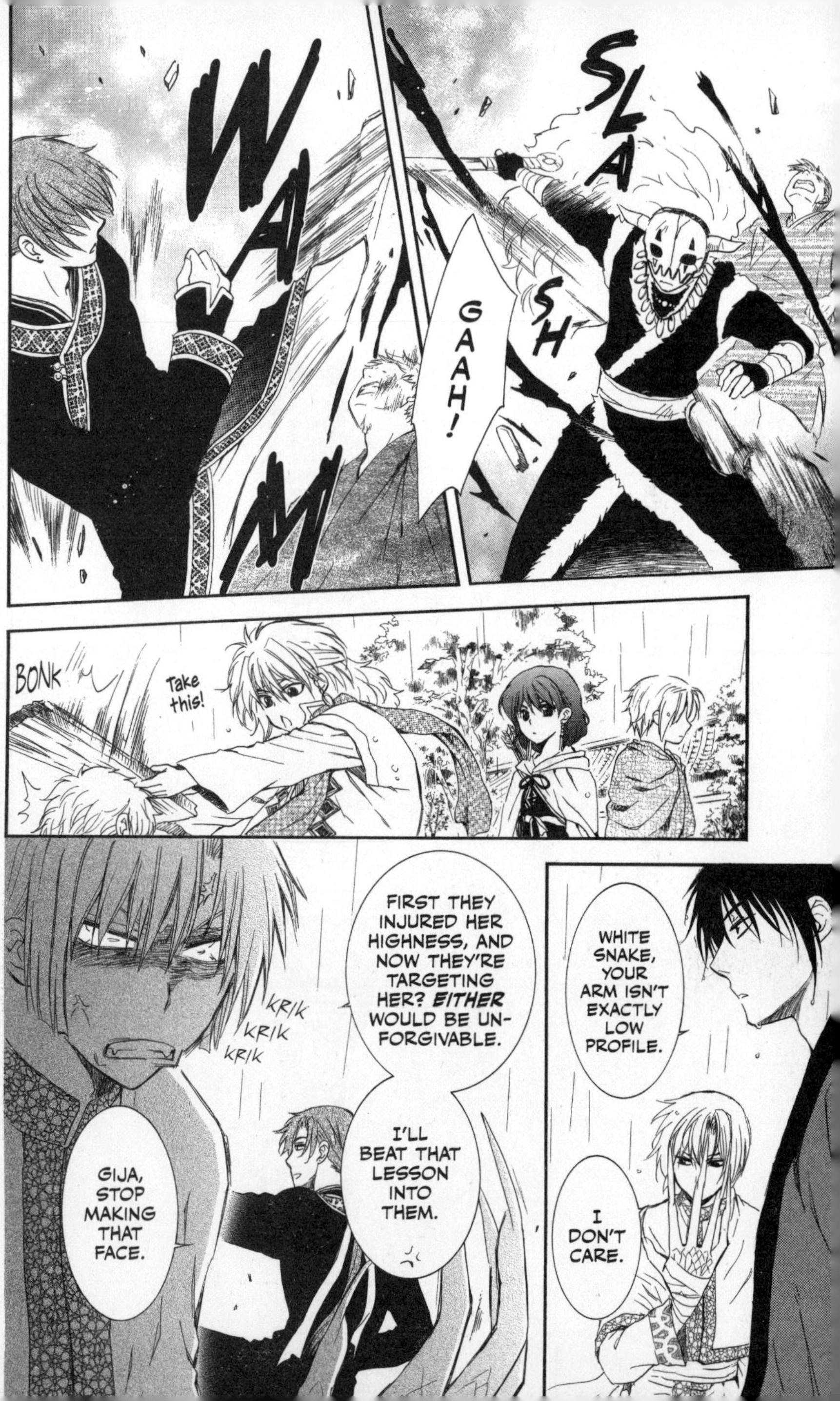
SLASH
GAAH!
WAM
Take this!
BONK
WHITE SNAKE, YOUR ARM ISN'T EXACTLY LOW PROFILE.
I DON'T CARE.
FIRST THEY INJURED HER HIGHNESS, AND NOW THEY'RE TARGETING HER? *EITHER* WOULD BE UN-FORGIVABLE.
I'LL BEAT THAT LESSON INTO THEM.
KRIK KRIK KRIK
GIJA, STOP MAKING THAT FACE.

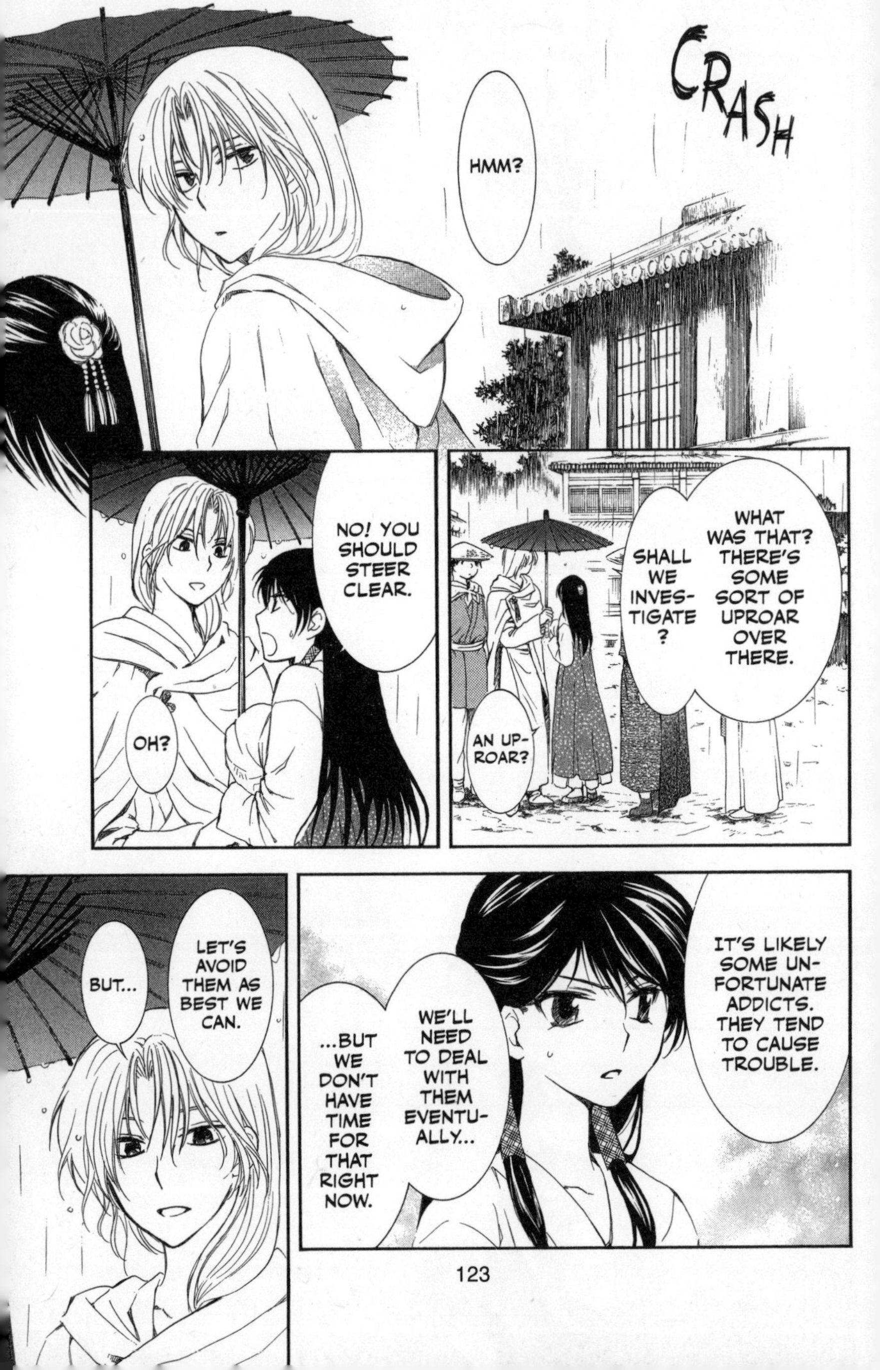
CRASH
HMM?
WHAT WAS THAT? THERE'S SOME SORT OF UPROAR OVER THERE.
SHALL WE INVESTIGATE?
AN UPROAR?
NO! YOU SHOULD STEER CLEAR.
OH?
IT'S LIKELY SOME UNFORTUNATE ADDICTS. THEY TEND TO CAUSE TROUBLE.
WE'LL NEED TO DEAL WITH THEM EVENTUALLY...
...BUT WE DON'T HAVE TIME FOR THAT RIGHT NOW.
LET'S AVOID THEM AS BEST WE CAN.
BUT...

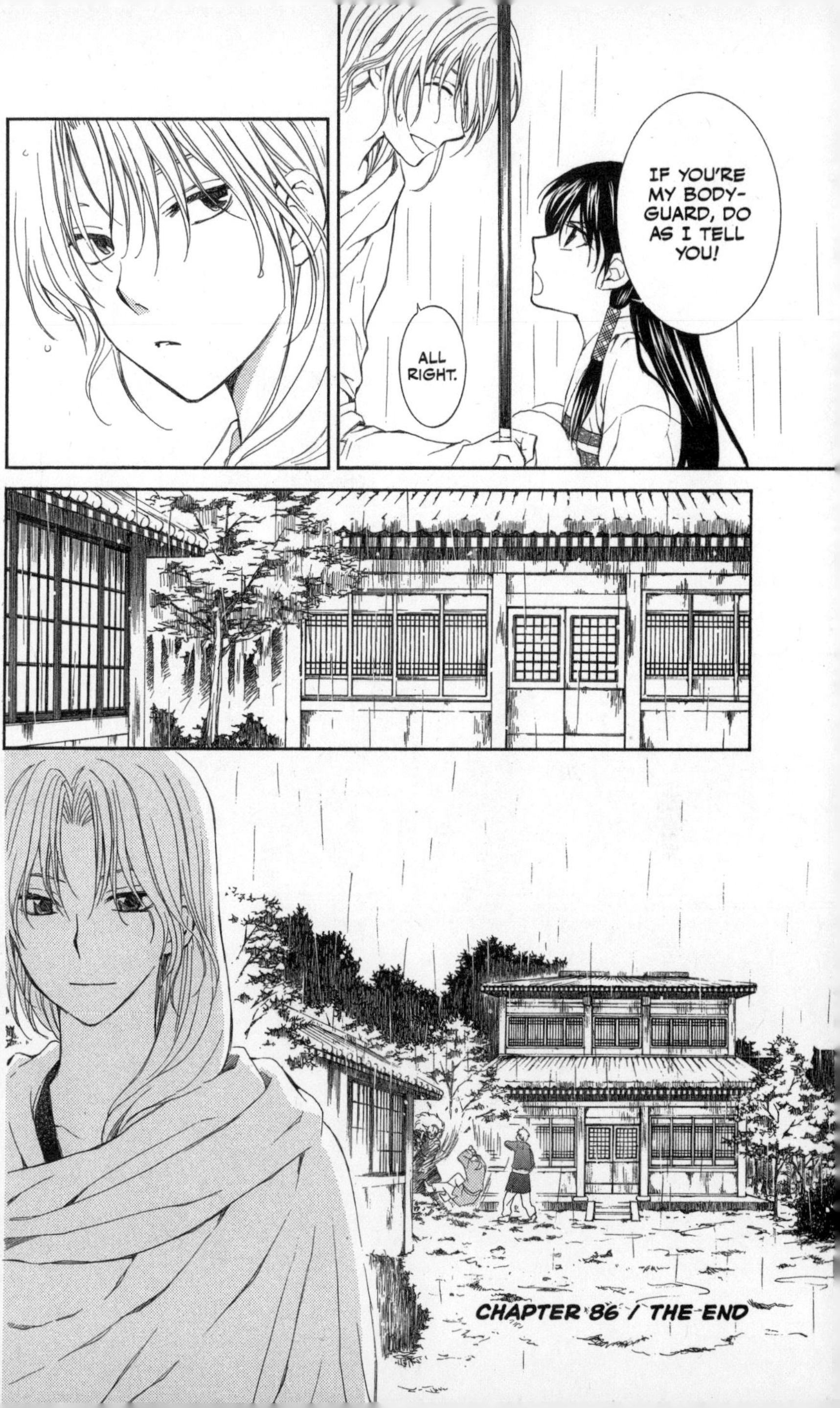
IF YOU'RE MY BODY-GUARD, DO AS I TELL YOU!
ALL RIGHT.
CHAPTER 86 / THE END

This is one of the art pieces I didn't use for the cover (of volume 15). There were too many characters here to fit on the cover of a graphic novel.
I thought I could use it as a title page, but the opportunity never came up. People have expressed interest in seeing Ayura and Tetra in color, but I wasn't able to make it happen. Sorry about that.

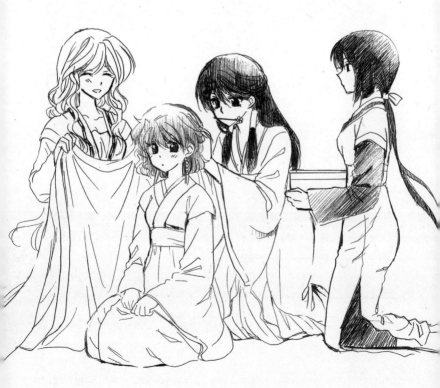

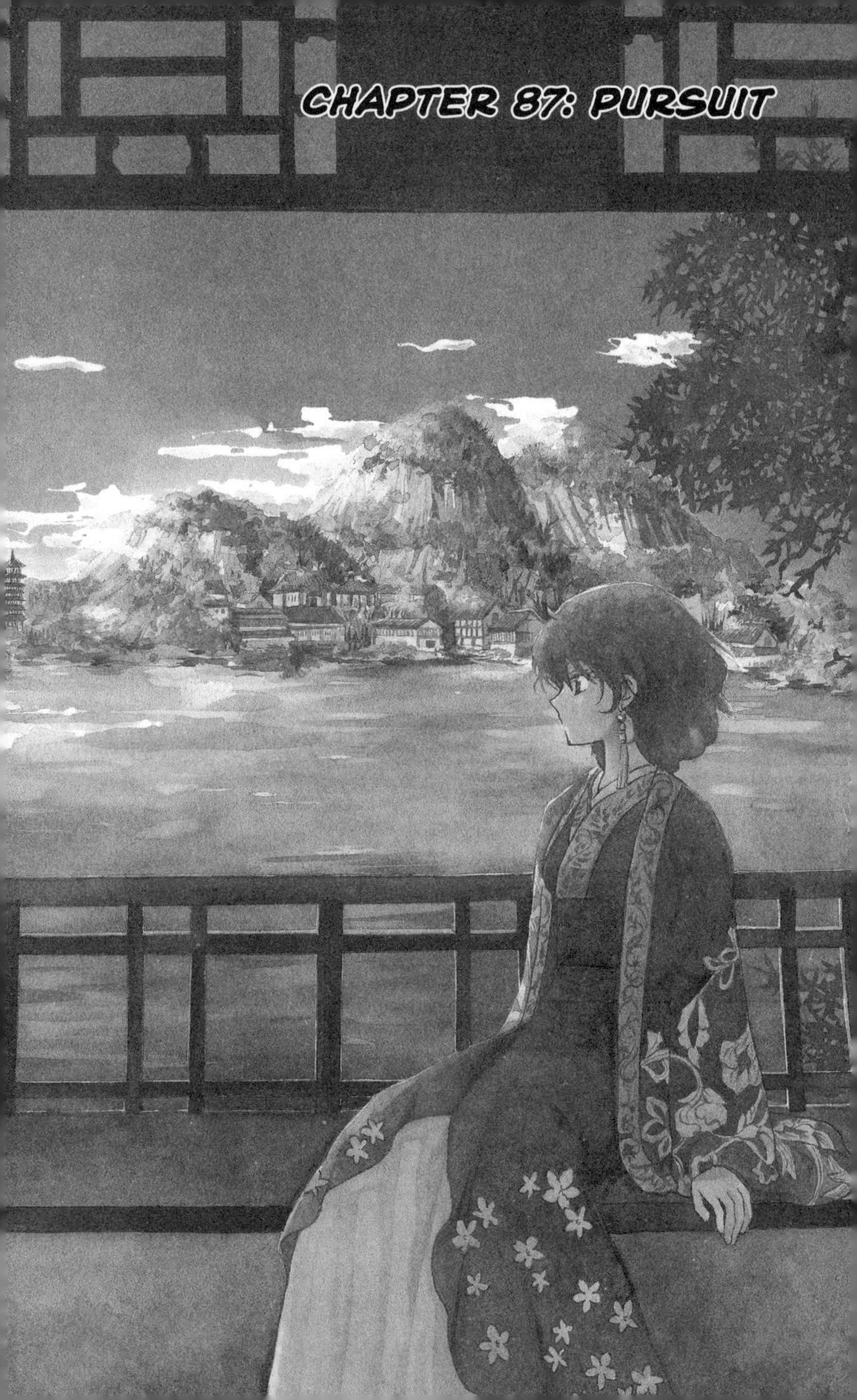
CHAPTER 87: PURSUIT

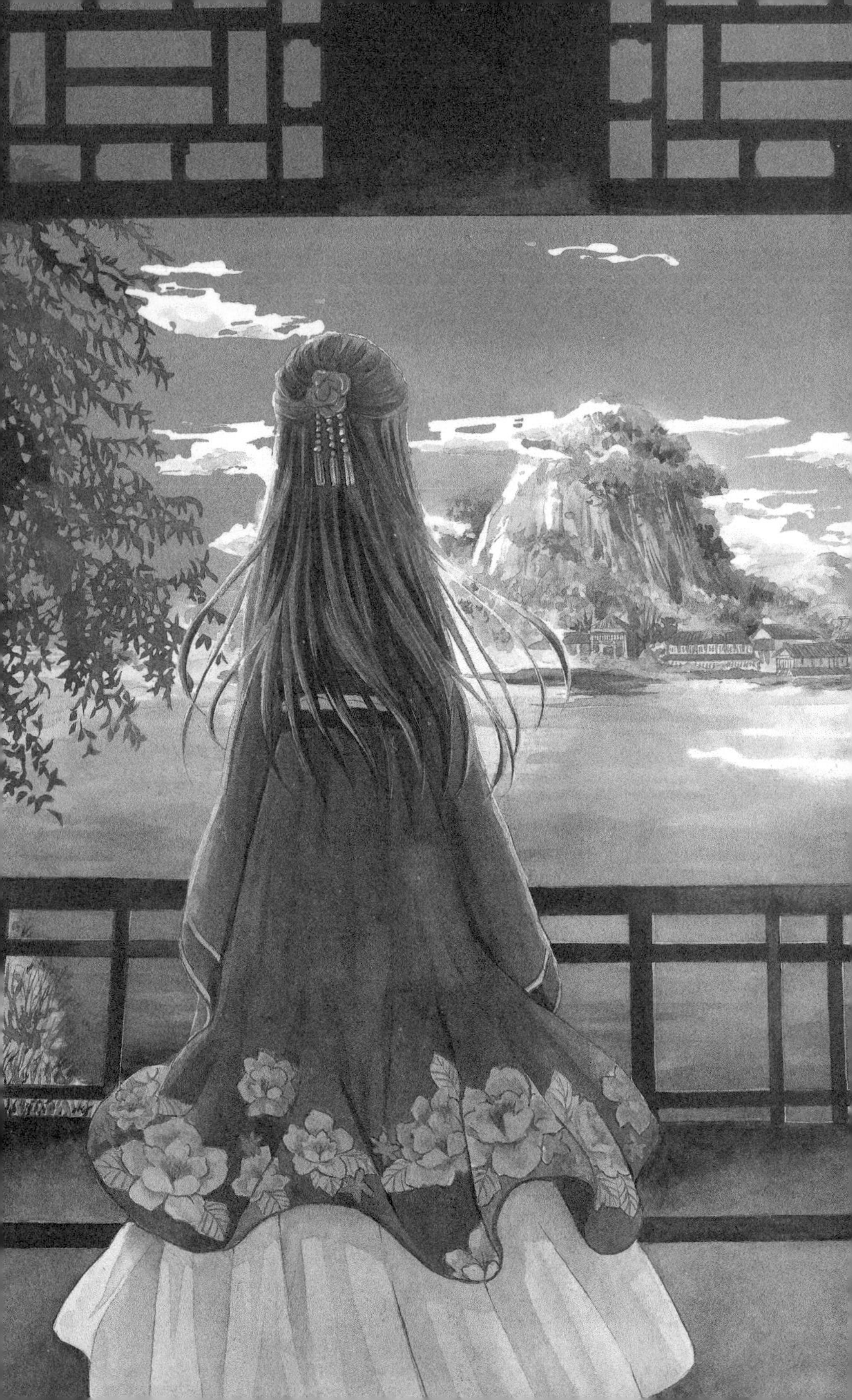

I'm fascinated by the traditional Vietnamese ao dai.

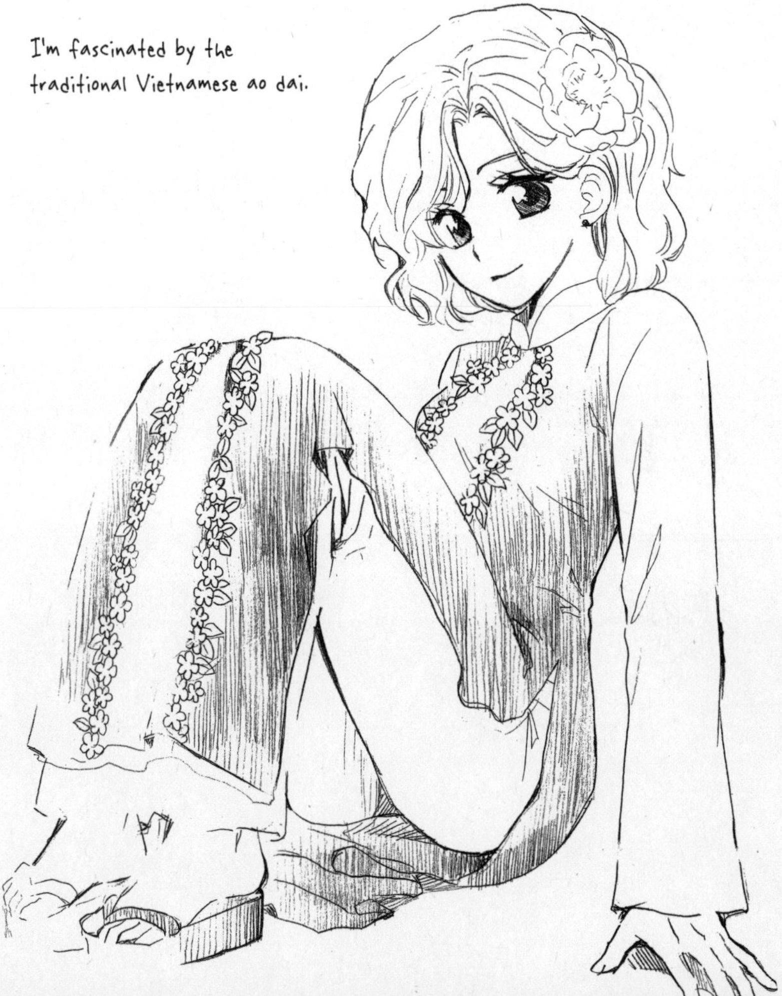

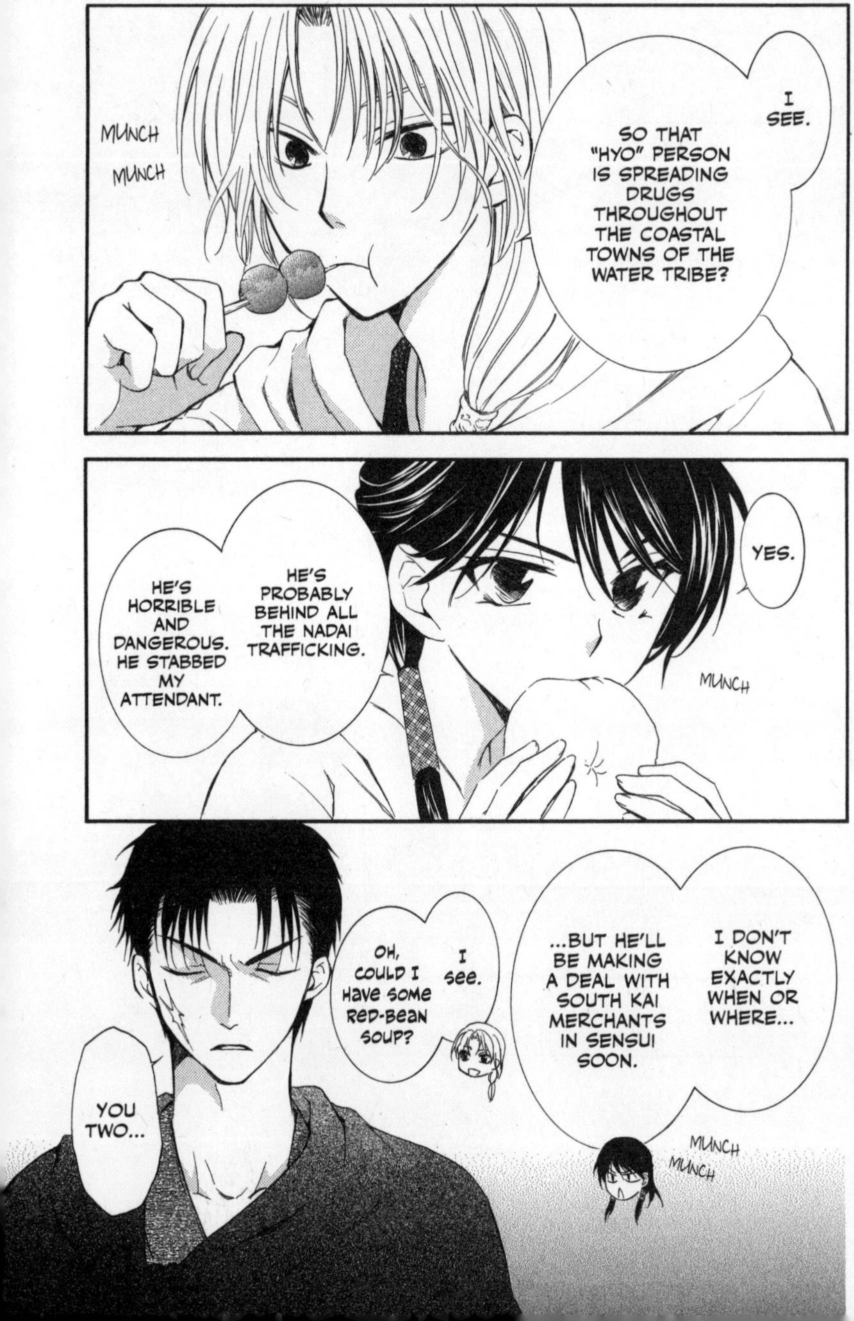
I SEE.
SO THAT "HYO" PERSON IS SPREADING DRUGS THROUGHOUT THE COASTAL TOWNS OF THE WATER TRIBE?
MUNCH MUNCH
YES.
HE'S PROBABLY BEHIND ALL THE NADAI TRAFFICKING.
HE'S HORRIBLE AND DANGEROUS. HE STABBED MY ATTENDANT.
MUNCH
I DON'T KNOW EXACTLY WHEN OR WHERE...
...BUT HE'LL BE MAKING A DEAL WITH SOUTH KAI MERCHANTS IN SENSUI SOON.
MUNCH MUNCH
I see.
Oh, could I have some red-bean soup?
YOU TWO...

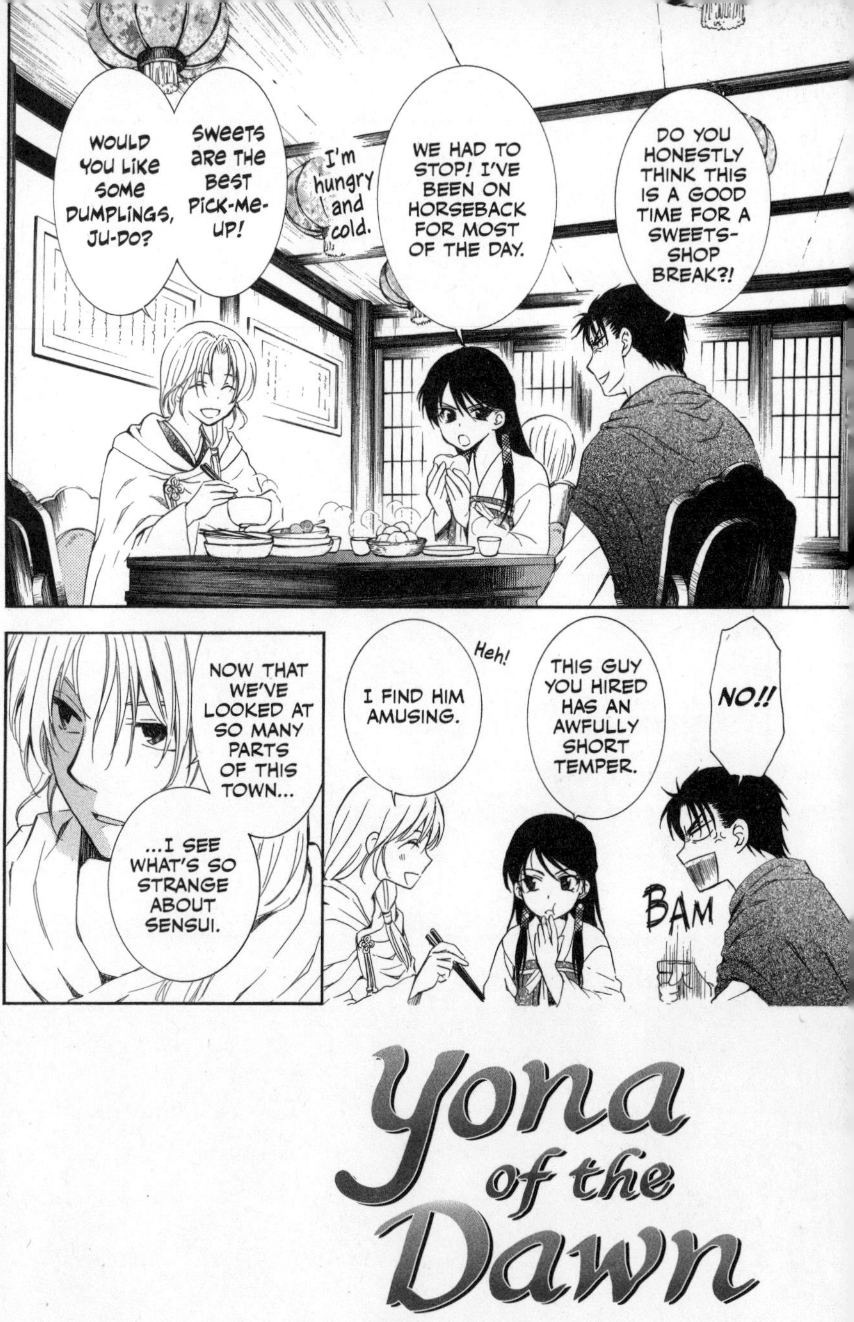
DO YOU HONESTLY THINK THIS IS A GOOD TIME FOR A SWEETS-SHOP BREAK?!
WE HAD TO STOP! I'VE BEEN ON HORSEBACK FOR MOST OF THE DAY.
I'm hungry and cold.
Sweets are the best pick-me-up!
Would you like some dumplings, Ju-Do?
NO!!
BAM
THIS GUY YOU HIRED HAS AN AWFULLY SHORT TEMPER.
Heh!
I FIND HIM AMUSING.
NOW THAT WE'VE LOOKED AT SO MANY PARTS OF THIS TOWN...
...I SEE WHAT'S SO STRANGE ABOUT SENSUI.

Yona of the Dawn

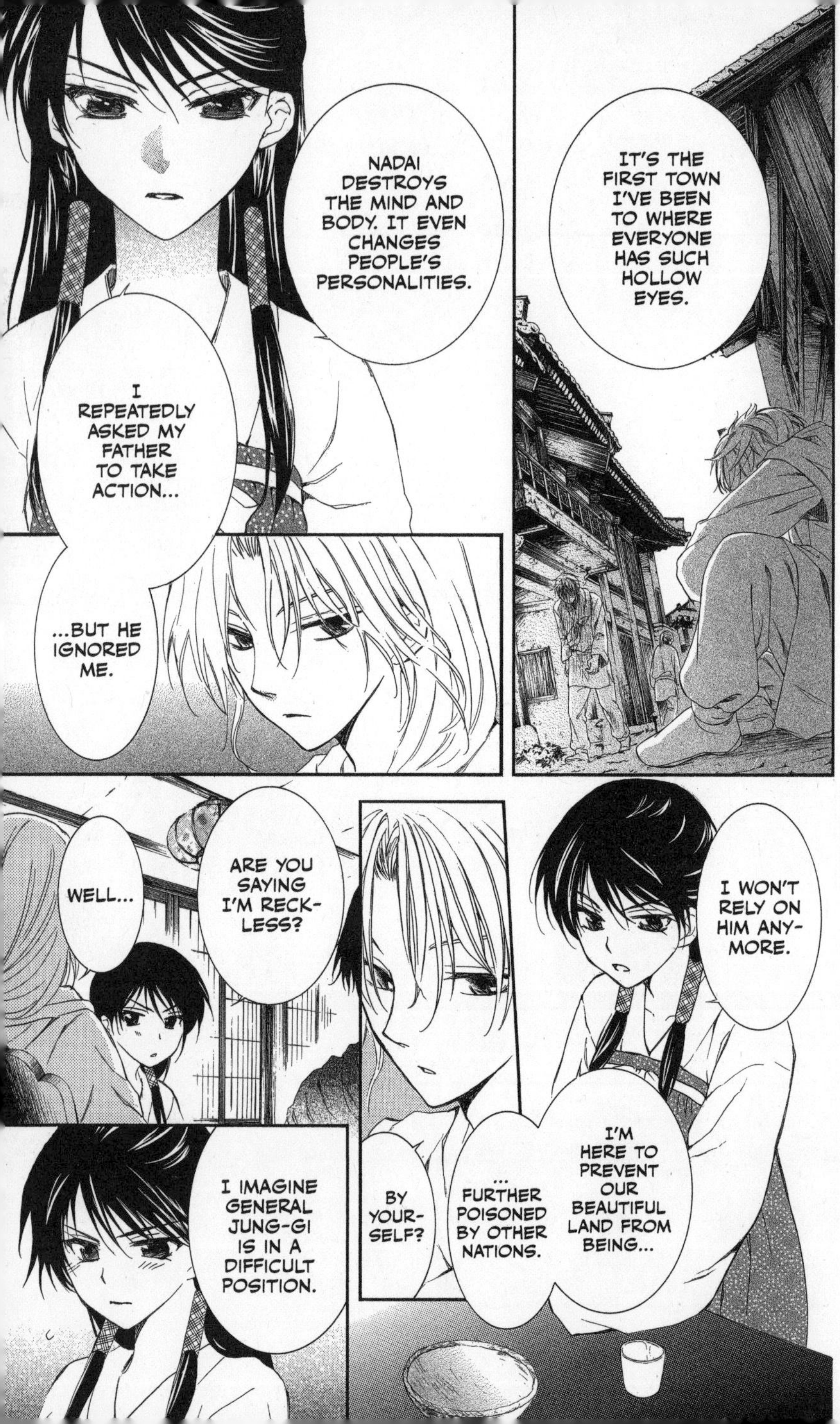
IT'S THE FIRST TOWN I'VE BEEN TO WHERE EVERYONE HAS SUCH HOLLOW EYES.
NADAI DESTROYS THE MIND AND BODY. IT EVEN CHANGES PEOPLE'S PERSONALITIES.
I REPEATEDLY ASKED MY FATHER TO TAKE ACTION...
...BUT HE IGNORED ME.
I WON'T RELY ON HIM ANY-MORE.
I'M HERE TO PREVENT OUR BEAUTIFUL LAND FROM BEING...
...FURTHER POISONED BY OTHER NATIONS.
BY YOUR-SELF?
ARE YOU SAYING I'M RECK-LESS?
WELL...
I IMAGINE GENERAL JUNG-GI IS IN A DIFFICULT POSITION.

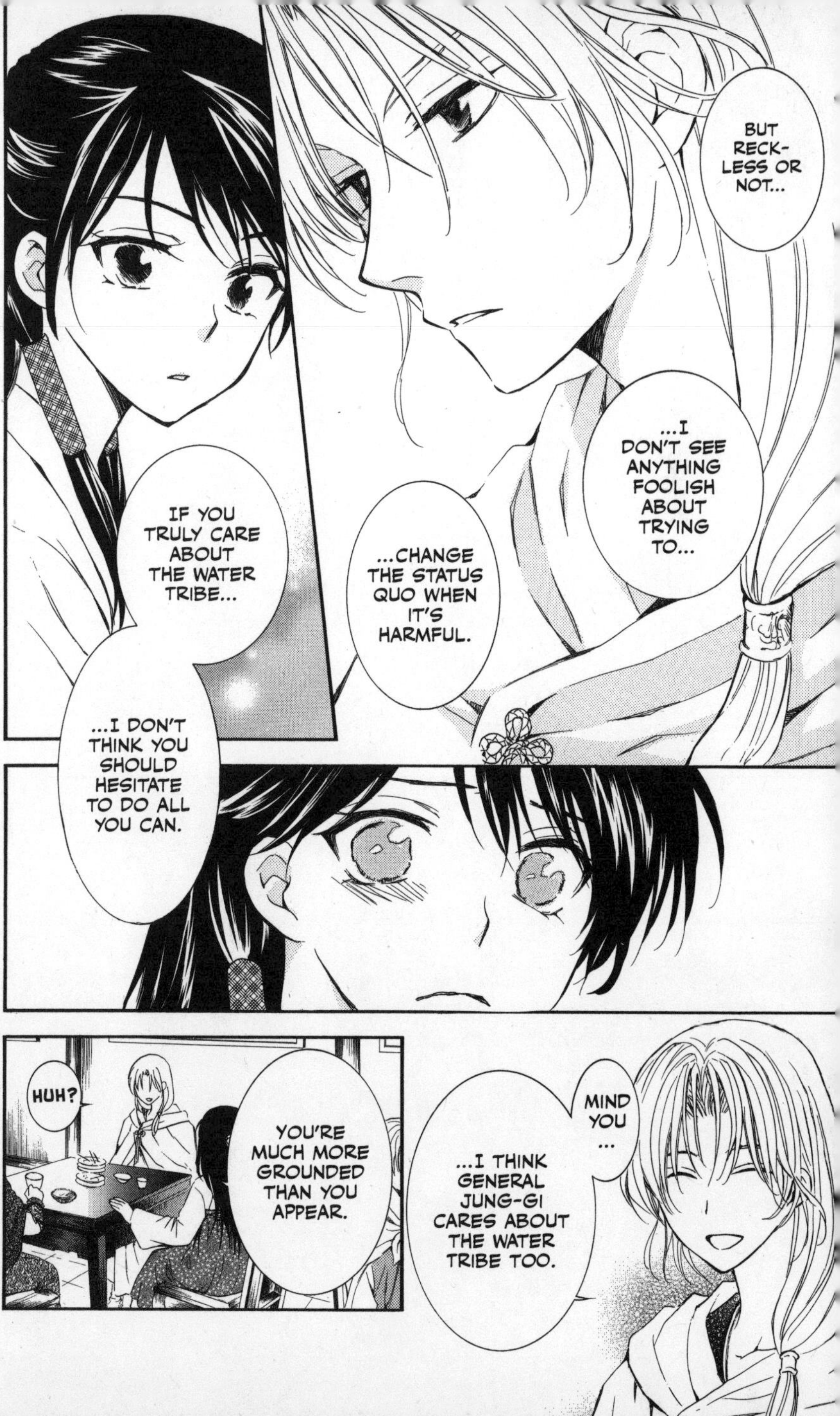
BUT RECKLESS OR NOT...
...I DON'T SEE ANYTHING FOOLISH ABOUT TRYING TO...
...CHANGE THE STATUS QUO WHEN IT'S HARMFUL.
IF YOU TRULY CARE ABOUT THE WATER TRIBE...
...I DON'T THINK YOU SHOULD HESITATE TO DO ALL YOU CAN.
MIND YOU...
...I THINK GENERAL JUNG-GI CARES ABOUT THE WATER TRIBE TOO.
YOU'RE MUCH MORE GROUNDED THAN YOU APPEAR.
HUH?

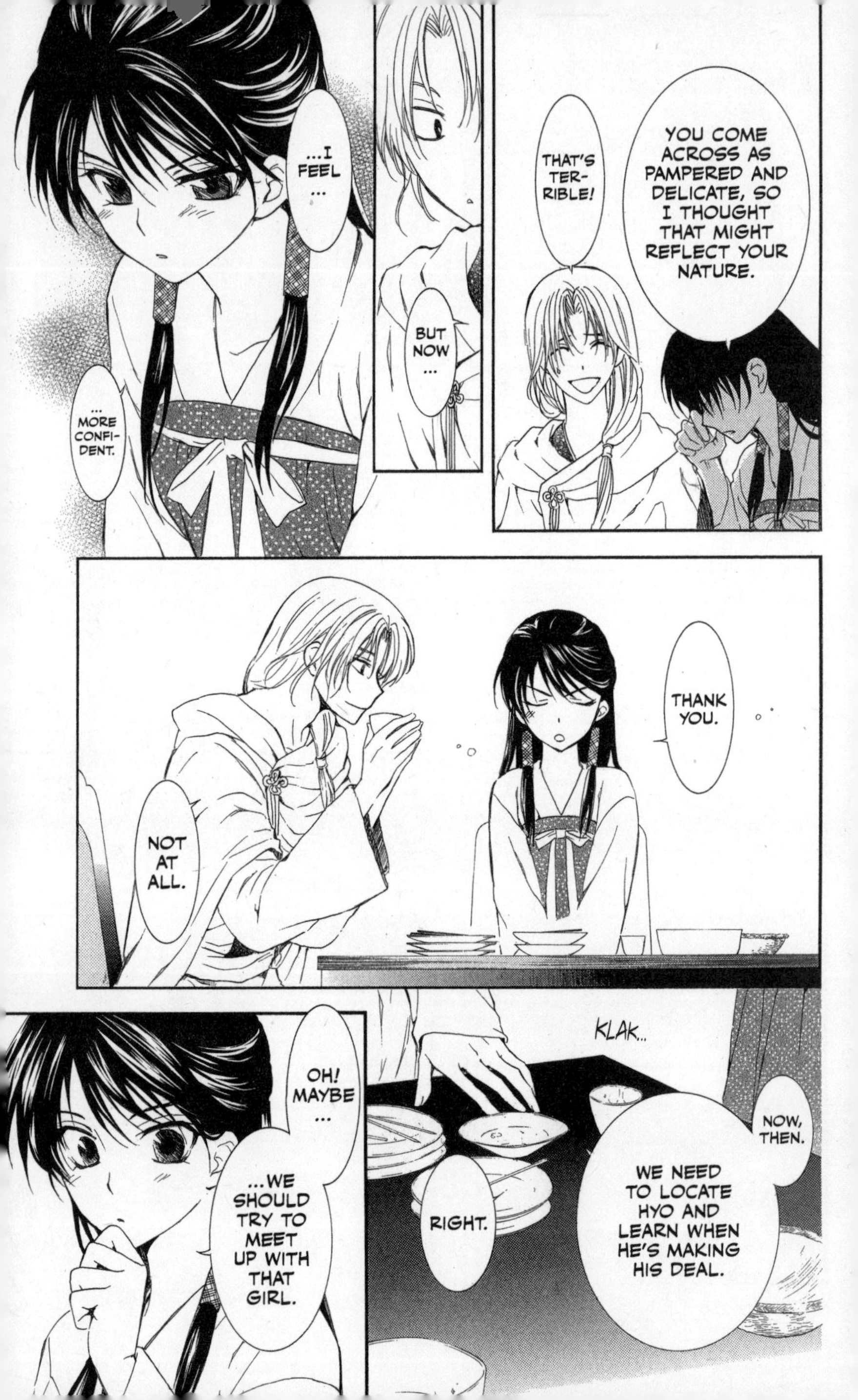
YOU COME ACROSS AS PAMPERED AND DELICATE, SO I THOUGHT THAT MIGHT REFLECT YOUR NATURE.
THAT'S TER-RIBLE!
BUT NOW ...
...I FEEL ...
... MORE CONFI-DENT.
THANK YOU.
NOT AT ALL.
KLAK...
NOW, THEN.
WE NEED TO LOCATE HYO AND LEARN WHEN HE'S MAKING HIS DEAL.
RIGHT.
OH! MAYBE ...
...WE SHOULD TRY TO MEET UP WITH THAT GIRL.

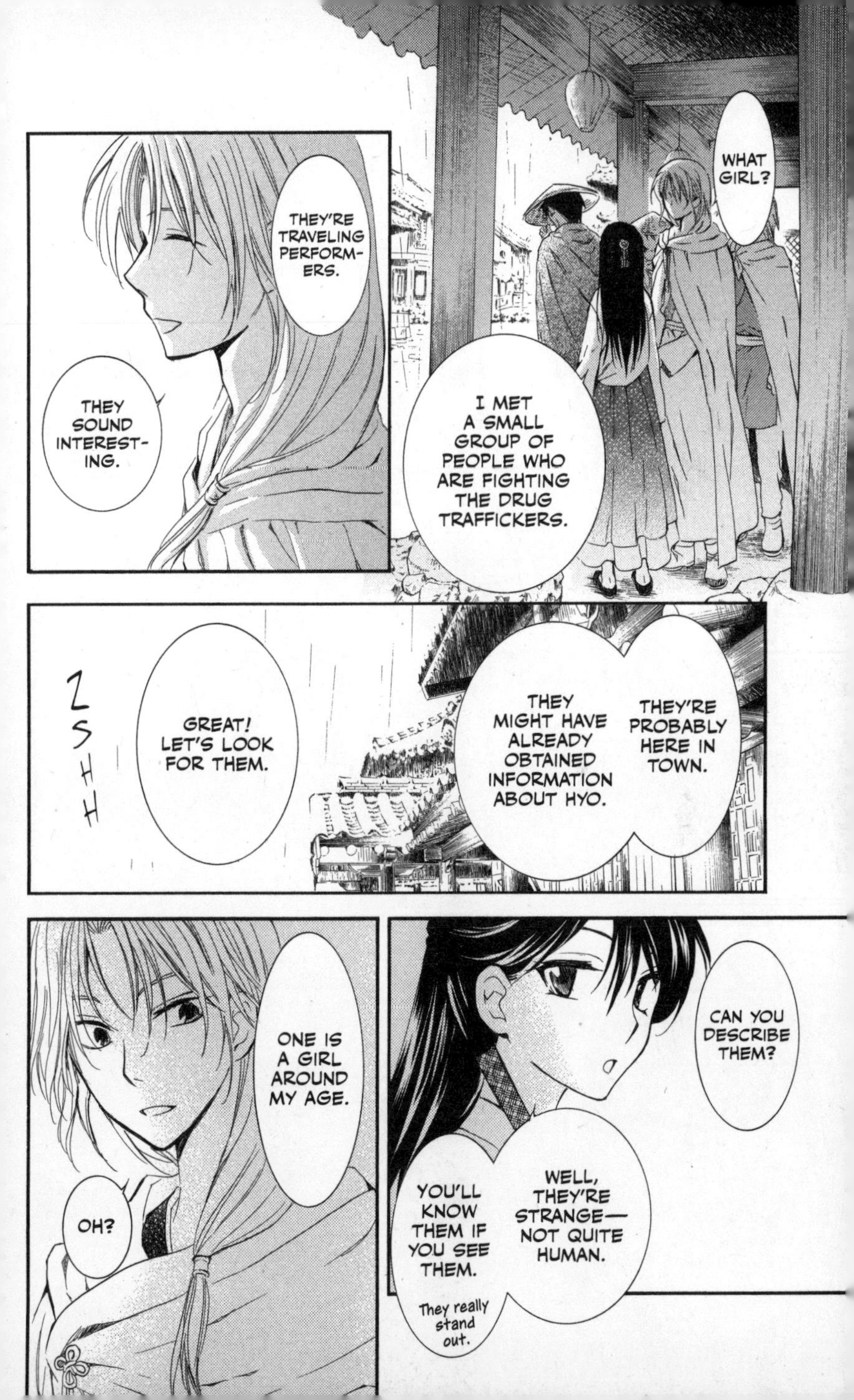
WHAT GIRL?
I MET A SMALL GROUP OF PEOPLE WHO ARE FIGHTING THE DRUG TRAFFICKERS.
THEY'RE TRAVELING PERFORM-ERS.
THEY SOUND INTEREST-ING.
THEY'RE PROBABLY HERE IN TOWN.
THEY MIGHT HAVE ALREADY OBTAINED INFORMATION ABOUT HYO.
GREAT! LET'S LOOK FOR THEM.
ZSHH
CAN YOU DESCRIBE THEM?
WELL, THEY'RE STRANGE— NOT QUITE HUMAN.
YOU'LL KNOW THEM IF YOU SEE THEM.
They really stand out.
ONE IS A GIRL AROUND MY AGE.
OH?

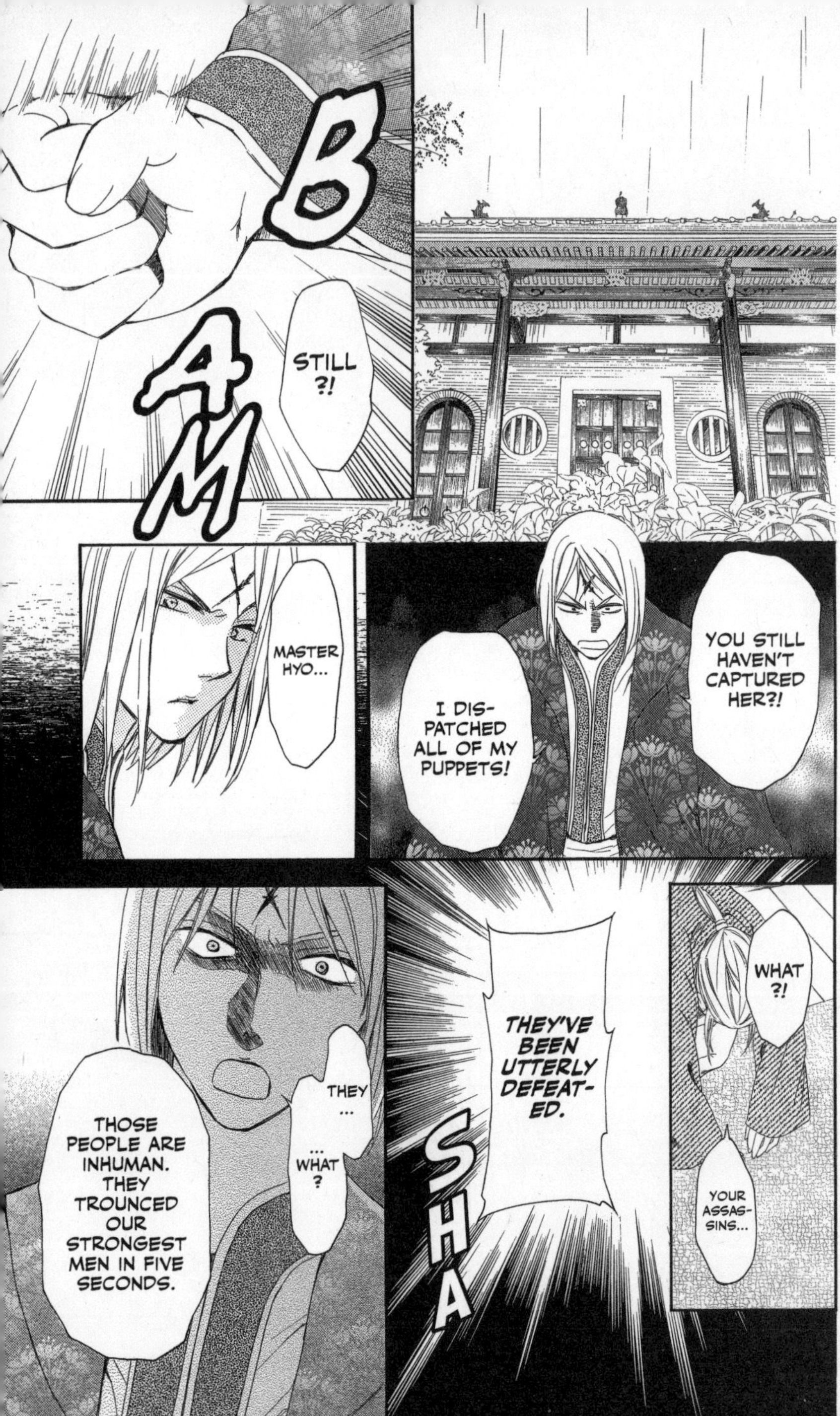
BAM
STILL ?!
YOU STILL HAVEN'T CAPTURED HER?!
I DIS-PATCHED ALL OF MY PUPPETS!
MASTER HYO...
WHAT ?!
YOUR ASSAS-SINS...
THEY'VE BEEN UTTERLY DEFEAT-ED.
SHA
THEY ...
... WHAT ?
THOSE PEOPLE ARE INHUMAN. THEY TROUNCED OUR STRONGEST MEN IN FIVE SECONDS.

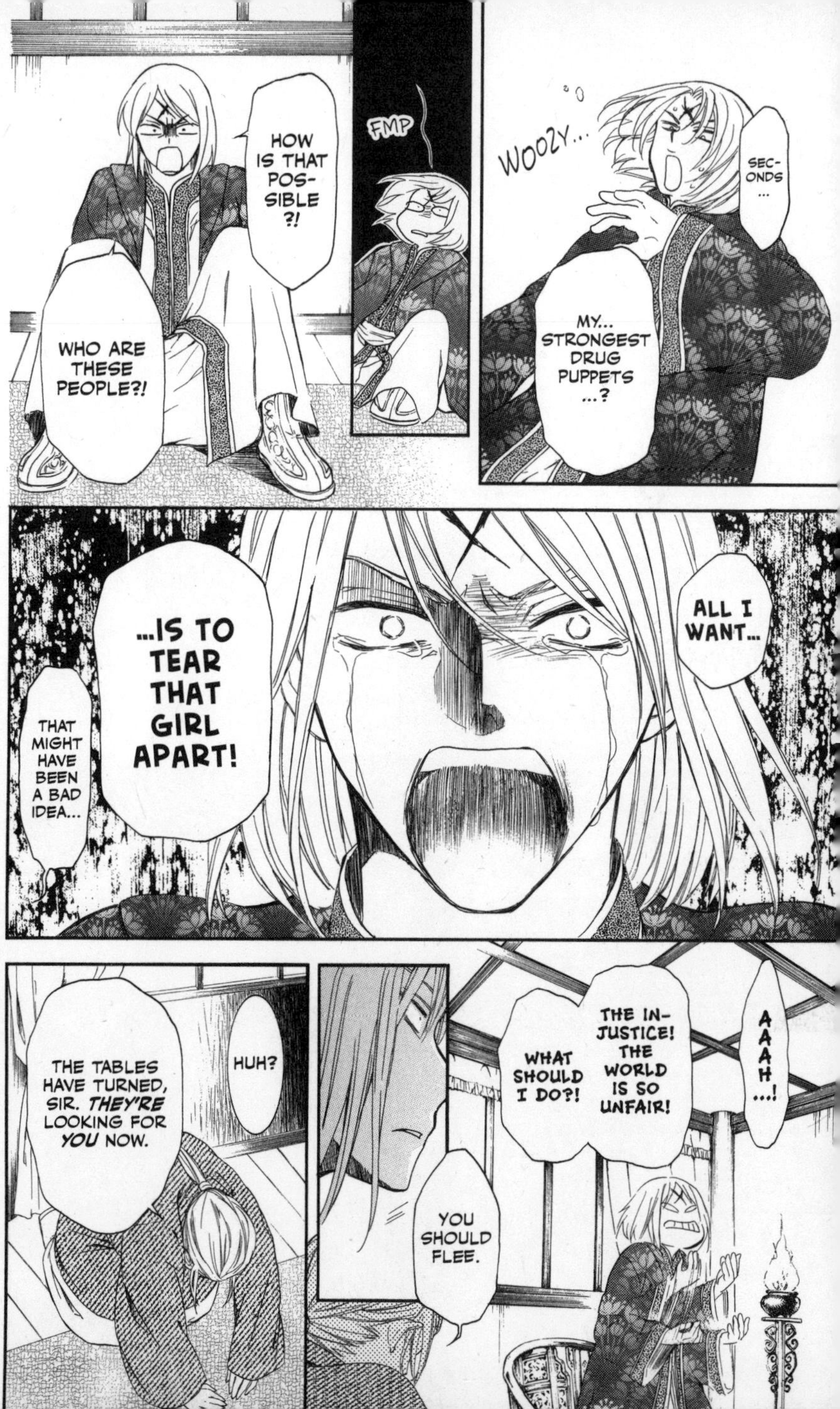
SEC-ONDS...
WOOZY...
MY... STRONGEST DRUG PUPPETS ...?
FMP
HOW IS THAT POS-SIBLE ?!
WHO ARE THESE PEOPLE?!
ALL I WANT...
...IS TO TEAR THAT GIRL APART!
THAT MIGHT HAVE BEEN A BAD IDEA...
AAAAH...!
THE IN-JUSTICE! THE WORLD IS SO UNFAIR!
WHAT SHOULD I DO?!
YOU SHOULD FLEE.
HUH?
THE TABLES HAVE TURNED, SIR. *THEY'RE* LOOKING FOR *YOU* NOW.

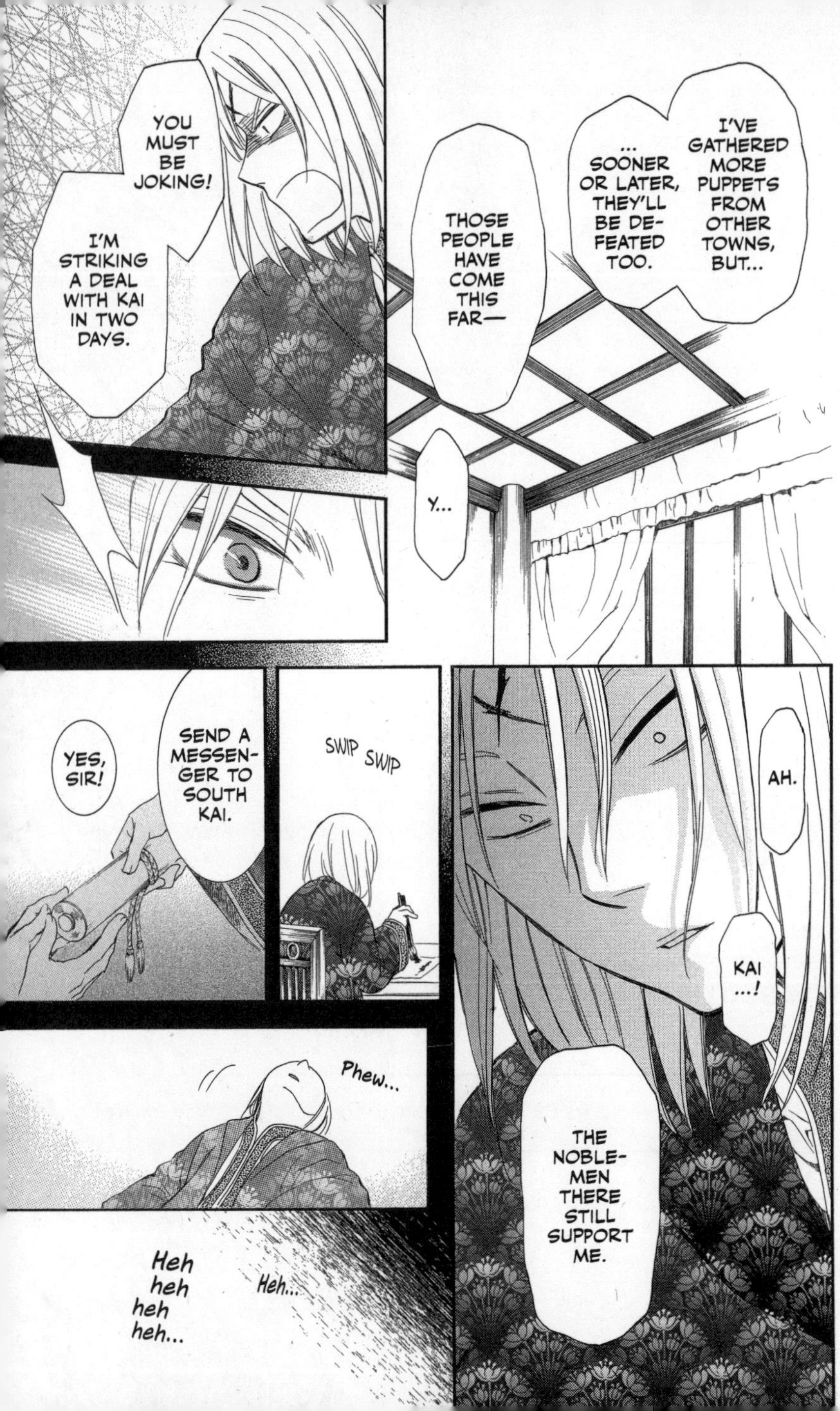

I'VE GATHERED MORE PUPPETS FROM OTHER TOWNS, BUT...
...SOONER OR LATER, THEY'LL BE DEFEATED TOO.
THOSE PEOPLE HAVE COME THIS FAR—
Y...
YOU MUST BE JOKING!
I'M STRIKING A DEAL WITH KAI IN TWO DAYS.
AH.
KAI ...!
THE NOBLEMEN THERE STILL SUPPORT ME.
SWIP SWIP
SEND A MESSENGER TO SOUTH KAI.
YES, SIR!
Phew...
Heh...
Heh heh heh heh...

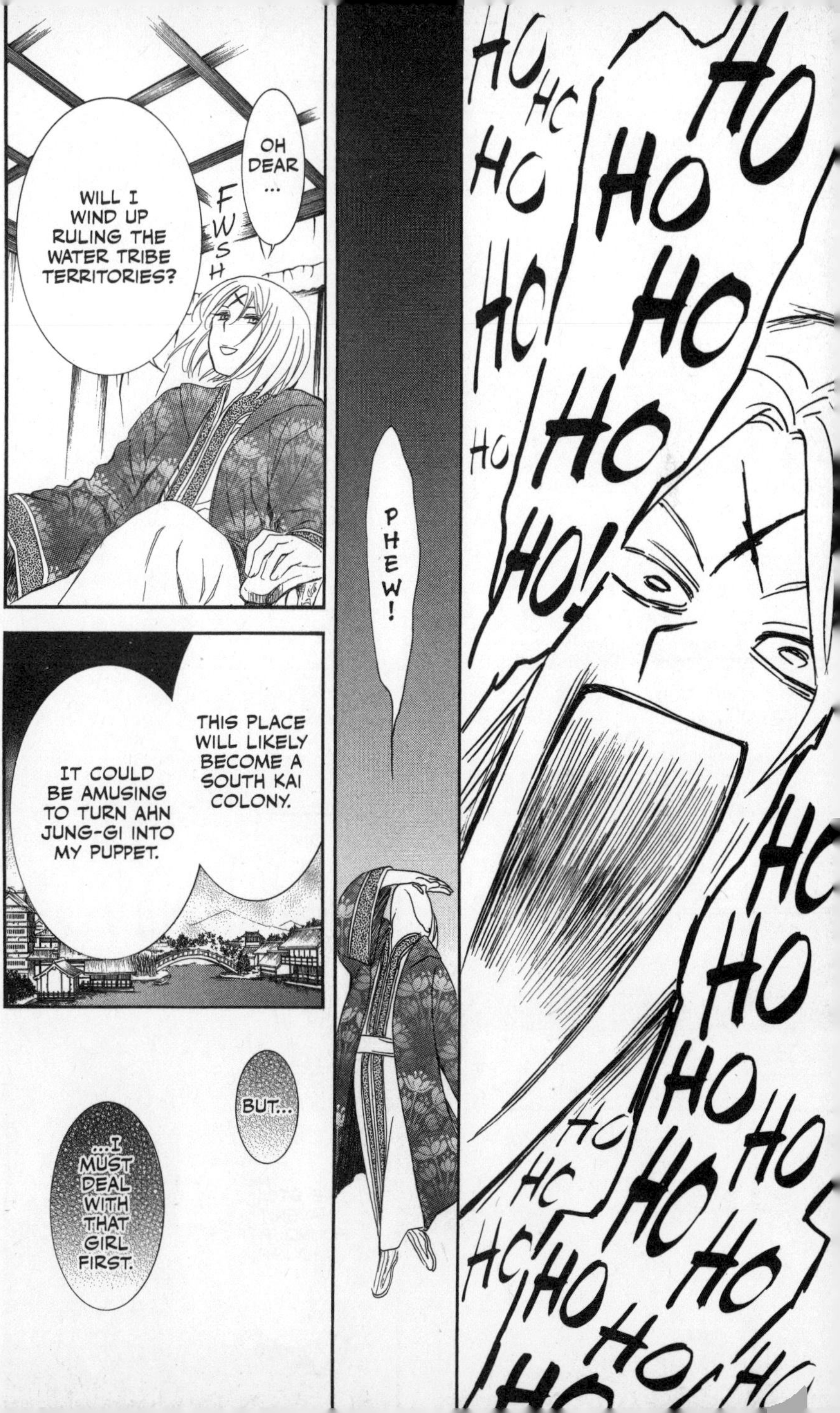
HO HC HO HO HO HO!
HO HO HO HO HO!
HC HO HO HO HO HO HO HO HC HC HC HC
PHEW!
OH DEAR...
FWSH
WILL I WIND UP RULING THE WATER TRIBE TERRITORIES?
THIS PLACE WILL LIKELY BECOME A SOUTH KAI COLONY.
IT COULD BE AMUSING TO TURN AHN JUNG-GI INTO MY PUPPET.
BUT...
...I MUST DEAL WITH THAT GIRL FIRST.

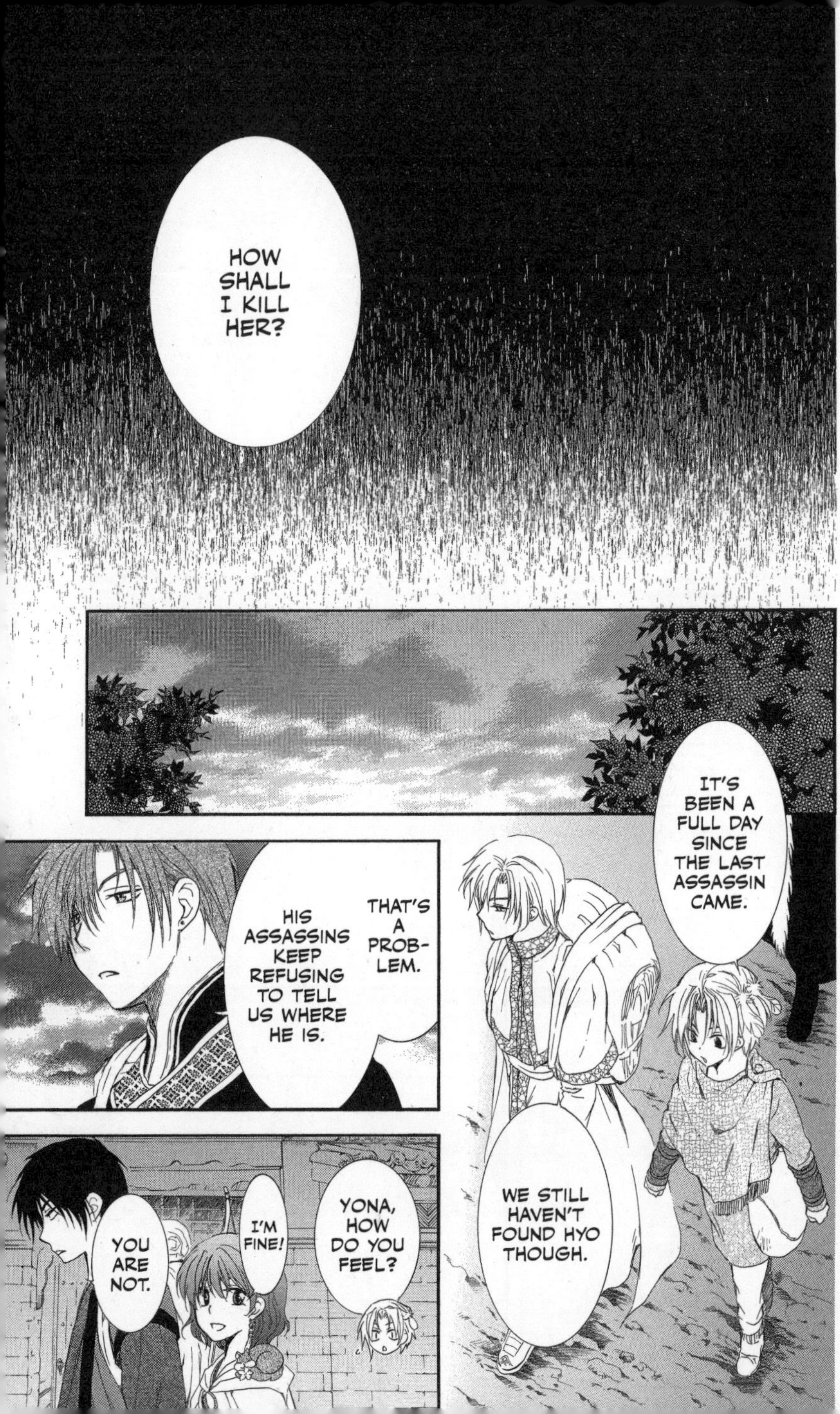
HOW SHALL I KILL HER?
IT'S BEEN A FULL DAY SINCE THE LAST ASSASSIN CAME.
WE STILL HAVEN'T FOUND HYO THOUGH.
THAT'S A PROB-LEM.
HIS ASSASSINS KEEP REFUSING TO TELL US WHERE HE IS.
YONA, HOW DO YOU FEEL?
I'M FINE!
YOU ARE NOT.

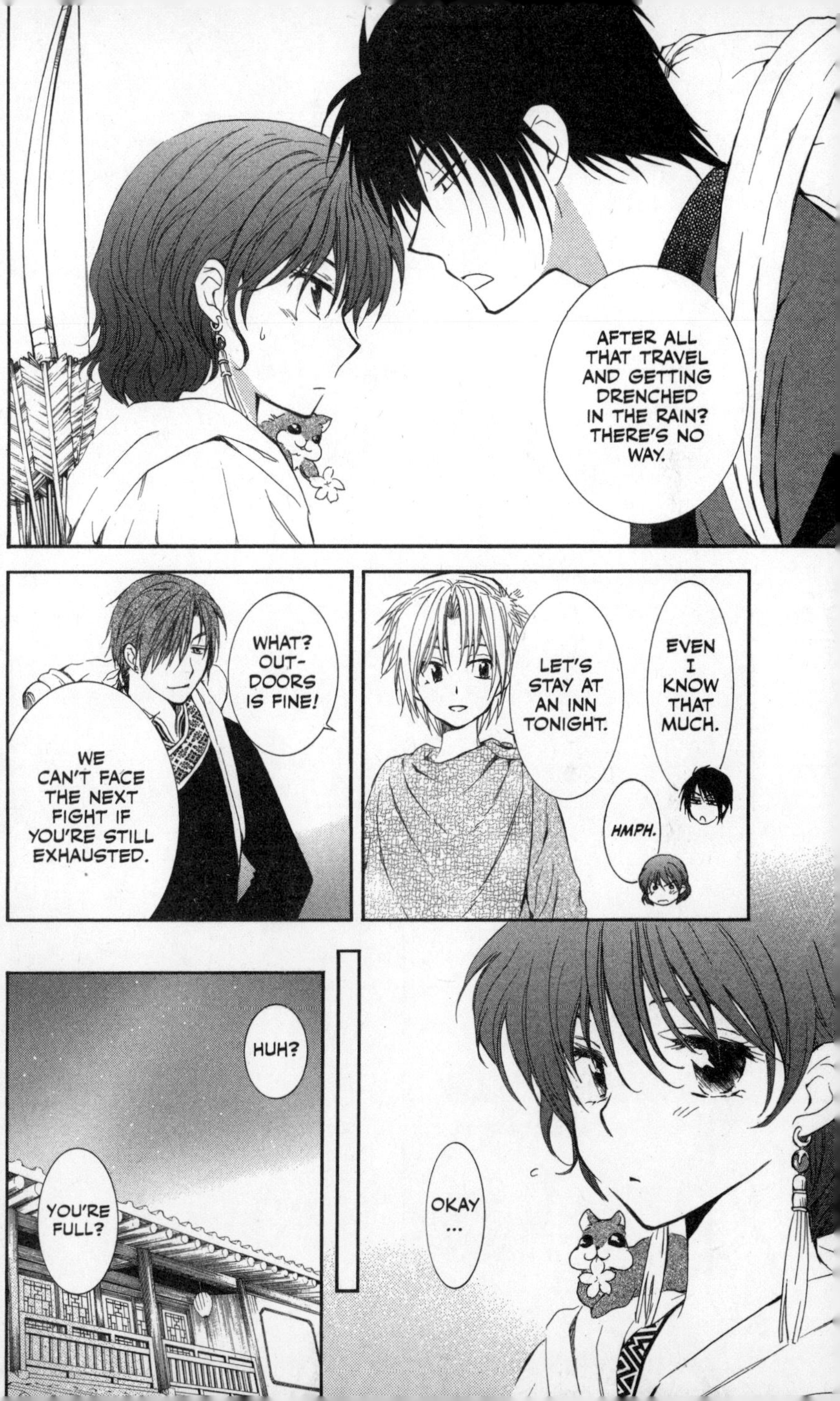
AFTER ALL THAT TRAVEL AND GETTING DRENCHED IN THE RAIN? THERE'S NO WAY.
EVEN I KNOW THAT MUCH.
LET'S STAY AT AN INN TONIGHT.
HMPH.
WHAT? OUT-DOORS IS FINE!
WE CAN'T FACE THE NEXT FIGHT IF YOU'RE STILL EXHAUSTED.
OKAY...
HUH?
YOU'RE FULL?

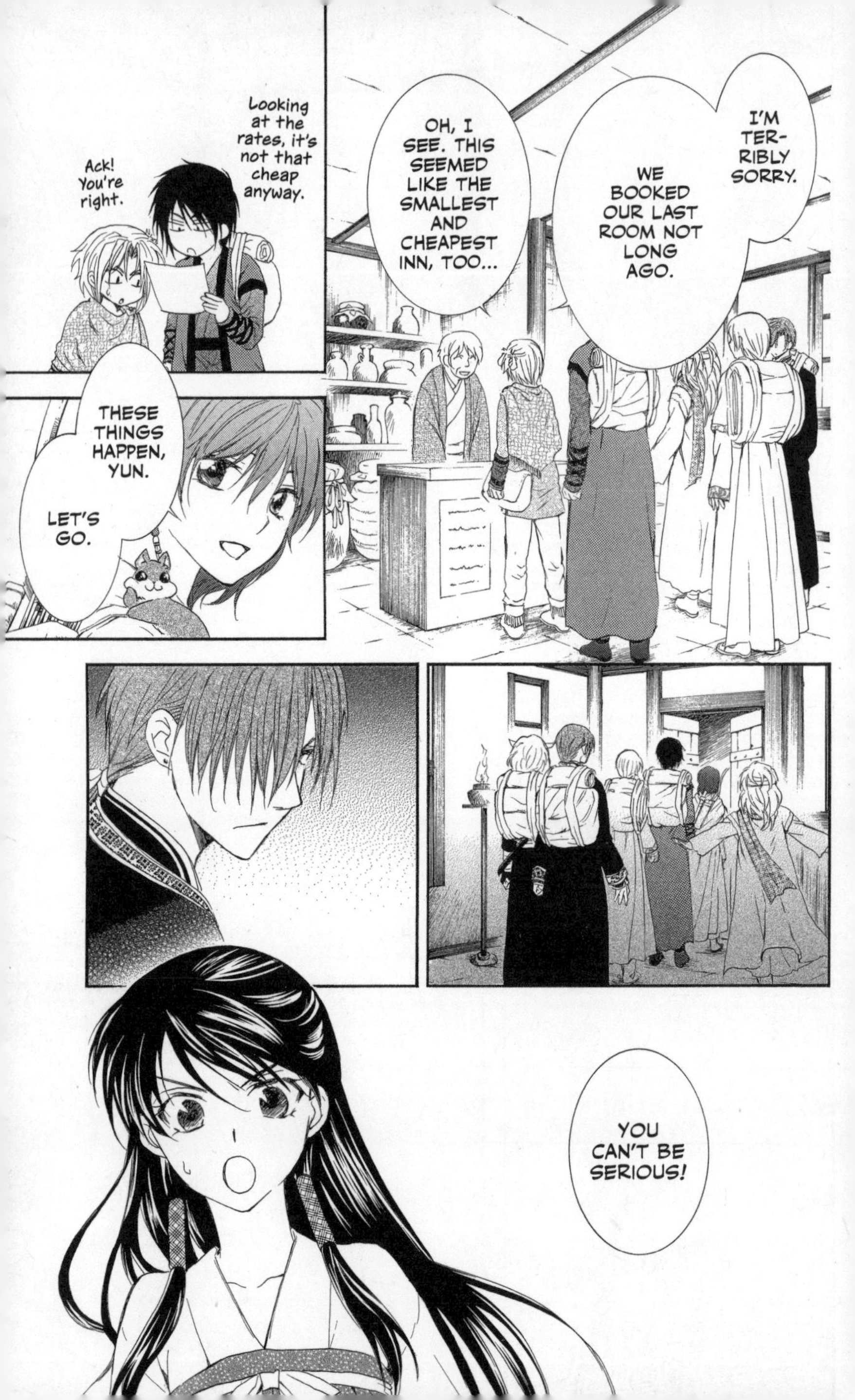
I'M TERRIBLY SORRY.
WE BOOKED OUR LAST ROOM NOT LONG AGO.
OH, I SEE. THIS SEEMED LIKE THE SMALLEST AND CHEAPEST INN, TOO...
Looking at the rates, it's not that cheap anyway.
Ack! You're right.
THESE THINGS HAPPEN, YUN.
LET'S GO.
YOU CAN'T BE SERIOUS!

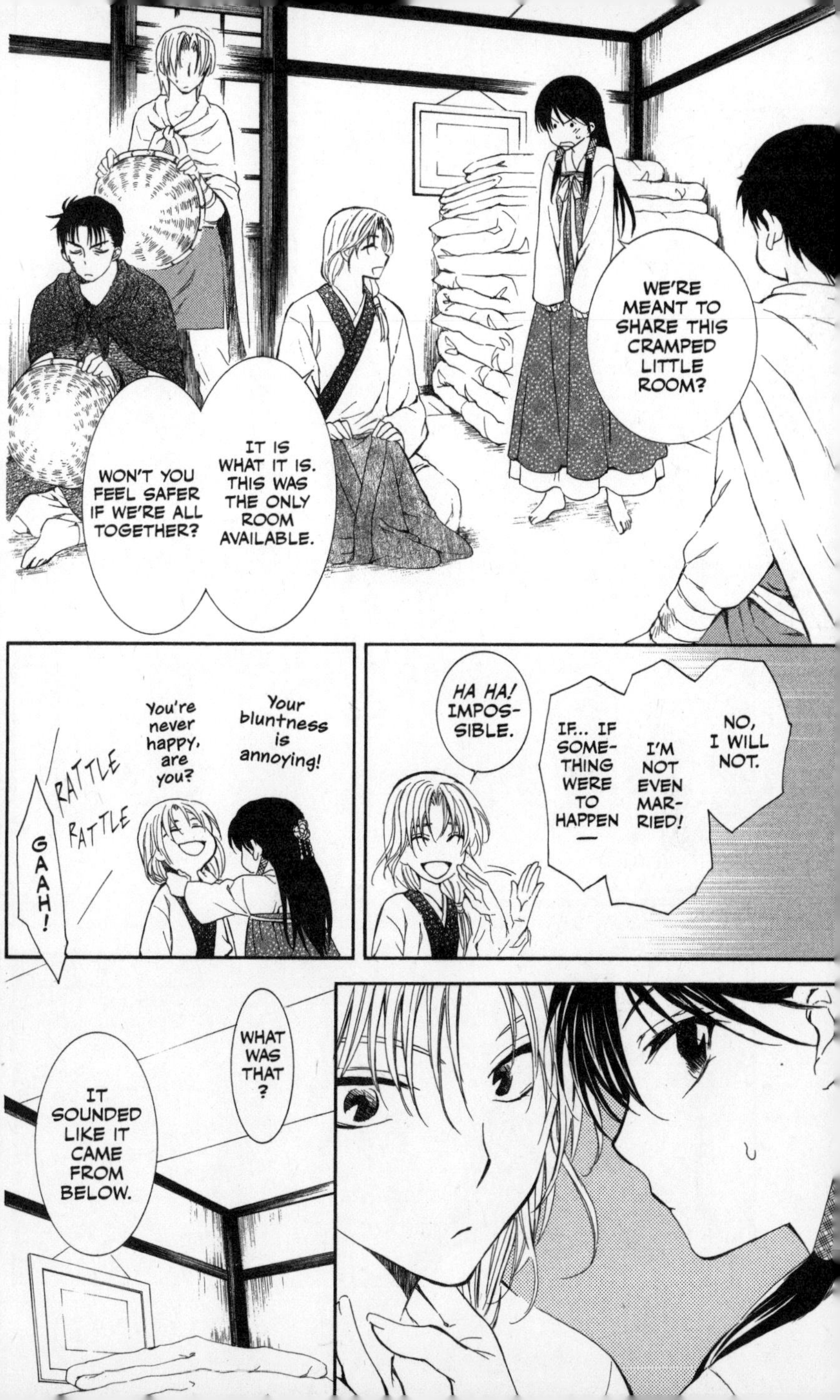
WE'RE MEANT TO SHARE THIS CRAMPED LITTLE ROOM?
IT IS WHAT IT IS. THIS WAS THE ONLY ROOM AVAILABLE.
WON'T YOU FEEL SAFER IF WE'RE ALL TOGETHER?
NO, I WILL NOT.
I'M NOT EVEN MARRIED!
IF... IF SOMETHING WERE TO HAPPEN—
HA HA! IMPOSSIBLE.
Your bluntness is annoying!
You're never happy, are you?
RATTLE RATTLE
GAAH!
WHAT WAS THAT?
IT SOUNDED LIKE IT CAME FROM BELOW.

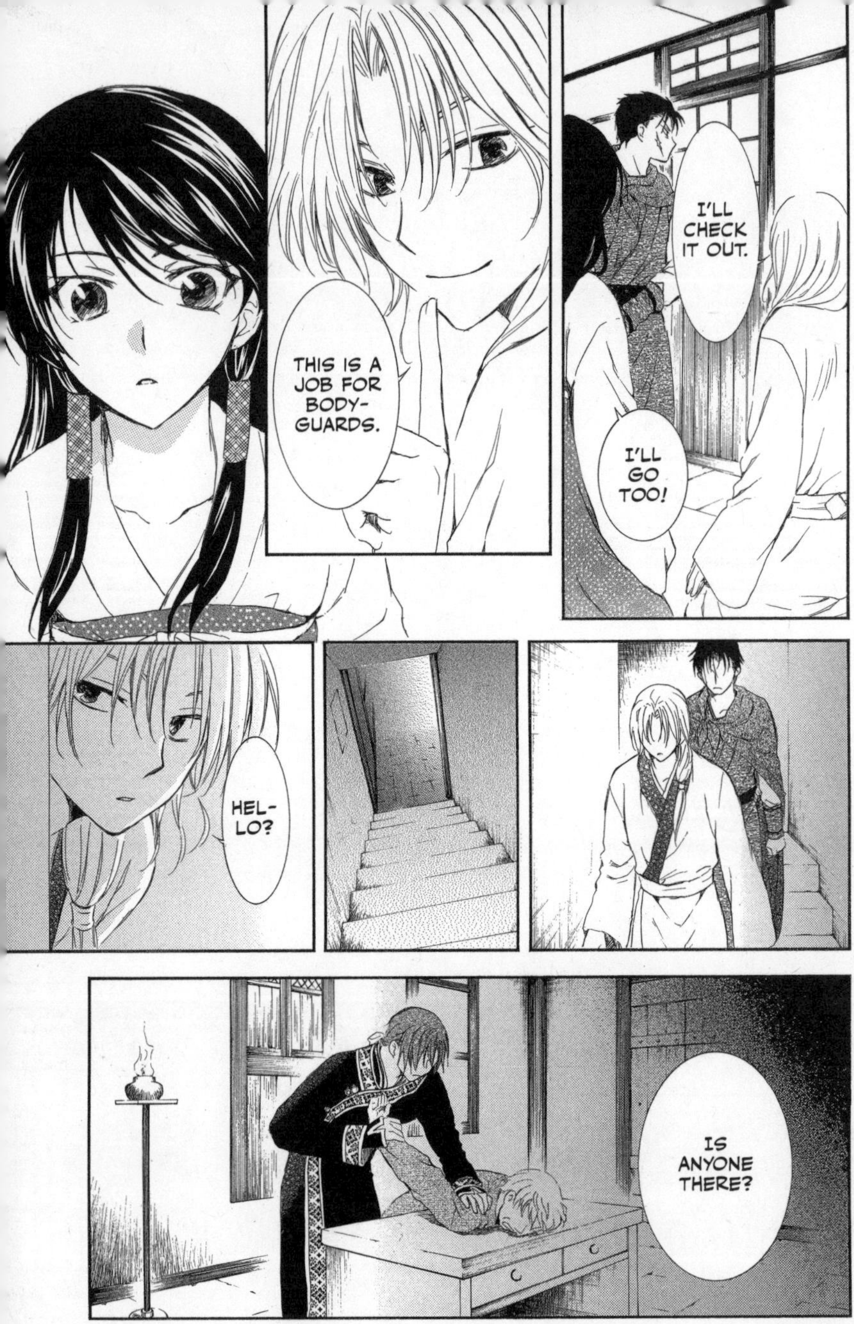
I'LL CHECK IT OUT.
I'LL GO TOO!
THIS IS A JOB FOR BODY-GUARDS.
HEL-LO?
IS ANYONE THERE?

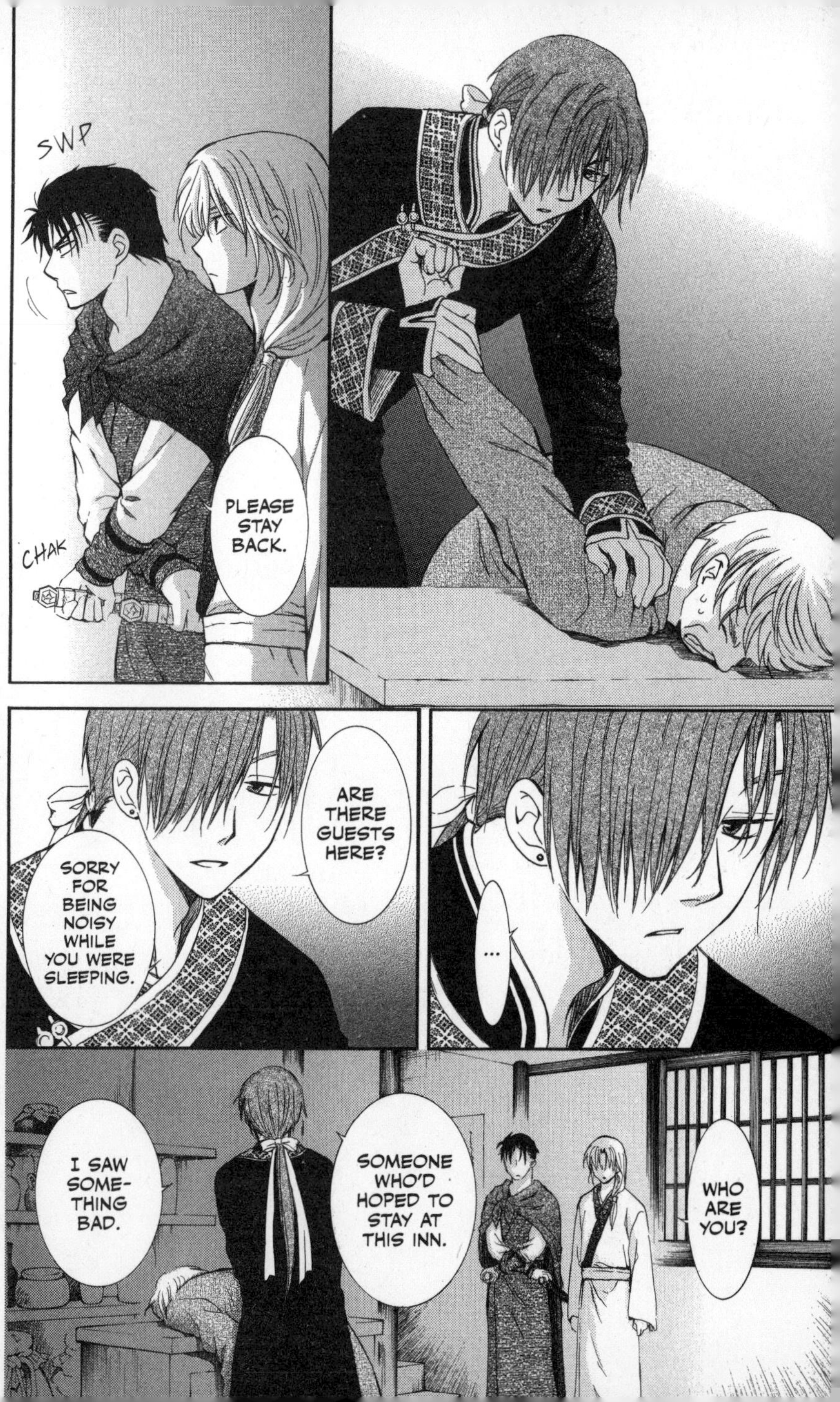
SWP
PLEASE STAY BACK.
CHAK
...
ARE THERE GUESTS HERE?
SORRY FOR BEING NOISY WHILE YOU WERE SLEEPING.
WHO ARE YOU?
SOMEONE WHO'D HOPED TO STAY AT THIS INN.
I SAW SOME-THING BAD.

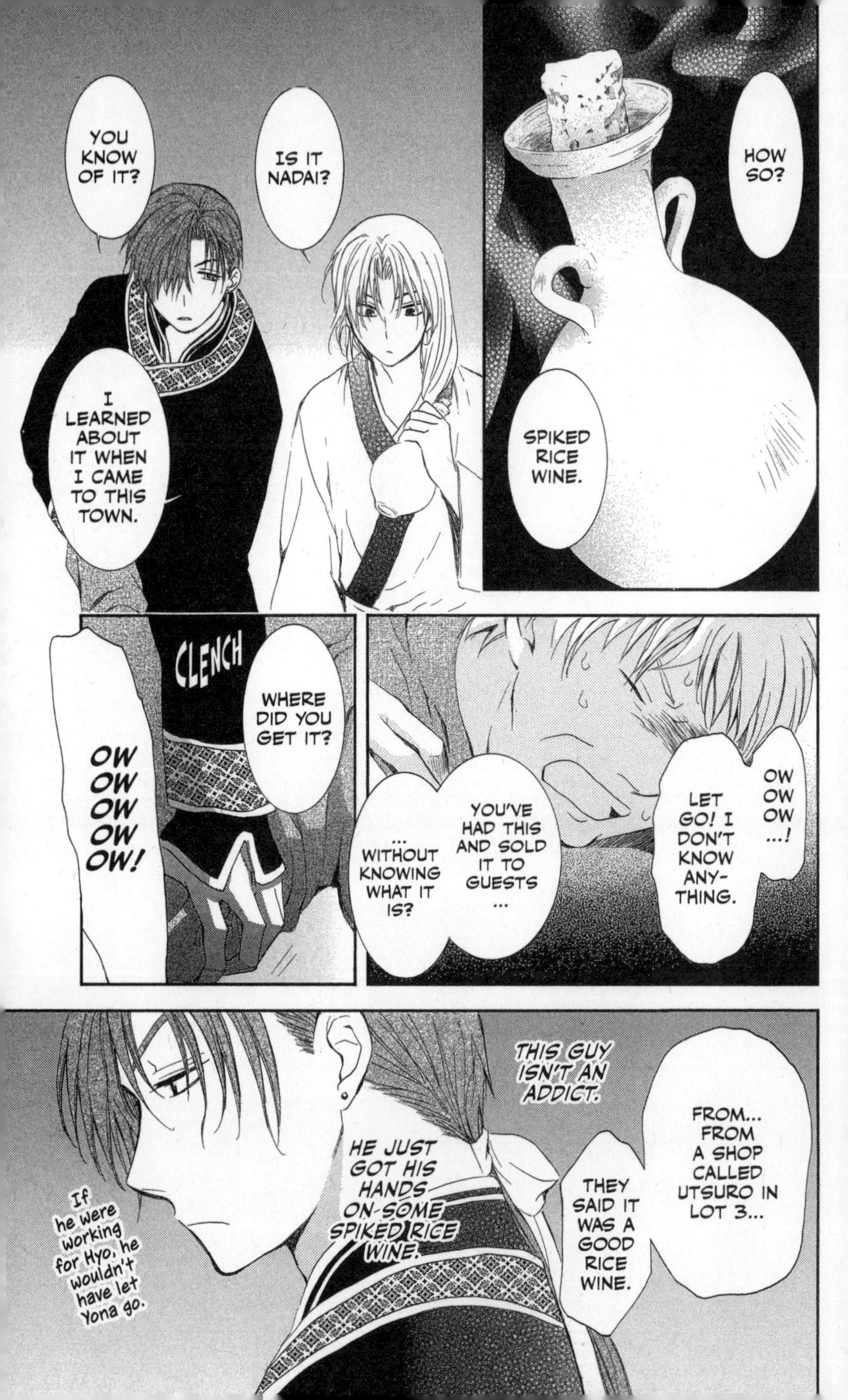
HOW SO?
SPIKED RICE WINE.
IS IT NADAI?
YOU KNOW OF IT?
I LEARNED ABOUT IT WHEN I CAME TO THIS TOWN.
OW OW OW ...!
LET GO! I DON'T KNOW ANY-THING.
YOU'VE HAD THIS AND SOLD IT TO GUESTS ...
... WITHOUT KNOWING WHAT IT IS?
WHERE DID YOU GET IT?
CLENCH
OW OW OW OW OW!
FROM... FROM A SHOP CALLED UTSURO IN LOT 3...
THEY SAID IT WAS A GOOD RICE WINE.
THIS GUY ISN'T AN ADDICT.
HE JUST GOT HIS HANDS ON SOME SPIKED RICE WINE.
If he were working for Hyo, he wouldn't have let Yona go.

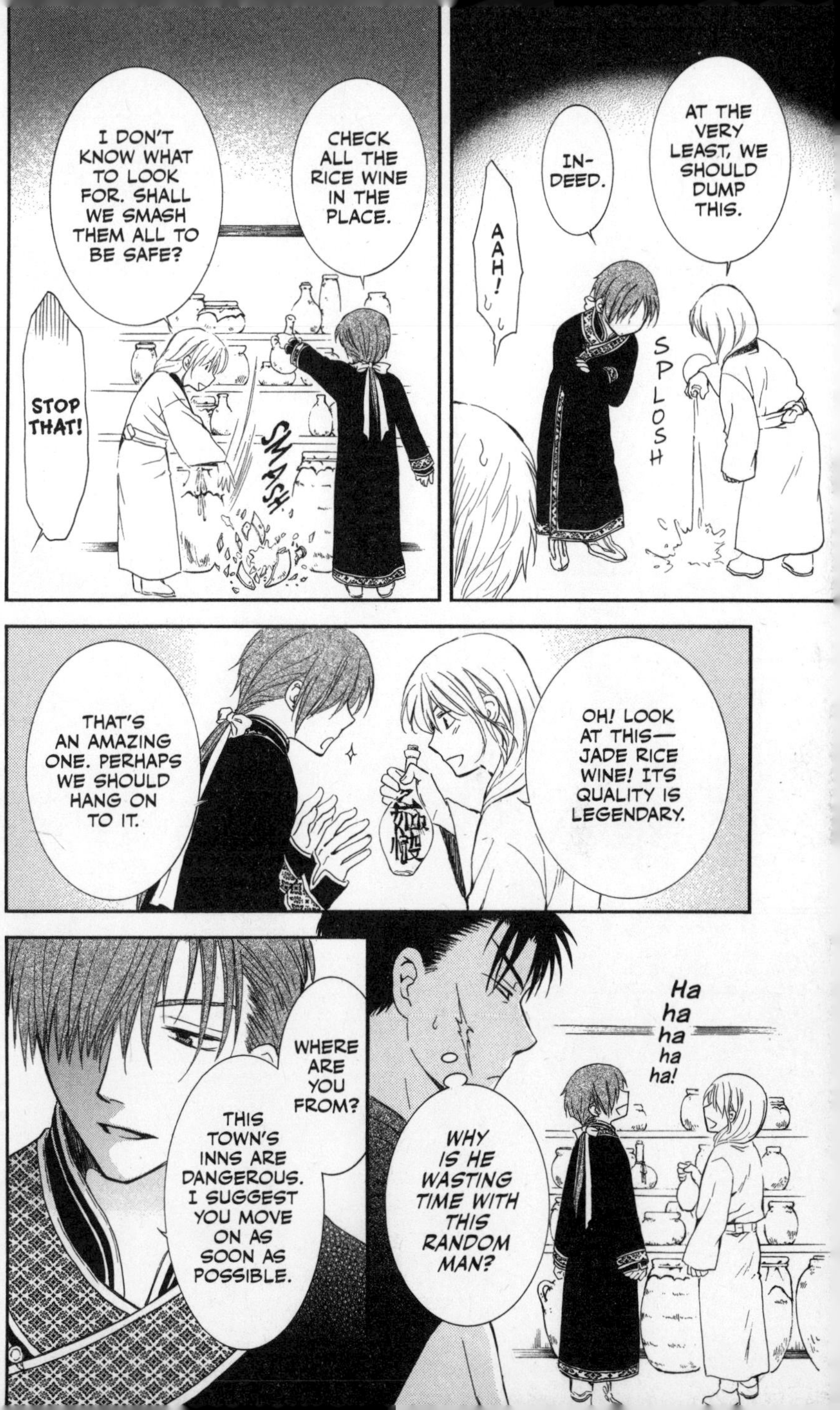
AT THE VERY LEAST, WE SHOULD DUMP THIS.
IN-DEED.
AAH!
SPLOSH
CHECK ALL THE RICE WINE IN THE PLACE.
I DON'T KNOW WHAT TO LOOK FOR. SHALL WE SMASH THEM ALL TO BE SAFE?
STOP THAT!
SMASH
OH! LOOK AT THIS—JADE RICE WINE! ITS QUALITY IS LEGENDARY.
THAT'S AN AMAZING ONE. PERHAPS WE SHOULD HANG ON TO IT.
Ha ha ha ha ha!
WHY IS HE WASTING TIME WITH THIS RANDOM MAN?
WHERE ARE YOU FROM?
THIS TOWN'S INNS ARE DANGEROUS. I SUGGEST YOU MOVE ON AS SOON AS POSSIBLE.

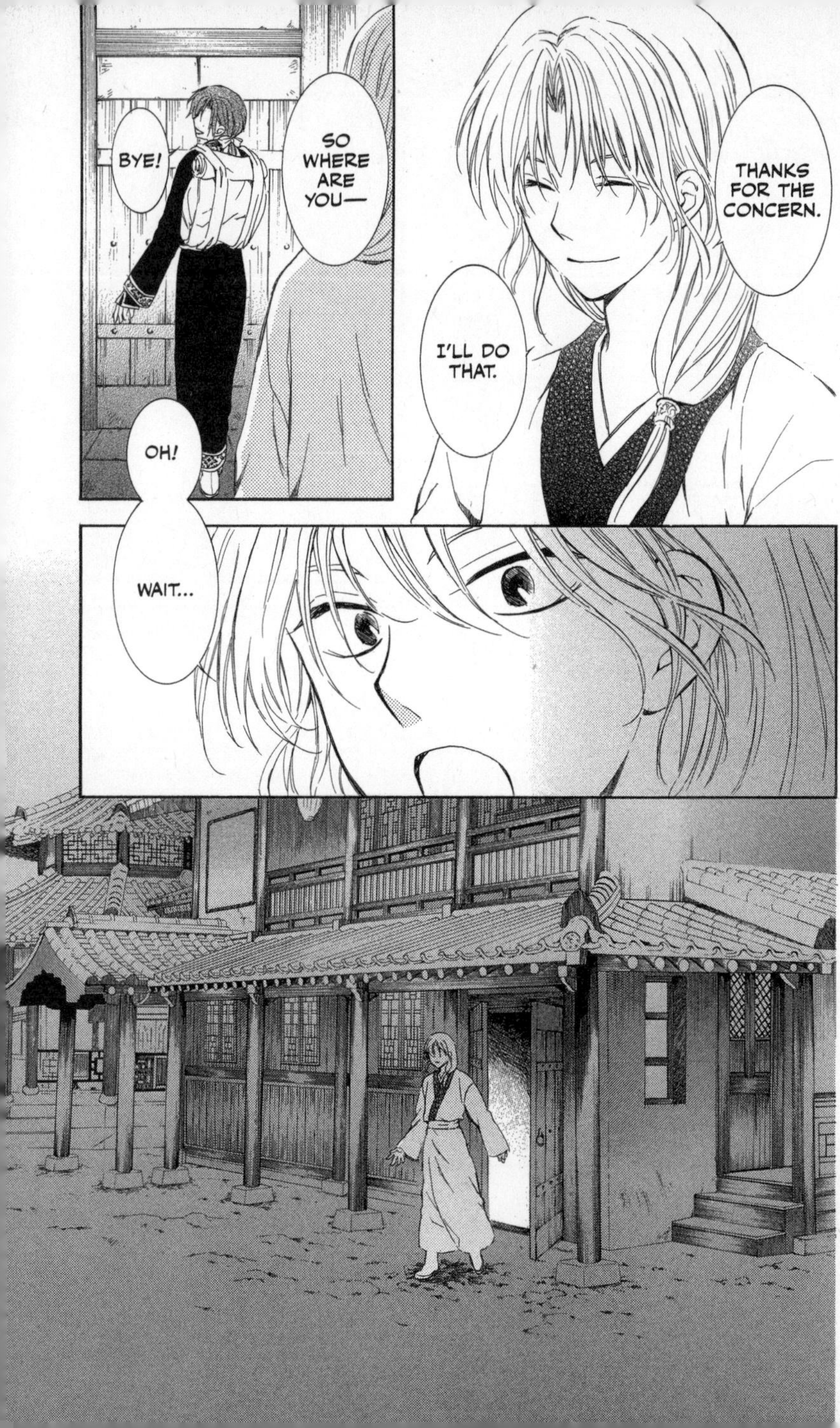
THANKS FOR THE CONCERN.
I'LL DO THAT.
SO WHERE ARE YOU—
BYE!
OH!
WAIT...

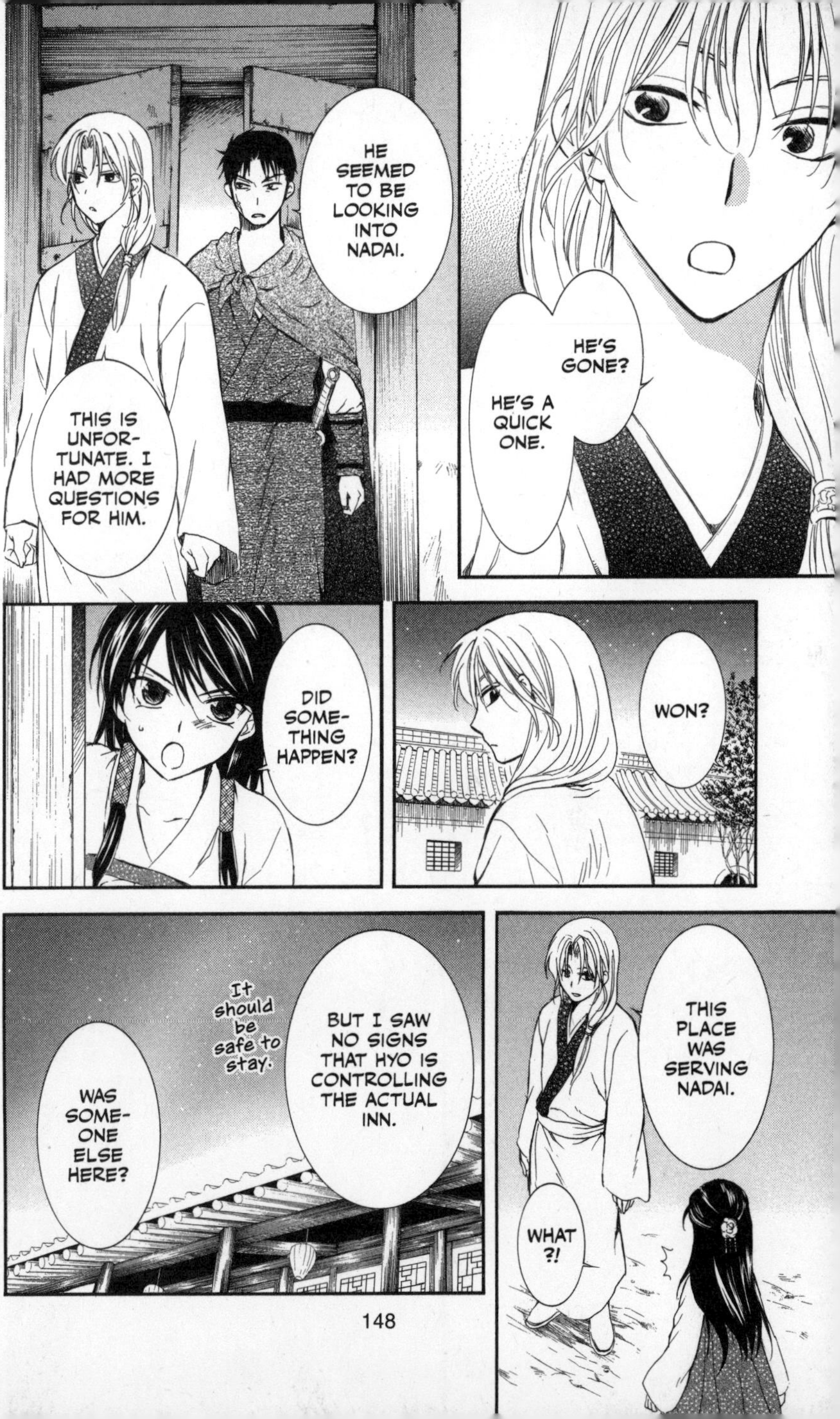
HE'S GONE?
HE'S A QUICK ONE.
HE SEEMED TO BE LOOKING INTO NADAI.
THIS IS UNFOR-TUNATE. I HAD MORE QUESTIONS FOR HIM.
WON?
DID SOME-THING HAPPEN?
THIS PLACE WAS SERVING NADAI.
WHAT?!
BUT I SAW NO SIGNS THAT HYO IS CONTROLLING THE ACTUAL INN.
It should be safe to stay.
WAS SOME-ONE ELSE HERE?

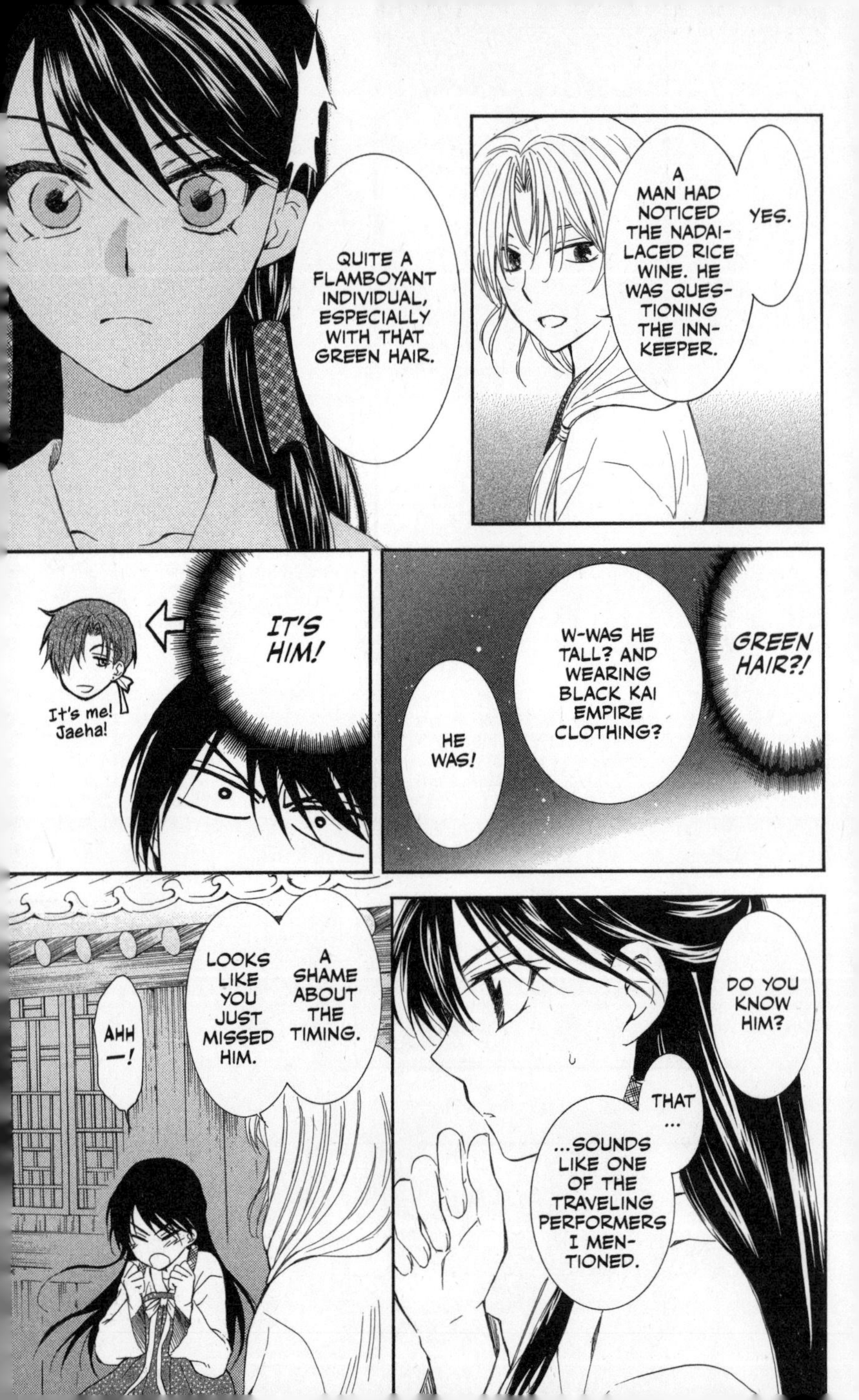
YES.
A MAN HAD NOTICED THE NADAI-LACED RICE WINE. HE WAS QUES-TIONING THE INN-KEEPER.
QUITE A FLAMBOYANT INDIVIDUAL, ESPECIALLY WITH THAT GREEN HAIR.
GREEN HAIR?!
W-WAS HE TALL? AND WEARING BLACK KAI EMPIRE CLOTHING?
HE WAS!
IT'S HIM!
It's me! Jaeha!
DO YOU KNOW HIM?
THAT...
...SOUNDS LIKE ONE OF THE TRAVELING PERFORMERS I MEN-TIONED.
A SHAME ABOUT THE TIMING.
LOOKS LIKE YOU JUST MISSED HIM.
AHH—!

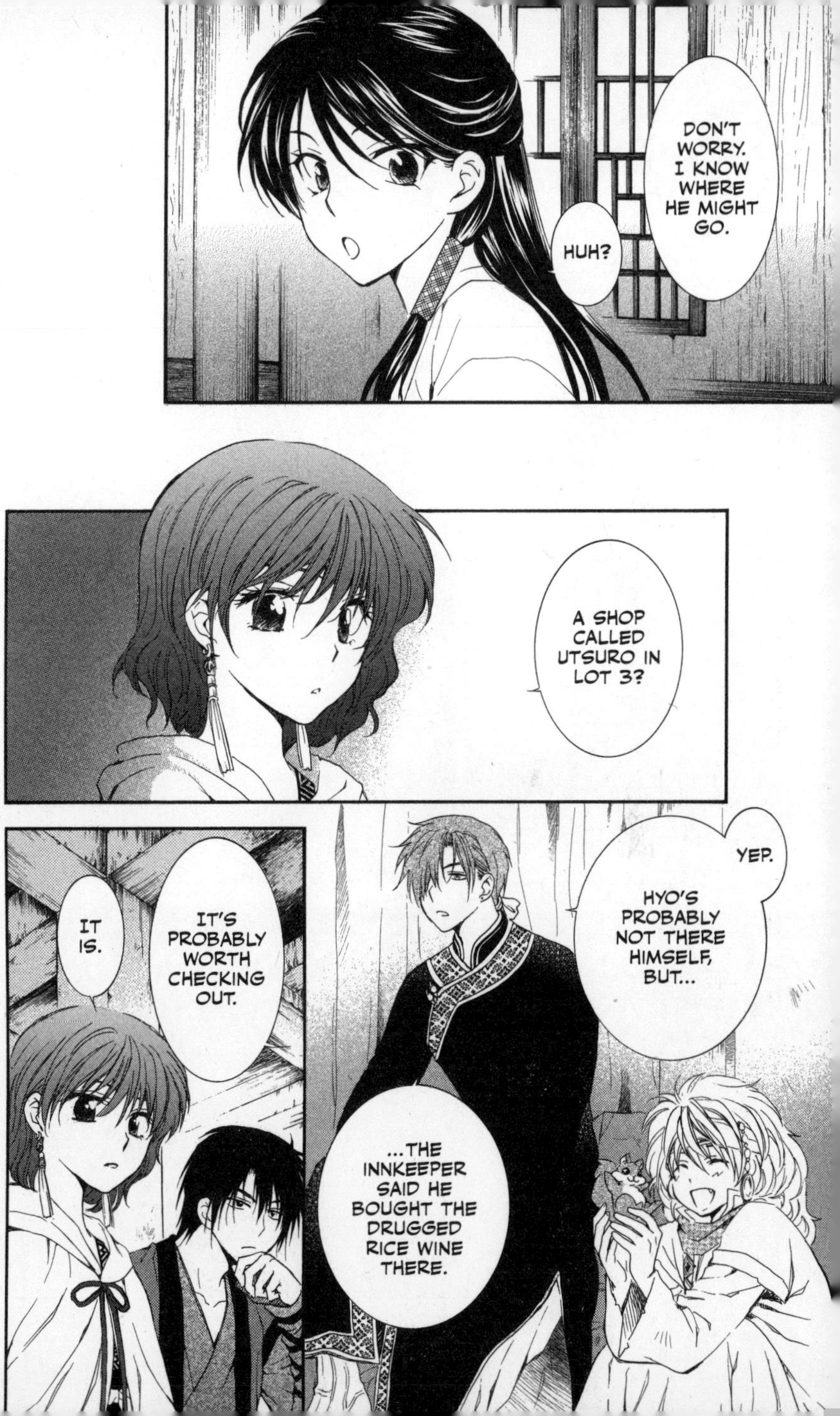
DON'T WORRY. I KNOW WHERE HE MIGHT GO.
HUH?
A SHOP CALLED UTSURO IN LOT 3?
YEP.
HYO'S PROBABLY NOT THERE HIMSELF, BUT...
...THE INNKEEPER SAID HE BOUGHT THE DRUGGED RICE WINE THERE.
IT'S PROBABLY WORTH CHECKING OUT.
IT IS.

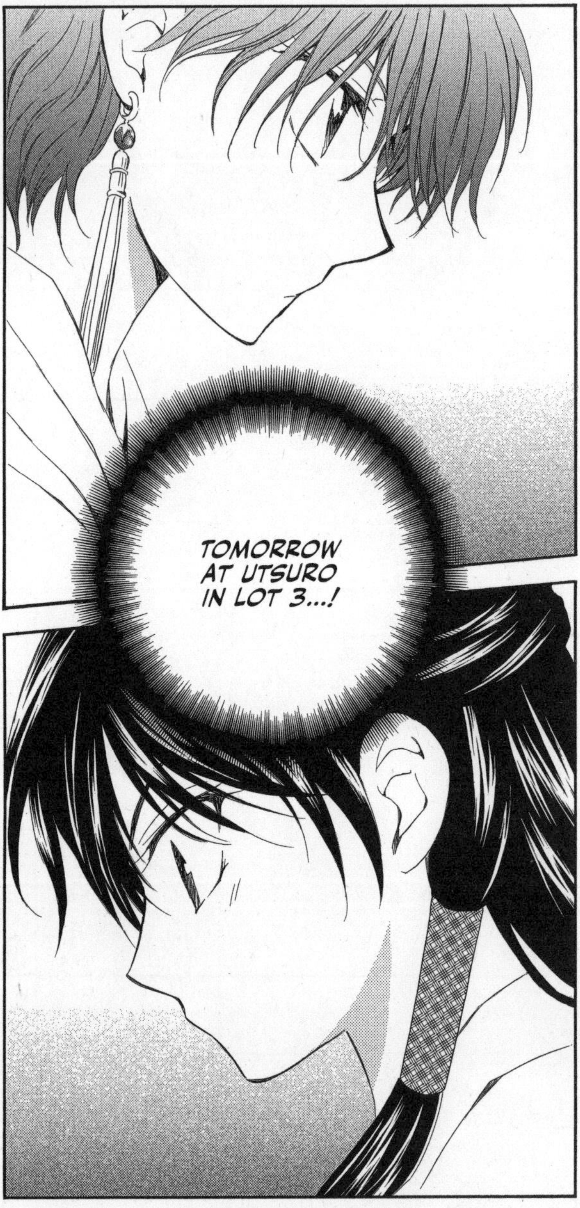
TOMORROW AT UTSURO IN LOT 3...!

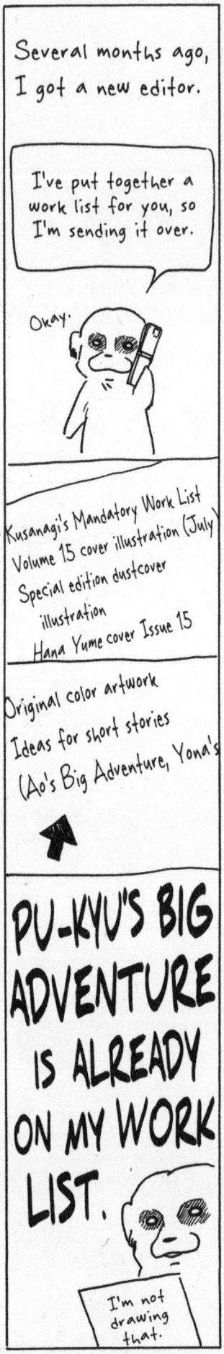
Several months ago, I got a new editor.
I've put together a work list for you, so I'm sending it over.
Okay.
Kusanagi's Mandatory Work List
Volume 15 cover illustration (July)
Special edition dustcover illustration
Hana Yume cover Issue 15
Original color artwork
Ideas for short stories
(Ao's Big Adventure, Yona's
PU-KYU'S BIG ADVENTURE IS ALREADY ON MY WORK LIST.
I'm not drawing that.

Does Kusanagi have a rule that says she has to reject the idea of Pu-kyu's Big Adventure?

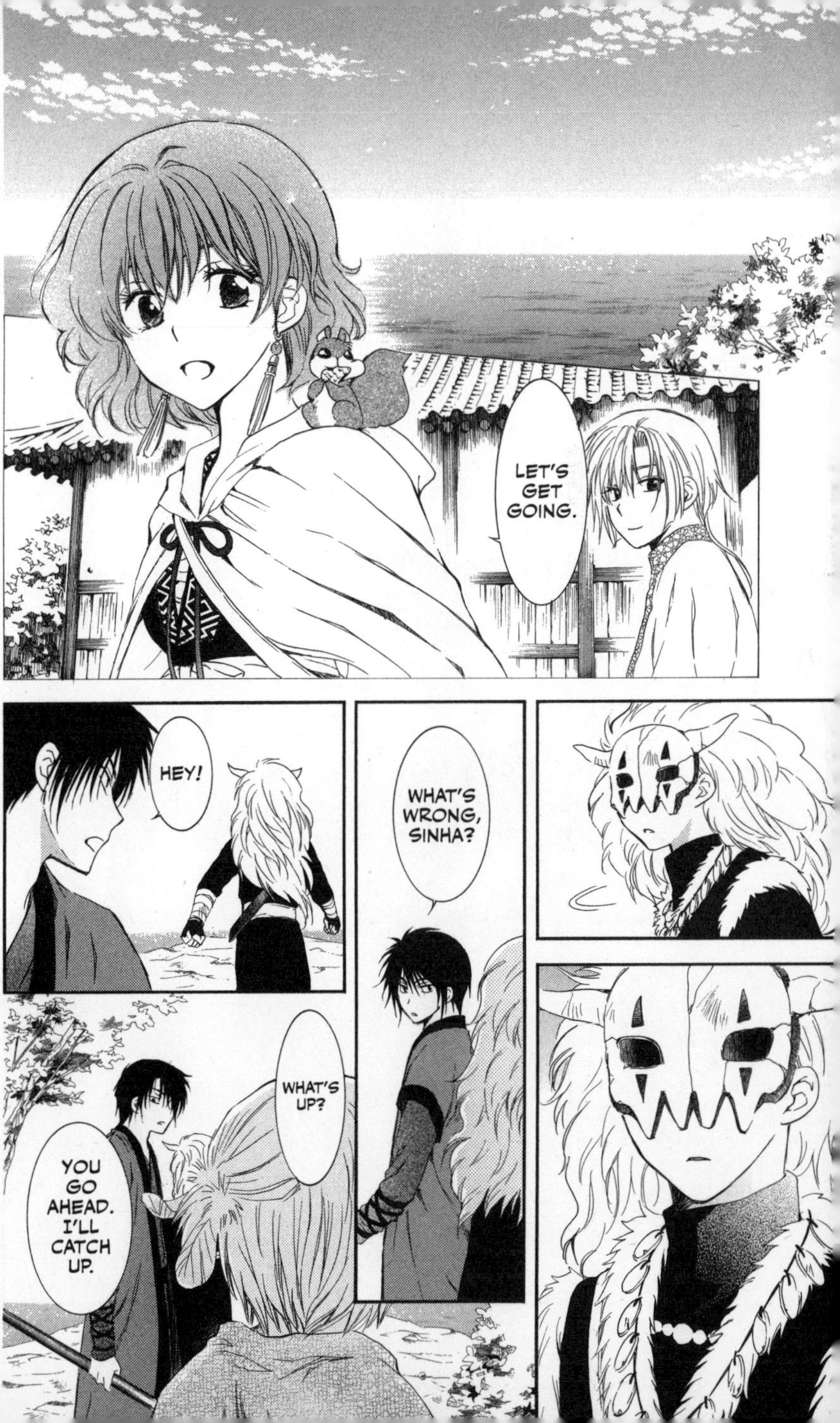
LET'S GET GOING.
WHAT'S WRONG, SINHA?
HEY!
WHAT'S UP?
YOU GO AHEAD. I'LL CATCH UP.

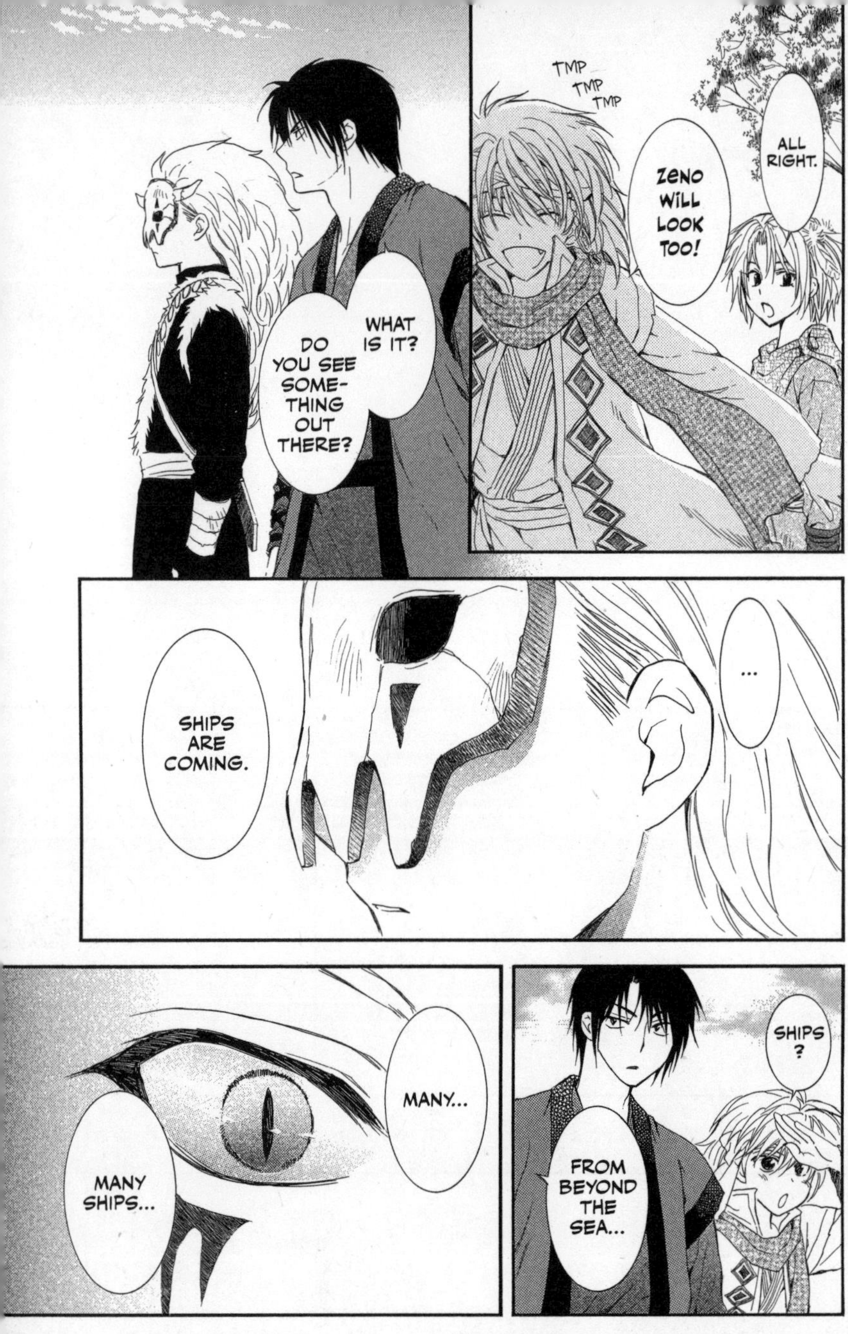
ALL RIGHT.
TMP TMP TMP
ZENO WILL LOOK TOO!
WHAT IS IT?
DO YOU SEE SOMETHING OUT THERE?
...
SHIPS ARE COMING.
SHIPS?
FROM BEYOND THE SEA...
MANY...
MANY SHIPS...

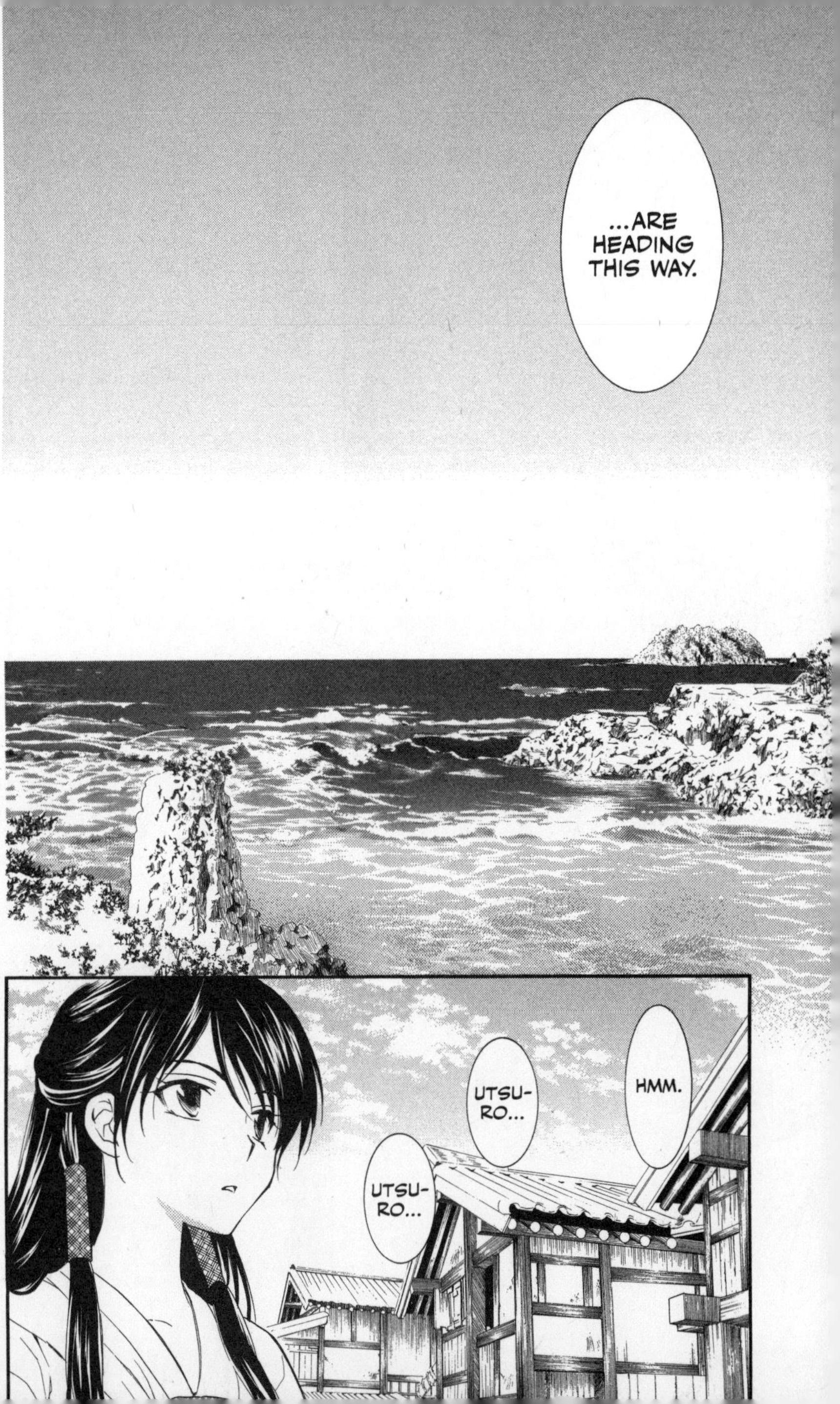
...ARE HEADING THIS WAY.
HMM.
UTSU-RO...
UTSU-RO...

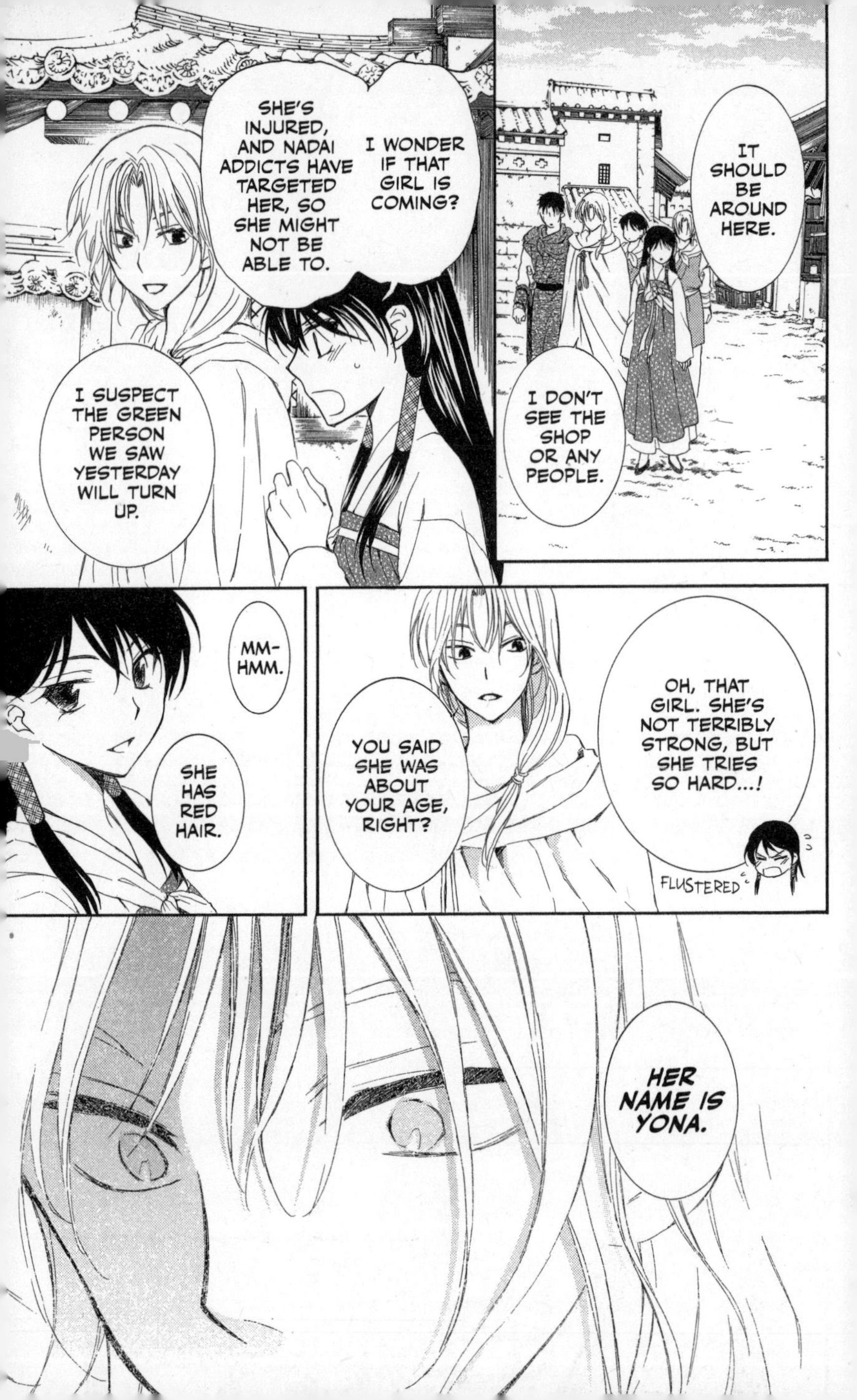
IT SHOULD BE AROUND HERE.
I DON'T SEE THE SHOP OR ANY PEOPLE.
I WONDER IF THAT GIRL IS COMING?
SHE'S INJURED, AND NADAI ADDICTS HAVE TARGETED HER, SO SHE MIGHT NOT BE ABLE TO.
I SUSPECT THE GREEN PERSON WE SAW YESTERDAY WILL TURN UP.
OH, THAT GIRL. SHE'S NOT TERRIBLY STRONG, BUT SHE TRIES SO HARD...!
FLUSTERED
YOU SAID SHE WAS ABOUT YOUR AGE, RIGHT?
MM-HMM.
SHE HAS RED HAIR.
HER NAME IS YONA.

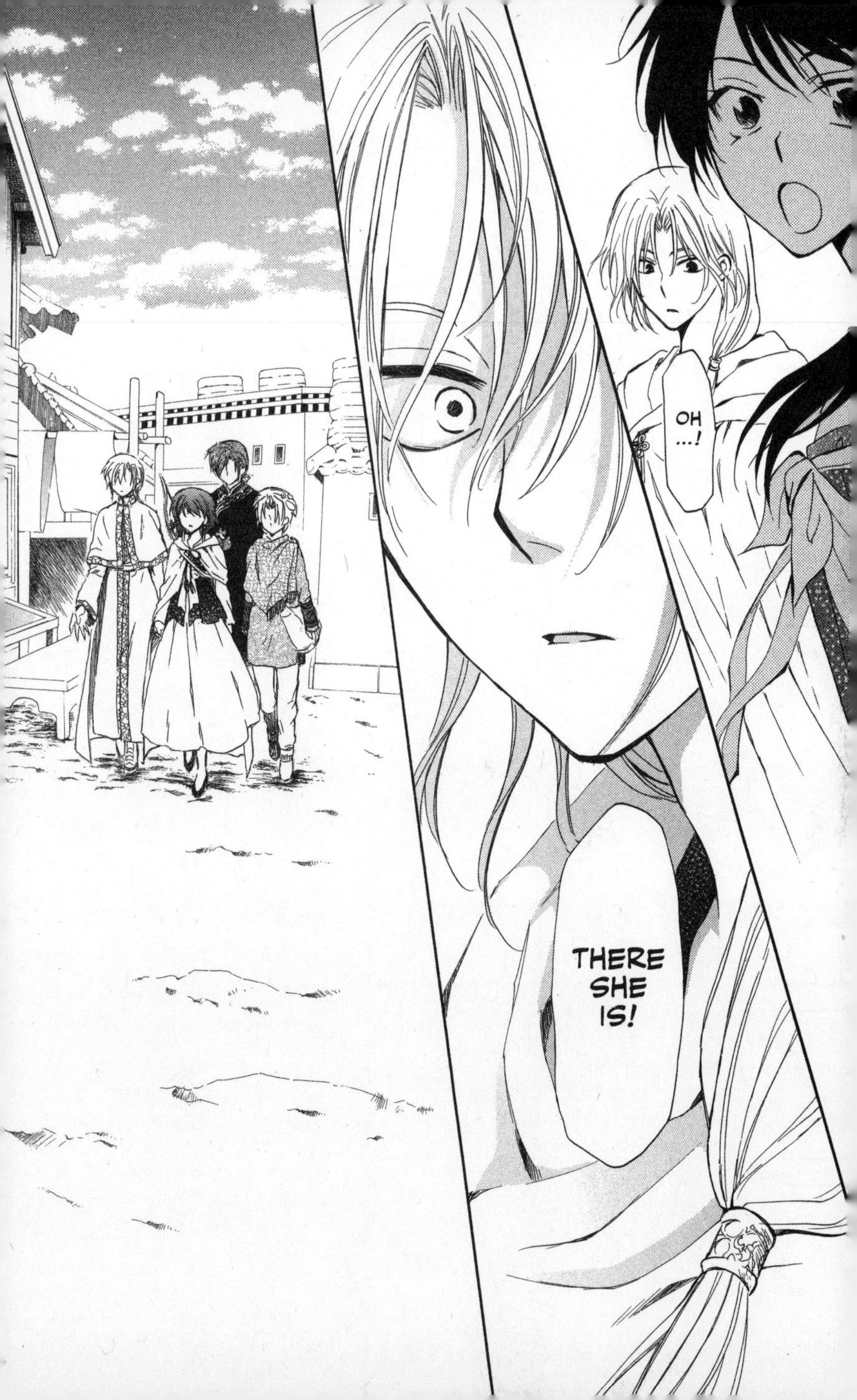
OH ...!
THERE SHE IS!

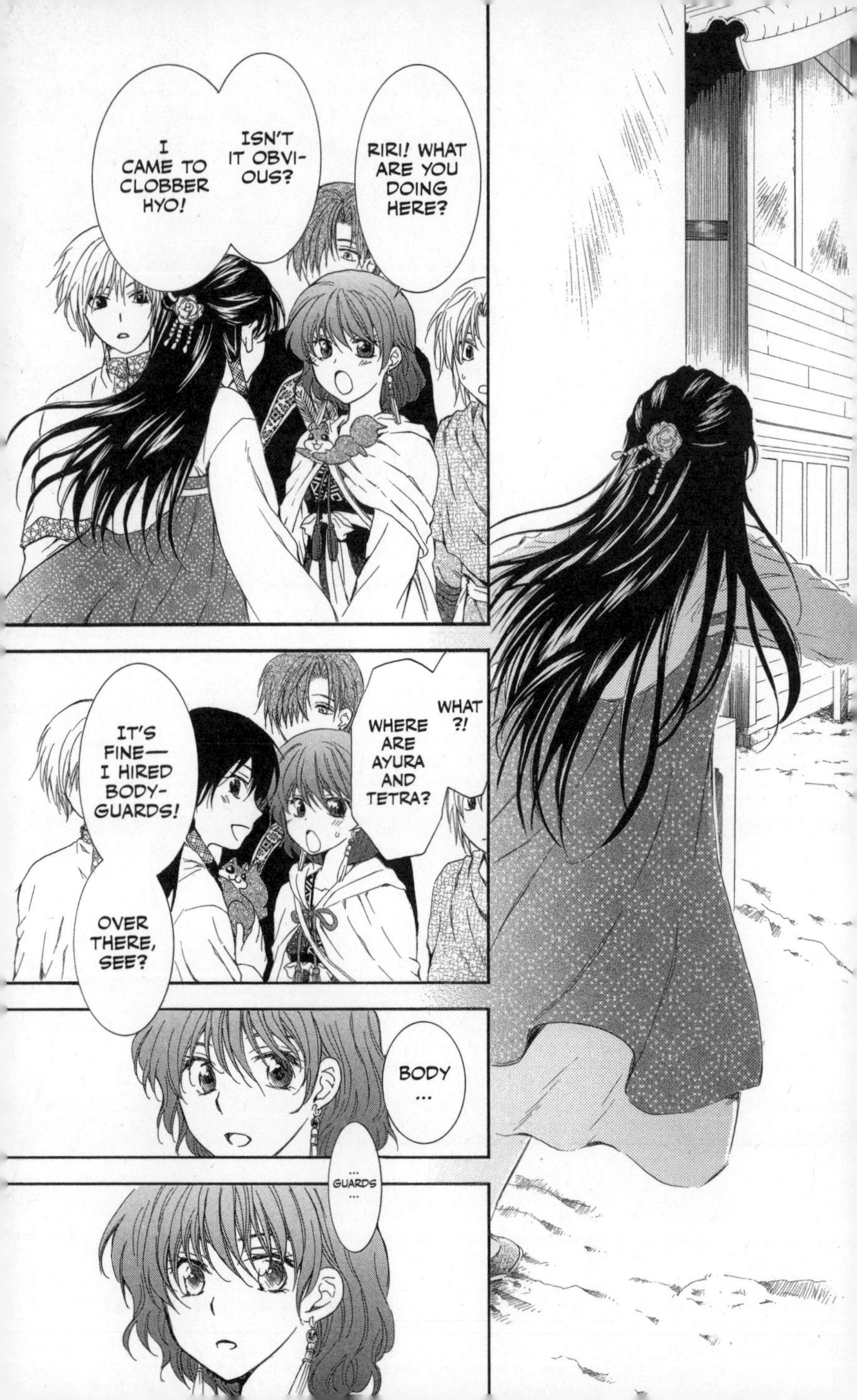
RIRI! WHAT ARE YOU DOING HERE?
ISN'T IT OBVIOUS?
I CAME TO CLOBBER HYO!
WHAT?!
WHERE ARE AYURA AND TETRA?
IT'S FINE— I HIRED BODY-GUARDS!
OVER THERE, SEE?
BODY ...
... GUARDS ...

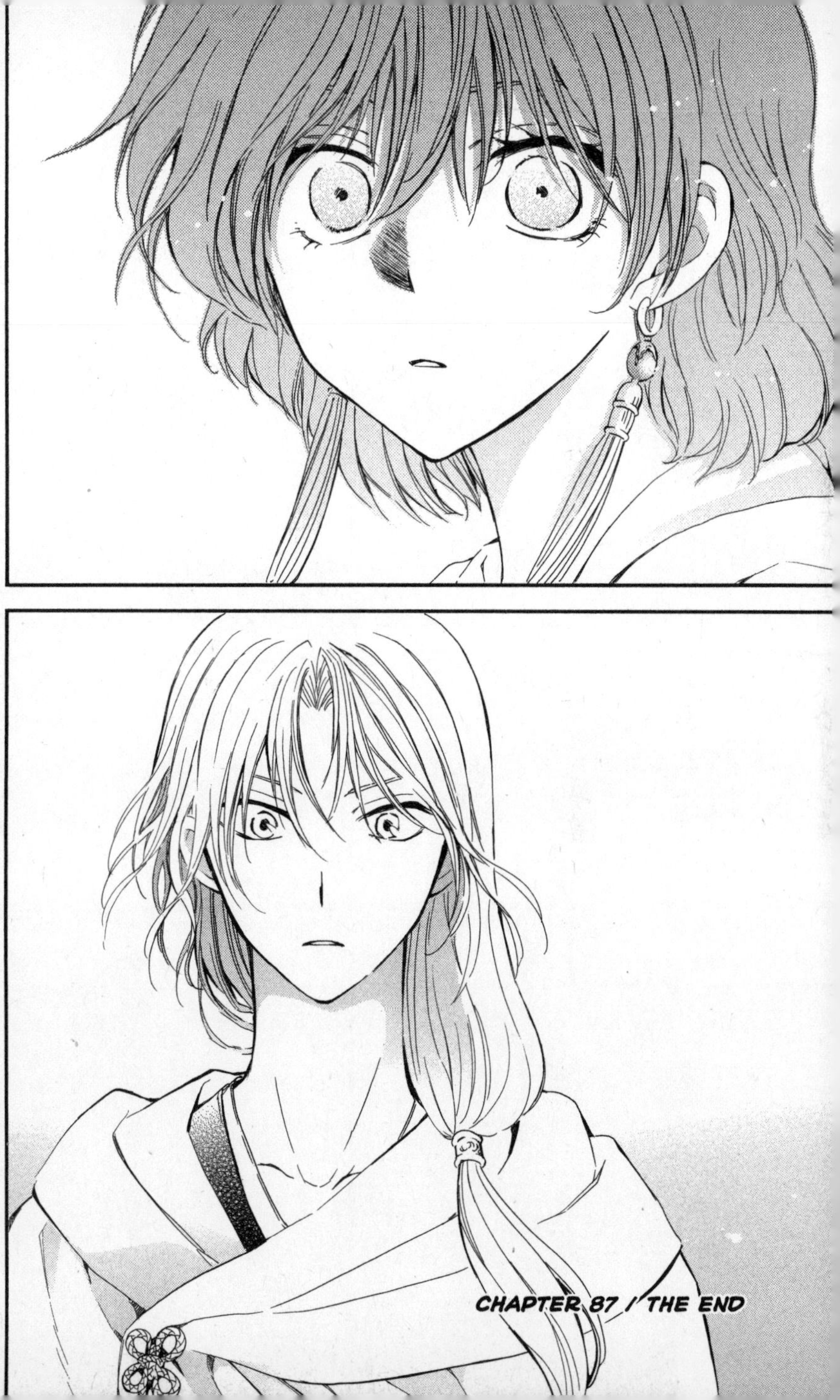
CHAPTER 87 / THE END

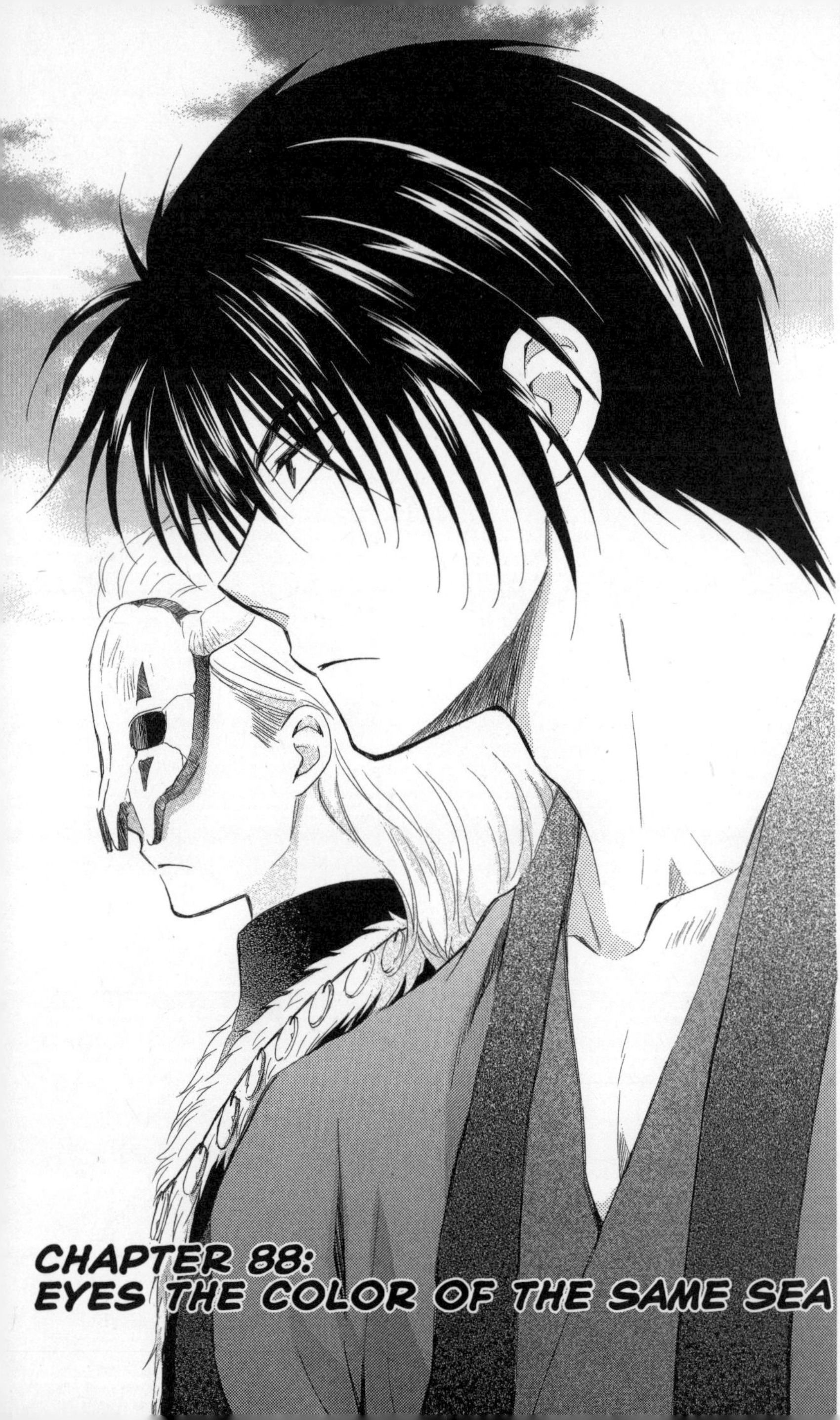

CHAPTER 88:
EYES THE COLOR OF THE SAME SEA

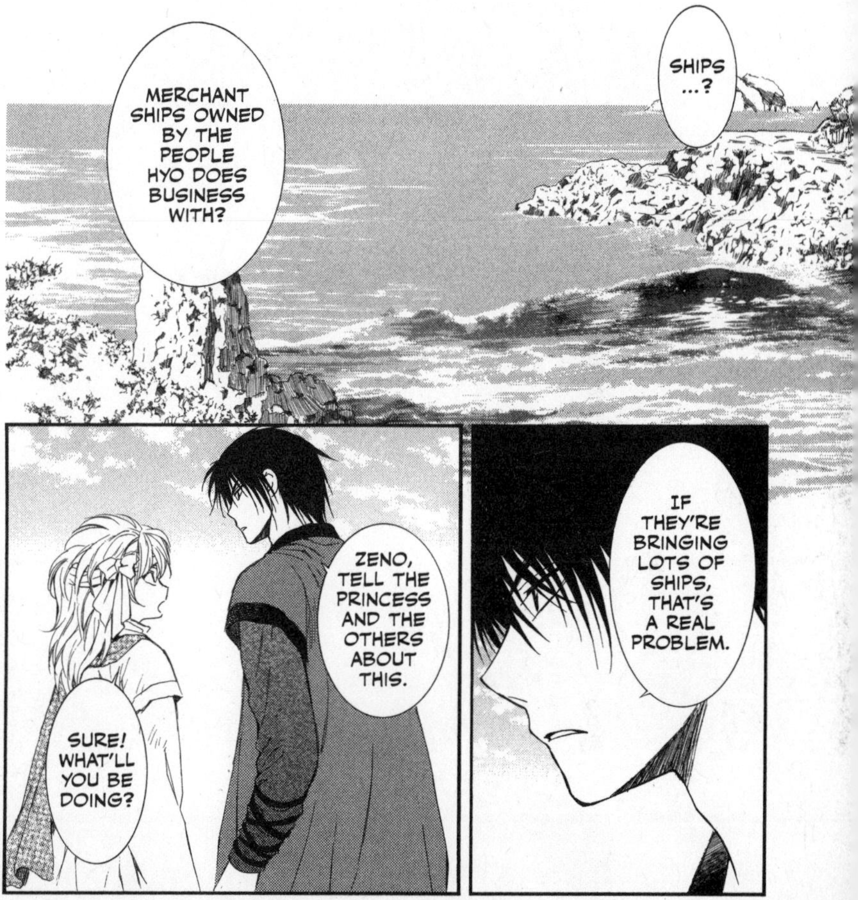
SHIPS ...?
MERCHANT SHIPS OWNED BY THE PEOPLE HYO DOES BUSINESS WITH?
IF THEY'RE BRINGING LOTS OF SHIPS, THAT'S A REAL PROBLEM.
ZENO, TELL THE PRINCESS AND THE OTHERS ABOUT THIS.
SURE! WHAT'LL YOU BE DOING?

Special thanks to all the people who've helped me!
My assistants → Mikorun, Ryo, Awafuji, C.F., Oka, Kyoko and my little sister...
My editor → Takizawa, my previous editors and the *Hana to Yume* editorial office...
Everyone who's helped me create and sell this manga...
Family and friends who've always supported me...
And of course you, for reading this! Thank you so much.
I'll do my best to repay your faith in me!

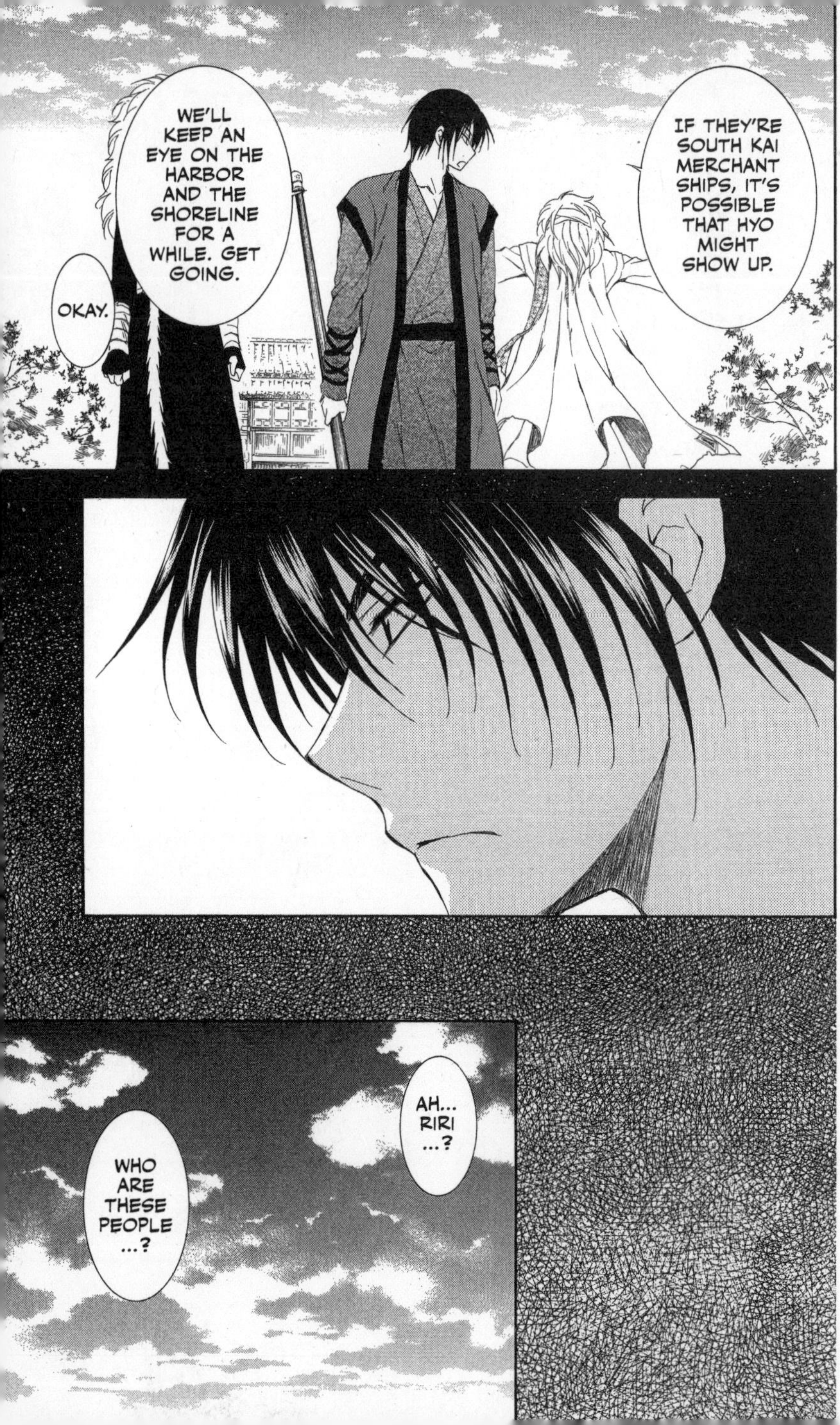
IF THEY'RE SOUTH KAI MERCHANT SHIPS, IT'S POSSIBLE THAT HYO MIGHT SHOW UP.
WE'LL KEEP AN EYE ON THE HARBOR AND THE SHORELINE FOR A WHILE. GET GOING.
OKAY.
AH... RIRI ...?
WHO ARE THESE PEOPLE ...?

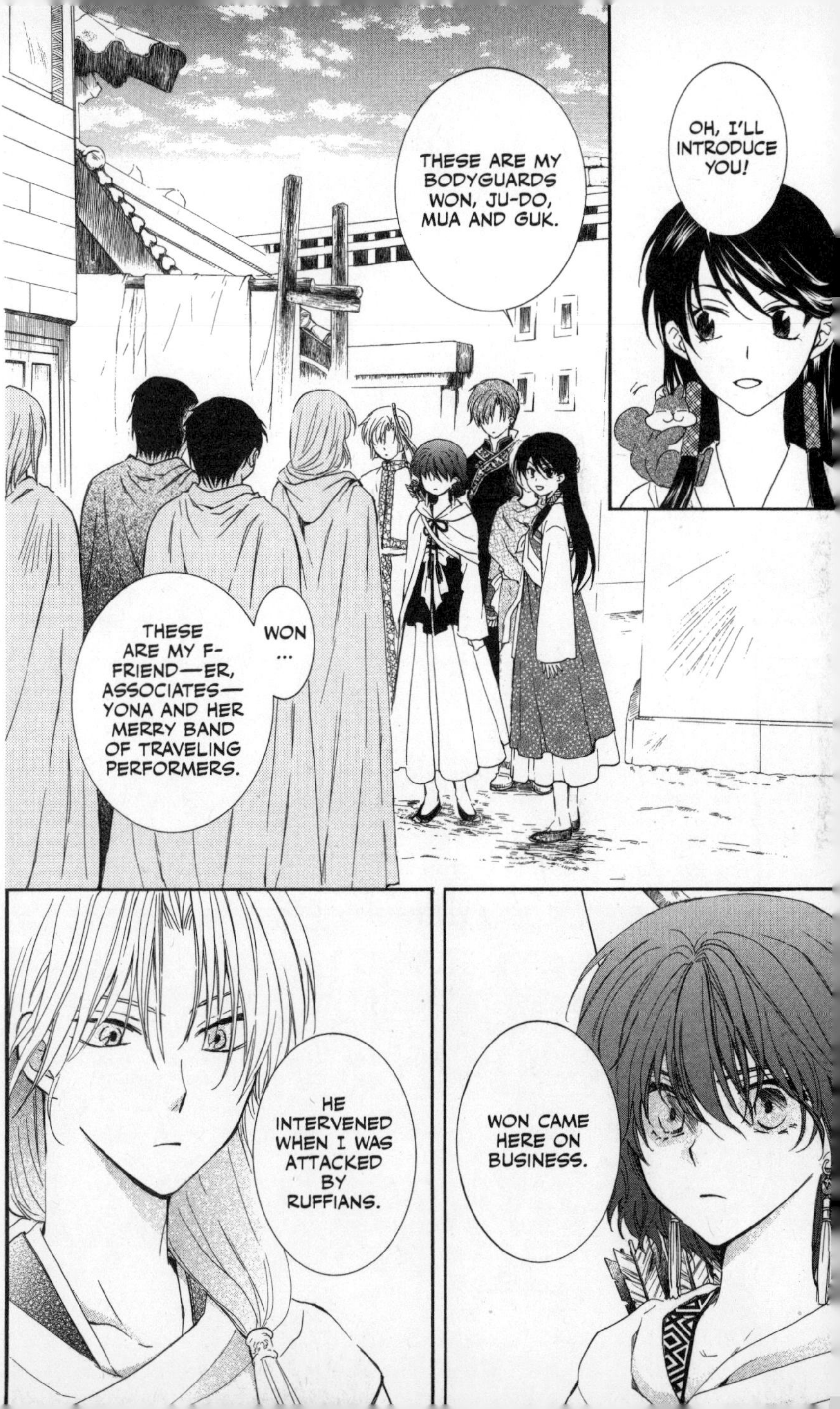
OH, I'LL INTRODUCE YOU!
THESE ARE MY BODYGUARDS WON, JU-DO, MUA AND GUK.
WON ...
THESE ARE MY F-FRIEND—ER, ASSOCIATES—YONA AND HER MERRY BAND OF TRAVELING PERFORMERS.
WON CAME HERE ON BUSINESS.
HE INTERVENED WHEN I WAS ATTACKED BY RUFFIANS.

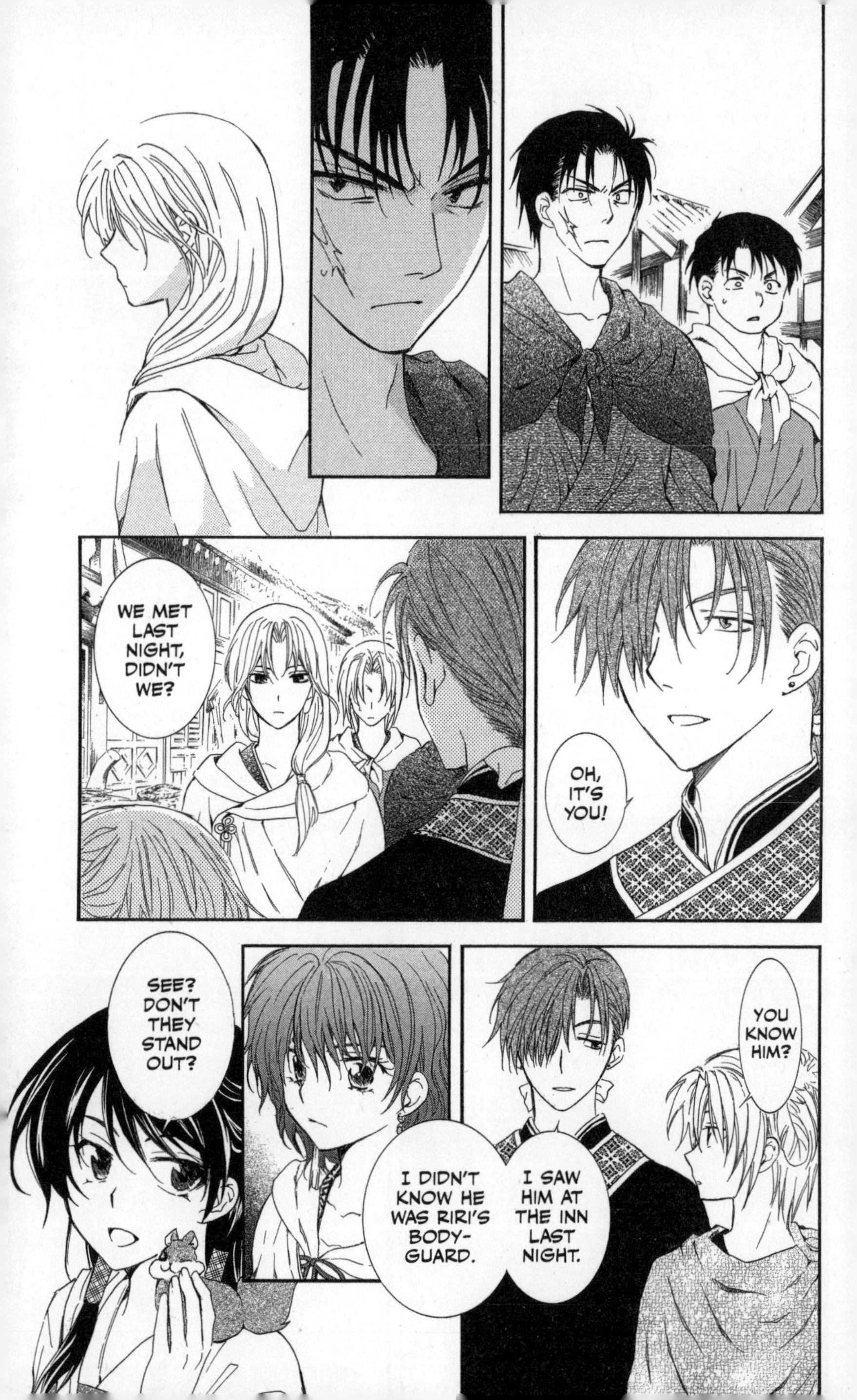
OH, IT'S YOU!
WE MET LAST NIGHT, DIDN'T WE?
YOU KNOW HIM?
I SAW HIM AT THE INN LAST NIGHT.
I DIDN'T KNOW HE WAS RIRI'S BODY-GUARD.
SEE? DON'T THEY STAND OUT?

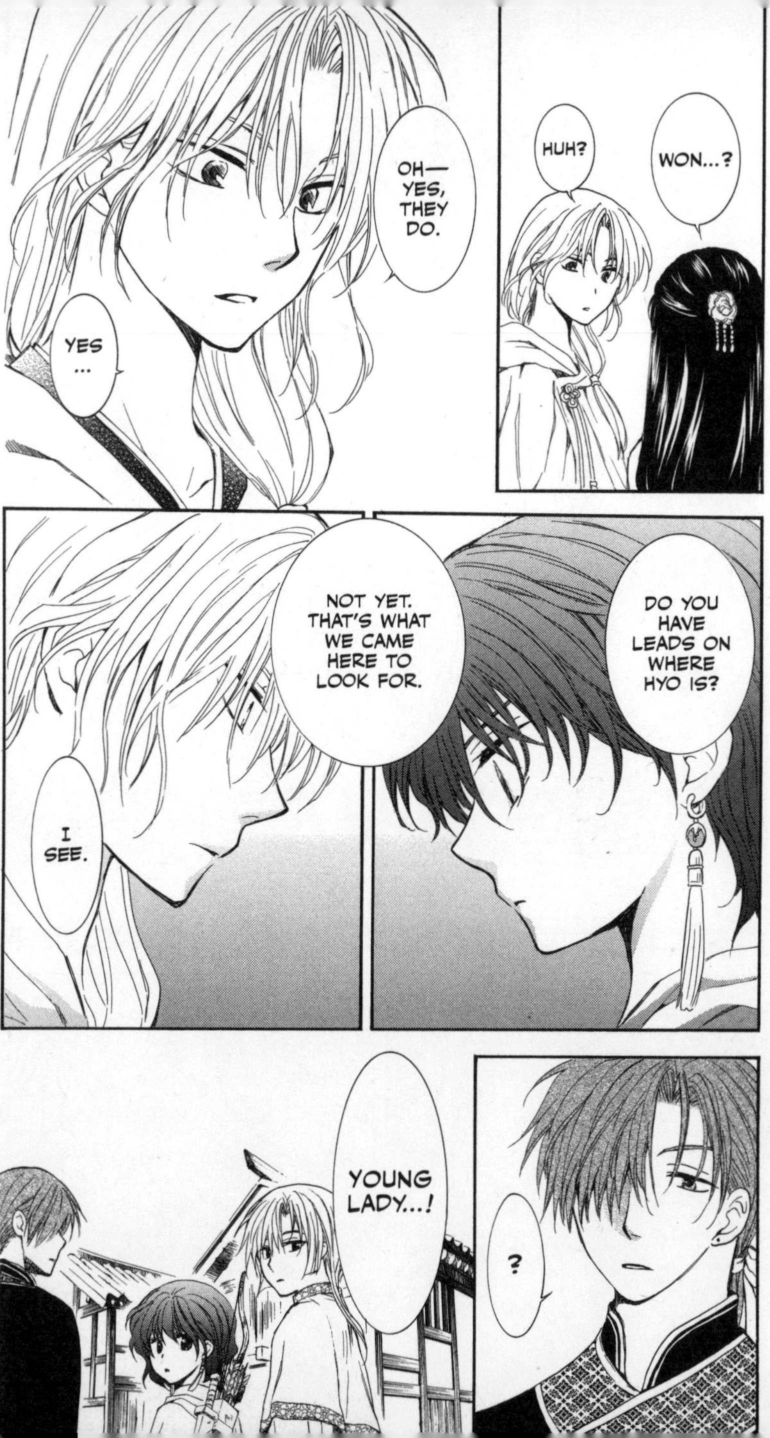
WON...?
HUH?
OH— YES, THEY DO.
YES ...
DO YOU HAVE LEADS ON WHERE HYO IS?
NOT YET. THAT'S WHAT WE CAME HERE TO LOOK FOR.
I SEE.
?
YOUNG LADY...!

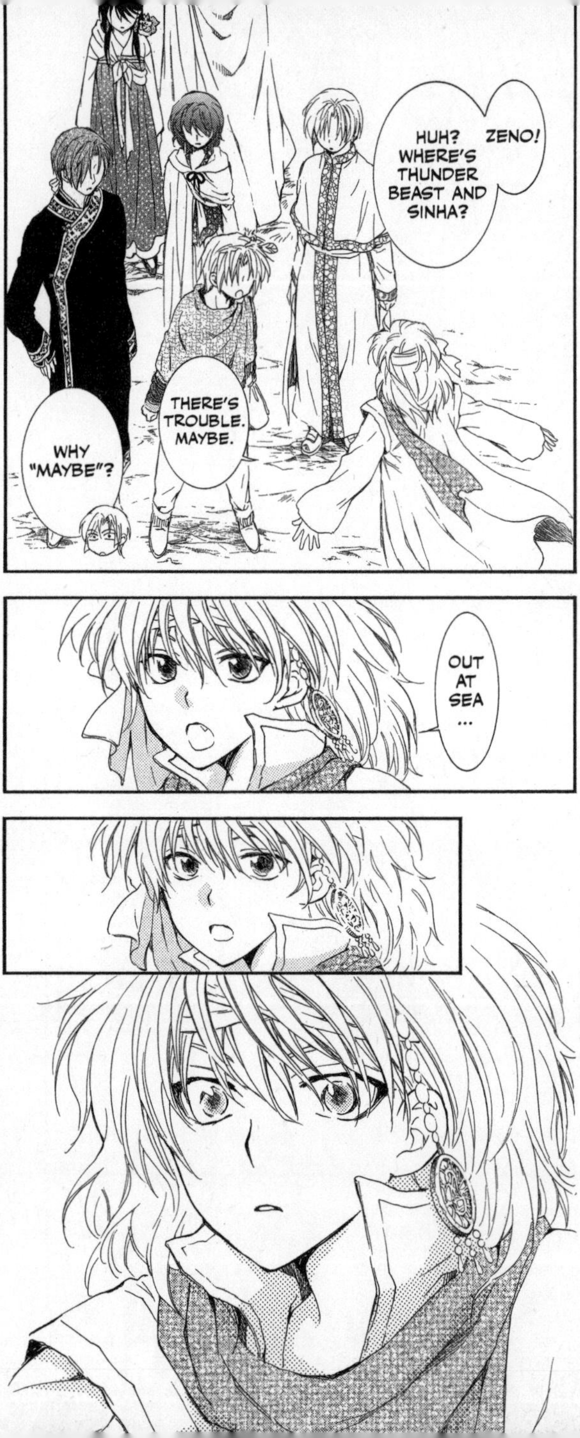
ZENO!
HUH? WHERE'S THUNDER BEAST AND SINHA?
THERE'S TROUBLE. MAYBE.
WHY "MAYBE"?
OUT AT SEA ...

For info on the anime, check out the official website and Twitter account, which are up now. (You can access them from *Hana to Yume*'s *Yona of the Dawn* page.) I also plan to release info on the anime and CDs on my personal blog and Twitter account (which I just started) as well.

I'm sorry there aren't many new stories in the collected volumes. I have a set number of pages, so I don't have much space. I can't often do things like in volumes 12 and 13. Instead, I've been doing some color artwork and artwork for gift items. So if you read *Hana to Yume*, please check them out!

I'm doing my best. The Water Tribe arc ends in the next volume.

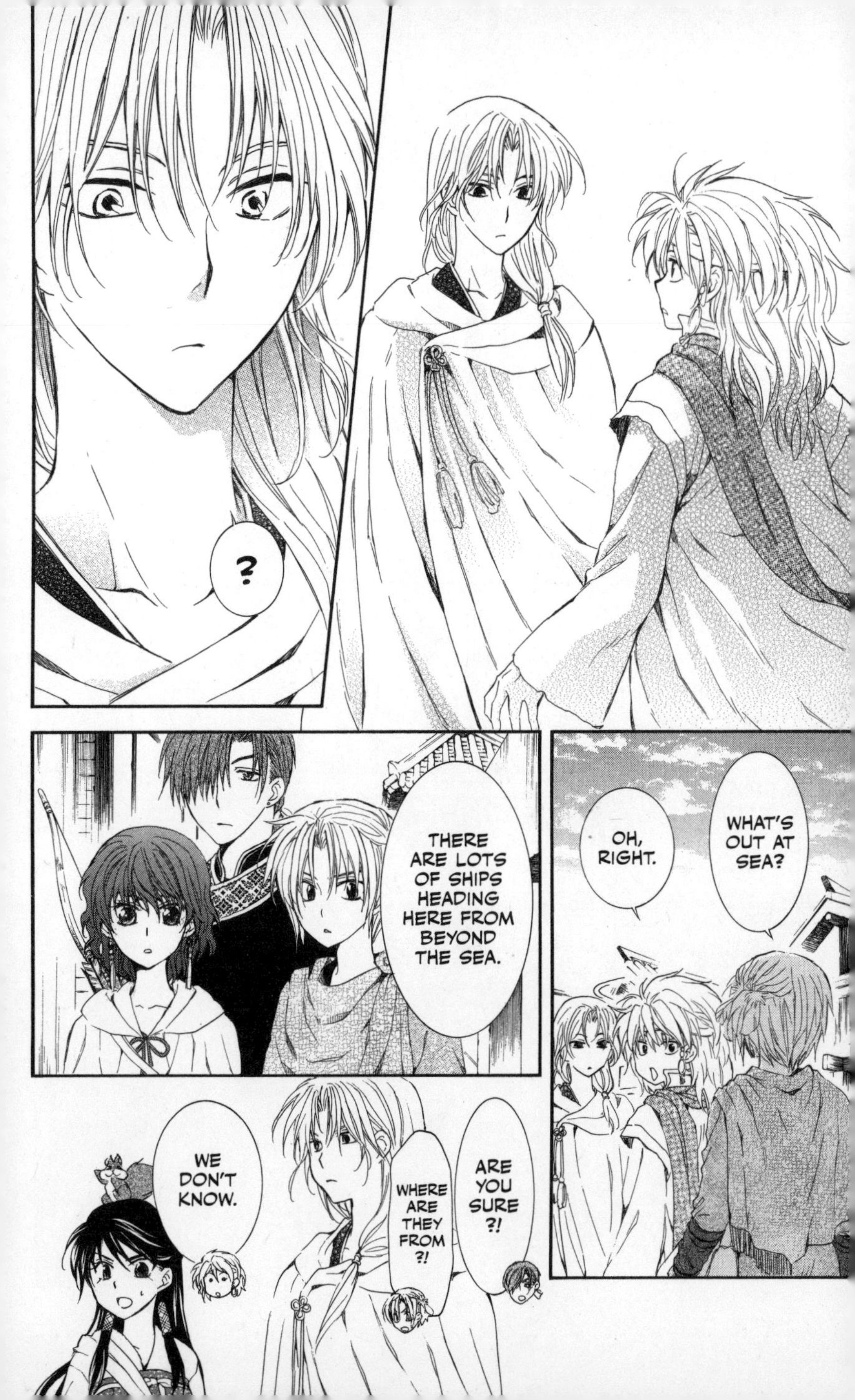
?
WHAT'S OUT AT SEA?
OH, RIGHT.
THERE ARE LOTS OF SHIPS HEADING HERE FROM BEYOND THE SEA.
ARE YOU SURE?!
WHERE ARE THEY FROM?!
WE DON'T KNOW.

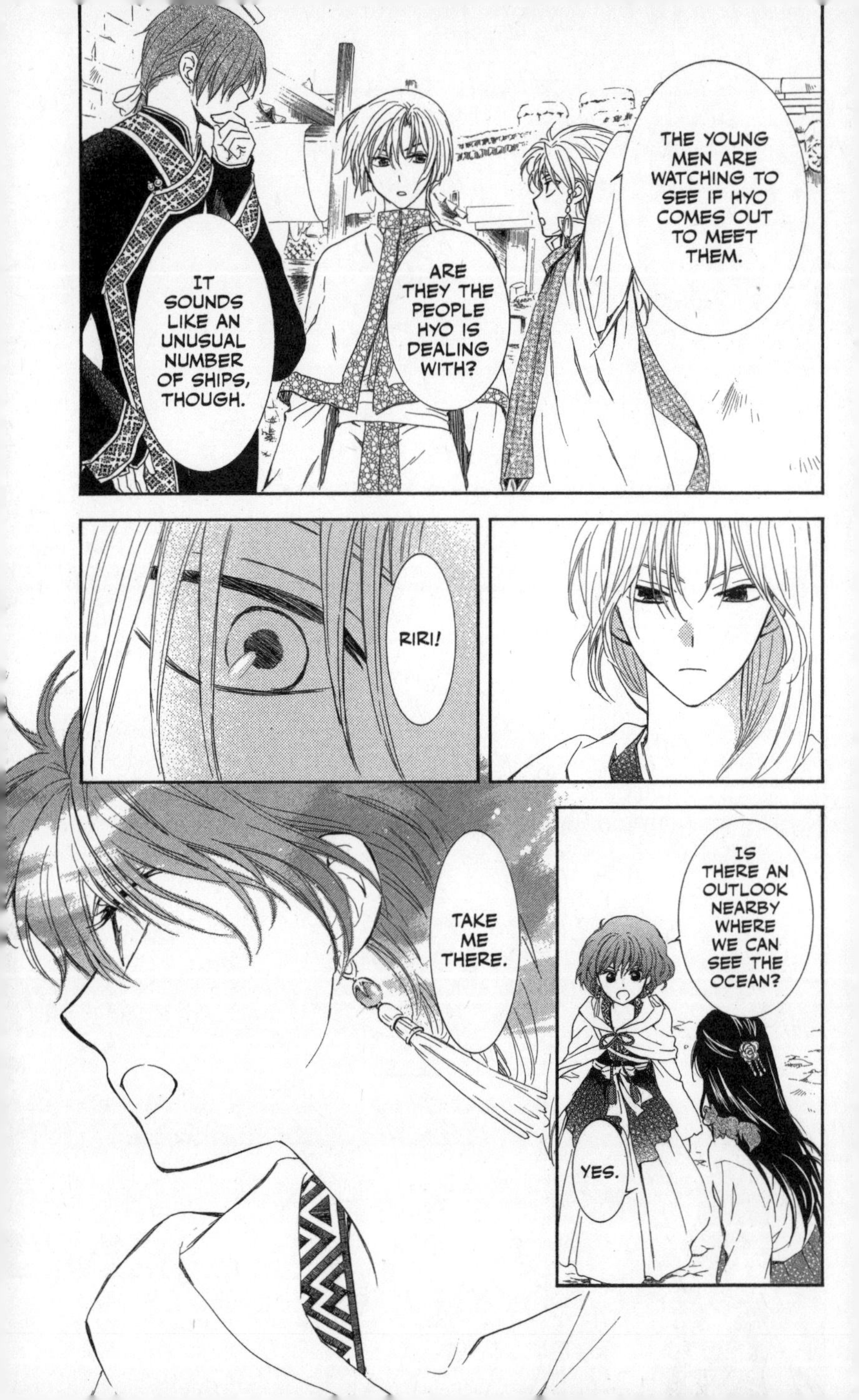
THE YOUNG MEN ARE WATCHING TO SEE IF HYO COMES OUT TO MEET THEM.
ARE THEY THE PEOPLE HYO IS DEALING WITH?
IT SOUNDS LIKE AN UNUSUAL NUMBER OF SHIPS, THOUGH.
RIRI!
IS THERE AN OUTLOOK NEARBY WHERE WE CAN SEE THE OCEAN?
YES.
TAKE ME THERE.

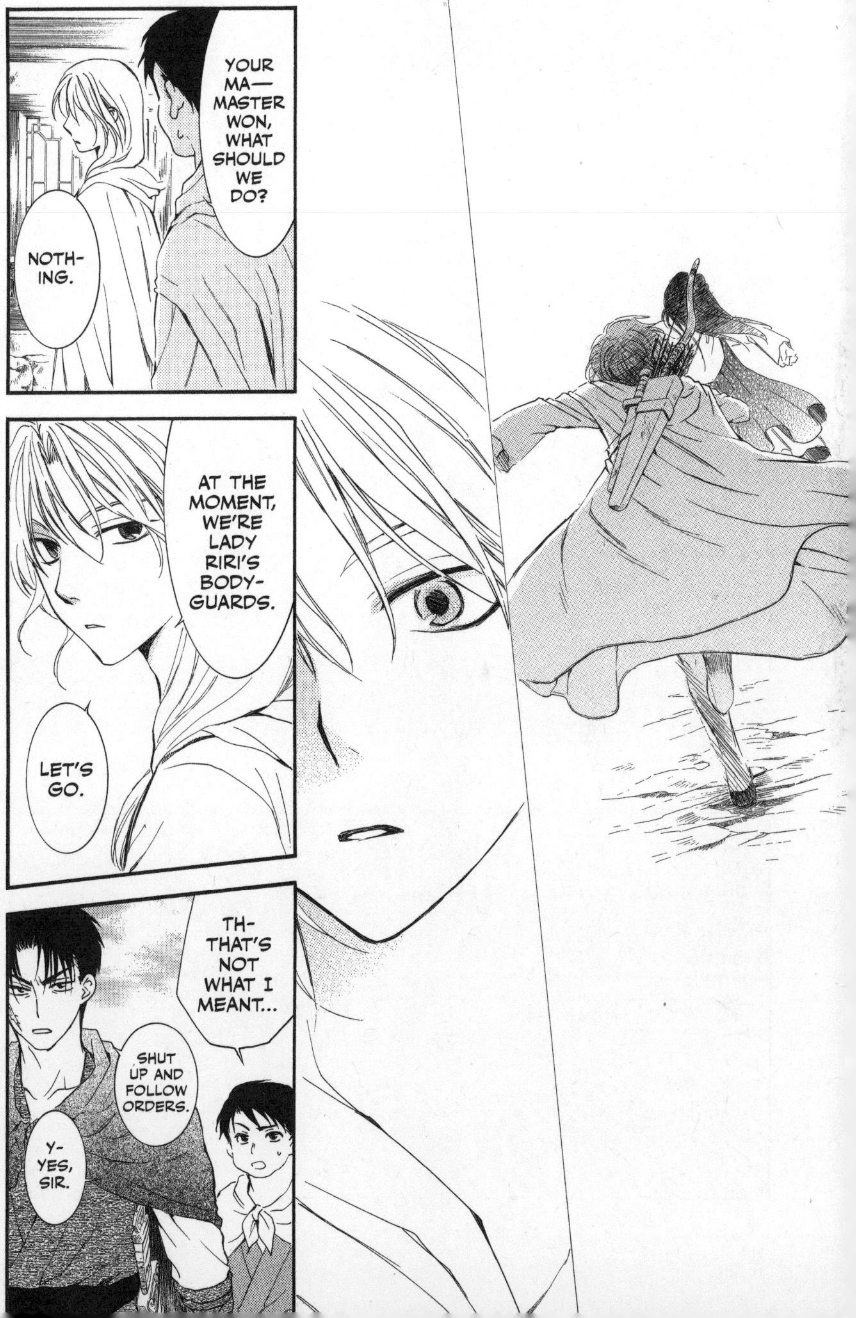
YOUR MA— MASTER WON, WHAT SHOULD WE DO?
NOTHING.
AT THE MOMENT, WE'RE LADY RIRI'S BODYGUARDS.
LET'S GO.
TH-THAT'S NOT WHAT I MEANT...
SHUT UP AND FOLLOW ORDERS.
Y-YES, SIR.

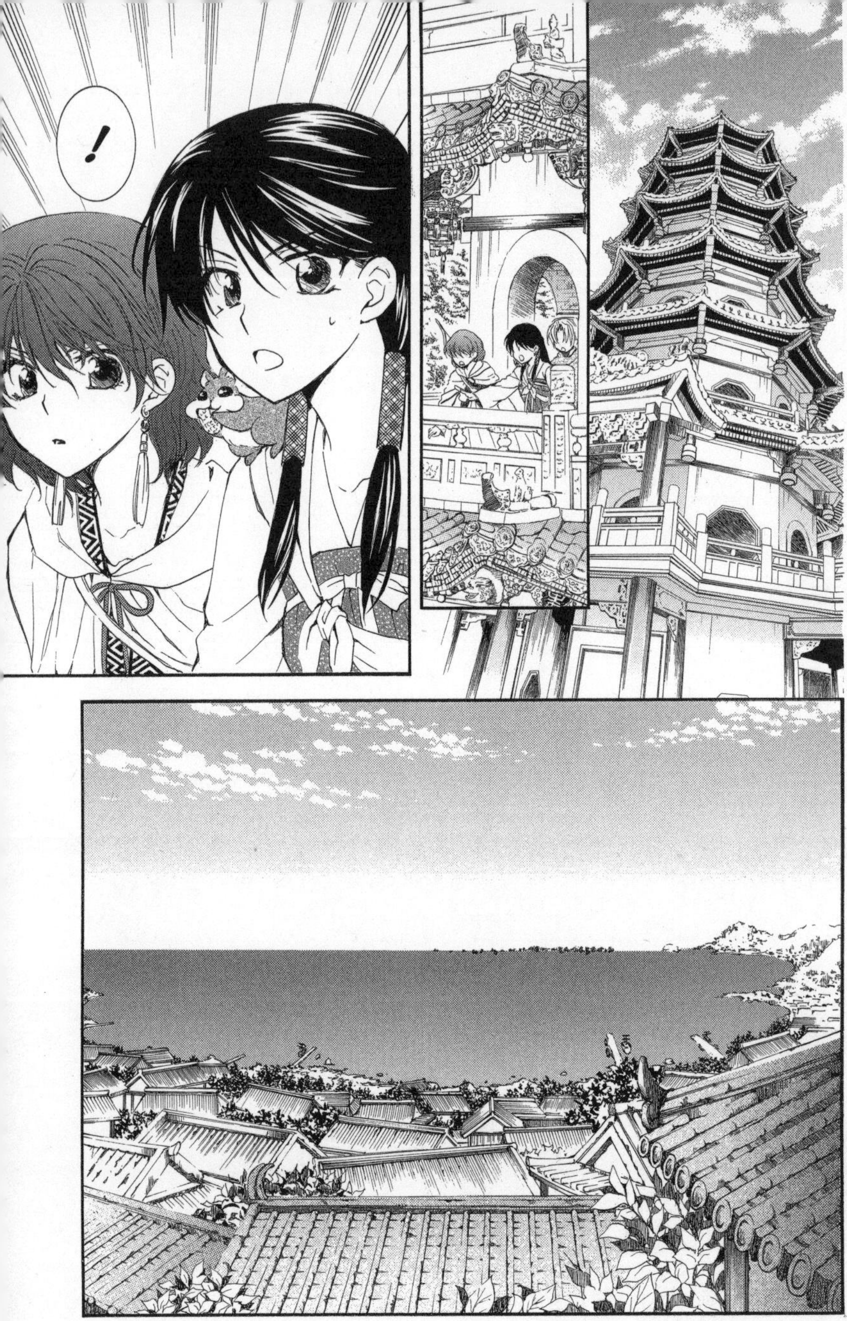
!

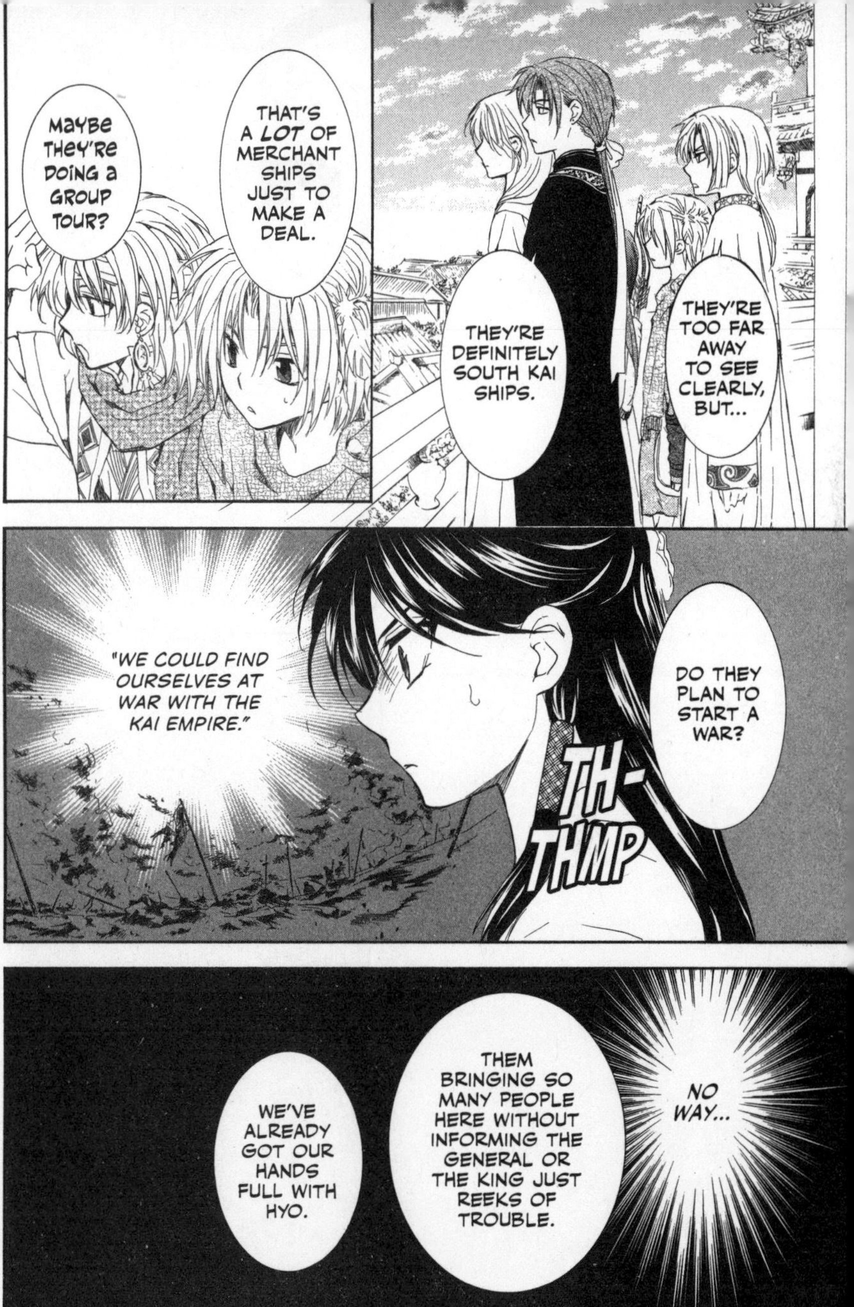
THEY'RE TOO FAR AWAY TO SEE CLEARLY, BUT...
THEY'RE DEFINITELY SOUTH KAI SHIPS.
THAT'S A *LOT* OF MERCHANT SHIPS JUST TO MAKE A DEAL.
MAYBE THEY'RE DOING A GROUP TOUR?
DO THEY PLAN TO START A WAR?
TH-THMP
"WE COULD FIND OURSELVES AT WAR WITH THE KAI EMPIRE."
NO WAY...
THEM BRINGING SO MANY PEOPLE HERE WITHOUT INFORMING THE GENERAL OR THE KING JUST REEKS OF TROUBLE.
WE'VE ALREADY GOT OUR HANDS FULL WITH HYO.

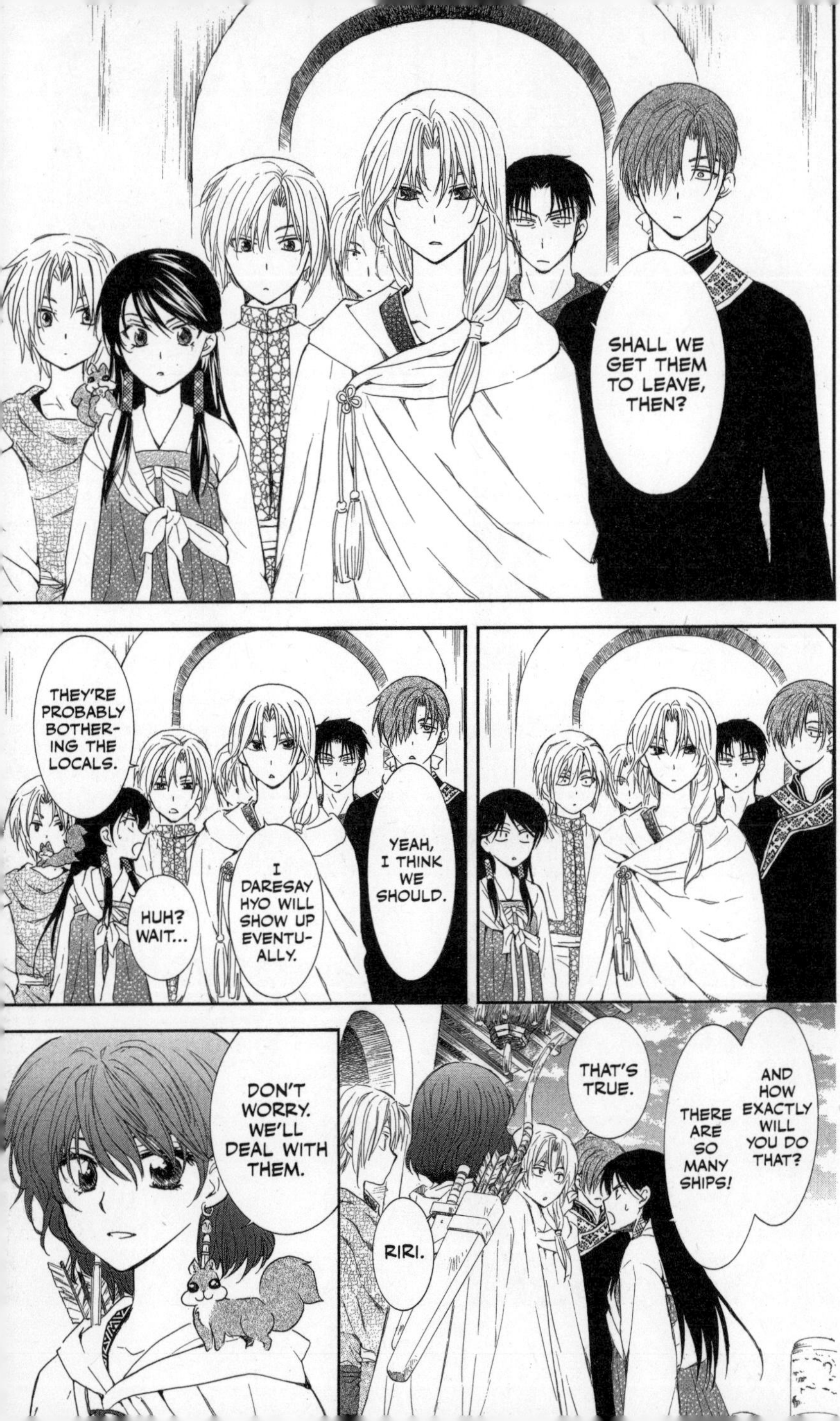
SHALL WE GET THEM TO LEAVE, THEN?
YEAH, I THINK WE SHOULD.
I DARESAY HYO WILL SHOW UP EVENTU-ALLY.
THEY'RE PROBABLY BOTHER-ING THE LOCALS.
HUH? WAIT...
AND HOW EXACTLY WILL YOU DO THAT?
THERE ARE SO MANY SHIPS!
THAT'S TRUE.
RIRI.
DON'T WORRY. WE'LL DEAL WITH THEM.

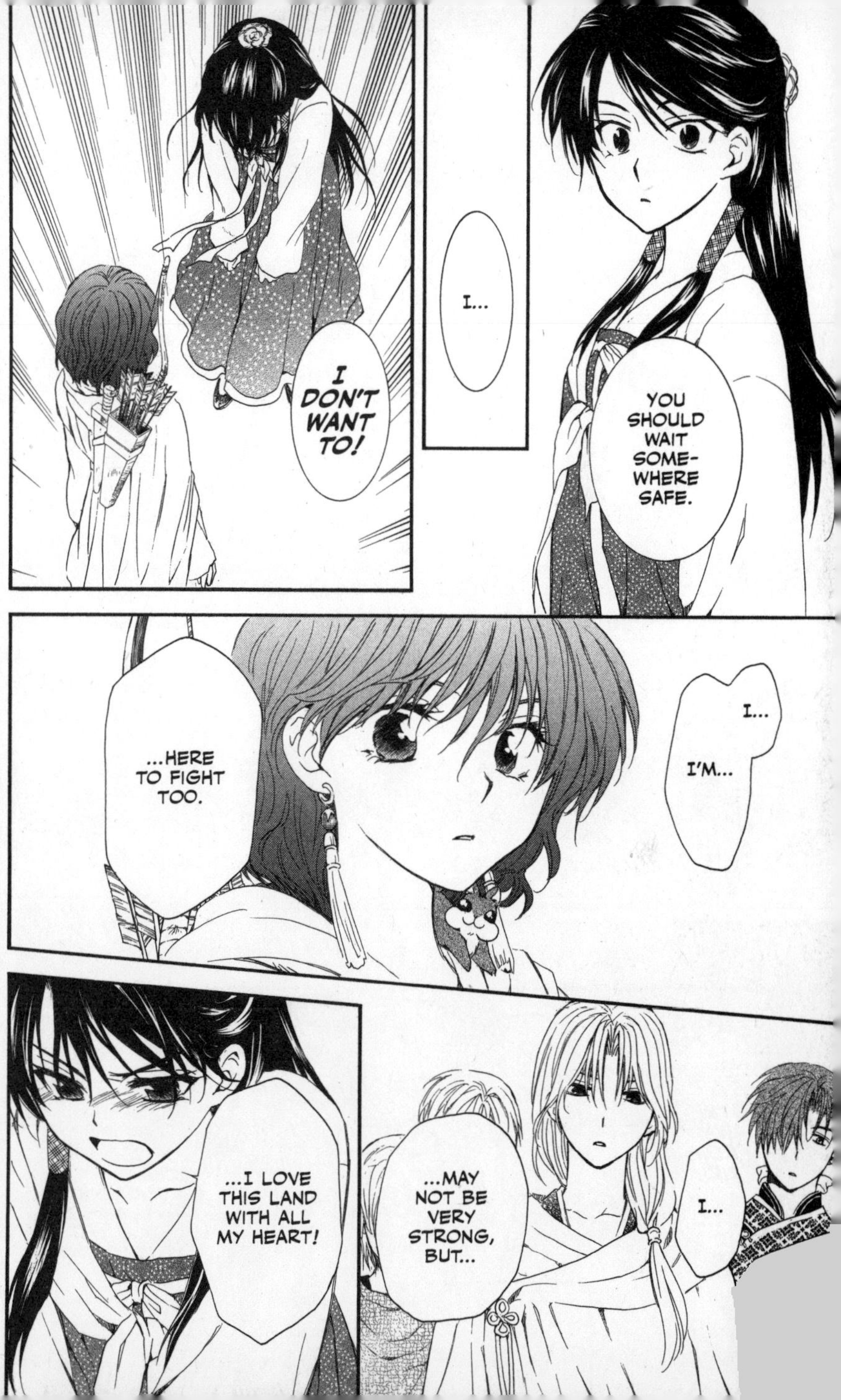
YOU SHOULD WAIT SOME-WHERE SAFE.
I...
I DON'T WANT TO!
I...
I'M...
...HERE TO FIGHT TOO.
I...
...MAY NOT BE VERY STRONG, BUT...
...I LOVE THIS LAND WITH ALL MY HEART!

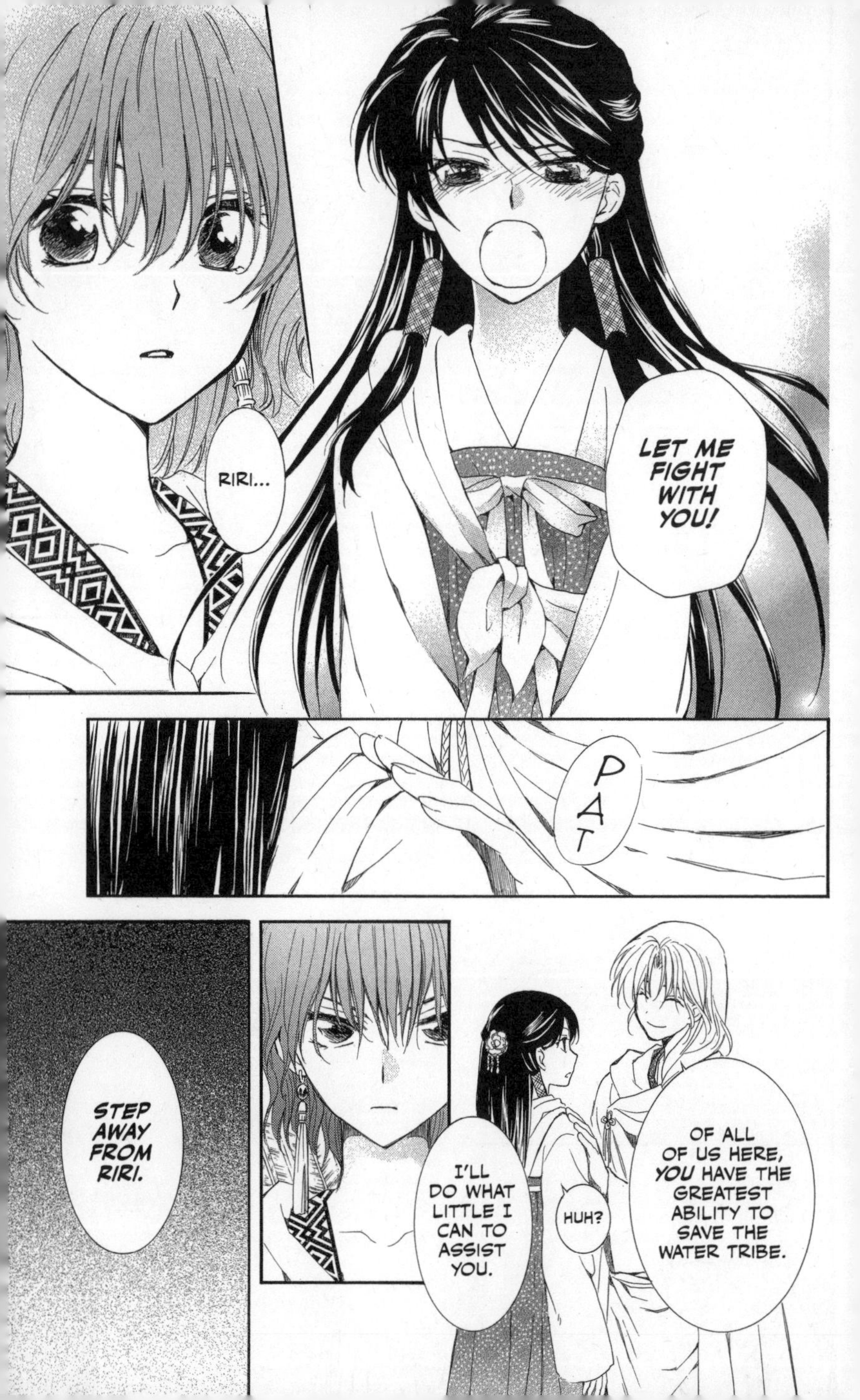
LET ME FIGHT WITH YOU!
RIRI...
PAT
OF ALL OF US HERE, *YOU* HAVE THE GREATEST ABILITY TO SAVE THE WATER TRIBE.
HUH?
I'LL DO WHAT LITTLE I CAN TO ASSIST YOU.
STEP AWAY FROM RIRI.

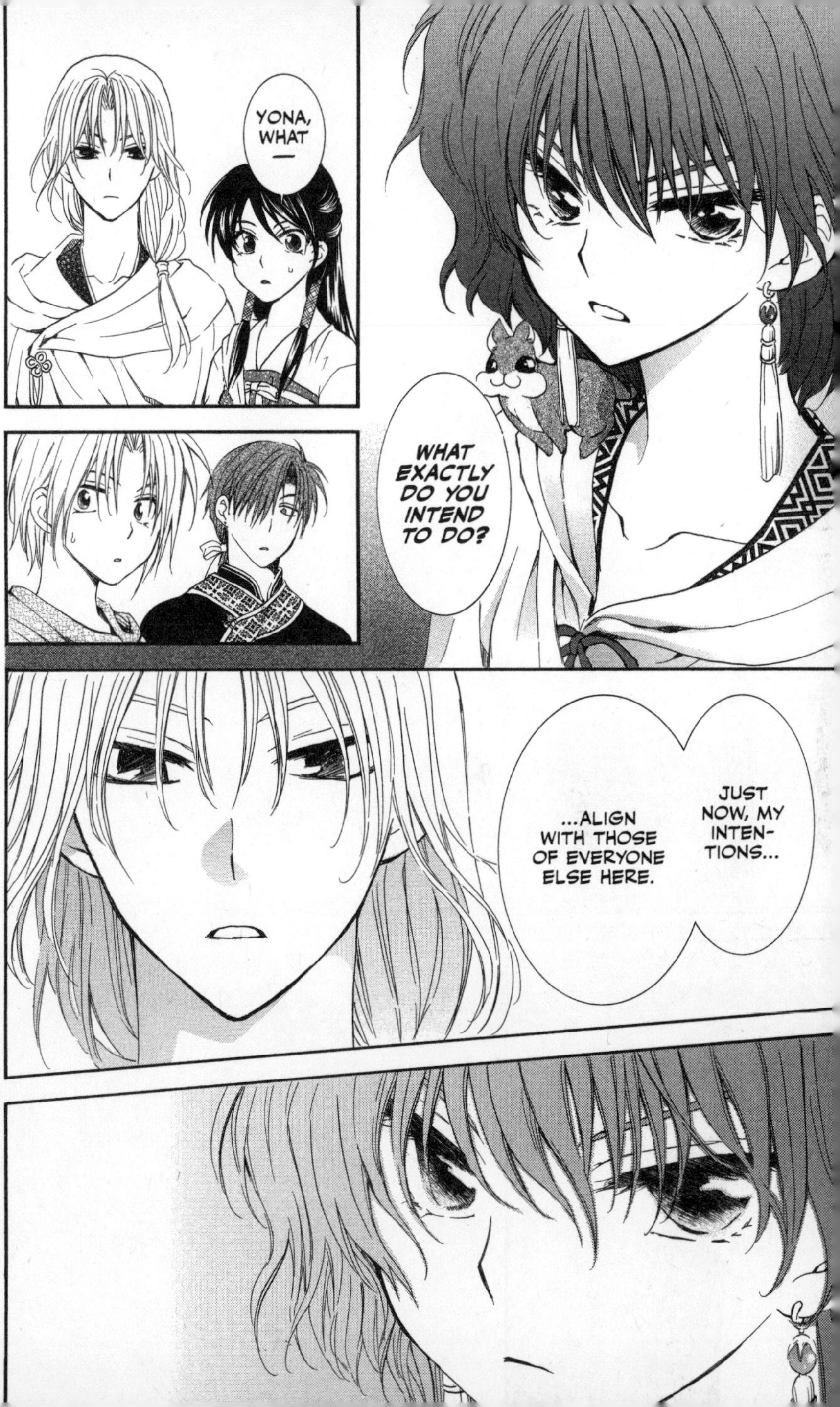
WHAT EXACTLY DO YOU INTEND TO DO?
YONA, WHAT —
JUST NOW, MY INTEN-TIONS...
...ALIGN WITH THOSE OF EVERYONE ELSE HERE.

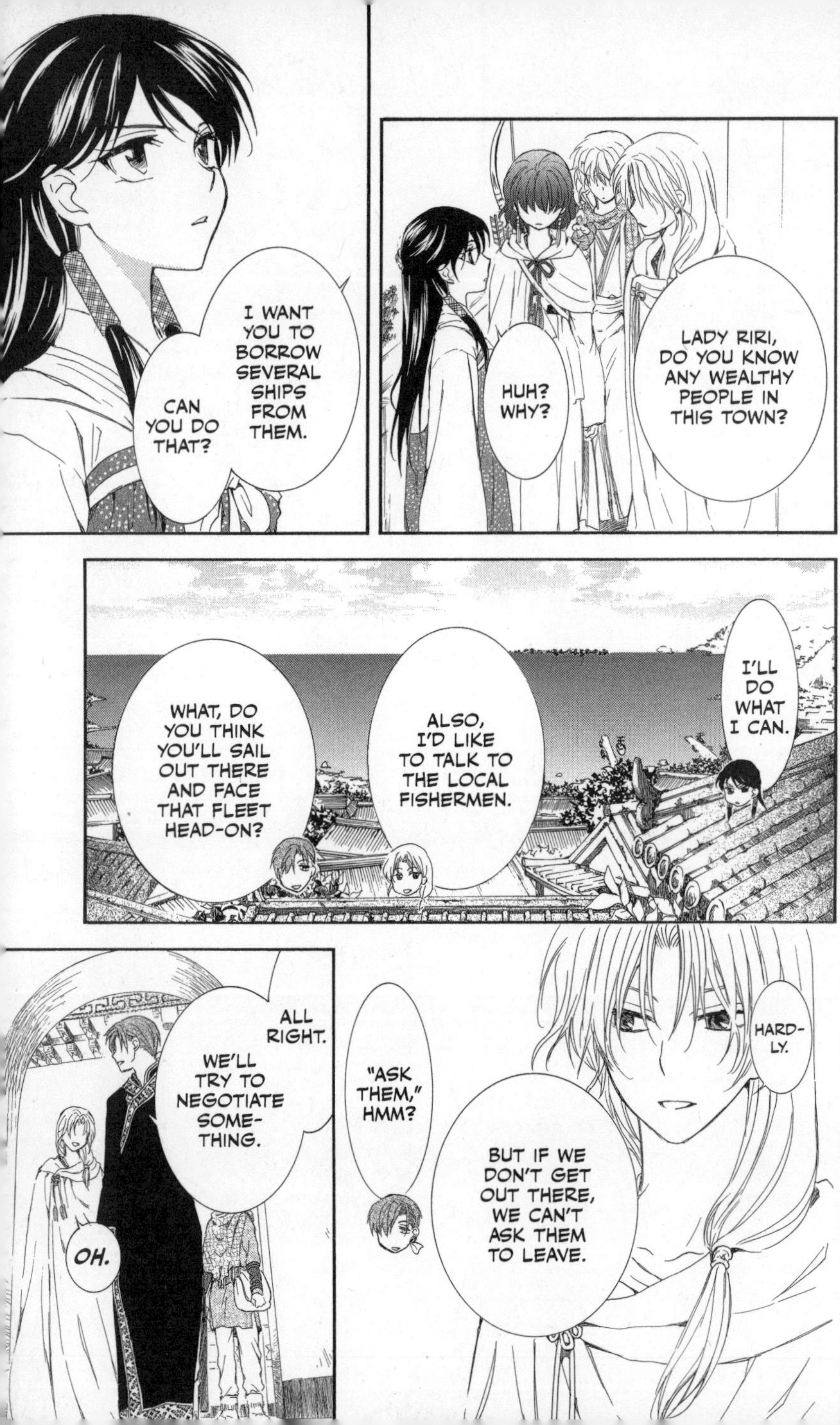
LADY RIRI, DO YOU KNOW ANY WEALTHY PEOPLE IN THIS TOWN?
HUH? WHY?
I WANT YOU TO BORROW SEVERAL SHIPS FROM THEM.
CAN YOU DO THAT?
I'LL DO WHAT I CAN.
ALSO, I'D LIKE TO TALK TO THE LOCAL FISHERMEN.
WHAT, DO YOU THINK YOU'LL SAIL OUT THERE AND FACE THAT FLEET HEAD-ON?
HARD-LY.
BUT IF WE DON'T GET OUT THERE, WE CAN'T ASK THEM TO LEAVE.
"ASK THEM," HMM?
ALL RIGHT.
WE'LL TRY TO NEGOTIATE SOME-THING.
OH.

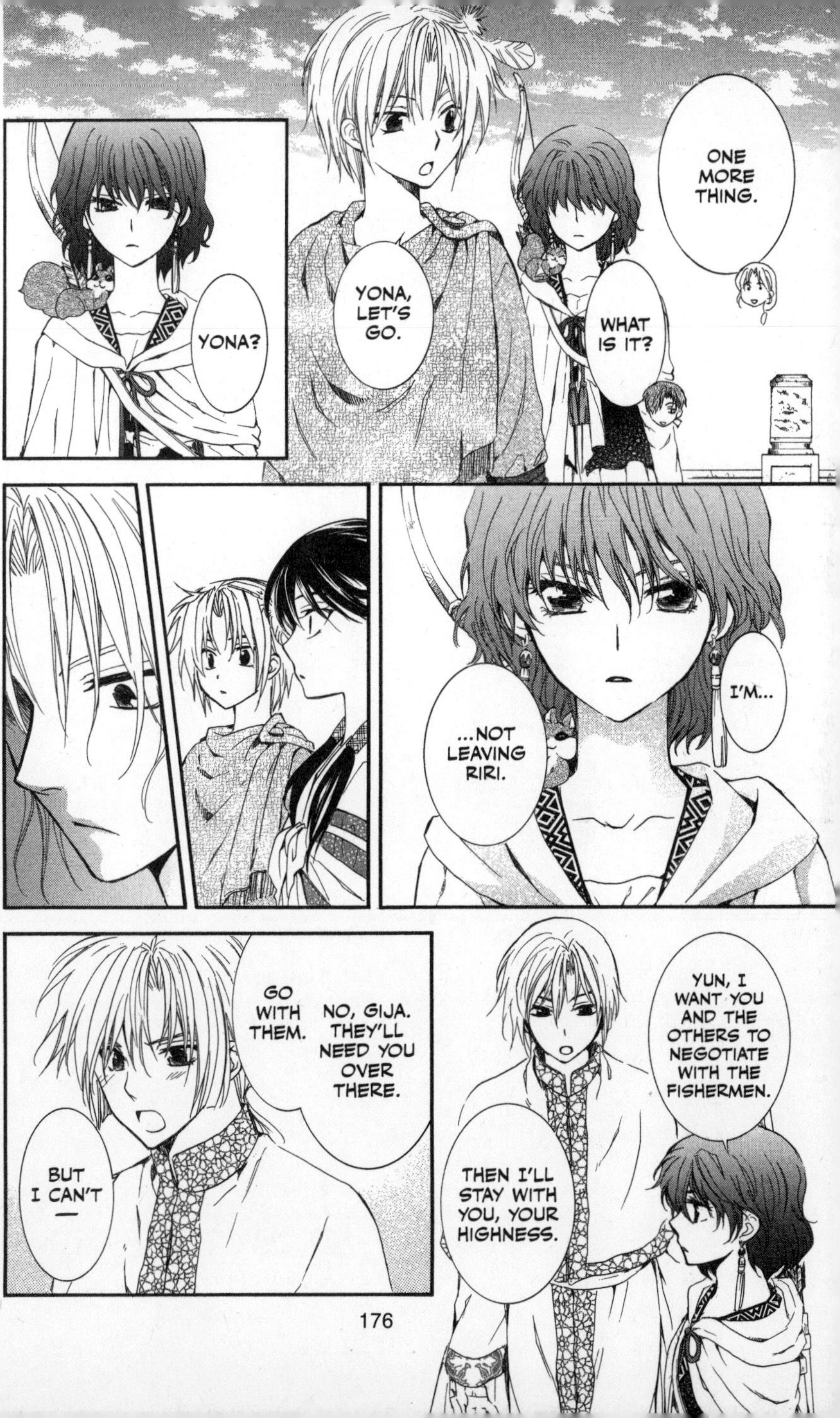
ONE MORE THING.
WHAT IS IT?
YONA, LET'S GO.
YONA?
I'M...
...NOT LEAVING RIRI.
YUN, I WANT YOU AND THE OTHERS TO NEGOTIATE WITH THE FISHERMEN.
THEN I'LL STAY WITH YOU, YOUR HIGHNESS.
NO, GIJA. THEY'LL NEED YOU OVER THERE.
GO WITH THEM.
BUT I CAN'T —

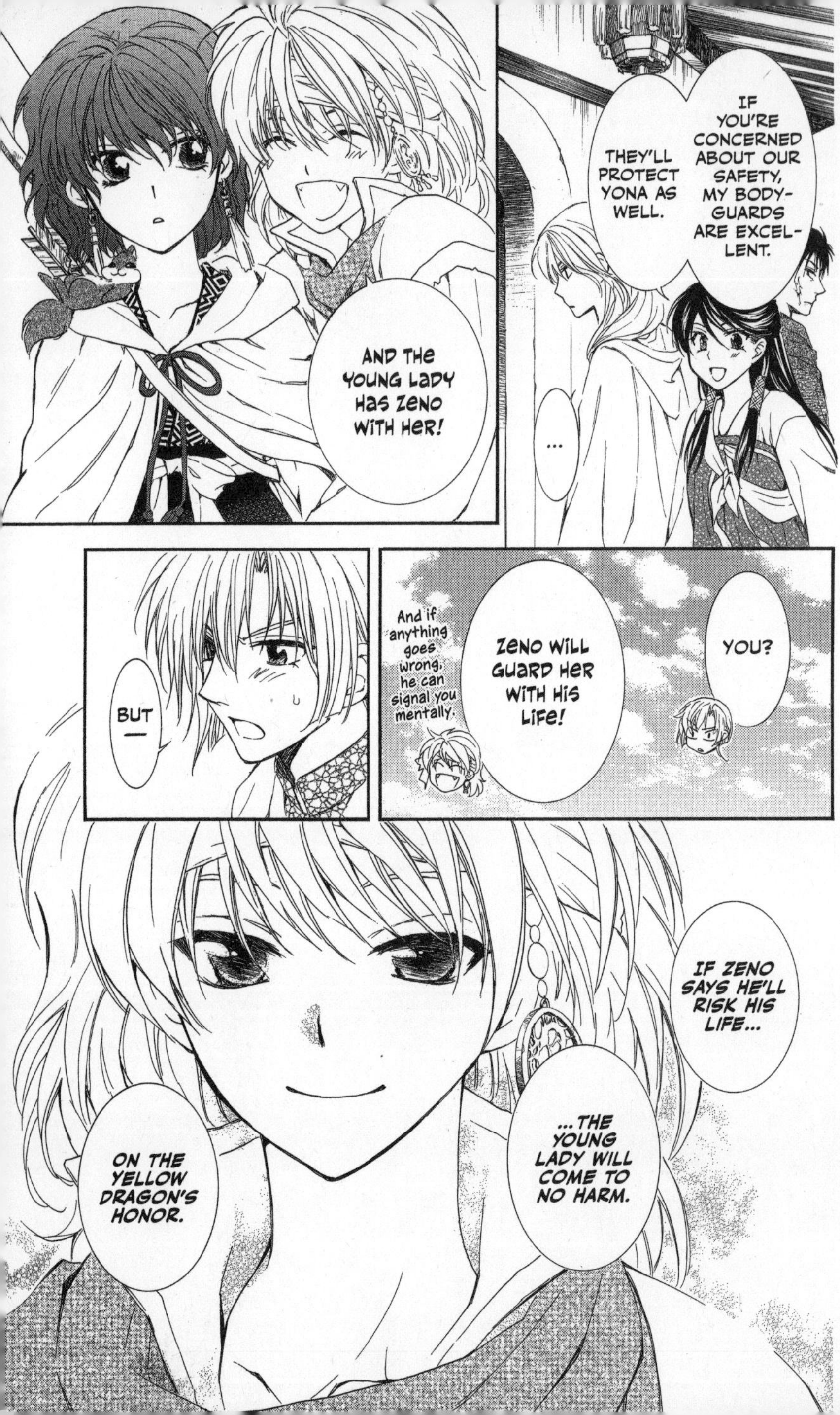
IF YOU'RE CONCERNED ABOUT OUR SAFETY, MY BODY-GUARDS ARE EXCEL-LENT.
THEY'LL PROTECT YONA AS WELL.
...
AND THE YOUNG LADY HAS ZENO WITH HER!
YOU?
ZENO WILL GUARD HER WITH HIS LIFE!
And if anything goes wrong, he can signal you mentally.
BUT —
IF ZENO SAYS HE'LL RISK HIS LIFE...
...THE YOUNG LADY WILL COME TO NO HARM.
ON THE YELLOW DRAGON'S HONOR.

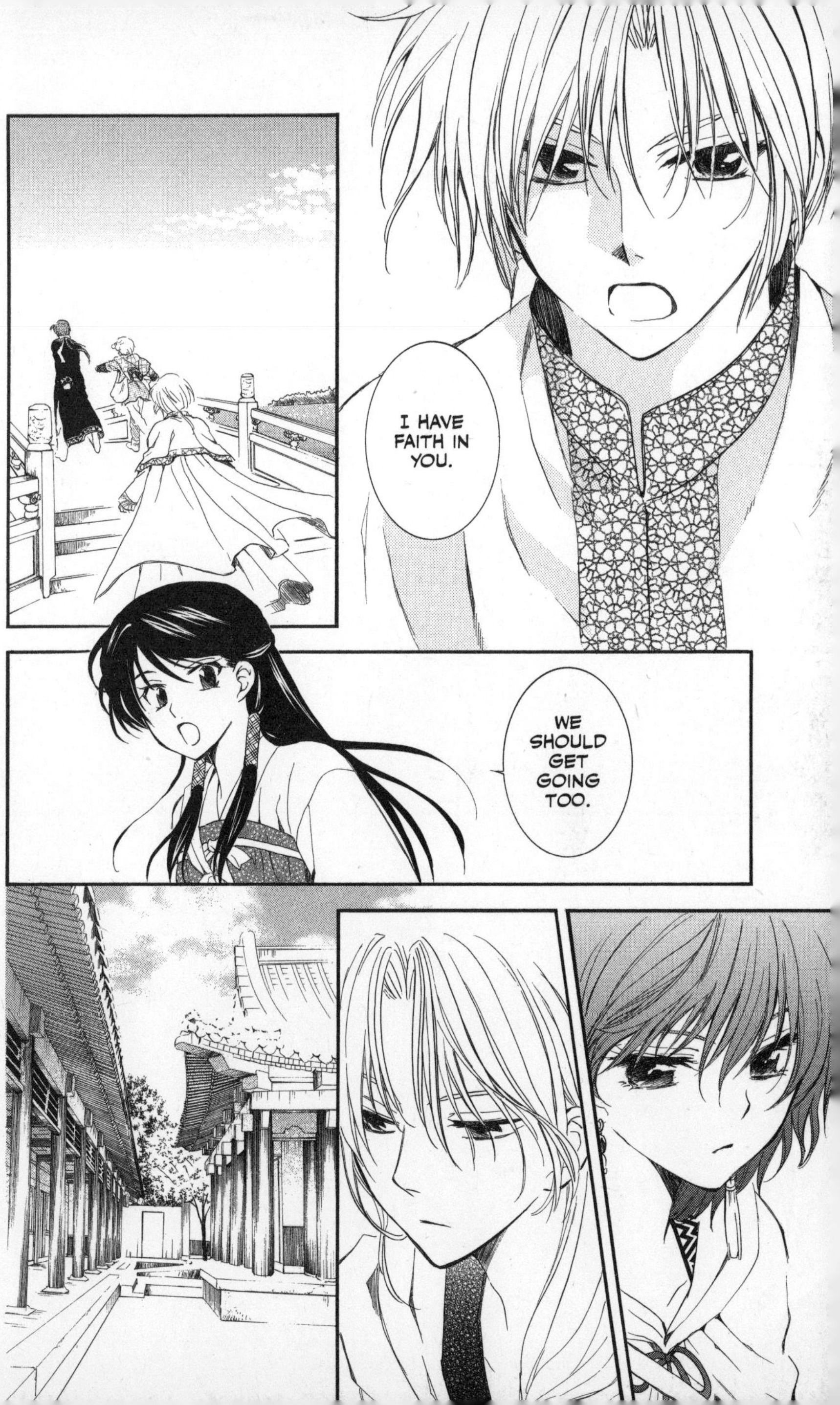
I HAVE FAITH IN YOU.
WE SHOULD GET GOING TOO.

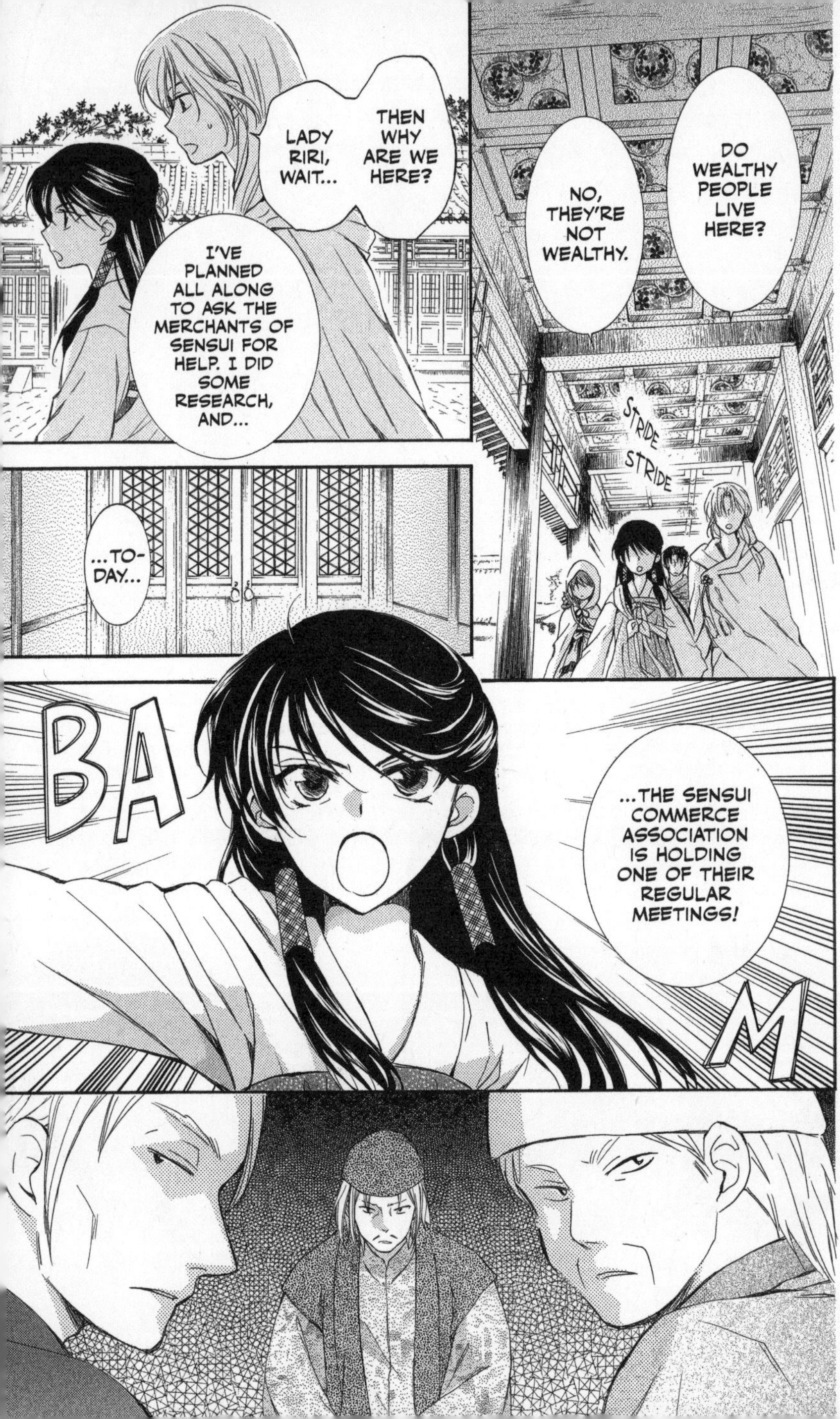
DO WEALTHY PEOPLE LIVE HERE?
NO, THEY'RE NOT WEALTHY.
STRIDE
STRIDE
THEN WHY ARE WE HERE?
LADY RIRI, WAIT...
I'VE PLANNED ALL ALONG TO ASK THE MERCHANTS OF SENSUI FOR HELP. I DID SOME RESEARCH, AND...
...TO-DAY...
...THE SENSUI COMMERCE ASSOCIATION IS HOLDING ONE OF THEIR REGULAR MEETINGS!
BA
M

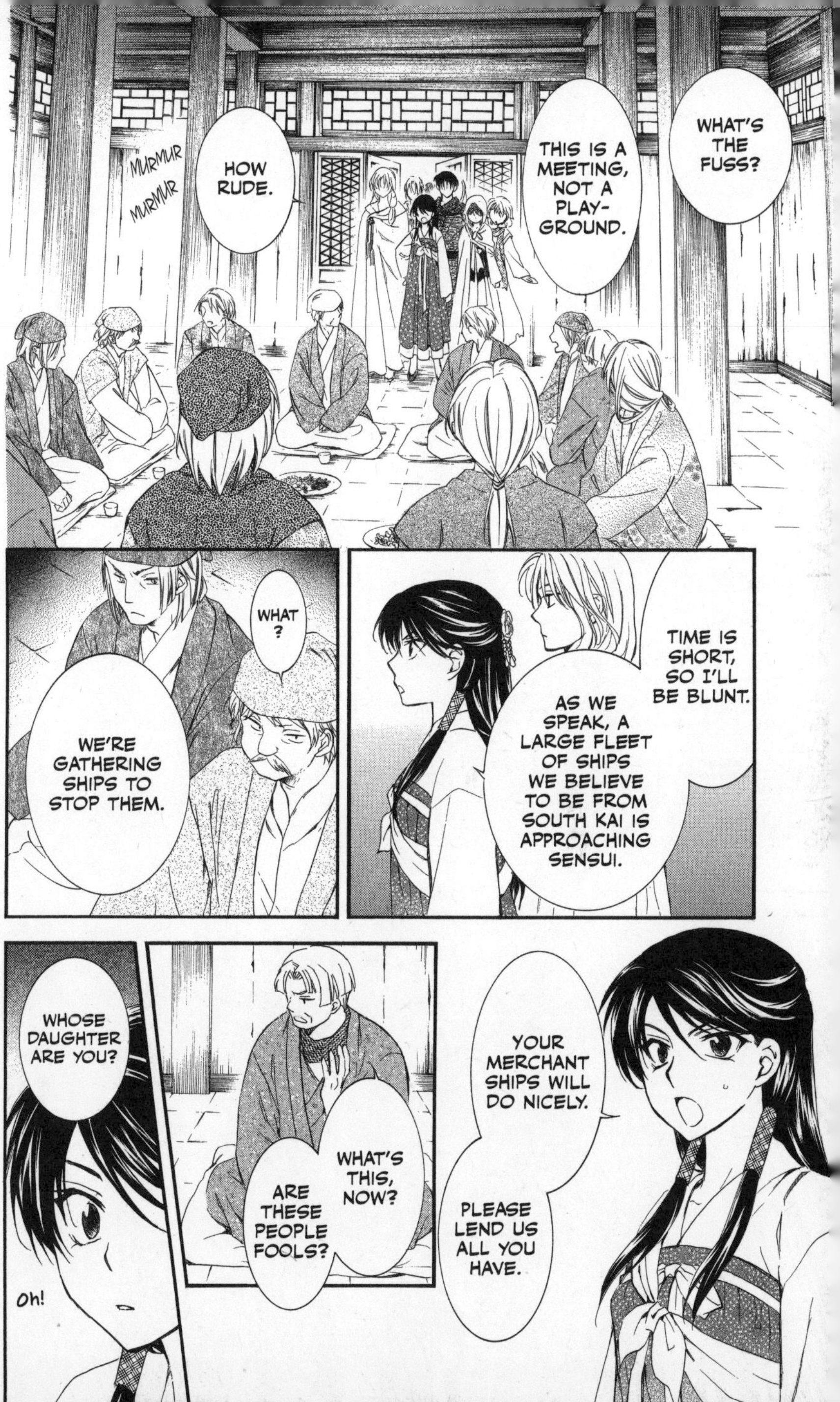
WHAT'S THE FUSS?
THIS IS A MEETING, NOT A PLAYGROUND.
HOW RUDE.
MURMUR
MURMUR
TIME IS SHORT, SO I'LL BE BLUNT.
AS WE SPEAK, A LARGE FLEET OF SHIPS WE BELIEVE TO BE FROM SOUTH KAI IS APPROACHING SENSUI.
WHAT?
WE'RE GATHERING SHIPS TO STOP THEM.
YOUR MERCHANT SHIPS WILL DO NICELY.
PLEASE LEND US ALL YOU HAVE.
WHAT'S THIS, NOW?
ARE THESE PEOPLE FOOLS?
WHOSE DAUGHTER ARE YOU?
Oh!

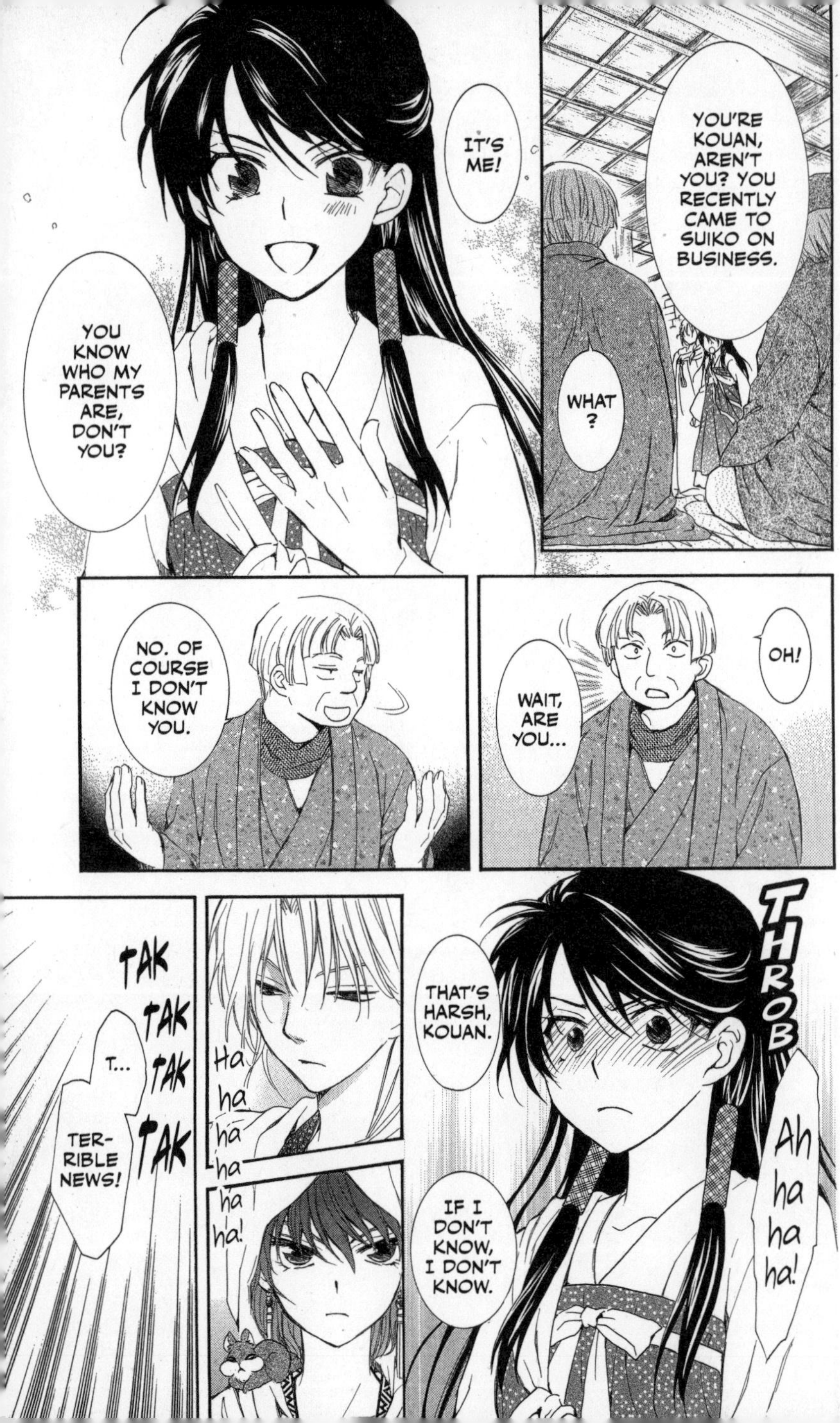
YOU'RE KOUAN, AREN'T YOU? YOU RECENTLY CAME TO SUIKO ON BUSINESS.
WHAT?
IT'S ME!
YOU KNOW WHO MY PARENTS ARE, DON'T YOU?
OH!
WAIT, ARE YOU...
NO. OF COURSE I DON'T KNOW YOU.
THROB
THAT'S HARSH, KOUAN.
Ah ha ha ha!
IF I DON'T KNOW, I DON'T KNOW.
Ha ha ha ha ha ha!
TAK TAK TAK TAK
T...
TER-RIBLE NEWS!

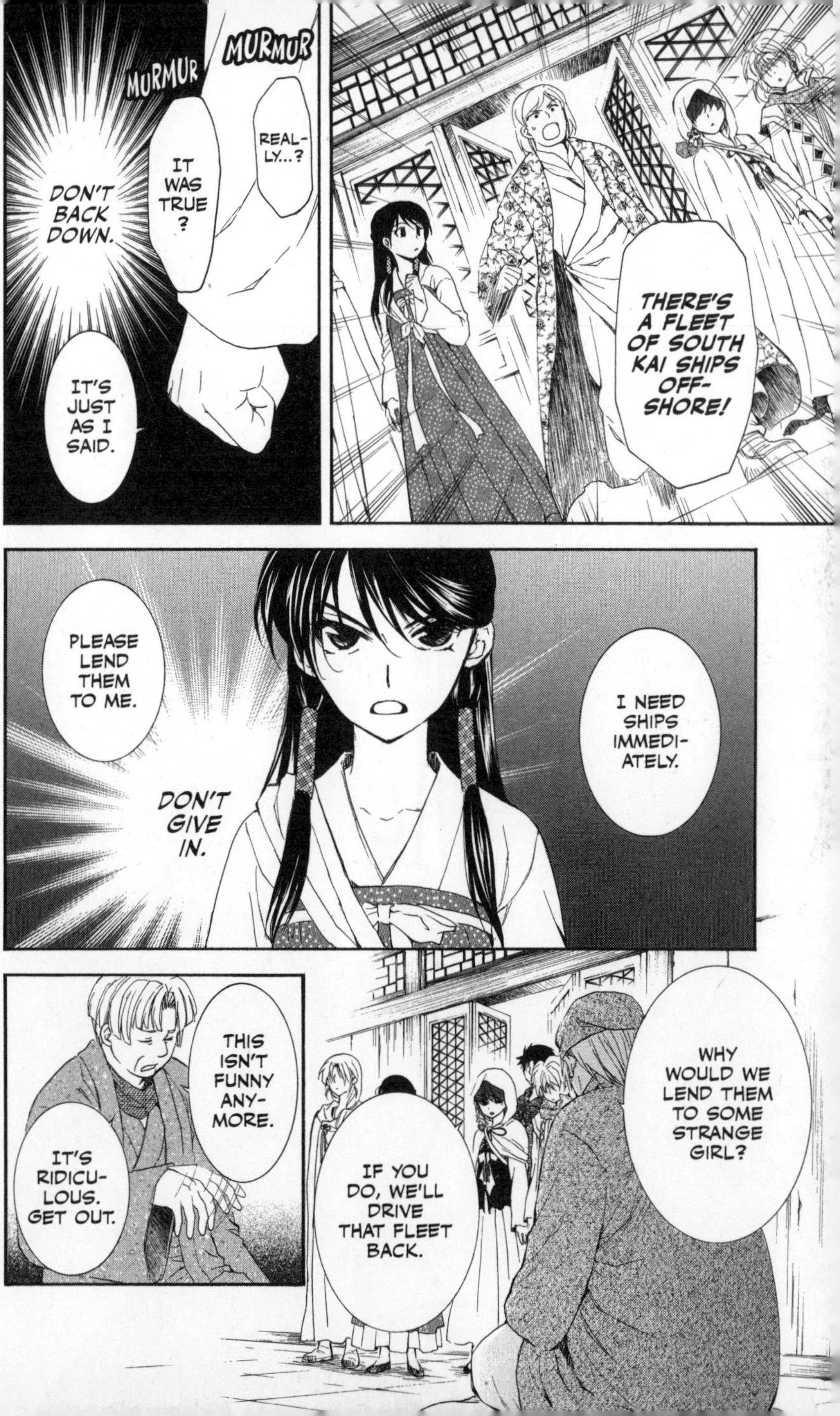
THERE'S A FLEET OF SOUTH KAI SHIPS OFF-SHORE!
MURMUR
MURMUR
REAL-LY...?
IT WAS TRUE?
DON'T BACK DOWN.
IT'S JUST AS I SAID.
I NEED SHIPS IMMEDI-ATELY.
PLEASE LEND THEM TO ME.
DON'T GIVE IN.
WHY WOULD WE LEND THEM TO SOME STRANGE GIRL?
IF YOU DO, WE'LL DRIVE THAT FLEET BACK.
THIS ISN'T FUNNY ANY-MORE.
IT'S RIDICU-LOUS. GET OUT.

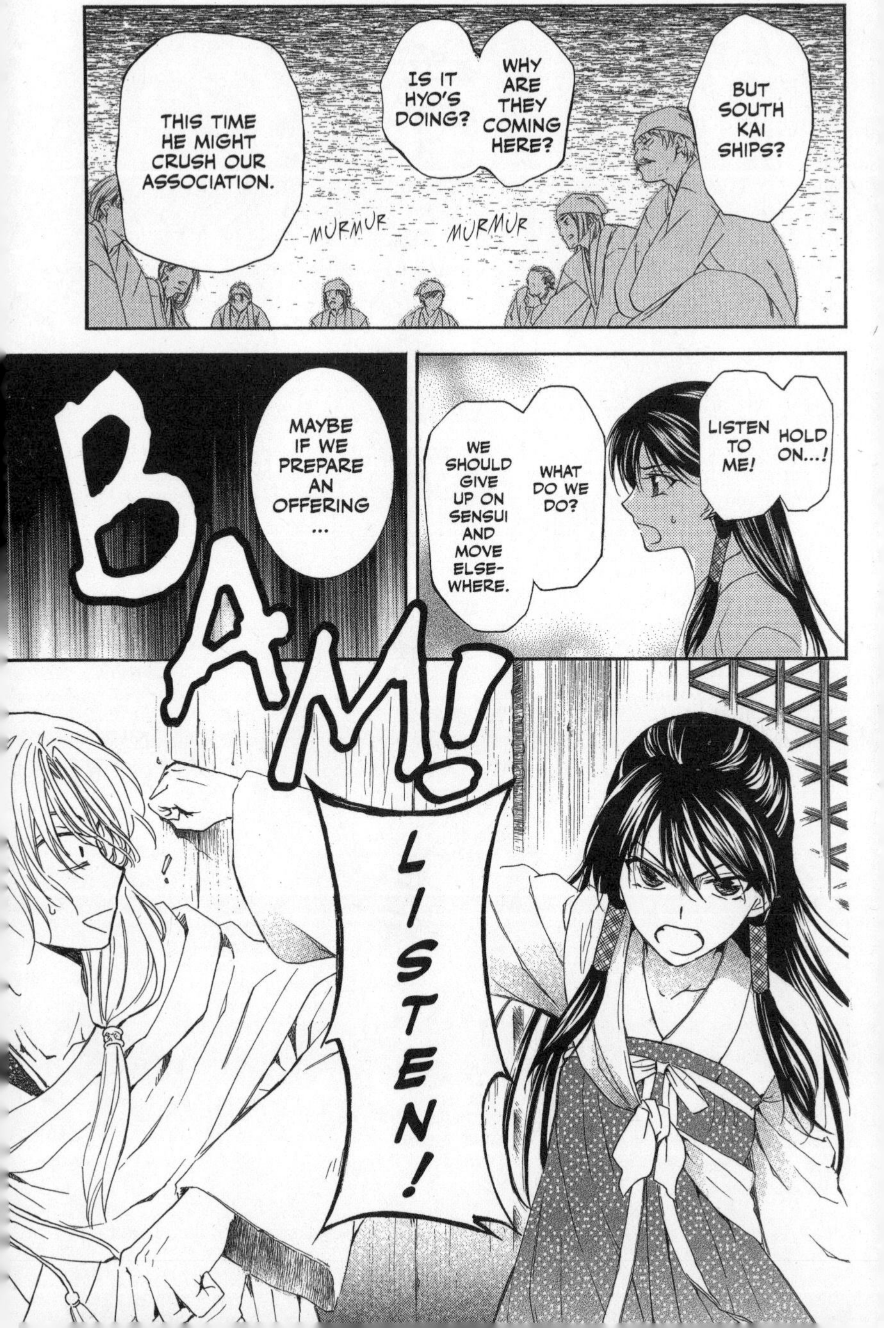
BUT SOUTH KAI SHIPS?
WHY ARE THEY COMING HERE?
IS IT HYO'S DOING?
MURMUR
MURMUR
THIS TIME HE MIGHT CRUSH OUR ASSOCIATION.
HOLD ON...!
LISTEN TO ME!
WHAT DO WE DO?
WE SHOULD GIVE UP ON SENSUI AND MOVE ELSE-WHERE.
MAYBE IF WE PREPARE AN OFFERING ...
BAM!
LISTEN!

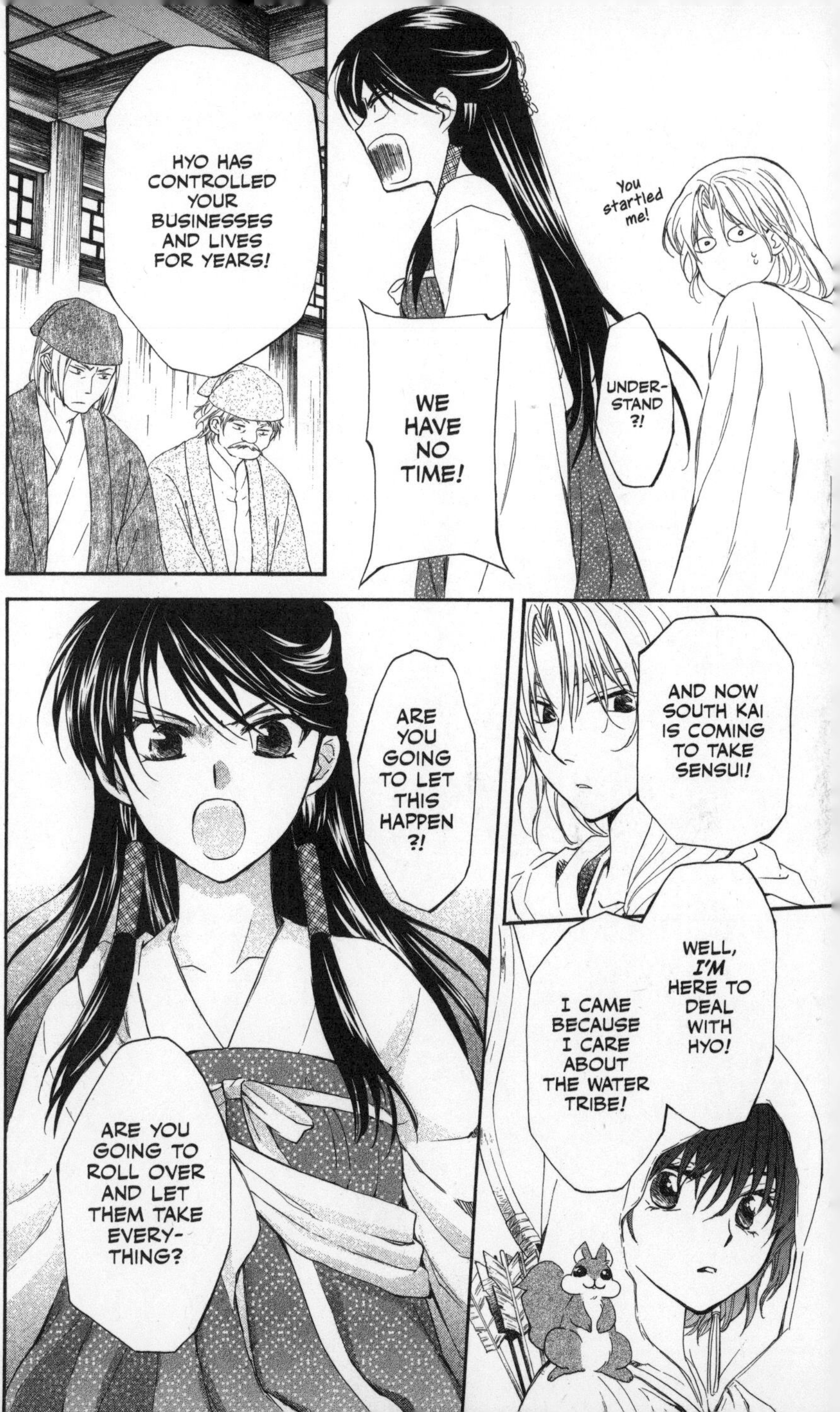
You startled me!
UNDER-STAND?!
WE HAVE NO TIME!
HYO HAS CONTROLLED YOUR BUSINESSES AND LIVES FOR YEARS!
AND NOW SOUTH KAI IS COMING TO TAKE SENSUI!
WELL, *I'M* HERE TO DEAL WITH HYO!
I CAME BECAUSE I CARE ABOUT THE WATER TRIBE!
ARE YOU GOING TO LET THIS HAPPEN?!
ARE YOU GOING TO ROLL OVER AND LET THEM TAKE EVERY-THING?

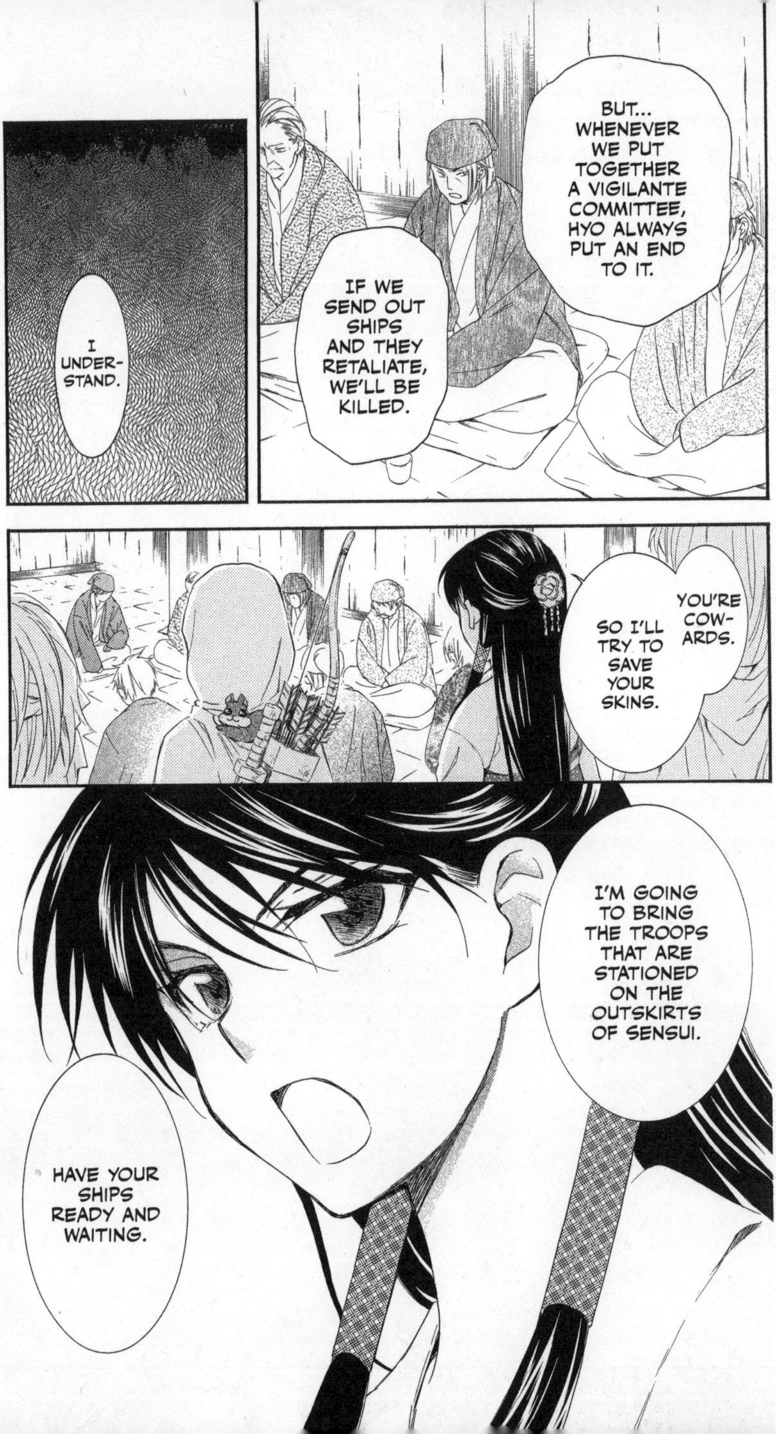
BUT... WHENEVER WE PUT TOGETHER A VIGILANTE COMMITTEE, HYO ALWAYS PUT AN END TO IT.
IF WE SEND OUT SHIPS AND THEY RETALIATE, WE'LL BE KILLED.
I UNDER-STAND.
YOU'RE COW-ARDS.
SO I'LL TRY TO SAVE YOUR SKINS.
I'M GOING TO BRING THE TROOPS THAT ARE STATIONED ON THE OUTSKIRTS OF SENSUI.
HAVE YOUR SHIPS READY AND WAITING.

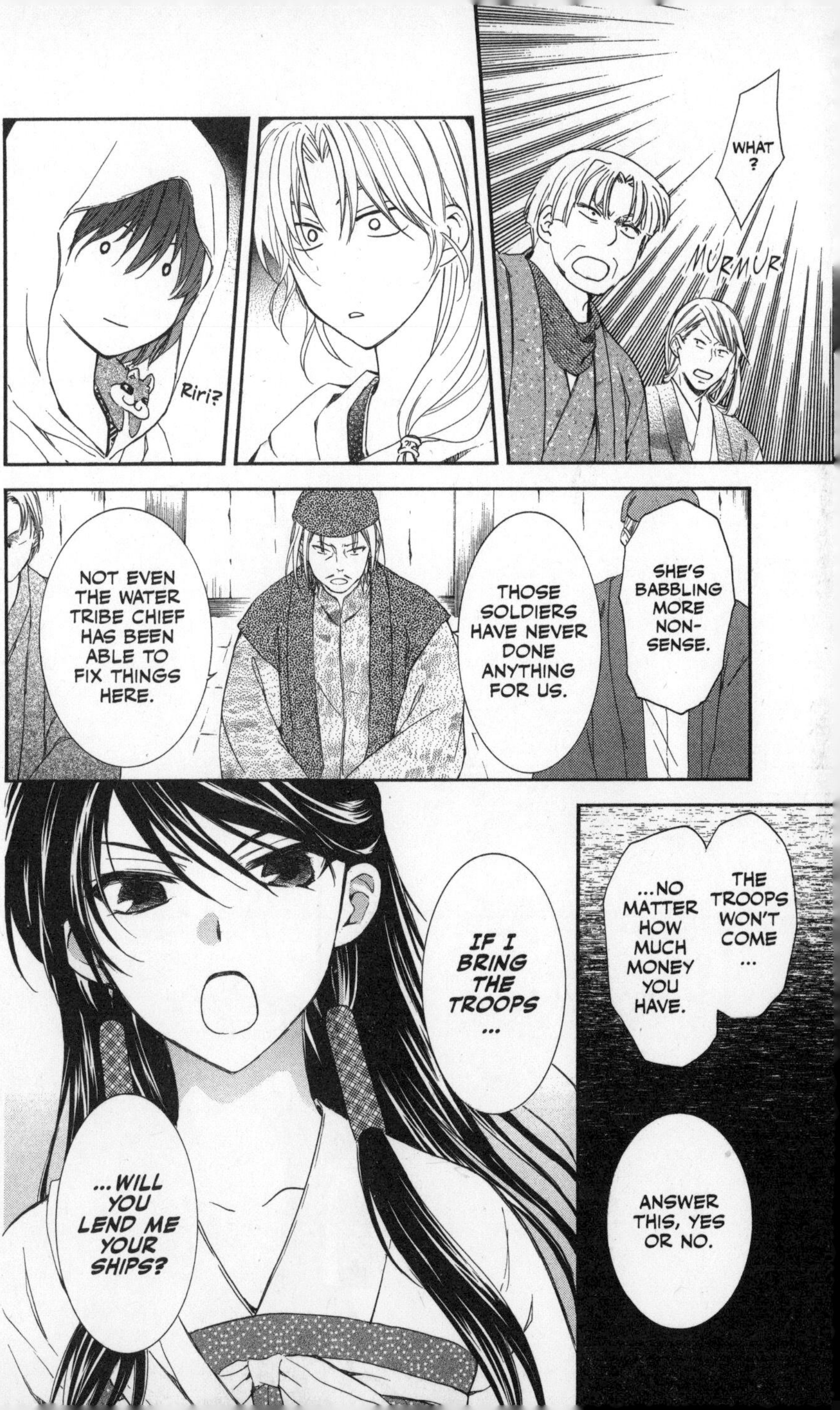
WHAT?
MURMUR
Riri?
SHE'S BABBLING MORE NON-SENSE.
THOSE SOLDIERS HAVE NEVER DONE ANYTHING FOR US.
NOT EVEN THE WATER TRIBE CHIEF HAS BEEN ABLE TO FIX THINGS HERE.
THE TROOPS WON'T COME...
...NO MATTER HOW MUCH MONEY YOU HAVE.
ANSWER THIS, YES OR NO.
IF I BRING THE TROOPS...
...WILL YOU LEND ME YOUR SHIPS?

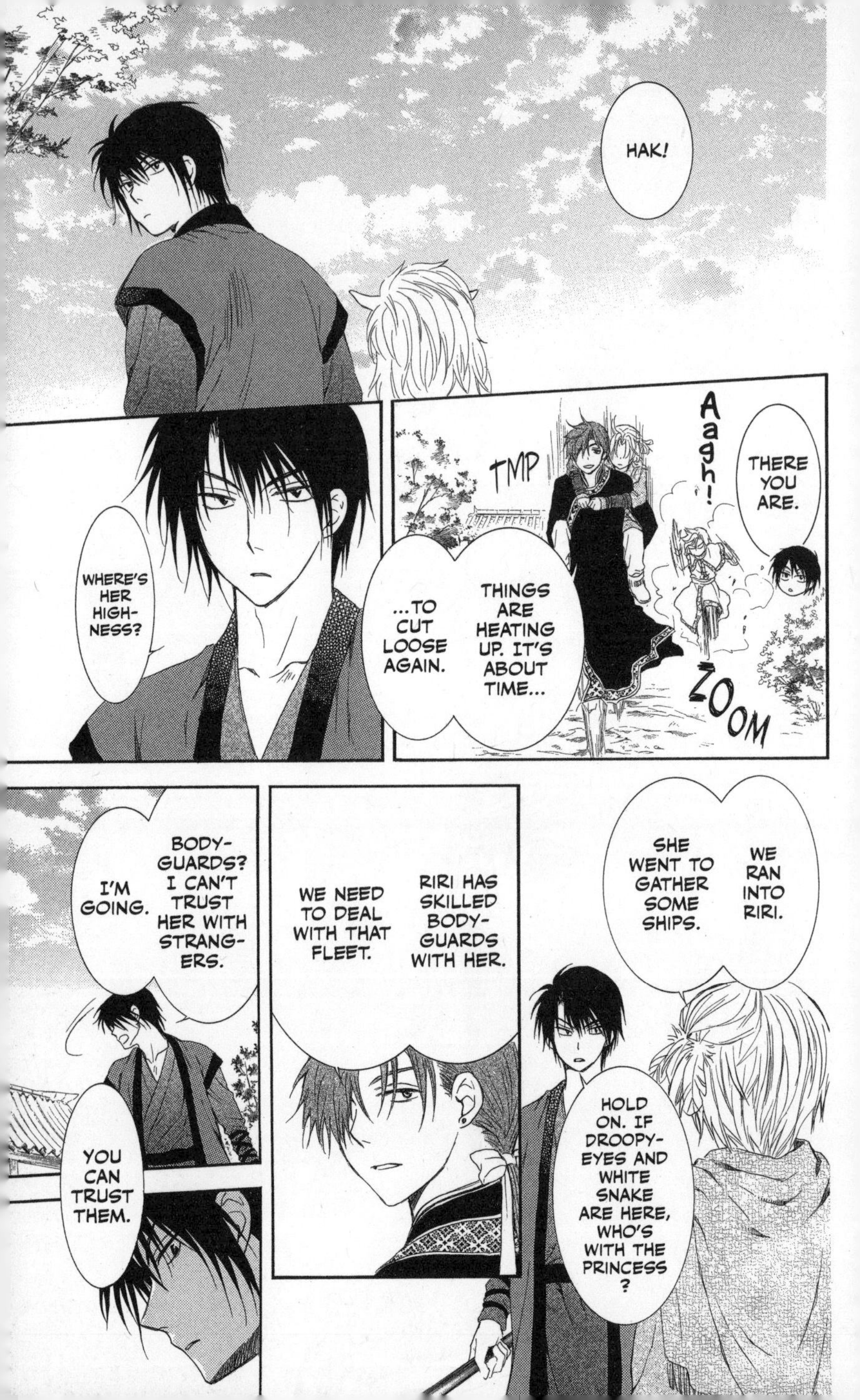
HAK!
Aagh!
THERE YOU ARE.
TMP
THINGS ARE HEATING UP. IT'S ABOUT TIME...
...TO CUT LOOSE AGAIN.
ZOOM
WHERE'S HER HIGHNESS?
WE RAN INTO RIRI.
SHE WENT TO GATHER SOME SHIPS.
HOLD ON. IF DROOPY-EYES AND WHITE SNAKE ARE HERE, WHO'S WITH THE PRINCESS?
RIRI HAS SKILLED BODY-GUARDS WITH HER.
WE NEED TO DEAL WITH THAT FLEET.
BODY-GUARDS? I CAN'T TRUST HER WITH STRANG-ERS.
I'M GOING.
YOU CAN TRUST THEM.

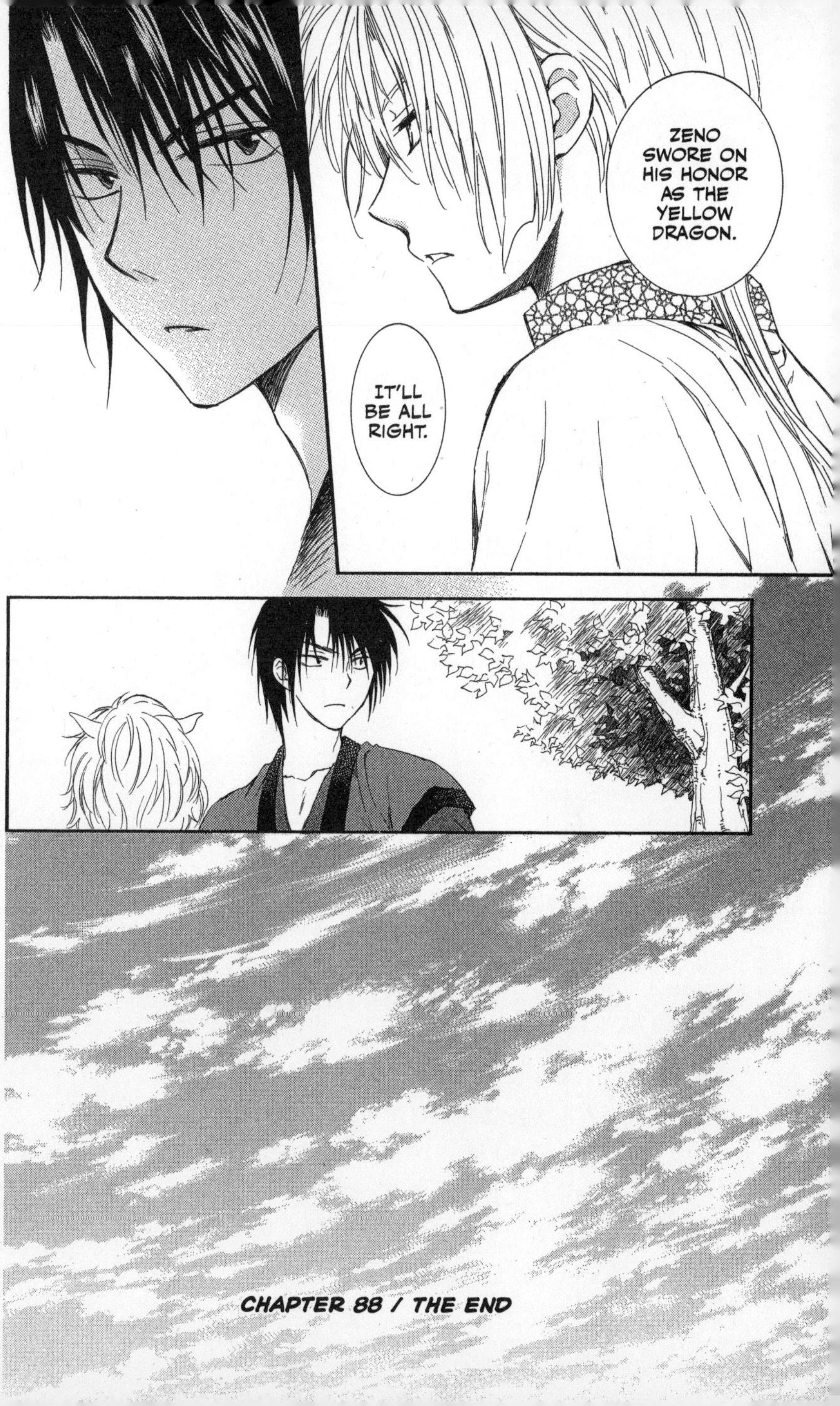
ZENO SWORE ON HIS HONOR AS THE YELLOW DRAGON.
IT'LL BE ALL RIGHT.
CHAPTER 88 / THE END

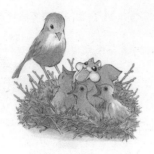

For the cover of this volume, I wanted
something very feminine with pink flowers,
but it turned into one that seems to say, "Come
near us and we'll cut you!"

—Mizuho Kusanagi

Born on February 3 in Kumamoto
Prefecture in Japan, Mizuho Kusanagi
began her professional manga career
with *Yoiko no Kokoroe* (The Rules of a
Good Child) in 2003. Her other works
include *NG Life*, which was serialized
in *Hana to Yume* and *The Hana to
Yume* magazines and published by
Hakusensha in Japan. *Yona of the Dawn*
was adapted into an anime in 2014.

YONA OF THE DAWN
VOL.15
Shojo Beat Edition

STORY AND ART BY
MIZUHO KUSANAGI

English Adaptation/Ysabet Reinhardt MacFarlane
Translation/JN Productions
Touch-Up Art & Lettering/Lys Blakeslee
Design/Yukiko Whitley
Editor/Amy Yu

Akatsuki no Yona by Mizuho Kusanagi
© Mizuho Kusanagi 2014
All rights reserved.
First published in Japan in 2014 by HAKUSENSHA, Inc., Tokyo.
English language translation rights arranged with
HAKUSENSHA, Inc., Tokyo.

Printed in the U.S.A.

Published by VIZ Media, LLC
P.O. Box 77010
San Francisco, CA 94107

10 9 8 7 6 5 4 3 2 1
First printing, December 2018

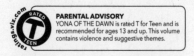

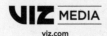

viz.com

shojobeat.com

This is the last page.

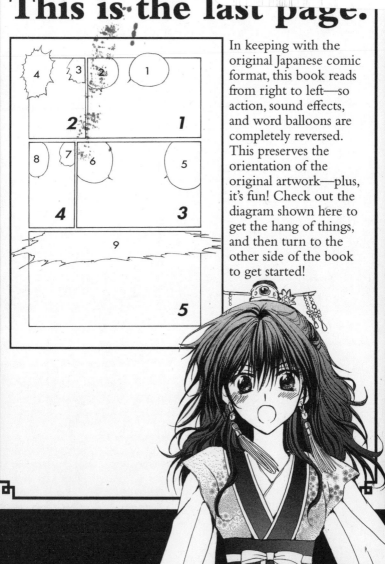

In keeping with the original Japanese comic format, this book reads from right to left—so action, sound effects, and word balloons are completely reversed. This preserves the orientation of the original artwork—plus, it's fun! Check out the diagram shown here to get the hang of things, and then turn to the other side of the book to get started!